JOHN APOSTAL LUCAS:
TEACHER, SPORT HISTORIAN, AND
ONE WHO LIVED HIS LIFE EARNESTLY

Mary Grundal,

John apostal Lucas

Teacher, Sport Historian, and
one who lived his life
earnestly

JOHN APOSTAL LUCAS:
TEACHER, SPORT HISTORIAN, AND ONE WHO LIVED HIS LIFE EARNESTLY

A Collection of Articles and Essays with an Autobiographical Sketch

By
John Apostal Lucas

Professor Emeritus
Pennsylvania State University

Eifrig Publishing
Lemont Berlin

Published by Eifrig Publishing,
PO Box 66, 701 Berry Street, Lemont, PA 16851, USA
Knobelsdorffstr. 44, 14059 Berlin, Germany.

For information regarding permission, write to:
Rights and Permissions Department,
Eifrig Publishing,
PO Box 66, 701 Berry Street, Lemont, PA 16851, USA.
publish@eifrigenterprises.com, +1-814-235-1501.

Library of Congress Cataloging-in-Publication Data

Lucas, John A., 1927-
    John Apostal Lucas: Teacher, Sport Historian, and One
    Who Lived His Life Earnestly. A Collection of Articles
    and Essays with an Autobiographical Sketch
p. cm.

ISBN 978-0-9795518-1-9

    1. Olympic Games 2. Track and Field 3. Marathon
    4. History 5. Pennsylvania State University
    6. 18th-20th centuries. 7. John Apostal Lucas, 1927-
I. Lucas, John A. (John Apostal), II. Title.

12 11 10 2009
5 4 3 2 1

Printed on acid-free paper. ∞

With love and respect
for the woman with whom
I have enjoyed 55 years of my life,
Joyce V. Lucas

J. A. L.

CONTENTS

Autobiographical Sketch

The esteemed American diplomat, writer, and world traveler, George F. Kennan (1904-2005), lived 101 years and was described as one possessing a puritanical character streak, "a categorical imperative of duty."[1] I seized upon this quote as something akin to my own essential being, childhood traits that I learned from my immigrant parents. My mother and father were born in nineteenth-century Albania—Europe's poorest country then, and it remains so in the twenty-first century. My mother, Antigone Mihaledes Zhitomi (born in 1898), and my father, Apostal Llukka, born a decade earlier, came from adjoining and remote villages high in the mountains along the northern Greek border and south of the Albanian town of Korce.

Someone read a poster in the town square to my father: "Earn five dollars a day in Henry Ford's automobile factory in America." The lure was immediate, even though misleading, and with only a few dollars in his pocket, he bought passage to America in 1909 to join an older brother already in Hudson, Massachusetts. The promise of a small fortune for a day's work, my father unfortunately learned, was for highly-skilled Ford Motor workers. He stayed put in Hudson, selling fruit and vegetables from a horse-drawn wagon. His brother died in about 1912, and his death was followed by difficult and lonely days for my father. He hired a scribe to write a letter to his mother, a marriage broker in the home village. She immediately found a teenage girl, Antigone, and the two bought lower-deck steamship tickets for an ocean crossing. In January of 1917, Antigone and her future mother-in-law arrived in Boston Harbor, and soon the two "strangers," Antigone and Apostal, were married.

Children soon arrived. Peter was born in December of that same year, followed by George in 1922, John in 1927, and Thomas in 1929. All four boys were baptized in the tiny local Albanian Orthodox Church, and all were given the middle name

"Apostal." My parents "slept apart" after that, and the young family moved to a small apartment at 356 Columbus Avenue in the immigrant haven of the South End of Boston, Massachusetts. Not even remotely does having the same parents or being from the same household assure clone-like siblings.

For Peter followed decades of hard work, first during the "Great Depression" working as a meat cutter in the Hotel Statler and then joining our dad in the small corner grocery store and candy-making business, where he remained for thirty-five years. George got his start in the same kind of work, but moved on in the 1950's to the burgeoning and profitable "supermarket" enterprise, spending more than twenty-five years doing creative re-modeling of markets, and also building homes and university dormitories in central Connecticut. George's intelligence and ever-present smile prompted some to say of him: "He's going to make it big. He deals with people every day, but never seems to make an enemy." He earned much more money than did his three brothers. Peter served domestically during the Second World War in the United States Air Force, while George was declared "4-F," unfit for war, due to a lingering childhood influenza attack.

I was the third of four sons and graduated from the nearby George Bancroft School in 1941.[2] In my eighth-grade "Elocution" class, I delivered a several-hundred word biography of Dr. Bancroft, received a "certificate of merit" from my teacher, and, I think, the approval by all for my presentation. For me, this was more valuable than gold, this recognition and small accolade.[3] Tom, the youngest son, who was perpetually drawing pictures during childhood, attended Boston Technical High School and then graduated from the two-year Boston School of Art. He went down to the town of Cohasset, taught art at the high school, founded the South Shore Art Institute, and spent many summers in rural Mexico, painting hundreds of excellent pictures, selling but a few. Four boys, four directions despite similar up-bringings. I graduated in 1945 from the Boston English High School, America's oldest free high school (1821), with good grades and four years on the track team, finishing with a two-minute, eight seconds eighth-place finish in the half-mile at the state championships. Without monies to attend college, I joined the United States Army in 1946, spending thirteen months as a private, then corporal, in the Army of Occupation in South Korea, a bitter cold isolation at the former Japanese air and sea base in Yosu, Korea, on the Yellow Sea.

Upon my return home, I entered the Boston University School of Physical Education for Men with government support provided through the G. I. Bill of Rights. I graduated first in my class, and I continued to run. Among other competitions, I participated in the unrivaled Penn Relays at the University of Pennsylvania. The Penn Relays, held in the spacious Franklin Field, began in 1895. The Relays consist of a long weekend, Wednesday through Saturday, with relays for boys, girls, men, and women—some awkward beginners, some multiple Olympic gold medalists. Now the drumbeat swoosh and staccato of runners, some with old sneakers and others with four ounce, $250 running shoes, race around the double track of sixteen lanes, hour after hour, for days. It is a nearly perfectly organized event, with 200 volunteer judges and referees and half-a-dozen paid starters. The number of spectators over the decades from the nineteenth century to the twenty-first is over three million, with nearly a half-million performers. The event has been precious to me since I participated as "middle leg" on the 1950 Boston University distance medley relay. Four years later, I took my Huntington Prep School there and won the two-mile relay in 1954.

As assistant coach at the University of Maryland, I was at the Relays from 1958-1961, and then as track and field coach at Penn State University from 1962-1968, I did not miss a Relay. From then until 2006, I was an official, helping the Penn Relays in their tradition, in what I call the world's greatest track meet—ten times bigger than the track and field competitions at the Olympic Games. It was at the Penn Relays that I made lifetime friends during this Quaker gathering of people of all races, color, creeds, and ethnicity.

While the Penn Relays have been important for my entire adult life, I spent only a short time after graduating from Boston University attending the University of Southern California, where I was rewarded with an academic scholarship in the School of Physical Education. The precious earned Master's degree included a challenging history-philosophy class, one in which I was asked to find someone who would debate the value of athletics to one's life. I invited a new friend and former multiple gold medalist at the Los Angeles Summer Olympic Games of 1932, Mildred "Babe" Didriksen, to be the lead in debating the positive side of competitive athletics. I thought I had a coup with the greatest woman athlete of the first half of the twentieth century. However, it was a raucous and revealing forty-minute talk by the poor kid from Texas, who grew to be Olympic champion and then the nation's top female golfer. Unfortunately for me, she said that the highly competitive athletics that she had participated in had probably injured her and made her sterile for life. She lost her final battle to cancer, at a relatively young age.

While studying at USC, I found time to help the Southern Cal hammer throwers prepare for the May 1952 American Olympic Trials in the magnificent Los Angeles Memorial Coliseum. In the early evenings for a year and a half, never missing a day, I ran 10 miles in the nearby low hills surrounding Los Angeles. No one was as surprised and pleased as I was in winning the early spring 1952 Southern California 10,000 meter championships in exactly 34 minutes, thus qualifying for the USA Olympic trials. I ran "bravely," finishing in 33 minutes, 30 seconds, almost "light years" behind the first three men destined for the Summer Olympics in Helsinki, Finland. These three athletes—fine men and champions—were Curtis Stone and Horace Ashenfelter (first and third) from Penn State University, and Fred Wilt, the durable "great" from Indiana University, in second place.

At USC, I ran out of money many months before finishing my degree, but I was fortunate to earn $100 for half days of work at the Metro-Goldyn Mayer Motion Picture Studios performing as a stunt man and extra. I played tiny roles in four films: Mario Lanza in "Because You're Mine"; Burt Lancaster in "Jim Thorpe— All-American"; Robert Taylor in "Quo Vadis"; and with Spencer Tracy and Katherine Hepburn in "Pat and Mike." I did not exactly "hob-nob" with these fine folks, but we did share box lunches on the sets. I collected my daily hundred dollars, fled back to campus and my real world of classes, study, and 90-minute runs in preparation for the '52 Olympic Trials.

The Lucas brothers—all earnest young men—did what they knew best: hard work, marriage, and families. Whatever one may say, their meaningful personal lives were not done without the help and succor from friends and family. Twice Pulitzer Prize winner, David McCullough, almost shouted at the absurdity of the so-called "self-made" person. "There's no such thing," he wrote, and added:

> We're all shaped by other people—by our parents, friends, teachers, and by people we never knew because they lived long before us. They wrote the books, painted the pictures, wrote the poetry, wrote the great works of

music that move us to our very souls and change our lives. We're shaped by our culture.

Back home from California in August of 1952, family and friends helped me get a last-minute teaching position in Natick, Massachusetts. During the six years in that vigorous town, I coached track and field at the Huntington (Boston) Preparatory School for Boys, winning all 77 competitions, including the National Indoor Championships in New York City's Madison Square Garden in the winter of 1957. Coach and players alike caught the eye of college athletic officials.

Somewhere in those halcyon years, I met Joyce Vaughan, from Minneapolis, then South Texas, and later the Christian Science Principia High School in Elsah, Illinois. She, her younger brother David, and their mother, Katherine, then moved to Boston, where Joyce was enrolled at Boston University. David joined the U.S. Air Force and served a distinguished quarter-century career, while Katherine found work at the Christian Science Publishing Society and a second marriage to Langley Carleton Keyes (Harvard University '24), businessman and scholar. Joyce and David lost their father years earlier. Ernest Wilson Vaughan fought in the First World War, was seriously wounded by mustard gas, worked as an artist for 20 years after the carnage, and died far short of old age. Joyce and I met in church, found ourselves compatible, and were married in July of 1955 in the old 1696 Congregational Church in Boston's Copley Square.[5]

After coaching for several years at the high school level, I became restless after my track and field team won the 1958 state championships at Natick High School. I decided to seek a doctoral program with an opportunity to coach at the college level and accepted a graduate degree opportunity at the University of Maryland. Our son, Mark Langley, was born in the summer of 1960, a full year after Joyce and I traveled to Turkey for a challenging four-month stint helping the Turkish Olympic team to prepare for the Rome Olympic Games of 1960. I was at these Olympic Games and watched the overmatched small team of Turkish men and women finish far behind in every event. I was invited by the Turkish delegation to a "victory party." "I don't understand," I said. "Not a single Turkish athlete finished higher than twenty-fifth place," I cried. The President of the Turkish Athletics Federation forgave my American naiveté, exclaiming that every single national track and field record for both men and women had been broken, and by large margins. It was a valuable lesson for me.

I was grateful, as well, to the Maryland track coach, Jim Kehoe, for alerting me to this well-paying American State Department assignment. To this day, so many decades later, I'm not only indebted to Jim Kehoe, but to my doctoral advisor at Maryland, Marvin Eyler, the most skillful teacher I have ever known. It was under Dean Eyler that I completed my 1962 doctoral dissertation, "Baron de Coubertin and the Formative Years of the Modern International Olympic Movement, 1883-1896."

Just prior to those steaming hot 1960 Olympic Games in Rome, where temperatures rose in the late afternoons to 100-103 degrees Fahrenheit, I spent three weeks in Lausanne, Switzerland, researching for scores of hours inside the home, "Mon Repos," of the Olympic Games Founder, Baron Pierre de Coubertin (1863-1937). My host was Lydia Zanchi, personal secretary to the Baron a quarter-century earlier. This good lady drove me over to a Geneva retirement home, introduced me to Coubertin's 100-year old widow, Marie Rothan Coubertin (1860-1964). She stared up at me from her wheelchair, eyes clear and mind alert, and answered my question: "Can you tell me something of your husband not found in books?" She replied in elegant French: "Yes, I believe I can." As best I can remember, and writing in my "Olympic Diary" that very evening, she said:

> Pierre spoke frequently of his "double dream," a coming together of athletes from every nation, and in so doing, to compete fiercely, honorably, learning something of one another, respecting one another, regardless of outward differences, all of which leads to greater internationalism, cosmopolitanism, and, over the ages, might make the Olympic Games a paragon of peace.

I collected my precious hand-written notes, took the night train over the Swiss and Italian Alps and on to Rome and my first Olympic Games. The Rome Games were special to me. I had befriended the brilliant Californian athlete, Rafer Johnson, already an Olympic silver medal winner in the decathlon in Melbourne, Australia in 1956. Almost without argument, the decathlon event in Rome was the greatest of all ten-events competitions—before or since. Late in the afternoon with long shadows in a half-filled stadium, C. K. Yang of Taiwan and his teammate from the University of California, Los Angeles, Rafer Johnson, were only a perilous few points apart as they approached the tenth event—the onerous 1500-meter run. C. K. Yang would be the gold medalist if he could finish ahead of Rafer by more than 40 meters. I sat anxiously in Row 1 of the Stadio Olympico as the decathletes circled the track in determined distress, in this near one-mile last event. Rafer "hung on" in greatest pain, joined in agony by his closest friend and competitor.

Yang didn't win the race, nor did he run ahead of "Raf" by more than twenty meters. Johnson won gold and C.K. the silver. I was whatever is beyond ecstatic, and I leapt out of the stands across the six-foot moat and embraced Rafer moments after the race. What then happened might be better told by Rafer, for he and I stayed friends for decades, culminating in his letter to me, dated July 16, 2007:

> I do remember the fact that we were roommates in Lousanne, and I'll never forget the long train trip to Rome for the Olympics. I also remember the fact that you were kind enough to get my starting blocks to me after the 1500 meters in the Olympic Stadium. Interestingly enough though, the thing I most vividly remember is you being carried off the Olympic Track by the Italian police.

Eight years later, I remember the practice track behind the 1968 Olympic Stadium in Mexico City. I was interviewing the famous and eccentric Australian coach, Percy Cerutty, when Joyce Lucas sauntered across the infield, and I introduced her to the bare-chested, bare-footed Percy. Joyce extended her arm, he took it, kissed her hand, wrist, forearm, and all the way up, placing a last greeting on her cheek.

I recall "everything" about Munich 1972, including a very early morning run out of our chalet, crossing the border into Austria, unchallenged by armed soldiers. Returning a bit later, the Germans refused to allow me to return into Germany. Several times they demanded my passport, repeating themselves several times. "I don't have my passport," I cried, adding "I must get back, in order to catch the train to the city," fifty kilometers away. No use; I threw up my hands and moved away from the armed constabulary, lacking their "OK" and half expecting some one-way disaster. They did not shoot. About a week later, following the ultimate horror of male Jewish athletes murdered inside the Olympic village, I witnessed the stadium-filled funeral ceremony, and the anger-awkwardness of speaker and International Olympic President Avery Brundage announcing: "The Games must go on."

Vaulting ahead to Athens at the 2004 Olympic Games: to my delight, I was allowed to enter the ancient pink-white marble Panathenaic Olympic Stadium for yet another pre-dawn 10,000-meter (6 ¼ miles) twenty-five lap run. Sixty-nine minutes is not "Olympian" in any way, but passable for a 77 year-old retired professor.

Olympic Games aside, I was pleased and privileged to complete 35 years of coaching and teaching in the Department of Kinesiology at Penn State University. Following my doctoral degree from the University of Maryland in 1962 and almost before the ink was dry on the diploma, I received a phone call from the athletic director at the University of Texas at El Paso, offering me, sight unseen, the position of head track and field coach. Joyce, young Mark Lucas, and I drove from College Park to El Paso. The downtown bank's huge clock and thermometer read "4:00 p.m. and 103 degrees Fahrenheit."

The athletic director and the head of the physical education department were pleased with my deportment, appearance, and commitment to my soon-to-be responsibilities. Before signing the papers, and in a way that, in retrospect, seemed surrealistic, I received a long-distance phone call from State College, Pennsylvania to El Paso, Texas. Ernest B. McCoy, athletic director and Dean of the College of Health and Physical Education of Penn State University, invited me to return East for an interview with him, President Eric Walker, and members of the Board of Trustees. I did just that, and with anticipation. After only a few hours, Dean McCoy offered me the possibility of coaching three sports: cross-country, indoor, and outdoor track and field. I phoned Joyce, exclaimed that the job was mine. I flew back to El Paso and we almost immediately drove East to University Park, but not before the most gracious El Paso folks wished us "bon voyage" and good luck.

During six school years and 12 seasons, I coached three sports. Our record was good but not stellar. We were a very good dual meet team, performed well in the Eastern intercollegiate league, the Intercollegiate Amateur Athletic Association of America (IC4A), won six individual championships in the National Collegiate Athletic Association championships, thanks in part to my assistant coach and dear friend, the late John Doolittle. Four

Nittany Lion trackmen represented their country at the Olympic Games, in the discus, the decathlon, the 3,000-meter steeple-chase, and in the harsh fifty-kilometer race walk.

I became increasingly restless. My doctorate in sport and Olympic Games history was "burning a hole" in my being, and at the end of the academic year 1968, I requested and received permission to enter the challenging, uncertain world of the non-tenured associate professor. It worked out marvelously, in part because of my own tenacity, serious intellectual efforts, and all-important decades of close association with the finest colleague in the world, Ronald A. Smith. I taught various courses, exercise classes, history of world physical education, American sport history, and a graduate course on sport philosophy.

In addition, I taught a course open to graduate and under-graduate students, the "History, Philosophy, and Politics of the Modern Olympic Games" for thirty years before retirement. Remarkably, I thought, I was invited to continue teaching this Kinesiology 443 course for many more years and beyond my eighti-eth birthday. I estimate that some 1,700 students have taken the Olympic Games course. It was beyond just satisfying to have been chosen the College of Health and Human Development "Teacher of the Year" in 1994 and five years earlier the "Researcher of the Year."

Well before these honors, I pledged to my mother and father that I would someday visit Albania to find the two villages in the remote mountain regions of their birth. I made the pilgrim-age in 1991, the year of Albania's liberation from the numbing regressive regime of Envir Hoja. I flew to Zurich and took the once-a-week flight to Tirana, where I was met by several happy and weeping relatives, some so poor that eight of them lived in a two-room apartment on the sixth level, without an elevator, in a ramshackle building close to the main center of Tirana, near my "pretend" five-star hotel, where very little functioned properly (elevator, lights, hot water, restaurant).

After visiting relatives, receiving their civilized and traditional greetings, and understanding much of their Albanian language, I told them of my plan to visit the villages of "Llousa" and "Lesheet-sa," a hundred miles to the south. I saw only puzzlement and some fear in their eyes and on their faces.

The next morning I hired a taxi and told the driver what I wished. He answered, "It is very far, very dangerous, and will cost you ten dollars American." We made the fifteen hour round trip in one day, found no extant villages, took a photo of myself kissing the ground of my parent's birthplaces, and returned to a "broken" Tirana, where I paid my brave driver with a brand new Andrew Jackson American twenty-dollar bill.

Eleven years later (2002), I returned to Tirana and stayed at the same ill-functioning hotel. Marxian Communism was gone, replaced by an ineffective government doing its best to "close the gap." I was with the brilliant German sport historian, Wolfgang Decker, to hold a series of lectures at the university, on the ancient and modern Olympic Games. At the three talks that filled the auditorium, my relatives sat in the back row, beaming.

To the immediate south lay Greece, the Peloponnesus, and the village of Olympia, with it 3,000-year-old ruins, and the modern-day International Olympic Academy (IOA). I lectured there in 1975 on "Pierre de Coubertin and his Vision of 'Muscular Christianity.'" I made seven more visits to the IOA, watching it grow in size and importance. I re-visited the Academy in June of 2007, where Professor David Young (University of Florida) and I received "busts" of Baron Pierre de Coubertin and delivered lectures to 180 young participants from 66 nations. Two of them, a young man and woman, were from Albania. Standing next to me as I spoke Albanian with them was my son Mark, who commented "I know now, Dad, where you were so often when I was a kid."

In 1992, IOC president, Juan Antonio Samaranch (1920-), awarded me the title of "Official IOC Lecturer," after reading my new 1991 book, *Future of the Olympic Games.* Somehow, while teaching my "level-best," I found the time and the motivation to lecture 233 times on three continents, including three trips to Australia.[6] My smallest group of listeners was a talk to fifteen elementary school children in Idaho Falls, Idaho. My largest audience may have been before 1,200 medical doctors and Ph.D. scientists, as the "D. B. Dill Historical Lecturer" at the American College of Sport Medicine in Cincinnati on May 31 of the Olympic Games year 1996. In that same year, at the Atlanta Olympic Games, I was invited into the private IOC meeting, where President Samaranch awarded me the "Olympic Order" and beamed, "You are the first school-teacher to be so recognized."

My more than fifty years of published research (1955-2008) can be categorized topically-chronologically in three segments: 1) historical reviews of Penn State University kinesiology-physical education, and aspects of the same in the United States, 2) historical and biographical observations on track and field at

Penn State University and in the USA, and 3) scores of essays on the Olympic Games, especially on Pierre de Coubertin and the other seven IOC presidents, as well as special attention to all the presidents and leadership personnel of the United States Olympic Committee 1906-2008. Some of these leaders were brilliant, some not, but for me, all had "interesting" personalities.

Family and church are of primary importance to Joyce and me, but I have not allowed it to dominate this autobiography. Joyce has at least three "passions": 1) helping to heal the "wounded spirits" of some friends, attending to this mission decade after decade; 2) cultivating her magnificent flower gardens, talking to the burgeoning buds, and watching them grow in variety and beauty; 3) traveling around the world, usually alone and always in cool to cold climates. Several of her thirty-three "voyages" have been to Iceland, Greenland, Svalbard-Spitsbergen, to the Isle of Skye, Tasmania, Nepal, Hokkaido Island, Tierre Del Fuego, along the ancient "Silk Route," a week on the Trans-Siberian Railroad, and over to Lake Baikal in Central Siberia. I suspect that she has not finished traveling. The two of us, from "Day One," have tried to practice the religion of Christian Science, to "pray without ceasing," as the Bible asks, and to try to be friends to all of humankind.

Our son Mark received his doctorate in Higher Education from Rutgers University and moved to the Columbia campus of the University of Missouri as the Director of Student Life. His wife, Pamela, was born in Hamilton, Ohio, spent formative years in Destin, and married Mark in that small city on the Florida Panhandle. They have two high-school-age children—Katherine Gail and Matthew John. Pam manages to work full-time at the University of Missouri Veterinary Hospital and enjoys her challenging, even exotic work very much.

Like everyone else, no one in my family can know the future. Nor could the ancient Greeks see more clearly than we do today. Their language did contain one word, however, "apokaradokia," which means "expectation of good" or "to catch sight of a distant object, to lift one's vision at the thought of good." I like to think that without ever previously knowing this word, I've tried to live my life in this manner.[7] In a way not possible for me to outline satisfactorily, my childhood reflected "apokaradokia," and this zest for life remained with me, affecting the very essence of my being.

Why in the world of reason would I remember that as an eleven-year-old child I won the summer playground "rebound ball" championship with 300 consecutive "hits"? It just felt good, as did that "A" grade received in a ninth-grade essay "How my homeroom teacher played in John Philip Sousa's band in the year 1900." Why can I not forget my eleventh-grade English teacher, Mr. Eccles, who congratulated me in front of the class for being the first student in twenty years to record fully and accurately every great name carved high atop the frieze on all sides of the Boston Public Library? Securing the names of several hundred great men and women in my notebook gave me a sore neck for days, but it was worth it. There was never a week that I failed to visit this first great public library in the United States, to gaze at the nineteenth-century giant mural paintings of French artist, Puvis de Chavannes.

Even as a child, I saw their pastoral and ethereal nature, never realizing that a hundred years earlier that very artist painted the inside wall of the Paris Sorbonne University, where in 1894, Baron de Coubertin created the International Olympic Committee, anticipating his and the Greek government's First Modern International Olympic Games. I had to wait until the celebration of the committee's hundredth anniversary to see Chavannes' murals in that Sorbonne auditorium. Seeing it made me recall my childhood wonderment back in Boston's "BPL."

I also recall taking part in the 1944 "Schoolboy Military Parade," dressed in full khaki uniform, passing the downtown statue of Paul Revere, along Beacon Hill's State Capitol building, and parallel to the Public Gardens, the Commons, both filled with imposing statues of the city's military, political, and literary heroes and heroines. In a mysterious manner, these impressions helped in forming the person that I became. Here is just one example: Our school military leader was the former Boston athlete and career military man, Colonel William H. "Bill" Meanix, once a finalist in the 440-yard hurdles at the American Olympic trials. He told us this story of "almost making the team." That same afternoon, I raced to "my" library, and with help, located the *AOC Report 1920*.[8]

In my penultimate story in this "looking back" exercise, I remember my first year as Penn State University's track coach (1962). I drove to Long Island in an effort to recruit the New York State high school cross-country runner, Steve Hayden. After talking with his parents, Steve and I took a long run along the Atlantic Ocean beach (probably against the present-day N.C.A.A. rules), stopping to say "hello" to Steve's friend, eighty-year old "Charles Atlas," legendary strongman of yesteryear, and in that year a handsome, muscular, white-haired, retired millionaire. He jogged with us, invited us for an ocean plunge, followed by a quarter-hour of "dynamic tension" exercises by the master. I drove back to school; Steve attended our university, was a "B" runner and "A" student, graduated and made the U.S. Olympic team, finishing twenty-first in the "50,000 meter race walk" in Munich, Germany 1972.

Lastly, but much earlier, on a Saturday afternoon "pick-up" football game in 1943, I sustained a serious compound fracture of my lower leg, shattering both bones. I was all of 110 pounds and 5'6" tall. At the free city hospital, I received the best attention; an aluminum pin and four screws were inserted, and the doctor warned: "Take it easy, you'll not be playing football again, and possibly no other sport." Several days later my brother George visited my hospital bed and gave me a battered paper-back book titled (I think) "How Glenn Cunningham Overcame Adversity and Became the Fastest Mile Runner in the World."[9] I didn't just read it. I memorized it and declared, silently, "If he can do it, so can I."

After my hospital release, I walked with crutches around Jamaica Pond in suburban Boston, walked slowly, laboriously around the water for months, and spent and additional half-year of slow jogging, on the famed 1¼ mile pond path. It was a full calendar year of recuperation before I could again join the high school indoor track team, never forgetting Cunningham. And I never stopped running: in college, as a club runner, and fifty-five additional years of running, during which I compiled a "Lucas Running Diary," and in a late 2007 notation, I had "run in circles" more than 150,000 miles.

What a pleasant and important interlude it was to travel to Westerly, Rhode Island, in late June of 2007, for a Lucas family reunion. Possibly, a hundred and forty folks, ages three weeks to eighty-four, spent an entire fair weather Saturday together. Joyce, Mark, and I moved about, enjoyed the wonder of so many similar personalities, so many colorful individual differences. Speaking strictly for myself, it was the best and possibly the last get-together of the "clan."

After all my years of work, fun, and reflection, I'm still not sure who I am, other than not an intellectual giant. Not many of my friends and colleagues, however, have surpassed me in "staying power." I'm proud of my heritage, of my modest sporting achievements, of my sixty years as a teacher; I am fortunate to be an American, filled with unalloyed joy about Mark Lucas and his family, and I am still in love with Joyce.

April 2009
State College, PA

NOTES

1 See John Lukas, *George Kennan, A Study of Character* (New Haven: Yale University Press, 2007), page 38.

2 George Bancroft (1800-1891), Harvard University historian, a Bostonian, and author of the 1840 three-volume *History of the United States*.

3 In that same grade Social Studies and elocution class, I recited in front of my teacher and peers the entire Psalm 19 from the *Holy Bible:* "The heavens declare the glory of God; And the firmament showeth his handiwork." Twenty-nine additional lines followed. My blue-ribbon award remained with me for years, but not as long as the "warm" memory of achievement and, even more, of recognition.

4 His commencement address titled "The Democratic Idea: Two Perspectives" is located in the Principia College Alumni magazine *Principia Purpose* (Spring 2007), page 6.

5 Joyce's mother remarried in 1954, to Langley Carlton Keyes, Harvard University Class of 1924, a successful Boston businessman and author of several books on the Transcendental thinker, Henry David Thoreau (1817-1862). One of his books, *Cape Cod*, so impressed Dr. Keyes that he bought a summer home on the "Cape" in order to emulate Thoreau, to escape excessive civilization where Thoreau and his followers saw so many leading "lives of quiet desperation."

6 I have in my study a six-foot wide space of "Olympic Diaries" of each of these far-flung lectures.

7 See Ron Mangelsdorf's essay in *The Christian Science Journal*, 125 (May 2007), 8.

8 See pages 178 and 194 for the results of the Antwerp, Belgium 440-yard hurdle "sweep" of gold, silver, and bronze by American athletes F. J. Loomis, J. K. Norton, and A. G. Desch, with C. D. Daggs, Los Angeles Athletic Club, in close attendance in fourth place.

9 Glen lived in rural Kansas. As a boy, his tiny home burned to the ground, both his legs seared to the bone. Doctors said he would be "crippled" for life. For eight years, he limped-walked the farm, then managed to win the mile run state championship and ran well at the University of Kansas. From 1930 through 1940, he competed in hundreds of races against the best in the world, winning a 4th place in the 1932 Los Angeles 1500 meter Olympic race, and a magnificent silver Olympic medal in the 1936 Berlin "1500"—a world record first place (3 min. 47.8 sec.) race by New Zealand's "Jack" Lovelock. I met Cunningham, a Ph.D. in exercise physiology, in 1979, but found no reason to share with him my own boyhood injuries.

1.
John Kelley—Marathon Champ*

The 1957 International Boston Marathon was won by John J. Kelley, America's all-time fastest long-distance and marathon runner. The ex-Boston University cross-country champion, a 26-year-old junior high school English teacher from Groton, Connecticut, put a convincing end to the foreign domination of the B.A.A. Marathon. Not since 1945 had an American-bred runner won the classic race.

Kelley's triumphant tour, which resulted in a remarkable run of 2 hours, 20 minutes and 5 seconds, was heralded by the greatest enthusiasm shown in more than a decade. The American sports public was jubilant. The Europeans and Asians, so accustomed to celebrating victory after this race, were stunned.

To those concerned with the future status of long-distance running in the United States, the story of John Kelley would be interesting and revealing. But first, something of this year's dramatic race—"A case of Kelley against the world."

Kelley could hardly have been classified as an underdog on the eve of the 61st running of the B.A.A. Marathon in 1956. He had run the slightly short course in 2 hours, 14 minutes, 34 seconds, finishing second, some few seconds behind Finland's Antti Viskari. He won the 1956 Yonkers race in 2 hours, 24 minutes, 52 seconds, smashing the old record of Nickolas Costes by six minutes. This year the Boston course was lengthened nearly 1,200 yards to give it the full 42,195 meters, or 26 miles, 385 yards.

Possibly the strongest foreign field of marathon runners in the race's history were present to answer the starter's gun. Three Japanese champions were present, including the former B.A.A. winner and record holder, Keizo Yamada. Also, there were three

*The Amateur Athlete, 28 (November 1957), 10-13.

Koreans, all of whom had run under 2 hours, 30 minutes, with Chung Wong Lim in 2 hours, 23 minutes, their country's fastest marathoner. Athletes from Mexico, Canada, Hawaii, and Puerto Rico were present. Back again were the Finns, Olavi Manninen, conqueror of Viskari, the 1956 champion, and Veikko Karvonen, who, at 31, was the most consistent and possibly the greatest marathon runner in the world.

The seventy-degree day was almost too warm for the more than 140 runners. At the six-mile checkpoint in Framingham, Massachusetts, the Korean Han was leading in 34 minutes, 54 seconds, with a small group of runners close behind. Kelley ran easily in tenth position along with Rudy Mendez of New York City. At Natick, the ten-mile mark (54:50), Kelley had moved up to fourth position behind Choi, Han, and Karvonen. At the halfway mark at Wellesley (1:10.56), Kelley, supremely confident of his conditioning and determined either to win or drop out, moved to the front. For the next three miles, Han, the Korean, and Karvonen matched strides with the lone American. Kelley took charge at the 16-mile mark (1:32:33) and began to wear out his chief challenger, Finland's Karvonen. Jerry Nason, sports editor of the *Boston Globe* and outstanding historian of the B.A.A. marathon, describes these last ten miles thus:

> At the end he had whirled away from the mighty Karvonen on the hills of Newton and gave that justly famous Finn the second worst beating of his illustrious career—3 minutes, 45 seconds, or about 1200 yards. And Han, a marine sergeant from the hills of Korea, who looked leggy and ominous, cracked up on the first of the Newton hills in his attempt to match Kelley's flight. Karvonen finished second, Han fifth—and spent. So fast did Kelley's amazing legs reduce the hot, black macadam miles, that he whipped Keizo Zamada, the first Japanese finisher (sixth) and former record holder, by a stunning 13 minutes, 17 seconds.

Kelley, the modern prototype of the speed distance runner, had completed the 26 miles, 385 yards in a record breaking 2 hours, 20 minutes, 5 seconds, an average of 5 minutes, 20 seconds for each mile.

Observers of Kelley's relatively long stride, his rolling out, side of the foot placement on the track or road, have described his action as similar to that of some former American Indian runners of the far West, and, more recently, of many Scandinavian champions.

A description of the Olympian's smooth and economical stride as depicted in the seven frames:

Frame No. 1 A fraction of a moment before John's slightly bent lead leg comes in contact with the ground, his ankle turns inward sharply, causing the stronger outside of the foot to strike the ground, heel first.

Frame No. 2 is a picture of the correct foot position fully under the body. In Kelley's "new look" style for marathon running, the kick-up behind is not a definite, deliberate kick, but simply allows the swing of the leg to follow through vertically, instead of a momentary pause and loss of motion of the trail right leg. Instead of pulling the trail leg forward, gravity takes a hand at the start of the forward leg movement, causing it to "fall" to the ground.

Frame No. 3 shows his upper body continuing to move forward over his left leg, the weight of the body being supported mainly by the bones of the outer edge of the foot. He continues this rolling or rocking motion, his center of gravity passing over and past his left leg and onto the ball of the foot. His knee lift is not excessive, but just sufficient to clear the corresponding foot in its forward swing.

Frame No. 4 illustrates the driving action of the left leg, not quite straightening and locking at the knee, driving him forward powerfully and smoothly, with no sign of wasteful "bounce." As his back left leaves the ground, his ankle relaxes, rests momentarily, the toe of his shoe perpendicular to the ground. Kelley's torso, with only a slight lean, shows his peculiar across-the-chest high arm carriage.

Frame No. 5 shows the middle of Kelley's stride. Here we see both feet off the ground. The lower part of the forward right leg swings like a pendulum into position for the start of the next stride. The rear leg is fully extended and about to begin its circular motion forward, just as shown in frames number 1 and 2. Again, this trail leg is not lifted forward, but is allowed to swing forward in a short pendulum arc. Except at the instant of driving forward, he is completely relaxed.

Frame No. 6 is similar to No. 3, showing the beginning of the relatively strong drive from the trailing leg, usually an exclusive characteristic of shorter distance runners.

Frame No. 7 is the same as No. 4, showing the left leg leading instead of the right, thus completing the full picture of Kelley's stride. Despite the rapid tempo and forward spring, Kelley's shoulders betray hardly any motion. He keeps his head up, eyes forward, as the stride is completed off the right toe, without a break in the rhythm of his running.

* * *

John Joseph Kelley was born December 24, 1930 in Norwich, Connecticut. He attended Bulkeley High School in New London, graduating in 1950, where he was chosen for the A.A.U. high school All-American team-with his 4:21.8 second mile performance. However, John's proclivity for long-distance running and his great natural ability were evidenced earlier, in 1948, when he won the national junior 25-kilometer championship as a tenth-grader.

Throughout his college career he continued running on the roads, in addition to track and cross-country. He combined seventh and fifth places in the B.A.A. marathon with first places in the New England and IC4A cross-country championships. The restless Boston University English major was formulating a philosophy toward running that was to always keep his mind and body free and enthusiastic.

Suited by temperament and desire to running on the roads, John Kelley has run all distances creditably, some distances very well, and still others fast enough to be considered among the world's best. Rarely can such a record of adaptability be found. He has run distances from the quarter mile to the marathon in the following times:

440 yards	52 sec.
880 yards	1:57 sec.
1,000 yards	2:19 sec.
¾ mile	3:10 sec.
1 mile	4:17 sec.
2 miles	9:17 sec.
3 miles	14:20 sec.
4 miles (road)	19:20 sec.
4 miles (cross-country)	19:40 sec.
4 miles	19:50 sec.
5 miles (road)	24:20 sec.
5 miles (cross-country)	24:50 sec.
6 miles	29:50 sec.
10,000 meters	30:50 sec.
15,000 meters (road)	45 min.
9 miles 564 yards)	
10 miles (road)	49 min.
12 miles (road)	60 min.
20,000 meters (road)	62 min.
(12 miles 752 yards)	
15 miles (road)	1 hr. 17 min.
52,000 meters (road)	1 hr. 19 min.
(15 miles 940 yards)	
30,000 meters (road)	1 hr. 35 min.
(18 miles 1128 yards)	
20 miles (road)	1 hr. 48 min.
marathon (road)	2 hrs. 20 min.

Kelley's style of running is radically different from traditional American long distance and marathon champions. His form is more like that of the middle distance runner, with an emphasis on relaxation. The low kick-up of the trailing leg, the flat-footed shuffle and the low arm carriage, so characteristic of most marathoners, are not evidenced in John Kelley.

John is a "speed" marathoner in its truest sense. His style of running, his body build, his delicate "sprinter-like" temperament, in addition to his great native ability and love of running, fully equip him as America's fastest runner above six miles.

Kelley is 5' 6" tall, 125 pounds, of Irish extraction. His legs are exceptionally long, well-muscled, lean from thigh to knee with powerful tapering calf muscles. His ankle is strong, loose and elastic, while his foot is bony, tough, and heavily calloused.

His unruly blond hair, lean face and high cheekbones, seem to perpetually wear a pained grimace in all stages of his running. Kelley's tempo on the highway is inexorable. In a ten-mile race, his stride tempo is between 180 and 185 steps per minute, each stride between six feet and six feet three inches long. During a marathon race his tempo is consistently between 160 and 165 steps per minute, his stride length being slightly less than six feet.

There is possibly no athlete in American history possessing such a love of running and passion for training as John J. Kelley. Such men as Nickolas Costes and Dean Thackeray (Kelley's marathon teammates at the Melbourne Olympics), may, over a brief period of months, have trained more intensely than John. However, over the past five years, possibly no one in America and few men in the world have run as many miles as the 1957 Boston Marathon winner.

John is always in good physical condition. He insists on a minimum of eight hours' sleep every night. There is no "off season," only a relaxing in the intensity of his training during the hot July and August months. He trains six days a week, twice a day, in the early morning and late afternoon, almost all year long. Since the Boston and Yonkers marathons and most of the national long distance championships occur during April, May, and June respectively, these months might be considered John's period of "mid-season" training. During his "restful" season of July and August, he trains once a day, early in the morning or late evening.

The months of September through November might be considered his "early season" training period, while the winter and spring months of December to March, his "late season" period, the later period seeing his greatest accumulation of mileage gradually progress to a period of intense speed training.

Competitive training for long distance running is a highly individualistic endeavor, depending upon many factors such as native ability, type of employment, time available, psychological, physiological and environmental differences. Thus, I shall outline typical weekly schedules for each of the four seasons of Kelley's training year without comment.

After years of thought, he has felt the following program is most suited to bringing him to the greatest degree of conditioning and speed for all distances above six miles. Excepting races, John never runs on the roads. All his training is done on grass or dirt. His morning workout is between 5:30 a.m. and 6:45 a.m., while his training period in the afternoon is usually between 4:00 p.m. and 6:00 p.m. It is significant to note that at no time in any of his workouts, even during his periods of restful jogging, does he permit himself to slow up to less than 6:40 seconds per mile. In addition, he makes a practice of doing 20 push-ups every morning.

Mid-Season
  Monday
  a.m. – 11 miles at 6:40 sec. per mile
  p.m. – 12 miles with 10 accelerations of 35 seconds
  (at least 220 yards)
  Tuesday
  a.m. – 11 miles steady at 6:40 per mile
  p.m. – 5 miles at 5:20 per mile
  Wednesday
  a.m. – 11 miles steady at 6:40 per mile
  p.m. – 8 miles with 5 accelerations of 70 seconds
  (about 440 yards)
  Thursday
  a.m. – 11 miles steady at 6:40 per mile
  p.m. – 8 miles at 5:15 per mile
  Friday
  a.m. – 4 miles steady at 6:40 per mile
  p.m. – 4 miles steady at 6:40 per mile
  Saturday
  Race – Total distance for the week approx. 100 miles

Restful Season
Train once a day six days per week. Consists mainly of relaxed runs of 5 miles at 5:40 per mile or 8 miles at 6:40 per mile.

Total distance for week approximately 40 miles.

Early Season
 Monday
 a.m. – 12 miles at 6:40 per mile
 p.m. – 8 miles at 5:20 per mile
 Tuesday
 a.m. – 12 miles at 6:40 per mile
 p.m. – 8 miles with 5 two-minute accelerations
 Wednesday
 a.m. – 12 miles at 6:40 per mile
 p.m. – 8 miles at 5:20 per mile
 Thursday
 a.m. – 12 miles steady
 p.m. – 8 miles with 12 accelerations of 35 seconds each
 Friday
 a.m. – 12 miles steady
 p.m. – 8 miles steady
 Saturday
 a.m. – 6 miles steady
 p.m. – 14 miles at 5:20 per mile
 Total distance for week 120 miles.

Late Season
 Monday
 a.m. – 8 miles steady at 6:40 per mile
 p.m. – 18 miles—6 miles in 32 minutes, jog 6 miles at 6:40 per
 mile – repeat 6 miles in 32 minutes
 Tuesday
 a.m. – 11 miles at 6:40 per mile
 p.m. – 10 miles with 10 seventy-second accelerations
 Wednesday
 a.m. – 8 miles
 p.m. – 15 miles—3 miles in 15 minutes—jog 3 miles—repeat 3
 miles in 15 minutes
 Thursday
 a.m. – 10 miles steady at 6:40
 p.m. – 12 miles with 12 accelerations of 45 seconds
 Friday
 a.m. – 8 miles steady
 p.m. – 10 miles steady
 Saturday
 p.m. – 20 miles at 5:30 per mile (road)

Total distance for week 130 miles.

During the late season, Kelley averages about 350 miles per month and during the course of an entire year runs some 3,500 miles during practice and competition.

Kelley never tires of running. His dedication to training and his boundless natural ability in addition to a well-rounded professional and social life, help toward a freshness of thinking, a zest for year-round training and competition. As John himself puts it, "One should make running a joyful activity throughout life. The peaceful solitude of workouts, the arduousness of training, and the sense of achievement of a job well done, are fundamental lessons of life to be learned from running."

2.
Pedestrianism and the Struggle for the Sir John Astley Belt, 1878-1879*

During the eighth decade of the nineteenth century, the American sporting scene was enriched by a series of five fabulous international pedestrian races. Sir John Astley, the English sporting Baron, inaugurated the transatlantic six-day and six-night marathon races. These quintuple struggles roused nationalistic pride and sporting blood on two continents, were witnessed by tens of thousands, and resulted in feats of unprecedented human endurance.

No more incredible sport event has ever taken place in New York's old Madison Square Garden than that of six-day marathon running. Of all terrestrial creatures, the one animal officially having recorded the greatest feats of endurance running is man himself. The combination of muscle, lungpower, indomitable will, and powerful incentives is more than a match for any beast. No greater proof can be found than in some of the remarkable exploits of late- nineteenth-century six-day marathon runners.

Pedestrianism, or the art of rapidly covering great distances on foot, originated in England. From 1765 to 1820 the names of Steward, Foster Powell, the legendary Captain Barclay, Abraham Wood, and Daniel Crisp were widely known to the sporting public of Great Britain.[1] Organized foot racing arrived in America in 1835 at the Union Race Course, Long Island on April 24.[2] Forty thousand spectators saw Henry Stannard exhibit "genuine Yankee agility and bottom," and become the first American

The Research Quarterly, 39 (October 1968), 587-594.

to run 10 miles in less than an hour.³ On October 16 and November 19, 1844, two international long-distance matches took place at the Beacon Course near New York City. The London and New York press considered them headline news.⁴ Between 1845 and 1862, two Americans traveled to England for a series of profitable races. William Howitt, alias William Jackson, better known as "The American Deer," and Louis Bennett, who took the pseudonym "Deerfoot," rewrote the record book at distances up to 20 miles.⁵ The arrival of Edward Payson Weston marked a new era in American pedestrianism. From 1861 until his last race in 1913, it is estimated that he covered over one hundred thousand miles in competitive pedestrian tramps. It was Weston who first accomplished 500 miles on an indoor track in less than six days and six nights.

For one brief decade, 1875-1885, the professional sport of pedestrianism reached heights of intense interest in several of the major cities of the United States. The five contests for the famous Sir John Astley Belt during 1878 and 1879 brought together the finest walkers and runners from Europe and America in a sort of international "world series." Never before or since has the harsh and peculiar art of alternately walking and running hundreds of miles been so popular.

Sir John Dugdale Astley, Baronet, member of the British parliament, announced in January, 1878, a series of six-day "go-as-you please" walking and running contests for the "long distance challenge championship of the world." Sir John, the "Sporting Baron," guaranteed $4,000 in prizes and a belt of great price and beauty to the winner of the first match. Each of the proposed five contests was to be carried on with the understanding that the winner was to defend his claim against anyone, of any nationality, "civilized or barbarian." The stage was set. Tens of thousands of Londoners and New Yorkers crowded Agricultural Hall and Gilmore's Madison Square Garden during the five races spread over an 18-month period.

The First Astley Belt Competition

Preparations had been completed in London for the clash of England's best versus Daniel O'Leary, the undefeated Irish-American race walker. He had emigrated to America in 1866 and immediately gained fame for his feats of endurance. In April 1875, he became the second man ever to cover 500 miles on an indoor track during a six-day and six-night marathon contest.

He duplicated the feat in November of that year, winning $5,000 and vanquishing the great Edward Payson Weston with a score of 501 1/4 miles.[6]

Seventeen Englishmen began walking on a track measuring seven laps to the mile while O'Leary walked in solitary splendor on an inner track measuring eight laps to the mile. The scene was laid in London's Agricultural Hall. Trainers, coaches, advisers, masseurs, physicians, dieticians and chefs, timers, lap counters, and judges all were on hand to play their respective roles. The English sport had reached a point of sophistication that was the envy of its American counterpart. At 1 a.m., Monday morning, March 18, 1878, the race began. The athletes tramped endlessly and in the beginning, effortlessly, around the circular path. They rarely rested more than a few hours of every twenty-four.

At one o'clock on the morning of March 23, Daniel O'Leary had covered 457 miles and was resting in his tent located on the infield. Harry Vaughan of Chester, England, had closed the gap by completing 443 miles and three laps. The Englishman "Blower" Brown was in third place, with more than 400 miles. O'Leary resumed running but was soon near collapse. He managed to hold off both Englishmen and at noon was 21 miles in the lead. Hopes of a close finish were dashed when Vaughan was forced to stumble to his tent and rest, being absent from the track exactly fifty-one minutes. O'Leary now held a 24-mile lead and, though in great pain, kept moving. There were nine hours remaining in the short week of 144 hours.

Vaughan got within 20 miles of O'Leary at 6 p.m.. By 7 p.m. it was 497 miles for Vaughan and 516 miles for O'Leary. At exactly 7:38 p.m. Vaughan completed his 500th mile amidst great cheers from the partisan crowd. The ordeal finally ended with O'Leary's winning total of 520 miles completed in 139 hours.[7] Vaughan had scaled Olympian heights in surpassing 500 miles while the colorful veteran, "Blower" Brown, had a hard-earned total of 477 miles. None of the others finished and therefore they earned no prize money. Daniel O'Leary took his small fortune and already famous Astley Belt home to Chicago and declared he would not part with it "till some better man come and fetch it away." Sir John's belt was made of five solid plates of silver with a solid gold buckle in the center. The gold centerpiece contained the words "Long Distance Champion of the World," while the fine silverwork showed figures of walkers and runners.

Second Encounter for the Astley Belt

Sir John Astley decreed that Daniel O'Leary's newest challenger would be John Hughes, the well-known New Yorker, by way of Tipperary, Ireland. The match was scheduled in New York from September 30 to October 5, 1878. The belt, a $10,000 first prize, a generous portion of the gate receipts, side-bets, and the adulation of the mob awaited the winner. Over 30,000 spectators found their way into Madison Square Garden during the abbreviated week's contest. O'Leary, the "perfect runner," completely outclassed his rival and returned home a wealthy man.[8]

At the start of the unusual two-man affair, O'Leary struck off at a long body-swinging walk while Hughes fled the first five miles in thirty-five minutes and forty-one seconds, two miles ahead of his rival. There were two tracks, O'Leary selecting the longer one-eighth of a mile surface, while Hughes worked on the inner nine-laps-to-the-mile track. Members of the Harlem Athletic Club kept the scores in three separate books, each lap being called out distinctly to both men. Hughes had a tent erected at one end of the arena, where he was attended by his wife and trainer. O'Leary occupied one of the rooms in the main building.

It was evident that the champion was working more to beat Hughes than to break any records. The match was concluded at eleven o'clock on Saturday night, October 5th, by which time O'Leary had covered 403 miles and Hughes 310. During the last hours, a gold watch was presented the winner, to add to his already impressive earnings.[9]

The Crucial Third Match

One more victory and O'Leary would be permanent owner of the coveted Astley Belt. Ever since it had left the United Kingdom, English pedestrians had anxiously inquired as to who should attempt regaining the prize. Sir John consulted with his sporting friends, Lord Balfour and the Prince of Wales. Both enthusiastically endorsed young Charles Rowell, boat keeper and part-time pedestrian, who was destined to be one of England's greatest nineteenth century athletes.

Four athletes took their places at the starting line at 1 a.m., March 10, 1879. Madison Square Garden was jammed at this incongruous hour. The police had difficulty restraining a mob of several thousand that had been refused admittance. The thirty-one year old Daniel O'Leary, 5'8", 148 pounds, was on hand to defend his championship belt. The tiny twenty-five year old ex-boatman, Charles Rowell, was a "sprinter" at 20-50-mile races and had never attempted a six-day "go-as-you-please" grind. John Ennis, thirty-seven, veteran walker, had had but one experience at this type of major competition. The fourth man was Charles A. Harriman, a young man, big for the sport at 6' ½" and 170 pounds. His reputation had been made as Massachusetts champion at 100-mile and 36-hour runs.

The most competent judges in the city were on hand, including the famous American sportsman, William B. Curtis. Hourly bulletins of the pedestrians' progress were posted in the city's hotels, barbershops, barrooms, cigar stores, and corner grocery stores. The New York press carried daily, full-page spreads of the world's championship match. As soon as the race began it became evident that O'Leary was not well and by Wednesday he was unable to rest or retain food. The Irish-American champion was forced to retire with only 215 miles, but denied persistent rumors that he had been drugged. The three remaining runners were averaging eighty miles a day through Thursday.

On Friday morning, although the admission fee had been raised to one dollar, the crowds increased. Amidst cheers and the beat of the band, the trio walked and ran endlessly around the sawdust-tanbark track. By Friday evening, Rowell had accumulated 417 miles to 390 for Harriman and 387 for John Ennis. The final day was Saturday and the unruly crowd spilled onto the track and taunted the plucky Rowell. Both Ennis and Harriman instantly addressed the audience and threatened to abandon the contest should harm come to the leader of the race. The three men clasped hands amidst thunderous applause and circled the track together.[10]

As always, the exhausting extended marathon had taken its toll. At 8:45 p.m., Saturday evening, an utterly spent Harriman stopped the self-inflicted torture as he completed his 450th mile. At 9 p.m., Charles Rowell completed 500 miles amidst "utmost enthusiasm" and stopped. Ennis kept at it. The veteran, who was to continue competing well into the next century, was presented with flowers as he completed his 474th mile. In appreciation, he immediately began sprinting. The delighted crowd cheered as he spun around the track, racing the last mile in 6 minutes and 55 seconds.

The unprecedented throngs resulted in a fantastic $20,000 being paid to the new champion, Charles Rowell. Ennis took home $11,800, while Harriman was content with $8,200. Rowell, the man who could "strike a 7 mph dog trot and keep it up for an interminable period," had won a fortune. As he left the stadium draped in the American flag and weighted down with the gold and silver belt, Sir John was heard to quip that it was, "a pretty good haul for a man who seldom had two sovereigns to rub against each other.[11] Waiting at the exit to immediately lodge a formal challenge was possibly the greatest pedestrian the world has ever known, the American, Edward Payson Weston.

Weston and the Fourth Astley Belt

Edward Payson Weston was the supreme showman of the pedestrian world and he was ready for this race. Born in Providence, Rhode Island, on March 15, 1839, he was the most famous "ped" in the world, and was known as the "Father of American Pedestrianism." His record-breaking feats of endurance on two continents were legendary. He could sprint a hundred miles with the best or walk twenty hours a day for a month. During the drama of the third Astley Belt match, Weston was engaged in an incredible journey on foot throughout Great Britain. He walked 2,000 miles in exactly 1,000 hours, a physical feat of nearly unbelievable proportions. During that time, he never walked on Sundays and he delivered a brief temperance lecture in almost every community he passed through.[12] In April 1879, Weston finished fifth in a six-day go-as-you-please race in London. He totaled 450 miles, while the winner, the indefatigable "Blower" Brown, logged an impressive and record-breaking 542 miles.

The fourth match began on Monday morning, June 16, 1879, at Agricultural Hall, London. Four contestants were prepared to match strides with one another. "Blower" Brown was installed as favorite. Weston was the choice of Sir John. John Ennis and William E. Harding were on hand for a piece of the money. The great Charles Rowell sat glumly in the audience, having "run a peg into his right heel," while the physically exhausted Daniel O'Leary had temporarily retired.

Weston, the temperate health faddist, could run as well as walk and he charged through 120 miles in the first day. The magnificent Brown kept with him every mile. By Tuesday, Harding was already "looking very queer," and Ennis was seized with cramps. On Wednesday morning at the impossible hour of 3 a.m., Brown wrested the lead from Weston, opening a gap of 7 miles with a total of 227 record-breaking miles. During the next twenty-four hours, the great Weston kept within striking distance of the veteran Englishman. On Friday, the fifth day, Weston made his move, covered 73 miles, and took the lead. He was impressive as he alternately walked and ran the endless laps with an inexorable and fluid stride, a portrait of "iron-like legs and indomitable will." Brown succumbed under the ordeal, his swollen knee forcing him off the track for five hours, following repeated pleas from his doctor.

Weston never faltered and a few minutes before 11 p.m., Saturday, he completed "the greatest pedestrian task of which the world has any knowledge."[13] He had covered 550 miles in less than six days. Brown had run 452, Ennis 180, and Harding 147, the last two having dropped out early in the week.[14] Weston was $8,000 richer and looked forward to the inevitable challenge, this time from the previous belt winner, Charles Rowell. The fifth and final match for the Sir John Astley Belt was arranged.

The Fifth Astley Belt

The familiar scene was the Garden in New York City, shortly after midnight on Monday, September 22, 1879. Weston and Rowell were on hand as was the perennial Ennis. George Hazael of England, George Guyon of Canada, and Peter Panchot had records of running more than 400 miles in this kind of competition. Also seeking fame and fortune was the Negro champion from Boston, Frank Hart. Fred Krohne of Germany and Samuel Merritt of Bridgeport, Connecticut, with successful pedestrian backgrounds, were entered, while lesser personalities named Taylor, Jackson, Federmeyer, and Dutcher completed the group of thirteen starters. Daniel O'Leary, still in poor health, was in the stands and kept close watch over his protégé, Frank Hart.

The capacity crowd of 7500 had been undaunted by the one-dollar admission fee. They were in a betting mood and the ever-present gamblers were doing a brisk business. The odds offered were one and one-half to one against Rowell, two and one-half to one against Weston and three to one against Hazael. The New York papers had given full-page descriptions of the pending match.[15] Thirteen tents had been assigned to the athletes and were neatly arranged around the track. Here they would rest, eat, sleep and receive medical treatment during the six days and nights. Few would allow themselves more than eighteen hours in their tents during the torturous 144-hour contest. The eight-laps-to-the-mile track had a foundation of fine tanbark with an eight-foot wide surface of well-groomed and hard-packed loam.

It was pronounced in excellent shape. After twenty-four hours of walking and running, Rowell had covered 127 miles and had won a $200 bonus, a solid silver card case lined with gold, and a silver plate bearing his name. All the major contestants except Weston had beaten 100 miles that day.

On Tuesday, Rowell, Hazael, Guyon, and Ennis continued a pitched battle for the lead. Hazael, thirty-five years old, round-shouldered and powerfully built, ran with the "long lope of a deer." Rowell, the other tough-muscled Englishman, ran with a methodical jog-trot that never seemed to tire him. Guyon was by far the most graceful in his walking and running, but soon found himself 7½ miles behind the leader, Charles Rowell. Frank Hart walked in the image of his teacher, O'Leary, and was doing well. Rowell's inexorable pace resulted in a record 176 miles in 36 hours. At 48 hours, the score stood at Rowell, 215 miles; Guyon, 200; Merritt, 197; Hart, 194; Hazael, 185; Ennis, 180; Weston, 173; and Krohne, 160.

Nearly nine thousand tickets were sold on Wednesday, the third day. Rowell still led with 310 miles while a four-way battle for second place saw Merritt, Hazael, Hart, and Guyon some thirty miles back. Weston was in sixth place and incurred the wrath of many fans and the press with his cane-swinging, carefree air, "absurd antics and idiotic grimaces." His retirement of eight hours from the track disgusted those who had backed him "for a walking rather than a sleeping match," and the betting odds against him rose to 50-1. It was later discovered that Weston had been ill throughout the entire match but chose not to quit or reveal his condition. The crowd favorite, Frank Hart, kept close and received a wreath of flowers bearing the motto, "Go it, Black Dan."

On Thursday, ten men remained on the track. Excitement was high and thousands of dollars were bet on who would take second place. Bulletins of the runners' progress were posted "from the Harlem Bridge to the Battery." Six thousand paid customers were on hand that night plus 300 street urchins who had gained entrance to the Garden through a narrow coal hole on 27th Street. Even bets were made that Weston's record would stand. The Tribune reporter stated that "$225,000 covered all the books in the betting up to 8 p.m." By 1 a.m. Friday morning, the score read Rowell, 402 miles; Hazel, 368; Merritt, 367; Guyon, 345; Hart, 339; and Weston, 322.

A major crisis occurred late Friday morning. Rowell had failed to emerge from his tent following one of his infrequent and always brief rest periods. The crowd, especially the bookmakers, waited anxiously. Finally, after six hours, he emerged, shaken, ill, and in convulsions. The brave Englishman immediately set out in pursuit of Merritt, who had closed the gap to 8½ miles. At 8.58 p.m., Merritt broke into a fast run. Rowell, shaken as he was, accepted the challenge and followed close on his heels. The crowd loved it and a "perfect storm of cheers followed them around the track." They continued this way into the night, with the ever-present metallic ring of the bookmaker's voice hawking his wares. The crowd around the betting table was dense. At one o'clock in the morning of the last day, over 6,000 enthusiasts remained in the stands. Rowell now led Merritt 452 to 442, while Hazael, Guyon, Hart, and, surprisingly, Weston, had all totaled more than 400 miles.

The last day of the match, Saturday, September 27, 1879, saw nine men on the track. Federmeyer had quit, complaining that the tempo was "more for hares than turtles." All morning the silent shuffling continued. Rowell reached his 500th mile at 1:02 p.m., amidst cheers and "God Save the Queen" from the band. The doughty Rowell sprinted a lap in acknowledgement. A storm of applause greeted Merritt at 4:10 p.m. as he finished his 500th mile. At 8 p.m. the Garden was packed with the largest audience of the match. Hazael scored 500 miles at 8:03 p.m. The crowd became unruly and many slipped under the guard rails and onto the narrow track. Spectators elbowed past the police in an effort to see the finish. The protracted torment finally ended at 9:48 p.m., some 140 hours after the start. Trainers and physicians escorted the nine men to their hotels for treatment. Rowell was the winner again with 530 miles. Merritt had completed 515 miles and Hazael an even 500. Frank Hart, the Boston favorite, managed 482 and Guyon 471, Weston 455, both Ennis and Krohne 450, and Taylor an undistinguished 250 miles. Nearly $56,000 was divided among them with Rowell receiving $30,000 for his week's work.[16]

Decline of Pedestrianism

The inherent ills of professional sport are greed, callousness, and an insatiable tendency toward blatant and often brutalized gladiatorial display. Without a regulator, professional sport contains the seeds of its own destruction. Professional pedestrianism in the United States was guilty of these abuses and slowly began to ebb in popularity after the intriguing series of five matches sponsored by Sir John Astley. Six-day foot racing did not give in to the flashier and faster six-day bicycle racing for several years and not without a struggle. During the declining years of the sport, with vicious exploitation of the athletes by promoters and gamblers plus the athlete's self-realization of his own vast physical potential, the public saw some marvelous performances. Inevitably, the world's record fell time and again.

In February of 1880, "Blower" Brown covered 553 miles and broke Weston's record. In New York City, from April 5-10, 1880, Frank Hart ran 566 miles. Rowell also did 566 miles in London that same year. Over the Christmas holiday in 1881, Patrick Fitzgerald upped the "go-as-you-please" record and the Madison Square Garden record to a prodigious 582 miles. On March 3, 1882, in New York, George Hazael of England became the first human to officially run 600 miles in six days and six nights. In that same race, his countryman Charles Rowell totaled a staggering 150 miles in the first twenty-four hours, a world record. In May 1884, Fitzgerald defeated Rowell 612 miles to 602 miles in a memorable race witnessed by 12,000 New Yorkers. On February 9, 1888, James Albert, alias "Cathcart," a Philadelphia alderman, logged his 621st mile and another record. Finally, the fastest six-day marathoner of them all, a tiny Englishman named George Littlewood, astonished the sports world and a knowledgeable New York audience with a performance of 623 ¾ miles in 139 hours and 59 minutes, a record unapproached to the present day.[17]

The sport died, but many of the runners continued their mesmeric tread on to the end of the century and well into the next. Weston had walked nearly 5,000 miles in 100 days in 1884.[18] He and his old rival Daniel O'Leary staged a comeback in 1896 by walking 2,500 miles across America in nine weeks. Charles Rowell completed a full 26-mile marathon in 3 hours and 4 minutes on March 26, 1909. John Ennis continued to walk till the eve of World War I. In 1909, the 71-year-old Edward Payson Weston made the headlines again by walking 3,895 miles from New York City to San Francisco in 104 days.[19] In 1913, on the fiftieth anniversary of his famous walk from Maine to Washington, D.C. (to attend Lincoln's inauguration), Weston duplicated the feat and astonished the accompanying doctors. Always the showmen, the six-day pedestrians of the nineteenth century represent a breed of men and a sport that is not likely ever to be seen again.

NOTES

1 "Pedestrian Feats," *Every Saturday,* July 11, 1868, pp. 46-50.

2 For interesting accounts of this important race, see Jennie Holliman, *American Sports (1785-1835)* (Durham, N. C.: Seaman Press, 1931), p. 154; Philip Hone, *The Diary of Philip Hone 1828-1851*, Allan Nevins, Ed. Vol. I. (Dodd, Mead and Co., 1927), p. 157.

3 *New York Times*, April 25, 1835, p. 2. This reference is from the old *New York Times*, founded May 12, 1834, which ceased publication October 17, 1837.

4 *The Spirit of the Times,* October 19, 1844, p. 402 and November 23, 1844, p. 462; *The Illustrated London Times*, January 11, 1845, p. 21.

5 Ralph H. Gabriel (Ed), *Annals of American Sport*, Vol. XV. "Early Professional Races," by John Alien Krout (New Haven: Yale University Press, 1929), p. 186; William B. Curtis, "By-gone International Athletic Contests," *Outing*, Vol. XXXVI (July, 1900), p. 350; and James S. Mitchell, "Athletic Giants of the Past, *Outing*, Vol. XXVIII (1901), p. 2 6 9.

6 William E. Harding, *The Pedestrian Manual. History of the Astley and O'Leary Belts* (New York: McGlew & Jacques, Publishers, 1880), p. 6.

7 Edward Plummer, *The American Championship Record and a History of Mixing Races* (New York: Snowden and Beaudine, 1881), p. 23.

8 "The Hughes-O'Leary Contest," *New York Sportsman*, October 5, 1878, p. 164.

9 "Walking for the Championship," *Frank Leslie's Illustrated Newspaper,* October 19, 1878, p. 115.

10 Two pages of illustrated materials and race commentary may be found in *Frank Leslie's Illustrated Newspaper*, March 29, 1879, pp. 48, 55.

11 John Dugdale Astley, *Fifty Years of My Life in the World of Sport at Home and Abroad* (London: Hurst and Blacken, Ltd., 1894), p. 156.

12 Walter H. Moler, "Weston and His Walks—the Wonderful Record of Edward Payson Weston," Souvenir program, 1910.

13 "Weston and the Championship," *The Turf, Field and Farm,* June 27, 1879, p. 410.

14 Further accounts of the Fourth Astley Belt race may be found in *Harper's Weekly*, July 12, 1879, p. 543; *The Turf, Field and Farm*, June 20, 1879, p. 396; and *New York Times*, June 22, 1879, p. 1.

15 The *New York Tribune* sports pages from September 23, 1879 through September 28, 1879 were dominated by detailed accounts of this memorable fifth contest. See also *The Daily Inter-Ocean*, Chicago, September 29, 1879, p. 3; and *The New York Sportsman*, October 4, 1879, p. 164.

16 Fifth Contest for the Astley Belt," *Frank Leslie's Illustrated Newspaper,* October 4, 1879, pp. 71-72.

17 Statistical details of all these record performances may be found in James I. Lupton, *The Pedestrian's Record* (London: W. H. Alien and Co., 1890).

18 "Weston's Temperance Tours," *The Times* (London) March 17, 1884, p. 10 and April 3, 1884, p. 6.

19 The *New York Times* carried extensive and daily columns in Weston's own words, beginning on March 16, 1909 and ending July 14, 1909.

3.
A History of the Marathon Race— 490 B.C. to 1975*

"Forty kilometers and then some— a marathon history from Pheidippides to Bill Rodgers"

Greek Antecedents

The marathon race is one of the greatest tests of individual endurance, and, in the western world, has resulted in an extraordinary history of physical prowess, courage, foolhardiness, drama and tragedy. The interesting word "marathon" may be used as a noun to describe any long distance foot race; in a twentieth-century context, it refers to an endurance contest of twenty-six miles, 385 yards. It is also a geographic location in Greece—made famous in 490 B.C. as the "Battle of Marathon." The word "marathon" may be used as an adjective in describing any phenomenon of great length, and it is commonly used in this manner. This paper will deal with the history of the marathon run—from its shrouded ancient origins to the extraordinary 1975 Boston Marathon victory of that New England free spirit— William "Bill" Rodgers. The even more perplexing problem of why men and women will spend years of preparation in order to run rapidly and without stopping more than forty-two kilometers will at least be alluded to in this document.

Highly organized competitive sport was invented by the Greeks. Homer's epic poem, the *Iliad,* is a tapestry of sport training and competition. Book XXIII, "The funeral rites of Patroclus, and how the games were held in his honor," is one of literature's most re-

Journal of Sport History 3 (Summer 1976), 120-138.

vealing insights into man's play and competitive instincts.[1] Later in 776 B.C., the Olympic Games were established to honor the gods, to pay homage to Greek warriors, and to emphasize and formalize a way of living that was to characterize these people for a thousand years. Herodotus immortalized this Greek penchant for sport in Book VIII of his *Histories,* where Greek deserters, brought before the Persians king, were asked what their countrymen were doing at that time.

> The Arcadians told him that they were keeping the Olympic festival and watching athletic contests and horse-races. The questioner asked what was the prize that they were contending for; and the Arcadians told him about the crown of olive that was to be won. Then Tigranes, son of Artabanus, said a most noble thing, though the king thought him a coward for it: for when he heard that the prize was a garland and not money, he could not hold his peace, but exclaimed in the hearing of all: "alas, Mardonius, what men are these that you have brought us to fight, who hold contests not for money but for the honor of winning."[2]

The Ancient Legend of Marathon

Nowhere in Greek sporting literature is there any mention of a twenty-six-mile marathon race. The Olympic multiple stade race probably did not exceed three miles. According to history and legend, the Persian king, Darius, attacked Greece to punish Athens for sending aid to the Ionian rebels. Herodotus says that Darius was so angered by the sack of Sardis that, during the rest of his life, he had a herald cry out to him thrice each day at dinner,—"O King, remember the Athenians!" The truth is that Persia was in a full career of conquest, and invasion was inevitable. The first expedition against Greece, 492 B.C., failed; in 490 B.C. the full strength of the Persian army and navy captured the Greek city of Eretria. Then the Persians landed on the plain of Marathon in Attica, prepared to punish Athens. In uncharacteristic fashion, Miltiades and the Assembly decided to leave the city, march out, and attack the Persians at once. Before they left the city, says Herodotus [ca. 484?-425 B.C.], the Athenian generals sent off a message of help to Sparta. "The messenger was an Athenian named Pheidippides, a trained runner still in the practice of his profession."[3] He reached Sparta the day after leaving Athens. "Men of Sparta," he is reported to have said, "the Athenians ask of you to help them, and not to stand by while the most ancient city of Greece is crushed and enslaved by a foreign invader."⁴

Apparently, Pheidippides (sometimes called Philippides) raced these 150 miles in vain—a rugged route between Athens and Sparta passing through the mountainous country of Arcadia. The Spartans, celebrating their festival of the Carneia, were unable to send their promised help before the full moon, which was probably six days away. Herodotus goes on to relate that during Pheidippides' return to Athens, he was stopped by the god Pan on Mount Parthenium, who promised to help the Athenians. The Greeks apparently believed the courier's message and, again, according to Herodotus, sought the gods' favor with yearly sacrifices and torch races. "After the full moon," says the great Greek story-teller, "two thousand Lacedaemonians came to Athens making so great haste to reach it that they were in Attica on the third day from their leaving Sparta. Albeit they came too late for the battle."⁵ The orator-pamphleteer, Isocrates [436-338 B.C.], in delivering his *Panegyric* before a crowd assembled for the Olympic games in 380 B.C. agreed with Herodotus on the speed of the Spartans, noting that "the Lacedaemonians in three days and as many nights covered 1200 stadia in marching order."⁶

The task of disentangling marathon fact from legend and myth, of seeing through the romance of marathon literature, and of discarding fiction about Greek long-distance running feats is a formidable one. There seems little doubt that a courier was sent from Athens to Sparta ... and that he returned with the discouraging message of delay by Spartan warriors. At this juncture—the fate of Pheidippides during and after the Battle of Marathon—is puzzling. Hammond's definitive study of the September struggle in 490 B.C. tells us little about the Athenian courier.⁷ Only the singular account of the Greek satirist, Lucian [ca. 120?-200?], some six hundred years after the fact, would indicate that Pheidippides was present at the Battle of Marathon and raced to Athens with the victory message. Lucian was reminded of the marathon story, when inadvertently greeting some friends, he said, "Health to you," instead of the more correct and ancient phrase, "Joy to you." He goes on to trace the origin of the latter phrase to:

> Philippides, the one who acted as courier, is said to have used it first in our sense when he brought the news of victory from Marathon and addressed the magistrates in session when they were anxious how the battle had end-

ed; "Joy to you, we've won," he said, and there and then he died, breathing his last breath with that "Joy to you."[8]

This is the only mention by an ancient writer declaring that it was Pheidippides who raced from Marathon to Athens. If one accepts this story, it must also be accepted that the messenger Pheidippides, or Philippides, raced the three-hundred-mile round trip between Athens and Sparta, marched to Marathon, and after the struggle, ran himself to death on his return to Athens. It seems unlikely.

Aristophanes [c. 448-388? B.C.], wrote the *Clouds* in 423 B.C., only sixty-seven years after the famous battle. The Athenian dramatist dwells at length on a certain Strepsiades and his vulgar and dissolute son, Pheidippides. It is unlikely that Aristophanes would have taken the name of the heroic Marathon courier for such unsavory a character as his Pheidippides of the *Clouds*. Lucian had attributed both runs to Pheidippides, but received no encouragement or confirmation in this position. Pliny the Elder [c. 23-79 A.D.], in his *Naturalis Historia,* calls Pheidippides's run from Athens to Sparta "a mighty feat."[9] Plutarch [c. 46?-120?] is more specific. The Greek biographer, in a famous discussion of Athenian military prowess as contrasted with Athenian wisdom (called "DeGloria Atheniensium), elaborated:

> Again, the news of the battle of marathon Thersippus of Eroeadae brought back, as Heracleides Ponticus related; but most historians declare that it was Eucles who ran in full armor, hot from the battle, and, bursting in at the doors of the first men of the State, could only say, "Hail! We are victorious" and straightaway expired.[10]

Pheidippides—Dubious Double Marathon Runner

There seems sufficient evidence to state that the Greek professional, Pheidippides, made the round trip from Athens to Sparta, but not the more famous, and shorter trial from Marathon to Greece. Harris relies heavily on Plutarch in stating that the Athenian Eucles, upon returning to Athens from abroad after the army had marched out to Marathon, "ran out to take his place in the ranks, arrived just in time to fight in the battle, and then ran back to announce the victory in Athens, dying as he did so."[11] A "modern confusion," says Gardiner, has resulted in the wrong man receiving credit for the victory run from the plain of

Marathon to Athens.[12] Ehrenberg goes further by labeling as "romantic invention" the idea that the same warrior-athlete made both runs.[13] Herodotus makes no mention of a messenger from Marathon to Athens—a courier who shouted "nike!" (victory!) with his last breath as he fell dead in the agora. The modern historian, Swain, conjectured that "Miltiades had every reason to let the city learn of his victory at the earliest possible moment ... yet we find no reference to [a] runner until more than six hundred years later."[14] The whole marathon race is commemorative of a legend of doubtful authenticity. Provost C. Henry Daniel of Worcester College, Oxford, concluded that "there is no mention of the presence of Pheidippides at Marathon, nor of any special messenger carrying the news of the victory to Athens."[15] Another scholar, writing in 1908, is of the opinion that Plutarch's six-hundred-year-old version is correct—that a certain Thersippus brought the news of the battle, expiring after he announced the victory. Lucian, also writing long after the fact, credited Pheidippides with both memorable runs. "A casual error of memory," on Lucian's part, said this same early-20th century writer in a letter to *The Times* of London.[16]

Noted historian, W. C. Lawson, writing during the American marathon "craze" of 1909, declared the alleged death run of Pheidippides as both untrue and absurd. "Even as a teleological myth," he says, "this is hardly a success ... it gives no encouragement to defenders of the heart-breaking long run."[17] Three scholars answered Lawson's accusation, but were more concerned with the accuracy of Greek translations, proper sources, and spelling, rather than the central matter of a Marathon to Athens run.[18] Herodotus never heard of Pheidippides, says Professor Lawson, in a reply to his three colleagues. "If, sixty years after the battle, any such tale had been current, surely the chronicler would have heard it from his Athenian friends and used it to gild his rather meager record...."[19] Poetic license and nineteenth-century romanticism are the culprits in crediting Pheidippides with the fabulous Marathon to Athens run.[20]

The Marathon as Nineteenth-Century Romantic Imagery

The European Romantic Movement began in the late eighteenth century, continuing well into the next period. The heroic struggle for independence by the Greeks, culminating in full liberation from Turkey in 1832, created a significant stir of romantic sympathy for the Greeks, and, especially, a renaissance of ancient Greek scholarship. Lord Byron [1788-1824] had participated in these early struggles and wrote in impassioned tones about the glory that was Greece. Standing amidst the Marathon battleground, he cried:

> The mountains look on Marathon—
> and Marathon looks on the sea;
> and musing there an hour alone,
> I dream'd that Greece might still be free,
> For standing on the Persian's grave,
> I could not deem myself a slave.[21]

In 1823, Byron set out to join Greek insurgents and died of fever at Missolonghi in April, 1824. Several years earlier he had finished his series of cantos, *Childe Harold.* In his youth Byron had toured Greece, and he remembered the country as a place of romance and unending beauty. Later, longing for Greek freedom, he exclaimed, "Ah! Greece! they love thee least who owe thee most—." In his Second Canto, Byron is shaken by "gray marathon":

> The sun, the soil, but not the slave, the same;
> Unchanged in all except its foreign lord—
> Preserved alike its bounds and boundless fame
> The Battlefield, where Persia's victim horde
> First bowed beneath the brunt of Hellas' sword,
> As on the morn to distant Glory dear
> When Marathon became a magic word.[22]

Robert Browning [1812-1889], English poet, had little formal education, apart from a year studying Greek at University College, London. Yet his experiments in diction and rhythm made him an important influence on twentieth-century poetry. Browning's dramatic idyll "Pheidippides" gives credit to the Athenian foot racer for both the Athens to Sparta 150-mile run, as well as the shorter "Marathon" from the battleground to Athens. The poet pays tribute to Greece and Pheidippides:

> First I salute this soil of the blessed, river and rock!
> Gods of my birthplace, daemons and heroes,
>   honor to all!
> Then I name thee, claim thee for our patron,
>   co-equal in praise.

"Run, Pheidippides, run and race, reach Sparta for aid!" implores an animated Browning. The familiar story of this "best runner of Greece"—as Miltiades called him—culminates in a blending of heroic fact and legend:

> Unforeseeing one! Yes, he fought on the Marathon day:
> So, when Persia was dust, all cried "To Akropolis!
> Run, Pheidippides, one race more! the mead [prize] is
>   thy due!
> 'Athens is saved, thank Pan,' go shout!" He flung down
>   his shield,
> Ran like fire once more: and the space 'twixt the Fennel-field
> And Athens was stubble again, a field which a fire runs
>   through,
> Till in he broke: "Rejoice, we conquer!" Like wine
>   through clay,
> Joy in his blood bursting his heart, he died—the bliss!
> So, to this day, when friend meets friend, the word of
>   salute
> Is still "Rejoice!"—his word which brought rejoicing indeed.
> So is Pheidippides happy forever,—the noble strong man
> Who could race like a God, bear the face of a God, whom
>   a God loved so well;
> He saw the land saved he had helped to save, and was
>   suffered to tell
> Such tidings, yet never decline, but, gloriously as he began,
> So to end gloriously—once to shout, thereafter be mute:
> "Athens is saved!"—Pheidippides lies in the shout for his
>   mead.[23]

Marathon poetry of less epic proportions continued into the present century. Alice E. Hanscom's "The Mound at Marathon,"[24] Fred Jacob's "The Marathon,"[25] and "The Athenian Battlehymn at Marathon,"[26] by Sir Francis Doyle, are examples. A recent novel— a skillful blending of ancient history and poetic license—is *Marathon* by Alan Lloyd. The author calls Pheidippides' acknowledged run to Sparta "a feat in the best tradition of Greek athleticism."[27] The author conjectures that Pheidippides returned from Sparta and was in the Athenian phalanx at Marathon "wielding a burnished blade." Lloyd concludes his tale by quoting Browning's heroic version of the exhausted Pheidippides' race from Marathon to Athens, the victory cry, and death. This last and most famous story has little historic substance, but is of enormous romantic proportions. Interesting historical vignettes continue to be associated with Marathon. For example, in 1895, a M. Dragoumis found in Salamis a stone which had long served as a doorstop to a peasant's cottage, and which was inscribed with the epitaph:

> Battling for Greece the Athenians at Marathon leveled the power of Persians, wearers of gold. With myriads three hundred here once fought from Peloponnesus thousands four.[28]

Marathon Feats through the Ages

Motivated by pride, patriotism, profit, glory, curiosity, and even by personal demons, men (and a few women) have performed fabulous trials of marathoning through the ages. Some stories are untrue—impossible, others are without substantiation, while many contain degrees of veracity from the possible to absolute fact. The ancient scribe, Pliny, tells of Alexander the Great's courier Philonides and the Spartan runner Anystis, both of whom ran the 148 miles inside the colosseum, while it is reported that "a boy of eight ran 68 miles between noon and evening." Guillaume Depping's revealing *Wonders of Bodily Strength and Skill* tells of Turkish foot-runners traveling the 120 miles from Constantinople to Adrianople in 24 hours. He also describes the Abbe Nicquet as the swiftest traveler of the sixteenth century, "who reached Rome from Paris in six days four hours, although the distance was 350 leagues."

Modern long-distance running or pedestrianism, as it was called, originated in Great Britain in the seventeenth century. From *The Diary of Samuel Pepys for the Year A.D. 1663* to today's countless British cross-country, road, and marathon races, these people, favored by climate and geography, have led the way in distance running. Two English footmen, running in Windsor Park in 1700, covered 22 miles in 2 ½ hours, while a few years later the teenaged Conrad Weiser ran footraces against Pennsylvania Indians. *The Secret Diary of William Byrd* reveals an early eighteenth-century footrace of three hours "for a wager of two guineas." The infamous "Pennsylvania Walking Purchase of 1737" saw the Delaware Indians cheated out of thousands of square miles as three highly trained white men raced 70 miles through dense forest in an agreed-upon eighteen-hour marathon. The legendary Foster Powell ran the 50 miles between London and Bath in seven hours the year after the 1763 Treaty of Paris. He continued running all over England for the next thirty years. At age sixty, he won a heavy wager for running the 402-mile roundtrip between London and York in five days 15 ¼ hours.

Marathon-like walks and runs punctuated the leisure hours of both English gentlemen and the working class for the entire nineteenth century. Largely responsible for the phenomena was Captain Allardyce Barclay who walked 1000 miles in 1000 hours—a continuous feat accomplished between June 1 and July 14, 1809. George Wilson, a tax collector, better known as the Blackheath Pedestrian, walked 1000 miles in 20 days in the year 1815. John Stewart [1749-1822], "The Celebrated Walking Stewart," toured on foot Europe, North America, and the Near East. Well-educated and philosophically inclined, the tall and handsome eccentric "refused to have his life recorded because his were the travels of the mind, and his object the discovery of the polarity of moral truth." A rash of American distance running performed on horse tracks began in 1824. Hoboken, New Jersey and Union, Long Island were the scenes of dozens of such affairs till the eve of war. *The American Farmer* of October 3, 1828, reported that a certain Cootes had broken Captain Barclay's record and logged 1250 miles in 1000 consecutive hours. The feat was surpassed several more times in the next half century. *The American Turf Register and Sporting Magazine,* during this antebellum period is filled with interesting and extraordinary marathon feats—mostly professional affairs.

Joshua Newsam was reported to have won $1000.00 by walking 1000 miles in 18 days in Philadelphia during November, 1830. Perhaps the most implausible adventure is that of the Norwegian sailor—Ernst Mensen—who ran from Paris to Moscow in less than 14 days [1831], and a round trip from Constantinople to Calcutta in two months [1836]. Sport magazines and New York City newspapers were filled with pedestrian feats during the 1840s and 1850s. Ten, fifteen, and twenty mile races—carefully supervised by officials and gamblers—produced nearly modern performances. Foreigners, Americans, and American Indians were improving records and earning handsome purses. *The Diary of Philip Hone, Spirit of the Times, Bell's Life in London,* and many other publications record man's seeming endless desire to run—for whatever reasons might engender the human species to such enterprises.

For some twenty years, between 1870 and 1890, English and American sport aficionados were caught up in six-day go-as-you-please contests. Profitable, exotic, and frequently dangerously exhausting, the names of Edward Payson Weston and Daniel O'Leary became synonymous with running 500 miles or more in six days and six nights. Hundreds of thousands of people paid from fifty cents to two dollars to see the sight. A score of "500" men emerged during the age until finally tiny George Littlewood raced 623 ¾ miles in 125 hours, 34 minutes, resting a total of 16 hours 26 minutes. It was all done in December of 1888, and on the little sawdust-tanbark track inside Madison Square Garden—an authentic Olympian marathon feat.

Both Weston and O'Leary walked on into the twentieth century, posting significant times even though well past seventy years of age. The unbelievable Weston walked the American continent during the spring of 1910. In England, 1921, George Cummings walked 420 miles from London to Edinburgh in 82 hours. The year before, 81 year-old Daniel O'Leary walked from Philadelphia to Atlantic City in 12 hours. During 1928 and 1929, entrepreneur Charles C. ("Cash and Carry") Pyle, organized cross-continent "Bunyun Derbies." The bizarre affairs—well orchestrated to catch the imagination (and monies) of thousands of Americans—culminated in an Oklahoma Indian's close victory over Joe Salo of Passaic, New Jersey. Nineteen-year-old Andy Payne staggered into New York City on June 1, 1928—90 days after leaving Los Angeles. He collected $25,000, Salo $10,000, eight others split unevenly the remaining $9,500. "The other 45 [finishers] received only a verbal citation for their guts and staying power."

Edward Payson Weston died at 90 years in 1929—the same year that Abraham Lincoln Monteverde, a 60-year-old bookbinder, walked from New York to San Francisco in 79 days. By this date, the compulsive South African runner, Arthur Newton, was setting records at ultra-marathon distances—50 miles in 6 hours and 100 miles in 14 hours, and 152 1/3 miles in 24 hours — all when past his fiftieth birthday. During the spring of 1960, two British soldiers and a Russian medical doctor, Dr. Barbara Moore, walked across the American continent. Fifty-year-old John Sinclair walked 216 miles in 47 hours 42 minutes without stopping once; he also walked from John O'Groats to Land's End (600 miles) in 19 days 22 hours.[29] Two years earlier in 1967, he walked 900 miles from Cape Town to Pretoria in 23 days. In 1964, Don Shepherd, another South African, walked and jogged alone across the United States in 73 days only to have his 1964 record broken by 8 days in 1969, by speed runner and British Olympian, Bruce Tulloh—whose 64 days, 21 hours, and 30 minutes remains the record at the present time.

Professional distance runner, Australian Bill Emmerton, has run some 150,000 miles in his eventful and bizarre career. In 1968, he ran across Death Valley, and repeated the feat again four months later. "Man believed sane runs through Death Valley," headlined the *Los Angeles Herald Examiner*. In October of 1969, John Tarrant of South Africa ran 400 laps on a track at Walton-on-Thames, England, in 12:31:10—a world record for 100 miles. It was promptly broken by 16 minutes in 1970 by Dave Box of South Africa. America's greatest super distance runner is Ted Corbitt, a New York City physiotherapist, who has accumulated a tenth of a million miles in 35 years of running. Clarence De Mar, John A. Kelley, John J. Kelly, Nicholas Costes, Browning Ross, Lou Gregory, are other Americans who have probably run 100,000 miles or more. There must be others. One of the greatest runs occurred on November 4, 1973, when Ron Bentley of England ran 161.3 miles in 24 hours, beating Hayward's record by two miles. That same month, an Irish-born Australian, Tony Rafferty, 34, ran 3686 miles from Fremantle on the west coast of Australia to Surfers Paradise on the east coast to break the 44-year-old world record by 21 miles. He did it in 74 days, averaging nearly 50 miles a day. In 1974, incorrigible Bill Emmerton ran 21 miles down and then up to the top of the Grand Canyon in 7 hours 45 minutes. Lastly, in March of 1975, a South African Kalahari bushman easily outdistanced a champion distance runner in a ten-miler across the desert.[30] Tokkelos, in his job as game tracker for Stoffel le Riche, chief ranger of the Kalahari game park, regularly runs eight hours nonstop, without food or water over soft desert sand and under a murderously hot sun. When tested by a physical education scientist at Stellenbosch University, the comment was made: "Staggering—his potential is simply staggering."

The First American Marathon, September 19, 1896

The fall meeting of the Knickerbocker Athletic Club took place in New York City's Columbia Oval on September 19, 1896. Yet the most historic event of the track meet was taking place in Stamford, Connecticut, exactly 25 miles away. As early as August 27, the *Stamford Advocate* showed considerable interest in this first American "Marathon."[31] World records were broken in the 600 yard dash and the quarter-mile hurdles, but it was the marathon finish that captured people's imagination. At 3:51 p.m. a woman screamed, "They're here! They're coming!"

The cry was taken up in the grandstand. Women who knew only that the first race of its kind ever held in this country was nearing a finish, waved their handkerchiefs and fairly screamed with excitement.... There was a pandemonium of joy. Judges stopped their work; athletes found time to become spectators.[32]

Pale-faced John J. McDermott of the Pastime Athletic Club had overcome fatigue and poor weather in 3:25:55.6, a half hour slower than the Athens Olympic victor of several months earlier. "The crowd was howling itself hoarse"—oblivious to the slow time—as the first two athletes circled the track and crossed the finish line. After all, history has been made—the first marathon race in America.

The Modern Olympic Marathon 1896-1972

Baron Pierre de Coubertin [1863-1937] conceived the idea of a modern version of the Olympic Games, but it was a French compatriot, Michel Breal [1832-1915], who thought of including a marathon race at the first Athens Games in April of 1896. Two years earlier, at the first meeting of the International Olympic Congress, delegate Breal "sent word to Baron de Coubertin recalling the legendary feat of Pheidippides and offering a trophy for a race to be run over the same course...."[33] Coubertin's autobiography confirms that "the marathon race was the creation of an illustrious member of the Institut de France,"[34] Breal, the brilliant semanticist and student of Greek mythology, probably had no idea how completely captivating his marathon idea would become. The world soon read of the Athens marathon victory by the Greek shepherd, Spiridion Louis; little was heard about the efforts of a certain Melpomene to enter this first Olympic marathon race. Her request was refused; accompanied by bicyclists, she nonetheless allegedly covered the 40 kilometers from Marathon to Athens in 4½ hours. The Greek paper, *Akropolis,* commented that "The Olympic Committee deserves to be reprimanded, because it was discourteous in refusing a lady's nomination. We can assure those concerned that none of the participants would have had any objections."[35]

All the Olympic marathon victors and their stories are included in John Hopkins' *The Marathon.*[36] The marathon distance in Paris in 1900, was 40,260 meters, in 1904, 40 kilometers, and at the unofficial 1906 Games in Athens the distance of about

26 miles was, apparently, slightly longer than the first Olympic race. The most famous of all Olympic marathon runs was the London affair of 1908. Pietro Dorando collapsed time after time within yards of the finish yarn. A compassionate official helped the semiconscious Italian across the line; Johnnie Hayes was then declared the winner and the western world became acutely aware of the marathon race. The distance of this race was 42.263 kilometers or 26 miles 385 yards. It seems that British officials, desirous of accommodating the King of England, started the race at Windsor Castle and finished at the Royal box in the Olympic Stadium—a distance of precisely 26 miles 385 yards.[37] The Queen of England awarded Dorando a special medal; his courage and deportment captured the sporting public. At Charing-Cross station, just before departing London, Dorando spoke to the London *Times* representative and a large crowd, pointing out the kindness of the English people, especially the Queen. "As the train left the station, the Italian national air was sung with great fervor."[38]

K. K. McArthur, a South African policeman, won a 1912 Olympic marathon race of 24 miles, 1725 yards in 2 hours, 36 minutes, 54.8 seconds. The remarkable Finn, Hannes Kolehmainen won an elongated 26½-miler in 2:36:54.8 at the Antwerp Olympics of 1920. Paris in 1924 witnessed the 26 mile 385 yard distance, and another Finn, 40-year-old Albin Stenroos, who won in 2:41:22.6. This marathon distance would remain the standard to the present day. Olympic marathon champions, thereafter, have been: El Ouafi of Algeria in 1928 (2:32:57.0), Zabala of Argentina in 1932 (2:31:36.0), and Kitei Son of Korea/Japan at Berlin in 2:29:19.2. The Games of the XIIth and XIIIth Olympiads were never held due to war. At London in 1948, an utterly exhausted Ettiene Gailly entered the Olympic stadium almost at a standstill, was passed by Cabrera of Argentina and Tom Richards of England—the South American winning in 2:34:51.6. Emil Zatopek of Czechoslovakia won gold medals at 5000 and 10,000 meters, and after several days rest won the 1952 Olympic marathon in 2:23:3.2. The element of speed had abruptly entered the traditional endurance event. Another Algerian, Alain Mimoun, won in 1956, running through the streets of Melbourne in 2:25. Abebe Bikila, "The Lion of Ethiopia,"—the only double winner in Olympic marathon history—sailed through the 1960 Rome race in 2:15:16.2 and ran a magnificent 2:12:11.2. in Tokyo. Mexico City in 1968 was the splendid scenery for another Ethiopian—Mamo Walde—who ran 2:20:26.4 through the city's thin mile-high air.

The United States, after 64 years of trying, was represented by the 1972 Olympic marathon champion—Yale University's Frank Shorter in 2:12:19.7. No pattern emerges except years of hard, intelligent work, gradual adaptation to a variety of external/internal stresses, and the slow apprehension by physicians and physiologists that a marathoner's greatness is all of the above plus the strong possibility of a genetically inherited talent.

The Illustrious Boston Marathon 1897-1975

J. J. McDermott won the first Boston Athletic Association Marathon race on April 19, 1897, in 2:55:10. AAU chief, James E. Sullivan, recalled that the fifteen starters "were at that time considered fit candidates for an insane asylum at the idea of running twenty-five miles."[39] Senior sports editor of *The Boston Globe,* Jerry Nason, has documented in capsule form every winner's performance from that first year through the 1965 record run of Japan's Morio Shigematsu (2:16:33).[40] Famous and colorful names and events are found in this classic event. Drama and pathos, a whole range of human emotions and experiences are wrapped up in this marathon—second only to the Olympic race. For example, in 1907 the talented nineteen-year-old Onondago Indian, Tom Longboat, elected to sprint through South Farmingham—only six miles into the race. It was a wise move as he had just managed to get past a railroad grade crossing as a long freight rolled by. The rest of the field was "log-jammed for two minutes." Longboat won by 3 ½ minutes. Clarence H. DeMar won the 1911 classic, and won again six more times. The 1923 race, won by DeMar, was the last at the shorter 25 mile distance. DeMar promptly won the 1924 version over a 26 mile, 209 yard course, and a 26 mile 385 yard course in 1927. Leslie Pawson in '33, '38, and '41, John A. Kelly in '35 and '45, Ellison "Tarzan" Brown in '36, and Gerard Cote in '40, '43, '44, and 1948, were several of the great pre and post war winners.

The foreign "invasion" began earnestly in 1946 with Stylianos Kyriakides, Yun Bok Suh in '47, Leanderson in '49, several Koreans, many Japanese, a Guatemalan, and an army of Finns. Anti Viskari won in 1956 (2:14:14), his countryman, Oksanen (2:17:56) was third. Two brilliant Americans, John "The Younger" Kelley (2:14:33) and Nick Costes (2:18:01) were second and fourth. Road re-measurements found the course 1183 yards short; it was lengthened and the meteoric Kelley promptly won the '57 classic in 2:20:05. Mihalic of Yugoslavia took the 1958 prize in 2:25:54; Oksanen returned to win the '59, '61, and 1962 races—all in fast times. Paavo Kotila, another Finn, won a 2:20:54 race in 1960, Belgium's Vandendriessche in 1963 and 1964 (2:18:58/2:19:59). Morio Sigematsu led an awesome Japanese sweep of 1-2-3-5-6 places; his 2:16:33 was a record in 1965.

In nearly unbelievable precision, Japanese marathoners took first through fourth places in the 1966 Boston classic—Kenjii Kimihara (2:17:11) only seconds ahead of the other three. In 1967, Dave McKenzie of New Zealand had to run a fast 2:15:45 to beat New York City's Tom Laris by a minute. This was also the year of the "mysterious entry," "K. Switzer of Syracuse." Kathy— the first known woman to run the race—had great difficulty with officials, made national headlines, and was a portent of the direction the marathon race would take. Surprising and popular was the 1968 victory of Wesleyan senior, Ambrose J. Burfoot (2:22:17). Hiroshima's Unetani lay to rest the notion of any other country but Japan as the world's greatest marathoning specialists during the 1960s. His 2:13:49 in 1969 was a record. Significant was the "mass marathon" syndrome, as 1152 men (and a few women not officially included) chose the protracted difficulties, challenges, and satisfactions of a twenty-six miler. Ron Hill of England, 31-year-old chemist and world champion, parlayed a scientifically harsh training program with a cool, moist, wind-blown day to win the 1970 race in a breath-taking 2:10:30—the second person in history to average under five minutes a mile. Eamon O'Reilly of the U.S.A. flew 2:11:12 in second place. Alvero Mejia of Columbia (2:18:45) beat Pat McMahon by only five seconds in 1971, while youthful Olavi Suomalainen of Finland took the 1972 prize in 2:15:39. Jon Anderson of Eugene, Oregon, ran an intelligent and courageous 2:16:03 in 1973; another American college student, Neil Cusak of Ireland, won the '74 race in 2:13:39. He had to run fast to beat the very strong Tom Fleming (2:14:25). Marathon fever was spreading rapidly, and despite time restrictions put on the race, 1705 men and 36 women officially ran that year's Boston marathon.

Back in December of 1967, towering 6' 2", 160 pound, Irish-born Australian, Derek Clayton, became the first person to run a full 26 mile 385 yard marathon in under 130 minutes—a seemingly impossible task. He won the prestige Fukuoka Marathon in 2:09:36. A year later, "this massive muscleman" ran to a 2:08:33 all-time clocking at Antwerp in May of 1969.[41] Few would have thought that William "Bill" Rodgers of Wesleyan University and

Boston College would join this charmed circle even though he had won several major road races that spring—and in outstanding time. Cool weather and a significant 20 mph helpful breeze conspired to keep the 1975 marathon leaders from running ordinary times through the various check points. "At 10 miles I knew it was too fast. At 17 miles I was convinced of it," said the free-spirited winner. He plunged onward, through fatigue barriers, never sure for a moment that he would finish, let alone win. "When I heard the time [2:09:55] I didn't believe it. I still don't. It's a dream," blinked the unfettered 27-year-old.[42] Liane Winter of Wolfsburg, Germany ran 2:42:33—an incredible world's record for women. It was a day for records; 49 women entered the race while "in excess of 2000 men," raced, ran, jogged, and plodded from Hopkington to the Prudential Center in Copley Square, Boston. Steve Hoag ran 2:11:54, Tom Fleming (2:12:05), Tom Howard (2:13:23), Ron Hill (2:13:28) and fifty more remained under 2:25. "There's no athletic event like it," said Johnny Kelley, 1957 winner. His 2:34:11 was good for 167th place. Kelly, Sr. (no relation), 68 years, was in his 99th marathon, Keizo Yamada of Japan, winner of this same B.A.A. race twenty-two years earlier, raced 2:34:54, and, nearly beyond comprehension, Bob Hall pushed a wheelchair all the way in 2:58!

The Present Status of the Sport

The "Marathon Craze" of 1908-1912 that swept the Continent and North America[43] was confined to a handful of professional long-distance runners. This small fraternity of marathon artisans bears little resemblance to the army of running zealots, the thousands of marathon devotees in America and Europe today. *"Runner's World* noted that in 1968 there were 38 marathons held in the U. S.; in 1974, there were 135."[44] The nature of running 26 miles without stopping and its mass popularity makes the effort one fraught with hazards. As long ago as 1948, correspondent Willy Meisel held the view that the marathon race "fathered by a sentimental classical scholar, and nursed by headline-hungry journalists, should never have been introduced into athletic contests."[45] There is some truth here, yet the fascination and challenge remains for increasing numbers, and with long, loving, and correct physical preparation, a surprisingly wide range of people may aspire to and succeed in running "forty kilometers and then some."

Encapsulated in this *2-5* hour run are an astonishing variety of individual experiences. The agonistic struggle, self-fulfillment, progress toward fitness, recovery from illness, and the search for beauty through both pain and pleasure are all valid reasons given by men and women. Pain is an absolutely integral part of a marathon runner's endeavor. And yet, as Francis W. Keenan, sport philosopher, says, "Even painful experience, both physical and mental, can be beautiful. When the distasteful can be perceived as a means for further development and cultivating an experience, it may be viewed as aesthetic and enjoyable."[46] Jonah J. "Bud" Greenspan, author and television producer, asked a recent Boston Marathon finisher why he had run the torturous 26 mile 385 yard distance without hope of victory. "Man," said the nineteen-year-old, "I finished!"[47] A. E. H. Winter, in his history of England's Poly Marathon race, is convinced that, for a few, it is an attempt at immortality. "And Hope is still the answer that Encouragement has given to us," he concludes. "The Hope that men will continue to come in peace, inspired only by a simple wish—to see their names engraved upon a silver statue forever."[48]

A plethora of marathon races take place in most parts of the world—and this does not include the feats of informal, non-competitive wonders from East Africa, the Japanese salt-flat runner-peasants, and those tireless joggers, the Taramahua Indians. Institutionalized marathon races exist today in all parts of the world and on all continents. The rationale ranges from the ridiculous to the sublime. "Real-life Walter Mitty success stories," said one writer in attempting to evaluate the accumulated fortitude he had witnessed in a single marathon race.[49] One sports writer pointed out that most Boston runners will arrive early "because this is important, because this probably is the biggest day of his entire year."[50] George Sheehan, remarkable runner, physician, philosopher, sees the race as a form of physical, but especially spiritual endurance. The marathon is a microcosm of life, he says.

> The marathoner can experience the drama of everyday existence so evident to the artist and poet. For him all emotions are heightened.... I believe every human must have this capacity [to endure] and could find it if he tried. And there is no better place to discover it than a marathon. For the truth is that every man in a marathon is a survivor or nothing, including the winner.... I do not intend to pause, or rest, or rust. Descendants of Ulysses... I will survive.[51]

Clarence DeMar, grandest old man of the sport, and marathon marvel, put it just as eloquently, no less honestly, and just as accurately, when he told *Boston Herald* columnist, Bill Cunningham, that training for and running in marathons "is no cheap and passing emotion."

> It's a supreme feeling of perfection and closeness to the Infinite I can't express very well.... To me it's more than a race. It's a very personal thing—a sense of supreme well being.[52]

NOTES

1 Homer, The *Iliad,* trans. by W. H. D. Rouse (New York: A Mentor Book published by the New American Library, 1938), pp. 265-282.

2 Herodotus, *The Histories of Herodotus of Halicarnassus* (London: Oxford University Press, 1962), pp. 501-502.

3_____, *The Histories*, trans. by Aubrey de Selincourt (Baltimore, Maryland: Penguin Books, 1966), p. 397.

4 Ibid., p. 398.

5 Herodotus, *The Histories*, trans. by A. D. Godley, Vol. 3 (London: William Heinemann, 1928), p. 275.

6 *Isocrates*, trans. by George Norlin, Vol. 1 (London: William Heinemann, Ltd., 1928), pp. 171, 173.

7 N. G. L. Hammond, "The Campaign and the Battle of Marathon," *The Journal of Hellenic Studies*, 88 (1968), pp. 13-57.

8 *Lucian*, trans. by K. Kilburn, Vol. 6 (Cambridge. Mass.: Harvard University Press, 1959), p. 177. Classicists identify this passage of Lucian (Prolapsu 3) as "A Slip of the tongue in greeting" by Lucian.

9 Pliny, *Natural History,* trans. by H. Rackham, Vol. 2 (Cambridge, Mass.: Harvard University Press, 1943), p. 561.

10 Plutarch, *Moralia,* trans. by Frank Cole Babbit, Vol. 4 (Cambridge, Mass.: Harvard University Press, 1962), pp. 503, 505.

11 H. A. Harris, *Greek Athletes and Athletics* (Bloomington, Ind.: Indiana University Press, 1976), p. 76.

12 E. Norman Gardiner, *Athletics of the Ancient World* (London: Oxford University Press, 1967), p. 140.

13 Victor Ehrenberg, *From Solon to Socrates* (London: Methuen and Co., Ltd., 1968), p. 412 ftn.

14 Joseph Ward Swain, *The Ancient World*, Vol. 1 (New York: Harper and Bros., 1950). p. 379.

15 "Pheidippides," *The Times* (London), July 28, 1908, p. 10.

16 Ibid.

17 "The Birth of a Legend," *The Nation*, 88 (May 27, 1909), p. 533.

18 "The Original Marathon Runner," *The Nation,* 88 (June 3, 1909), p. 559.

19 "A Retreat from Marathon," *The Nation,* 88 (June 17, 1909), p.602.

20 See Francis G. Allinson, "The Original 'Marathon Runner'," *The Classical Weekly,* 24 (March 16, 1931), 152; also his *Greek Lands and Letters* (New York: Houghton Mifflin Co., 1931), pp. 138-159.

21 "Lord Byron: Don Juan," T. G. Steffan and W. W. Pratt (editors). Vol. 2 (Austin: University of Texas Press, 1957), p. 312.

22 _____, *Childe Harold* (London: George Bell and Sons, 1893), Second Canto, p. 139.

23 Robert Browning, "Pheidippides," in *The Complete Works of Robert Browning,* edited by Charlotte Porter and Helen A. Clark, Vol. 2 (New York: George D. Sproul, 1898), pp. 117-124.

24 Alice E. Hanscom, "The Mound at Marathon," *Chautauquan,* 31 (September, 1900), p. 625.

25 Fred Jacob, "The Marathon," *St. Nicholas,* 40 (November, 1912), 52-55.

26 Sir Francis H. Doyle in M. A. Hamilton, *Greece, A Short History* (Oxford at the Clarendon Press, 1926), p. 61.

27 Alan Lloyd, *Marathon* (New York: Random House, 1973), p. 47.

28 See G. W. Botsford and E. G. Sihler (editors) *Hellenic Civilization* (New York: Octagon Books, Inc., 1965), p. 200.

29 See Harold H. Hart, *Physical Feats that Made History* (New York: Hart Publishing Co., 1974), pp. 332-333.

30 See "Track Finds A Prospect in the Bush," *New York Times,* March 22, 1975,Sports Section, p. 6.

31 "Becoming Classic," *Stamford Advocate,* August 27, 1896.

32 "Great Athletic Records," *The New York Times,* September 20, 1896, p. 6.

33 Bill Henry, *An Approved History of the Olympic Games* (New York: G. P. Putnam's Sons, 1948), p. 34.

34 Pierre de Coubertin, *Memoires Olympique* (Lausanne: Bureau International de Pedagogic Sportive, 1931), p. 40.

35 See Eva Foldes, "Women at the Olympics," *International Olympic Academy Proceedings* 1964, pp. 112-113.

36 John Hopkins, *The Marathon* (London: Stanley Paul, 1966).

37 See "The Marathon Race" in *The Fourth Olympiad London 1908 Official Report,* Theodore Andrea Cook (ed.) (London: The British Olympic Association, 1909), pp. 68-84.

38 "Dorando's Departure," (London) *The Times,* August 10, 1908, p. 4.

39 James E. Sullivan, *Marathon Running* (New York: American Sports Pub. Co., 1909), p. 101.

40 Jerry Nason, *The Story of the Boston Marathon* (Boston: The Boston Globe, 1965).

41 "Briton Shatters Marathon Record," *The Boston Globe,* April 21, 1970, p. 1; also Dave Prokop, "Derek Clayton," *Runner's World,* 6 (January 1971), 14-20. The Antwerp course may have been short.

42 "Will" Rodgers in John Ahern, "Win, Record Surprised Rodgers, Too," *The Boston Evening Globe,* April 22, 1975, p. 37.

43 See John Lucas, "The Professional Marathon Craze in America, 1908-1909," *U. S. Track Coaches Quarterly Review* (December 1968), 31-36.

44 *Track and Field News,* 28 (June 1975), p. *43.*

45 Willy Meisel, "The Birth of the Marathon," *World Sport* (1948), p. 16.

46 Francis W. Keenan, "The Athletic Contest as a 'Tragic' Form of Art," *International Review of Sport Sociology,* 10 (1975), p. 40.

47 Bud Greenspan, "The Marathon," *The Olympian,* 1 (February 1975), p. 13.

48 A. E. H. Winter, *From the legend to the Living* (n.p., 1969), p. 40.

49 Barry Stavro, "26 Miles—One Step at a Time," *Yankee Magazine* (April 1973), p. 131.

50 Leigh Montville, "They Brace For Longest Day," *The Boston Globe,* April 20, 1975.

51 George Sheehan, "The Boston Marathon: 3 Hours for the Race, but Like a Lifetime for the Runners," *New York Times,* April 20, 1975. Sport Section, p. 2.

52 Clarence DeMar and Bill Cunningham, "Marathon More Than Race to DeMar," *Boston Herald,* June 7, 1958.

4.
EARLY OLYMPIC ANTAGONISTS:
*Pierre de Coubertin Versus James E. Sullivan**

International relationships between sovereign states cannot exist without elements of antagonism. Almost as frequent as the antagonisms, there exist singular common goals that tie the individuals together, and sometimes their countries. Such symbiotic relationships are not unknown in international sport. During the period 1900-1914, the most famous sports figure in France was the Baron Pierre de Coubertin, while in the United States, the most influential athletics administrator was James Edward Sullivan. They did not like one another, and this personal animosity contributed to the halting harmony between the United States and the International Olympic Committee during the four official and one unofficial games of the century's first dozen years.

Men of extreme intensity, especially those with a singular life-purpose, frequently have little patience with countervailing forces. In the autumn of 1893, Coubertin was commissioned by his government as an organizing committee member of the Chicago Exposition's French section. He was also designated as one of the honorary heads of the Exposition's Congress on Higher Education. Coubertin's premature plan for an Olympic Games revival had met with disaster at the Sorbonne Conference of 1892, and so for a variety of reasons he looked forward to another visit to the United States.[1] But with the exception of a visit with Princeton University's William Milligan Sloane, Coubertin's attempts

*STADION III, 2 (1979) 258-272.

to create an American interest in the idea of an international Olympic Games was met with massive indifference. America's sporting officials, he said, were too preoccupied with "the secret war between the colleges and the AAU."[2]

James E. Sullivan was the young, hard-line secretary of the American Amateur Athletic Union at the time, and was persuaded by AAU boss, Gustavus T. Kirby, to meet with the French Baron and form a U.S. Olympic Committee in order to send qualified athletes to the Athens games of 1896. Coubertin and Sullivan met for the first time at this November 1893 gathering in New York City's University Club; the American agreed to chair a committee made up of Kirby, Julian Curtis, A. G. and Walter Spalding, plus Caspar Whitney, the influential, opinionated editor of *Outing* magazine.[3] The precocious Coubertin was thirty years of age as he left for London and then Paris to drum up Olympic Games interest. No evidence has been found to show that the thirty-three-year-old Sullivan was even remotely interested in the idea of a revived Olympic Games—a concept conceived by most sportsmen in the United States as bizarre. The tiny American team, privately financed by the Boston Athletic Association, Princeton University, and personal monies, did remarkably well in Athens, no thanks to the AAU. And yet the fault may not have been one-sided, for Caspar Whitney strongly criticized Coubertin's newly formed International Olympic Committee as inefficient and mismanaged, incapable of informing athletes of "information vitally needed by clubs and colleges willing to join in the sending of American representatives."[4] From its beginnings in 1894, the IOC had decided that the United States would host the games of the Third Olympiad, following those in Greece and France, "the original trinity chosen to emphasize the world character of the institution and establish it on a firm footing."[5]

During the late 1890s, France suffered serious internal conflict with monarchists, clericals, and army men, on one hand, and progressives, anticlerical, and republicans on the other. France was further divided by the celebrated Dreyfus case. The condemnation of Captain Alfred Dreyfus as an alleged traitor, the famous Emile Zola letter, Zola's arrest, and trial after riots in Paris streets, and the imprisonment of Dreyfus, were all too much for Coubertin's Olympic Committee during these unsporting years of 1898 and 1899.[6] European sporting organizations expressed their discontent at the lack of Olympic planning during these difficult years. Coubertin had not even contacted the (in 1895) half-a-million-member German Turner organization, the

Deutsche Turnerschaft, one of the strongest and best-organized sport associations in the world. "Instead," wrote Arnd Krüger, "he contacted Berlin's high society Union Racing Club."[7] It was too often Coubertin's habit to seek help from this special segment of society. A Colonel Louis Hamburger of the AAU, representing the United States at the 1900 Paris Exposition, failed in his attempts to see Coubertin, returning home in disgust.[8] American Olympic Committee member, Caspar Whitney, expressed nothing but sympathy for Coubertin when control of the 1900 games was taken away from him by an Exposition committee. "What this committee does not know about sports would fill volumes; [...] The Dreyfus case is at the bottom of the trouble," pronounced Whitney.[9] The scholarly friend of Coubertin, William Milligan Sloane, erupted and called the Paris games committee "an organization of incompetents."[10] To say that the small international athletics competition held incidentally along with the Paris Exposition of 1900 was an "Olympic Games" is an exaggeration. They failed to fulfill the dream of the young idealist, Coubertin, who was slowly maturing beyond French patriot to that of world citizen. He complained bitterly that "whenever public authorities meddle with sport organizers they introduce the fatal germs of impotence and mediocrity."[11]

There was not a shred of cosmopolitanism in James Sullivan at the turn of the century, and he would remain an aggressive American patriot till his death in 1914. During the eleven-month period from July 1900 to May of 1901, an ill-defined, but vaguely interrelated series of events occurred on both sides of the Atlantic that widened the ideological gap between the tough-minded, uncultured Sullivan, and the dreamy, well-born Pierre de Coubertin. Sullivan was the power behind the American AAU and as such pushed for his favorite sport of athletics to organize an international federation. Sullivan failed to gain this recognition on July 27, 1900, in a Paris meeting at the office of the "Union des societes frangaises des sports athletiques" (USFSA). The always-touchy Coubertin was alarmed that any new international sporting organization not directly under his jurisdiction might take something away from his fragile Olympic Games. Coubertin biographer Marie-Therese Eyquem paraphrased a USFSA document, *Tous les Sports,* dated September 22, 1900, which announced the creation of the international athletics union. But, says Eyquem, the published report was careful not to mention that the union intended to take control of the Olympic Games, and, indeed, had already started recruiting the very ranks of the IOC."[12]

Sullivan, from his New York City office, was the driving force behind the creation of the international track and field union—an organization that Coubertin perceived (with some justification) as a threat to his Olympian Games. Although the International Amateur Athletic Federation (IAAF) was not founded until 1913, Sullivan was instrumental in making athletics the dominant Olympic Games sport. He did this by playing a key role in the near domination by the United States of Olympic Games athletic events from 1900 through 1912. On July 28, 1900, *The New York Times* noted that the University of Pennsylvania had negotiated with British authorities for the 1904 Olympic Games to be transferred to Philadelphia. It was bizarre, of course, for it was only track and field athletics that interested parties of the two organizations, and not a multiple sport festival as outlined by Coubertin and his handpicked IOC. No mention was made in this news bulletin of the Baron or his committee. It did state, however, that the American Olympic Committee (AOC) members Sloane, Whitney, and James Sullivan favored the idea of a Philadelphia Olympics.[13] Equally strange and certainly unsettling to Coubertin when he heard about it, was Sullivan's unilateral announcement that the Buffalo, New York Pan American Exposition would host an Olympian Games in 1901, under AAU auspices.[14] A somewhat optimistic Bill Henry stated that an emphatic Coubertin denial of any such venture effectively "silenced this attempt to interrupt the quadrennial sequence of the games."[15] Coubertin, looking back thirty years, recalled that his choice, right from the beginning had been for Chicago to host a 1904 Games, and the idea was gaining acceptance by the press "when a furious letter by James E. Sullivan was published" on November 13, 1900, in *The Sun.*

Sullivan's tirade was in response to a Coubertin bulletin issued from his Paris home on November n, 1900, in which the Baron, after consulting with his committee, announced that either Chicago or New York would be the site of a 1904 Olympic Games.[16] The pugnacious Sullivan was quick to answer what he considered a totally premature and unacceptable plan—one arrived at without consultation with a single American sports leader. Sullivan was very angry, pointing out that Coubertin had been stripped of his athletic powers by the French government and thus "no longer in control of international meetings." The new athletics union will take charge, he said, and conduct annual meetings, the first of which will be held at the 1901 Pan American Exposition in Buffalo. Sullivan was aware of the friendship between Baron de Coubertin and the University of Chicago's president, the highly respected William Rainey Harper (1856-1906), tossing crumbs to the Frenchman by allowing that there is nothing to prevent that city and its university from hosting a 1904 meeting, "provided the other delegates of the International Union agree to hold the games in the U.S. in that year, but President Harper will have to apply to the new union, as it will be impossible to hold a successful meeting without the consent of that body. Baron de Coubertin has no right to allot dates for such a meeting."[17]

Fundamental differences between Sullivan and Coubertin began to widen the chasm between the two men. The American was of lower middle class background, a blunt, no-nonsense pragmatist who avoided compromise and subterfuge, preferring an honest directness—no matter whom it hurt. The Baron de Coubertin was very different, not only by birth and education, but in temperament. Espousing egalitarianism, he was, nevertheless, for all his life, much more comfortable among the wealthy and aristocratic classes, finding small, closed meetings among his own kind much more to his liking than larger, open forums. Lastly, and very significantly, James Sullivan was totally involved in a realizable dream of making the United States of America the world's greatest track and field power. His vision never went beyond this narrow view, and he was hugely successful. Coubertin's idealized and grandiose Olympian plans, right from the beginning, were unrealizable, but he clung to them right to the end. The two men were never on the same intellectual, historical, or psychological wavelength. The gap widened between the two men when *The Sun* correspondent, in the November 12, 1900 release, stated that Coubertin had "received from President Harper of the University of Chicago an important letter which evidently makes the Baron feel in favor of Chicago." President Harper immediately denied ever having written such a letter.[18] James Sullivan, in Paris at this time, called Coubertin a powerless, pathetic figure in charge of an inept committee. We know that Coubertin was deeply angered by Sullivan's coarseness; the Frenchman's two autobiographies discuss the matter at length. The Baron struck back, stating that at the time European sport leaders had not taken Sullivan seriously, and that American IOC member William Milligan Sloane had written him on December 12, 1900, informing Coubertin that there definitely would be some kind of athletic competition, not necessarily Olympian, in Buffalo the next year, but beyond that "I can learn no more, as those who know the facts remain prudently quiet."[19] The Frenchman could be forceful in his own way, asserting that:

> At the end of 1900, the *Morning Telegraph* had written
> that all this was a campaign against Chicago; [...] the
> freezing horror of the situation can only be fully appre-
> ciated when it is seen that James Sullivan is not the
> American member of the IOC.[20]

"The fight was on," chortled Coubertin thirty years after the event. We do not know if he was so jovial in the difficult days of 1900-1901. The struggle for control of international sport prompted the Baron to say: "The success of an idea is to be judged by the number of people who claim credit for it."[21] Sullivan considered himself the ultimate authority on that most important of sports, track and field, while Coubertin was confident that the world would soon recognize that he was the originator of these new Olympic Games, and just as importantly, that his IOC was the ruling authority on international amateur athletics. In addition, he said, Mr. Sullivan is not even a member of the committee. Eyquem reports that a contemporary newspaper recognized that at the root of Sullivan's hostility toward Chicago as an Olympic Games site, was his unacceptability as an IOC member.[22] Coubertin may have won this early skirmish with Sullivan, for there never developed a 1901 Olympic Games in Buffalo; only a track meet in conjunction with the Pan-American Exposition was held.[23] A little earlier, in January of 1901, Coubertin's cause received a lift from an unusual corner. Sullivan's fellow American Olympic Committee member, Caspar Whitney, reminded his close friend that his AAU was not only without international jurisdiction, but that American college athletes, from which the great majority of the Olympic team would come, were also outside the control of the AAU. Whitney concluded that in his opinion the IOC was an organization of "high character."[24] Although somewhat out of character, Sullivan is alleged to have written Coubertin on March 21, 1901, that "I am always willing, if I think I have made a mistake, to acknowledge it."[25]

The athletically-minded Dr. Harper, of the University of Chicago, presided over a banquet on February 13, 1901, formally opening the campaign to win for his city the privilege of hosting the Olympic Games.[26] Little is known about Olympic activities during March and April of 1901, but we do know that on May 21, 1901, Coubertin and the IOC voted for Chicago rather than St. Louis as the site of the next Olympic Games—sending two telegrams to the Windy City's Henry J. Furber, Jr., President of the Olympian Games Association. Coubertin's cable read, "Chicago wins"; the second cable from prominent Paris attorney, secretary of the "Comite franco-americain pour le patronage des etudiants," and city of Chicago representative Henry Breal (author of *Lawyers in Literature)* was even more dramatically succinct. The single word "Oui" in his cable sent the Chicago press running to their desks; bon fires and celebrations on the University of Chicago campus followed, taking up the entire week. "Joy in Olympian Games," and "Games baptized in fire," headlined the *Chicago Tribune;* Furber, Harper, the famous physical educator-football coach, Amos Alonzo Stagg, and others joined in the festivities.[27] The exchange of letters between Harper, Furber, and Coubertin had convinced the IOC president of the suitability of Chicago.[28] "Everything was off to a good start," beamed the modern Olympic Games 'renovateur'. Two modern French scholars noted that "James E. Sullivan despaired at the choice," while contemporary Caspar Whitney dismissed Sullivan's abortive effort with the comment that: "There really never was deviation from the original plans."[29]

The great Louisiana Purchase of 1803 would soon celebrate its one-hundredth anniversary, and as part of a great Exhibition, some city planners perceived a great physical culture symposium and an international Olympian games as desirable. However, as late as winter and spring of 1902, the powerfully financed ($ 1,000,000) Furber Committee in Chicago made a number of European trips and visited with President Zemp of Switzerland, the king of Greece, England's Sir Thomas Lipton, and "an amicable talk at Munster, Alsace," between Coubertin and Furber.[30] A Chicago Olympic Games seemed assured, especially after an August, 1902 pledge by President Roosevelt in support of that city, although he voiced "regret that the United States cannot officially take charge or be responsible for the games."[31] The gist of this last remark is that president of the pending Chicago Olympian Games, Henry J. Furber, had publicly acknowledged Coubertin and his IOC as the ultimate authority for this kind of sporting event.[32] But beginning in the early months of 1902, Baron de Coubertin "noticed a certain disquiet and reserve in his letters." The early enthusiasm had waned in Mr. Furber's Chicago, and, as Coubertin recalls, "a certain wavering began to be noticed among the organizers." Another college president, Mr. David R. Francis of St. Louis University, was president of the Exposition planned for that city and openly sought a 1904 Olympic Games, in direct competition with Chicago. Henry Furber wrote Coubertin on November 26, 1902, that his Chicago Olympic Games venture was seriously threatened after learning that the St. Louis people had postponed their Exposition to 1904, in order to accommodate an Olympic Games. Rival athletic contests in the two cities would be disastrous, he said. Coming straight to the point, Furber suggested that: "Should you therefore, in view of the attitude and invitation of Saint Louis, desire to transfer to that city the Olympian Games of 1904, Chicago would, in the best interest of sports, cheerfully relinquish them."[33] In December of 1902, David Francis telegraphed Michael Lagrave, commissioner of the French exhibit at the Louisiana Exposition in St. Louis, requesting that he contact the IOC for a transfer of the Olympic Games from Chicago to St. Louis. Coubertin's committee met on December 23, 1902, and voted (14 in favor, 2 against, 5 abstentions) for the transfer. According to Coubertin, Sullivan warmed a little toward him at the news and said that a St. Louis games would be "the most splendid series of sporting events the world had ever seen."[34]

Coubertin, in a conciliatory and probably clever move, requested that Walter H. Liginger and James E. Sullivan, officers of the AAU, take administrative charge of the 1904 Games. Mr. Liginger immediately replied in March of 1903, considering "it a great pleasure to act in the capacity suggested in your letter of the 10th."[35] President of the United States, Theodore Roosevelt, approved of the transfer, so we are told in the Coubertin reminiscence *Memoires Olympiques*.[36] St. Louis was the unhandsomest city in America, according to Coubertin, who believed "that the Olympiad would match the mediocrity of the town." He did not attend these Third Games, nor did his committee, and few European athletes came. Europe was still a very great distance from the American mid-west. The St. Louis games were better than Paris in 1900, but neither pleased Coubertin, and he vowed never again to hold an Olympic Games in connection with a world's fair.[37] Nevertheless, the Baron must have felt some sense of gratitude toward his adversary Sullivan, awarding him a rare gold medallion for his organizational skill and dedication at the Games.[38] It was to be a long time before Sullivan saw his medal—another source of irritation between the two men.

Two consecutive Olympic Games failures were sufficient motivation for the IOC to seek an emergency alternative, and the Greek government seized Coubertin's offer of an out-of-sequence Athens Games in 1906—the tenth year of the modern revival. Sullivan approved of this fresh opportunity to display his country's athletic superiority, but he was most displeased with the dates, April 22 to May 2, 1906—the middle of the spring academic calendar for American intercollegiate athletes. Sullivan went to Athens in late November of 1905, to make sure things were right, and on March 9, 1906, lunched with President Roosevelt in the White House receiving his blessing as "boss" of the American team. Sullivan pledged a strong showing in Athens.[39] Meanwhile, the Baron de Coubertin, besieged by French Leftists, rejected by many of his fellow aristocrats, and alarmingly short of money, was unable to attend the successful Athens games of 1906. Actually, he was not keen on going, for these games were not truly "Olympic." He thanked the Greek committee for a job well done, assuring them that international games would continue to have a "salutary influence ... on civilization."[40] Sullivan, too, felt a sense of euphoria about his contribution "toward making honest and sturdy Americans."[41] The Americans were "keen" for the 1906 competition, he said. "As is customary in our country," he boasted, "our men were trained scientifically. We go into athletic sport with an earnestness that the other countries cannot understand." [42] Sullivan's bellicose and patriotic nature was reflected to an astonishing degree on the American team members from 1900 through 1912. Teddy Roosevelt understood it well and was pleased; he sent Sullivan and the 1906 team a cablegram: "Uncle Sam is all right." For Sullivan, these unofficial Olympic Games settled "the athletic supremacy of the world."[43]

James Sullivan was a "team" man all the way. Sport was a serious business to him, and international track and field athletic domination was a clear-cut manifestation of national strength. He was much appreciated in his time, and would be well understood in these last decades of the twentieth century. In a strong dictum to an American Olympian, Sullivan advised the young man to remember that "the team will go absolutely as an American team" and if they do so "this country will be victorious."[44] Immediately upon his return from Athens, Sullivan received a letter from Pierre de Coubertin—a "very kind and interesting communication," dated May 27, 1906. On June 26, Sullivan replied with an astonishing 2,000-word outpouring, alternately praising the Olympic leader and roasting him mercilessly. "I propose to be frank with you," was Sullivan's ominous initial comment to Coubertin. Sullivan mentioned conversations with IOC members at the recent games, resulting in a conviction "that you did not like me and that I thought the feeling between us was mutual." Sullivan quickly got to the sore point of his missing Olympic medallion of two years earlier. "I never received it," he complained, "and I presume that the Baron is dissatisfied with something I have done."

This personal note done, Mr. Sullivan got down to the castigation of the IOC and Coubertin, its "inept leader." Why, he thundered, had Coubertin capriciously struck "my name from your membership"? A long time hurt was revealed as Sullivan reminded the Frenchman that a decade of loyal service to the Olympic Movement was unrewarded and had not resulted in his appointment to the IOC. "I lost all interest in the Olympic Committee," he lamented, in an obvious moment of self-deception. Sullivan continued his anger at James Hazen Hyde, a mere insurance agent, replacing Caspar Whitney on the IOC. Why not himself, he asked. The action was "a monstrous joke." He turned his attention to William Milligan Sloane, original member of the IOC. Why is that "lovely gentleman" kept on, asked Sullivan. "He knows absolutely nothing about athletics ...; I doubt if he ever attended an important athletic meeting in America." Sullivan thus dispensed with two countrymen, and in so doing, seriously criticized Coubertin's rationale for selecting IOC members.

While in Athens, Sullivan said, several IOC members hoped he might join them in that select body, but he told them, "before I could accept anything like this, I certainly would want a letter from you." Sullivan's preoccupation with his missing gold medal returned mid-way through the letter. He lamented:

The letter which I received from you (27 May 1906) puts an entirely new tone to it. I did not know that it was necessary for you to hand me the medal voted. Had I known this, you can rest assured that I would certainly have made arrangements so that you could have presented it to me on some one of my trips abroad. Yes, I did stop a few days at Paris on my way to Athens, and I would have been delighted to have called on you had I the slightest idea that such a call from me would be appreciated by you, as you have not recognized me in the slightest way in your organization, or, in your good work you have never asked me for my cooperation; you have gone along with the idea that you could get along without America. You say you do not understand my ways and manners. Perhaps not. I don't think you have tried to understand me thoroughly; if you did I think we could become firm friends.[45]

Sullivan explained, to his own satisfaction, why he had attempted a rival organization to the IOC back in 1900. It was for the greater good of international sport, he said. Maybe, just maybe, said Sullivan, IOC membership for him might be unwise, "because I would disagree with you. I certainly will stand up for anything I think is right." In his concluding paragraphs, Sullivan had for Coubertin both "the greatest admiration" as Olympic innovator and also indirect criticism that the Baron had never given him and his AAU even a vestige of recognition. Sullivan promised unqualified support in all future Olympic ventures. Share this letter with your friends, ended Sullivan. "It's immaterial whether you or I can get along together," concluded Sullivan. "You can always count on America as being with you when it comes to having International sports."[46] "My dear Baron," was Sullivan's salutation in another letter dated July 31, 1906. He was really angry at a recent Coubertin letter of July 5 which purports to cast doubt on Sullivan's motives in attempting to gain membership in the IOC. The exasperated Sullivan erupted with: "You pass my entire letter off by saying that there was not one single word of truth in any of my statements ... well, I think that settles it! ... I am thoroughly convinced ... that we had better cease writing." [47] There is a great deal of evidence that Sullivan, unfulfilled in several personal goals, was most effective—almost too much so, in marshalling his country's athletic muscle at two Olympic Games and one Athens International, up to that time. At a 1907 testimonial, celebrating Sullivan's election to AAU presidency and attended by 200 athletes, *The New York Times* journalist called him "the greatest present force in athletics today." Former president of the New York Athletic Club, Barton Weeks, was the final speaker and declared that Mr. Sullivan's strength of character "is derived from the fact that he invariably tries to do right, no matter whom it aids or hurts."[48] The next month Sullivan practically demanded (but did not receive) $100.000 from the government in order to pay for the next year's London Olympic Games. "It is a question of national pride," said the new AAU president.[49] Caspar Whitney praised Sullivan to the sky as "a man who not only sees right, but has the courage to fight for it."[50] And fight he did. While much was right about the 1908 Olympic Games, there was a near-disastrous, continual verbal battle between American and English officials. Some of the fault must lie in Sullivan's belligerency. "We have come here to win the championships in field sports," he muttered, "and we are going to do it, despite the handicap [poor officiating] from which we are suffering."[51] Coubertin, who was also in London for the Games, had once again to defend the integrity of the IOC cooptation selection system as well as the quadrennial rotation plan.[52] Typically, Coubertin was busy defending, Sullivan preoccupied with attack. The Baron was deeply concerned about the internecine struggle between the Anglo-American nations. Looking back at the success and turmoil that was London in the summer of 1908, Coubertin remembered the American Olympic chief with bitterness: "I just could not understand Sullivan's attitude here. He shared his team's frenzy and did nothing to try and calm them down. This was followed on his return by a new betrayal; he persuaded the Amateur Athletic Union to appoint a commission for the purpose of forming a new International Olympic Committee and drawing up the statutes of future games. But this time, nobody listened to him."[53]

In a brief essay titled "American Ambitions," Coubertin recapitulated the three attempts in the previous ten years, 1899-1908, "that some American leaders have attempted to overthrow the Olympic Organization."[54] During these post-Olympic months, editor Caspar Whitney both defended and criticized the American Olympic and AAU leader, James Sullivan.[55] The fire of misunderstanding and animosity between the two fifty year old sports giants smoldered during the between years of 1910-1912. Some mellowing may have taken place, for in a letter dated November 4, 1910, Sullivan informed Coubertin of the progress on his new Olympic history book, giving Coubertin his due as the Games' founder. I am trying, said the American, "to keep away from the row we had in London, which was not a very nice row, as you will agree. It should never have happened." [56]

The 1912 Olympic Games—the Games of the Fifth Olympiad— were the most successful and pacific since their inception. They had arrived as a genuine international sport festival. Coubertin, writing under a symbolic double French and German pseudonym, won a literature gold medal at these Stockholm games. His "Ode au Sport" was a romantic hymn in nine stanzas, praising sport as the messenger of beauty, honor, joy, progress, and above all else, peace.[57] Somehow, the anger had softened, and in James Sullivan's new history of the 1912 Games, he dedicated the book to Baron Pierre de Coubertin, "to whom perseverance and zealous work for 30 years is due the ... final success of the Olympic Games."[58] The Baron lived another quarter-century of success and failure; Sullivan died of a heart attack while still young. His passing, on September 16, 1914, was not without one final irony, for in May of that same year, he traveled to France for an IAAF meeting and returned home in July with a precious trophy presented to him in person by Baron Pierre de Coubertin "on behalf of the IOC ... as a token of appreciation ... in promoting the Olympic Games."[59]

NOTES

1 For details of this trip, see Pierre de Coubertin's *Souvenirs d'Amerique etde Grece*, Paris: Librairie Hachette et Cie, 1897. The mixed reaction received by Coubertin is discussed by John Lucas in his doctoral dissertation, "Baron Pierre de Coubertin and the Formative Years of the Modern International Olympic Movement, 1883-1896," University of Maryland, 1962, 88-91.

2 Pierre de Coubertin, *Une campagne de vingt-et-un ans 1887-1908*, Paris: Librairie de l'education Physique, 1908, 92.

3 Gustavus T. Kirby as quoted in a personal interview fifty-eight years after the event. See Robert Korsgaard, "A History of the Amateur Athletic Union of the United States," Ed. D. dissertation, Columbia University, Teachers College, 1952, 183.

4 Caspar Whitney, "Amateur Sports," *Harper's Weekly*, 40 (April 18, 1896) 406.

5 Pierre de Coubertin, *Memoires Olympiques*, Lausanne: Bureau International de Pedagogic Sportive, 1931, 60.

6 The Dreyfus Affair showed the seamy side of French; the Exposition, of which the Olympian Games were a small part, attempted to show France at her very best, "as she wished to appear before the world." See Richard D. Mandell, "The Affair and the Fair; Some Observations on the Closing Stages of the Dreyfus Case," *The Journal of Modern History*, 39 (September, 1967), 255.

7 Personal letter from Arnd Krüger, June 23, 1977.

8 See Korsgaard's dissertation, 1856.

9 Caspar Whitney, "Outdoor Sports—What They Are Doing for Us," *The Independent*, 52 (May 31, 1900) 1363.

10 See the text of former IOC director Otto Mayer, *Retrospectives Olympiques*, Geneve: Pierre Cailler, 1961, 72-3.

11 Coubertin, *Une Campagne*, 152.

12 Marie-Therese Eyuem, *Pierre de Coubertin —L' Epopee Olympique*, Paris: Calmann–Levy, 1966, 175.

13 "Olympic Games in America," *New York Times*, July 28, 1900, 5.

14 "The Olympic Games at Buffalo," *Public Opinion* 29 (November 1, 1900), 567.

15 Bill Henry, *An Approved History of the Olympic Games*, New York: G. P. Putnam's Sons, 1976, 50.

16 "Olympian Games for America," *The Sun* (New York) November 12, 1900, 8.

17 "The Next Olympian Games," *The Sun* (New York) November 13, 1900, 5.

18 "Denial from Dr. Harper," *New York Daily Tribune*, November 14, 1900, 9.

19 See Coubertin, *Une Campagne*, 154.

20 Coubertin, *Memoires Olympiques*, 61-2.

21 Ibid., 62.

22 Eyquem, *Pierre de Coubertin*, 175.

23 Sullivan boasted that the Buffalo meet showed the U.S.A.'s emergence as a world athletic power. See his article: "Athletics and the Stadium," *Cosmopolitan*, 31 (September, 1901) 501-8.

24 Caspar Whitney, "International Athletic Organization," *Outing*, 37 (January, 1901) 473-4.

25 See Coubertin, *Memoires Olympiques*, 61.

26 See *Une campagne*, 153-4; also "Chicago Preparations for 1904," *Revue Olympique* (January, 1901), 11-12; and "Chicago Wants Olympian Games," *Chicago Daily Tribune*, February 14, 1901, I.

27 See the *Chicago Tribune*, May 22, 1901, 3 and May 26, 1901, 1.

28 See *Revue Olympique*, (July, 1901) 32-40.

29 See Guy Lagorce and Robert Pariente, *La Fabuleuse Histoire des Jeux Olympiques*, Paris: Editions Odil, 1972, 61; Caspar Whitney, "Olympian Games at Chicago ...," *Outing*, 38 (August, 1901) 587.

30 See the *New York Daily News*, January 19, 1902, 10; May 3, 1902, 4; August 2, 1902, 4; September 5, 1902, 4; September 14, 1902, 9; September 23, 1902, 9; October 22, 1902, 3; also *New York Times*, July 13, 1902, 12; and *Outing*, October, 1902, 120.

31 See *New York Times*, August 22, 1902, 9, and *New York Daily Tribune*, August 22, 1902, 14.

32 Henry J. Furber, "Modern Olympian Games Movement," *The Independent*, 54 (February 14, 1902) 384.

33 Henry Furber to Pierre de Coubertin, November 26, 1902; see *Revue Olympique* (February, 1903) 5.

34 Sullivan as quoted in Coubertin, *Memoires Olympiques*, 64.

35 See this letter in Revue Olympique (April, 1903) 19.

36 Roosevelt had taken office on September 14, 1901, eight days after the assassination of President McKinley at the Buffalo Pan-American Exposition—a celebration that co-director James E. Sullivan had hoped might be called an "Olympic Games."

37 See Charles J. P. Lucas, *The Olympic Games of 1904*, St. Louis: Woodward and Tiernan Co., 1905, 17.

38 Coubertin to Sullivan, October 19, 1904; see James E. Sullivan, *Spalding's Official Athletic Almanac for 1905—Special Olympic Number*, New York: The American Sports Publishing Co., 1905, 185.

39 "U.S. Representatives to Olympic Games; President Roosevelt appoints J. E. Sullivan," *New York Times*, March 10, 1906, 8.

40 Pierre de Coubertin in the *Bulletin du Comite des Jeux Athens* (April 10, 1906).

41 See Ralph D. PAINE, "A Very Worthy Tribute to James E. Sullivan," *Outing,* 48 (June, 1906) 362.

42 Sullivan, "American Athletes in Ancient Athens," *American Review of Reviews,* 34 (July, 1906) 44.

43 See Sullivan, "American Athletes Champions of the World" *Outing* 48 (August, 1906) 625-6; also Sullivan, *The Olympic Games of 1906 at Athens,* New York: American Sports Publishing Co., 1906, 44-45.

44 Sullivan to Marquand Schwartz, 8 March 1906, University of Illinois, Archives of the Alumni Association, Avery Brundage Collection, Box 103, International Olympic Committee Subject File, Pierre de Coubertin. For this reference and the next two Sullivan, 26 June and 31 July, 1906, special thanks to Dr. Arnd Kruger, Universitat Hamburg, one of the first scholars to do research at the University of Illinois Brundage Collection in 1976. The present writer spent eight profitable days in the library during the summer of 1978.

45 Sullivan to Coubertin, 26 June 1906. Ibid.

46 Ibid.

47 Ibid., 31 July 1906.

48 *New York Times,* January 10, 1907, 7.

49 See Sullivan "Wants Congress to Aid Athletes," *New York Times,* February 20, 1907, 9.

50 Caspar Whitney, "Right Man in the Right Place," *Outing,* 49 (March, 1907) 795.

51 Sullivan, *New York Daily Tribune,* July 19, 1908, 8.

52 See Coubertin, "Letter to the Editor," *The Times* (London) July 13, 1908, 12.

53 Coubertin, *Memoires Olympiques,* 92.

54 See *Revue Olympique* (December, 1908) 179.

55 See Caspar Whitney's comments, *Outing* 52 (September, 1908) 761; 53 (November, 1908) 244-9; *Outing,* 53 (February, 1909) 643-6.

56 Sullivan to Courbetin, 4 November 1910, University of Illinois, Archives of the Alumni Association, Avery Brundage Collection, Box 103: International Olympic Committee Subject File, Pierre de Coubertin.

57 Georges Hohrod et M. Eschbach, *Ode au Sport.* Prim6e au concours de Litterature Sportive de la Vieme Olympiade, Stockholm, 1912.

58 James E. Sullivan, *The Olympic Games, Stockholm 1912,* New York: American Sports Publishing Co., 1912.

59 "James E. Sullivan of AAU is Dead," *New York Tribune,* September 17, 1914, 14.

5.
Mabel Lee and Elmer Mitchell Reach Out and Touch One Another*

Past president of the American Academy of Physical Education Harold Barrow had a fine idea when he suggested (in April of this year) that Mabel Lee and Elmer Mitchell visit one another. These two oldest and most distinguished living physical educators talked for three hours and, predictably, it was an extraordinary and historically important occasion. John Lucas, historian-archivist for AAPE, was fortunate to be present. Update is grateful to John for this account.

Mabel Lee, the first woman to serve as president of the American Physical Education Association (1930) was born in 1886, the year after a Yale University physician founded our professional

*AAHPERD UPDATE (July-August 1980), p. 5.

organization. In 1936, this remarkably sturdy lady reminded Strong Hinman that a 50th year history of the profession was overdue. She wrote it. In 1960, Miss Lee was 74 years young, and her association had seen 75 years. She reminded president Art Esslinger that a new history needed to be written and, in collaboration with Bruce Bennett, wrote a "Heritage" history which occupied the entire issue of the April 1960 *Journal.*

This year, 1980, Mabel Lee, marvelously active in her 94th year, reminded American Academy of Physical Education members that the only living charter member of that honored society, Elmer Mitchell (born September 6, 1889), was still with us, living in Ann Arbor—only a short drive from the Detroit-based AAHPERD annual convention. It seemed the most natural thing in the world to bring the two very long-time friends and professional colleagues together.

Dr. Harold Barrow of Wake Forest University, the 1979-1980 president of the American Academy of Physical Education and author of the AAHPERD *Update* biographical essay on Elmer Mitchell (April, 1980), had worked tirelessly for weeks to arrange the Lee-Mitchell get-together. He wanted very much to see it all unfold, but with typical graciousness allowed John Lucas, Academy historian-archivist, to take his place.

At 9:00 a.m., April 11, 1980, we left the Detroit Plaza Hotel for a pleasant hour's drive to suburban Ann Arbor, Michigan. Driving was King McCristal, former dean of the University of Illinois College of HPER and ex-president of the Academy of Physical Education. His companion in the front seat was "Jack" Frost, retired department chairman at Springfield College and one of the most effective presidents of the Alliance.

I sat in the back seat, squeezed in between and listening to a physical education "stream of consciousness" between Miss Lee and Academy president Aileene Lockhart, department head at Texas Woman's University. Humane treatment of the aged, the legendary Luther Halsey Gulick, the elevated sport philosophy of professor Wilbur P. Bowen, the "brilliant and tragic giant in our field"—James Huff McCurdy, comparisons of the journals *Mind and Body* and the *American Physical Education Review* were backseat discussions. I may never know what the wise professors McCristal and Frost talked about in the front seat.

Ann Dailey (professor Mitchell's daughter) and Mr. Robert C. Dailey met us at the door and ushered us into their home. Both Mabel Lee and Dr. Mitchell smiled as they shook hands, as, undoubtedly, the flood of 65 years of professional memories began to take shape. Elmer Mitchell sat down first, the years having taken their toll on his once robust, six-foot tall frame. He needed a cane and a firm arm to lean on. Mabel Lee decidedly found comfort just in the latter.

Tea and cake in the midst of an extremely civilized pastel-green living room ended with Miss Lee and Elmer Mitchell sitting very close (their hearing is less acute than they would like), with the rest of us clustered about like disciples. Logically and with gracious-ness, Dr. Mitchell began with inquiries about Miss Lee's health and proceeded to tell us about his father Samuel and grandfather George, the latter an expert copper miner from Cornwall, England, who emigrated to America and the Lake Superior copper regions in the upper peninsula. Samuel Mitchell followed the same trade, and Elmer was born in '89 in the Chippewa Indian community of Negaunee ("Hell"), only an arrow shot away from the town of Ishpeming ("Heaven")—both close to the city of Marquette and Huron Bay.

Dr. Mitchell's gentle demeanor was confirmed by the assertive Mabel Lee, who noted that "Elmer was always a most diplomatic man; he never looked for a fight." Miss Lee was afforded no such luxury in the early days, and yet, to this day, is the epitome of the evangelist who never once forgot her manners. The two-hour conversation never lagged, with catalytic questions to both former Academy and Alliance presidents from Lockhart, McCristal, Frost, and Lucas. It occurred to me that, including my own 29 years as a teacher, there was an astonishing 300 years of professional experience in that small group.

Lee and Mitchell shared several secrets, only hinted at to their attentive younger colleagues. It was difficult, in only half a morning together, for the two of them to expand on such tantalizing comments as:

"I think Jesse Feiring Williams dropped out of the Academy because of my election to it. He didn't like me nor could he accept the new assertiveness by some women for equal professional opportunity." (Lee)

"1929 and 1930 were pivotal years in the profession. Dr. McCurdy was a great man, leader, and scholar, but he found it impossible to step down graciously as editor of the *Review*." (Mitchell)

"Jay B. Nash was the loveliest of men, but the most inefficient of Academy secretaries." (Lee)

"As new editor of the *Journal,* we were fortunate in gaining instant credibility by translating and publishing in Volume I, Jean

Chryssafis's "Aristotle on Physical Education" and "Aristotle on Kinesiology." (Mitchell)

"I feel sure that 'The Bernarr Macfadden Affair' was behind my temporarily being 'black-balled' from Academy membership." (Lee)

"Fielding 'Hurry-up' Yost was my friend, as was Amos Alonzo Stagg, and the greatest kicker of them all—Harry Kipke." (Mitchell)

"Yes, I remember Yost and Stagg. They teased me and always greeted me as 'Miss Nebraska.'" (Lee)

Both Miss Lee and Dr. Mitchell hesitated for a moment, then "cracked up" recalling Blanche Trilling's classic "faux pas" and unfortunate juxtaposition of words at the 1931 Academy Banquet. It seems that as toastmaster, she announced that guest speaker, Jay B. Nash, was taken quite ill and "confined to bed with a private nurse." "Jack" Frost, unable to restrain himself, reminded us that his own memory easily went back nearly 50 years to the legendary locker-room philosophy of Yost, who wrote on the blackboard: "Love football, your work, your teammates, your associates, and, most of all, love yourself."

Somehow the conversation turned away from "olden times" to some contemporary issues. Dr. Mitchell, an astute stock market broker after his retirement, predicted a mild depression, but economic upswing thereafter. Miss Lee nodded approval, hoping that the "upswing" would come soon (i.e., "before I check out") in order that she might personally supervise the orderly transfer of all her professional papers from Lincoln, Nebraska to Alliance Headquarters in Reston, Virginia.

"The AAHPERD financial crisis concerns me greatly, especially regarding the disposition of my papers," said Miss Lee. She reminded whoever would listen that the Alliance should organize a "Friends of the Alliance Archives" movement, since, as she said, "our organization must necessarily relegate archival records to a secondary priority."

Dr. Mitchell, first editor of the *Research Quarterly* and the *Journal,* inventor of "speedball," pioneer leader in the science of intramural athletic organization, and author of the germinal and creative *Theory of Play* appeared tired, and we all knew it was time to leave. Even so, we took 20 minutes to say "good-bye," and no one seemed to mind.

Our driver, King McCristal, on the return to downtown Detroit, overshot the city by eight miles; we were forced to double back. But no wonder. The conversation was animated, spirited, even though intractable. Dr. Lockhart was deeply moved in anticipation of her Gulick Award that evening. Mabel Lee, lost in reverie, chuckled at remembrances of Gertrude Moulton "floating in the sky." The always practical Miss Lee admitted, "Back then we needed people like that." Both McCristal and Frost recalled the remarkable Charles H. McCloy—the paragon physical education scientist and fitness enthusiast. The 94-year-old Miss Lee, recently (fully) recovered from a broken hip, returned to her condemnation of hospital staffs that purposely "rob old people of all dignity in order to render them utterly docile." It was manifestly obvious to me, sitting next to the neatly-groomed Mabel with her white gloves, pale green suit, and complimentary gold earrings, that she had been untouched by the exploiters.

We were getting close to the convention. I had welcomed the detour, hoping to hear more from Mabel about the "disgraceful 'falling out' between Clifford Brownell and J. F. Williams;" from Frost about "middle-aged Carl Schrader and his amazingly skillful giant-swing on the horizontal bar;" and King McCristal's anecdotes about Seward Staley, John Sundwall, and the late Jesse Owens. We were at the hotel door and the irrepressible Mabel Lee managed parting volleys on "The present disgrace of Rumanian female athletes on drugs," "The plight of Iran's women," "The vulgarity of some female athletic mercenaries," and "The national importance of the Alliance's 100th birthday in 1985."

No grass grows under this lady's feet, nor, for that matter, beneath McCristal, Lockhart, or Jack Frost's. As for me, I knew I had been in good company. I had been in the collective presence of several men and women professionals who had reached high places in our work without, at the same time, ever losing the dimension of the humane, the frequent touch of the divine.

6.

American Involvement in the Athens Olympian Games of 1906: Bridge between Failure and Success*

In the United States of America during the first dozen years of the twentieth century, the year 1906 marked that country's high point of social and political reform, and coincided with her decision to participate in the unofficial Athens Olympian Games, and in so doing, substantially aided in the strengthening of the whole Olympic movement. The first three Olympic Games in Athens, Paris, and St. Louis, proved that international sporting festivals were only marginally acceptable to the world community.[1] For ten years the question of a permanent Olympic Games site in Athens versus different locations among the world's great cities created uneasiness among Olympic Committee members, especially for its president, the Baron Pierre de Coubertin. Although clearly understood by the Baron and his small cadre of friends that these new games would rotate from city to city every four years, the enthusiastic acceptance of the 1896 games by all the Greek people helped revive a strong but latent Hellenic patriotism, resulting in persistent and irritating (to Coubertin) calls for a permanent Greek Olympic Games or a Panhellenic "Athenaia" on alternate years 1898, 1902, and 1906.[2] No less than the King of Greece, at the banquet following the Athens games of 1896, looked "forward with confidence to the next festival, to be held in our dear capital."[3] King George was only reflecting what the United States Consul of Greece, George Horton, called

*STADION, VI (1980) 217-228.

the recent "tidal wave of interest in physical culture" among Greeks, which converted all of them "into earnest partisans of this city as a permanent meeting place."[4] None of this sat well with Coubertin. Amidst the temporary euphoria of a permanent Greek site, he voiced his opposition,[5] and thirty-five years later, in his *Memoires Olympiques,* where he claimed that even at the time, he "realized with absolute certainty the impractical nature of such a plan, which could only be doomed to failure."[6] Prince George, the King's son, disagreed, as did the Greek president of the International Olympic Committee, Dimitrios Vikelas, who distributed a circular among its members, calling for permanent Greek games, every two years, alternating with the established festival. "I voiced my opposition to what appeared a too frequent Olympic Games," complained Coubertin.[7]

Coubertin's position as leader of the Olympic movement was quite tenuous in these very early days. A minor revolt by some IOC members[8] convinced Coubertin that compromise was necessary, and so he agreed to discuss with Greek authorities the possibility of permanent Greek games to be added to the already established rotating games. Coubertin claimed the idea of complementary games occurred simultaneously with the Crown Prince and himself.[9] The possibility of an annual Athenian sport festival was briefly discussed at the 1901 IOC Meeting in Paris, but serious military confrontations with Turkish troops and Cretan insurgents during the period 1897-1904 ruled out such an idea. Coubertin had his own troubles during this era, and they came from four directions: in the spring of 1898, the organizing committee of the Paris games of 1900 had forced the Baron to resign as a member; Greek nationalists, through their organ, the newspaper *Messager d'Athenes,* continued to label Coubertin an interloper into the Olympic Games, which to them was an essentially Greek modern movement; American sport officials, led by James E. Sullivan, challenged Coubertin's authority as president of the IOC; unceasing turmoil within the IOC resulted in near defections by several members. As early as November of 1900, *The Sun* of New York City declared that the Baron de Coubertin was no longer in control of international athletics and had "no longer any power to name the place at which Olympian Games ... shall be held."[10] Coubertin tried to set it all straight in his 1902 *Revue Olympique* article, "Une Rectification Necessaire," but he had to wait till the Brussels Congress of June, 1905, to at least resolve the issue of a rival Olympic Games in Athens. It was agreed that the IOC would "support additional Greek games in the year 1906."[11]

During the closing ceremonies of the Athens Olympic Games of 1896, the hugely successful band of Americans, led by the veteran James B. Connolly, "signed a petition that thereafter the Olympic championships be contested only in Greece." The Harvard University "drop-out" explained their decision as a result of "breathing the atmosphere of that atavistic occasion."[12] Although the next two Olympic Games in Paris (1900) and St. Louis (1904) were failures by a great many standards, the American success in what were essentially international track and field championships can be traced directly to the organizational genius of James E. Sullivan. His election to president of the all-powerful Amateur Athletic Union (AAU) in late 1906 came on the heels of Theodore Roosevelt's selection of Sullivan as official United States representative to Athens in the spring of that year. "The name of Mr. Sullivan," pontificated *The New York Times,* was the only one considered, "he embodying in the minds of all present, every desiderata of the position."[13] And more than that, the American Olympic Committee (AOC) made it clear that "in matters of competition, Mr. Sullivan is to be in charge and that his decision shall be final."[14]

To say that the American public, even that smaller segment, the sporting public, was preoccupied with the out-of-sequence Olympic Games in Athens during the spring of 1906, would be exaggeration. American baseball dominated the sports pages during these months, while the headlines, editorials, and special sections screamed the unsettling news of cataclysmic earthquakes, volcanic eruptions, far-flung military campaigns, and of course, unceasing national political news. The year 1906 marked the mid-point and high water mark of American's grand experiment in social reform. This "Era of Reform," was marked by journalistic expose, progressive legislation, zealous and humanistic outpourings, and prideful awe at the emerging universal technological giant—the United States of America. The brilliant Henry Adams, upon setting eyes on the 1904 Louisiana Purchase Exposition (also the site of the Olympic Games that year), marveled that "a third-rate town" like St. Louis could do what European cities had shrunk from attempting. Adams saw the new America as "the servant of the power house, as the European of the twelfth century was the servant of the Church."[15] Most Americans during this first decade of the twentieth century were impressed with the nation's expanding horizons; most harbored hopes of personal rising expectations and fortunes; the more thoughtful were convinced of the country's manifest destiny—on the threshold of the world's leadership. The embodiment of all these attributes, and more, was Jim Sullivan—ruler of the American Olympic team about to steam out of New York harbor headed for the city of Athens.

Pierre de Coubertin was president of the IOC in 1906, and yet did not share the same enthusiasm for the coming Athenian festival as did his antagonist from the USA—James Edward Sullivan.[16] Rather than go to Athens, Coubertin scheduled a "consultative Conference on Art, Letters, and Sport." The Paris meeting coincided exactly with the Olympian festival in Athens, and thus, he said, "would be an excuse for not going to Athens, a journey I particular wished to avoid."[17] But it was full-steam ahead for the cocky, well-trained American contingent. Private American monies ($14,000) plus a gift of $1,500 from the Athens organizing committee assured the Yanks of their overseas passage. American newspapers gave them small attention. Much more important news was the unrest in China, Alice Roosevelt's marriage to Nicholas Longworth, the threat of strikes in the mines and railroads, the death of 1,219 men in a Courriere, France, coal mine, American gunboats in Nanchang, and the passing of the revered Susan B. Anthony.

By March 25, 1906, twenty-seven track and field athletes and four swimmers—all men—had been selected and labeled "almost the strongest possible for America to assemble."[19] Several days later, C. B. Parsons, Francis B. Connolly (brother of James B. Connolly), and Thomas E. Cronan were added to the team, and 2,000 spectators saw them off from Hoboken, New Jersey, on April 3 aboard the North German Lloyd steamship "Barbarossa." James Sullivan was already in London, conferring with British Amateur Athletic Association (AAA) officials on the creation of an international athletics organization—a move calculated to strip the IOC of what little power it possessed at this time.[20] The traditional route to Athens was a stop at Gibraltar, disembarkment at Naples, a slow train ride to Brindisi on the heel of the Italian boot, and a final boat passage across the Adriatic Sea to Piraeus and on to Athens by train. During the long 16-day voyage, natural aberrations on the high seas and two geological upheavals impacted on the small band of athletes and caused world-wide death and destruction.

On Wednesday, April 4, just the second day at sea, the "Barbarossa" ran into very heavy seas. Six athletes went to the extreme bow of the ship "to see if they couldn't get sick," when a huge wave nearly swept marathoner Harvey Cohen overboard. Eye-witness and Olympian jumper-hurdler, Hugo M. Friend of the University of Chicago, recalled that "It was only through the quick action of Bornamann, who drew Cohen back over the railing, that a serious accident was averted."[21] The brilliant Syracuse University sprinter-jumper, Myer Prinstein, in a May 4, 1906 letter to his fiancée, recalled that only minutes before the accident, he had gone below decks to enjoy dancing with several of the girls. Harvey had been caught by the foot just before being swept overboard, he said. "Jim Mitchell had his left shoulder dislocated, and he wasn't washed over because his shoulders got stuck between the railings," wrote Prinstein.[22] Cohen was badly bruised about the legs, as was Harry Hillman, Olympic champion and world record holder in the 400 meter hurdles, the latter eventually suffering water on the knee by the time the team enjoyed a six-hour "shake-out" at Gibraltar on April 13.

On Sunday, April 8, 1906, the famed volcanic mountain, Vesuvius, exploded, engulfing Italian towns, and "Visiting Death and Destruction to the City of Naples."[23] Strong earth tremors accompanied the disaster, indicating a major earthquake. On April 16, the ship carrying the American Olympic team docked in Naples harbor; some of the athletes visited the slopes of the mountain "amidst scenes of desolation," and thick layers of choking dust that covered the ground. Young Myer Prinstein was horrified by it all, including the "crowds of beggars, all shouting for money.... We were glad to get out of there."[24] They made it to Brindisi the next day, and set sail on the "Montenegro." The crippled athletes were not doing well; the team was met by the advance group of American athletic officials, plus the German team came aboard at the Italian port.[25] Remarkably, on the day the group arrived in Athens, April 19, 1906, one of the world's great natural disasters occurred, as *The New York Herald* screamed, "Earthquake and Fire Devastate San Francisco; 1,000 Lives Lost."[26] While death and destruction leveled most the American city, Athenian citizens, caught up in the euphoria of their very own second Olympic Games, gave the Americans a tumultuous welcome as the exhausted athletes rode to the Zappeion Athletic Club in decorated carriages. *Boston Globe* correspondent and American hammer thrower, Robert Edgren, murmured, "It was a hard trip."[27] That same day, obscuring the events in Athens, inch-high headlines cried, "San Francisco Doomed, Flames Sweep Unchecked, and Historic Residences of Nob Hill are in Ashes; City in Darkness, has no water; Terror everywhere."[28]

The American athletes strongly objected to accommodations at the Zappeion. As beautiful as it was, outwardly, said Prinstein, "the sleeping quarters were mere stalls ... and we all moved to the Hermes Hotel." German athlete, Johannes Runge, remembered that the Americans didn't like the Greek food, either, and after moving, "set up an American kitchen for themselves."[29] Far away, in Paris, Pierre de Coubertin made the best of what he considered an unfortuitous Olympic Games, sent his regrets for not being there, and wished good luck to the organizing committee: "Hours of work have insured the continuance of the Games and the salutary influence they have and will continue to have on civilization; please accept my profound gratitude."[30]

It seemed that most citizens of Athens were present on the opening day, April 22, 1906. Nearly a tenth of a million people filled the beautiful but inefficient marble stadium and covered the high ground outside. Almost the entire Greek and British royal families were present in anticipation of seeing approximately 900 athletes from 22 different countries. There were 36 Americans present, including the all-powerful Sullivan and the manager of the team, Matthew P. Halpin. The latter was enormously impressed on this first day and cabled the New York *Evening Mail* that the whole affair was like a king's coronation, and "When I dipped the Stars and Stripes passing the royal box, the King staked me to a smile that made me feel that I belonged."[31] Halpin played a starkly secondary administrative role to that of Sullivan and was accused by the first American Olympic champion, James B. Connolly, of being "a relic of the old days.... This man had never in his life done anything which might indicate that he could even half fill the job. Long before he reached Athens he proved himself an incompetent trainer, a man of impossible manners, a child in travel...."[32]

Even if true, leadership was not missing from the USA team. The single-minded Sullivan was ever-in-command. For example, before the team left for Greece, Sullivan wrote a letter to Marquard Schwartz, "a capital short and middle distance swimmer," representing the Missouri Athletic Club, that he had been selected for the Olympic team. Begin intensive training, ordered Sullivan, and be reminded "that in matters of competition, and all details related thereto.... Mr. James E. Sullivan, shall be in charge and his decision shall be final.... The team will go absolutely, as an American team.... You are now in a responsible position, for the eyes of the American public will be on you, and I feel confident, that if each man will remember that he is working for the good of the entire team and for the success of America, this country will be victorious."[33]

Competition began on Monday, April 23, 1906, in gymnastics, lawn tennis, rowing, weight-lifting, Greco-Roman wrestling, shooting, football, rope-climbing, tug-of-war, bicycling, fencing, swimming, diving, and, as far as Sullivan was concerned, the only real sport—track and field (athletics). All the others, he said, are "minor sports" and "do not figure prominently at all in connection with the games."[34] Despite Sullivan's earlier patriotic admonition to Marquard Schwartz, that young man and his teammates Joseph Spencer and Frank A. Bornamann, failed to score in the individual swimming events and, despite Charles M. Daniels' anchor leg, finished fourth in the 4 x 200 meter freestyle relay.[35] Daniels won the 100 meter freestyle in 73.4 seconds, the only American scorer outside of track and field. Wrestler Isidor Miflot was eliminated, and D. A. Sullivan failed to survive the two-hour long first round of the Greco-Roman wrestling competition.[36] Sullivan had his way, and the rest of his team dominated the athletics events.

The British invented modern track and field, but by 1906, their most adept pupils, the Americans, had surpassed the world. Only athletes from these two nations, noted a *Washington Post* journalist, train hard and intelligently, such that nothing will "interfere with their practice and diet."[37] Americans train scientifically, boasted U.S. Commissioner, Sullivan. "We go into athletic sport with an earnestness that the other countries cannot understand."[38] Yankee enthusiasm, self-confidence, and attention to science, he added, tend to "develop the good that is in men from their boyhood up."[39] The 100 meter dash finals proved Sullivan not only a chauvinist but an accurate analyst. Americans Archie Hahn, Fay Moulton, William D. Eaton, and Lawson Robertson went 1, 2, 4, 5 in the short sprint and 1, 4, 5, 6 in the "400," by Paul Pilgrim, Harry Livingston Hillman, Charles Bacon, and Moulton. The aptly named James Lightbody finished inches behind Pilgrim in the 800 meters, with Bacon in sixth place. Lightbody won the "1500," with James P. Sullivan and George V. Bonhag in fifth and sixth places. No less dominating were American high hurdlers Robert G. Leavitt and Hugo Friend, who took first and fourth places while Bonhang, in his first walking race ever, won a much disputed 1500 meter race in which the confused jury, made up of the Greek royal family, disqualified most of the competitors.[40] More damaging was James B. Connolly's accusation that since Sullivan was chief judge of that event, "it would be safe to skip the corners" and cheat one's way to victory. "The American officials gave the race to Bonhag," confessed Connolly.[41]

The American athletes in Athens needed no such extra aid, as alleged by the angry Connolly. Their runners, jumpers, and throwers were the best in the world, although there were notable individual exceptions such as the superb Peter O'Connor, triple jump winner over a field that contained Thomas Cronan and Francis Connolly of the U.S.A. At the flag-raising ceremony, O'Connor attempted to hoist the flag of Ireland instead of the British colors, but he was restrained from doing so.[42] Possibly the most gifted all-around athlete in the world at the time was Martin J. Sheridan of New York City's Irish-American Athletic Club. At these 1906 games, after he won the shot put, discus throw, finished second in the standing long jump, the stone throw, the standing high jump, and a fourth place in the Greek style discus, he sent a telegram home: "Don't worry; the team is sure to win for 'Old Glory's' sake."[43] It was reported that the Greek crown prince declared that the American flag had been upraised so often, "they needed another set."[44] Ray Ewry won the standing high jump and the standing long jump while Herbert Kerrigan, Thomas Cronan, and Lawson Robertson were prominent scorers in these and other field events. Myer Prinstein injured himself during competition, but still won the long jump over O'Connor and the U.S.A.'s Hugo Friend. Theodore Andrea Cook saw it all and concluded that "the Americans almost swept the board in the Stadium events, but they paid for specialization by doing very little else."[45]

The Canadian, William John Sherring's victory in the classic marathon received an unbelieving and cool reception by the stadium crowd and some calls of "Barbarian," but the royal family's enthusiasm for the victor quickly changed their attitude to one of unreserved support. William G. Frank of New York City was third, two minutes behind John Svanberg of Sweden. French athletes had done very well; the Italians, Swiss, Danish, British, and Scandinavian athletes had proven themselves winners, but American victory after victory at the packed stadium appeared to most as a clarion call of Yankee superiority at these Olympic Games. The Americans continued to be enormously popular at the early Olympic Games. King George summoned James Sullivan, congratulated his "marvelous athletes" and expressed "regret that President Roosevelt, whom I admire greatly, is not here to enjoy them."[46] Theodore Roosevelt, in turn, sent a telegram to his friend, Sullivan, rendering "Hearty congratulations to you and the American contestants. Uncle Sam is all right."[47] The Athenian newspaper *Estia* was puzzled by the message and asked "Who is this 'Uncle Sam'?"[48]

For nearly two weeks, most Athenians had been euphoric about these second Greek games. Parties, receptions, banquets, classical plays in ancient theaters and atop the Acropolis, exhibitions, fireworks, athletic demonstrations, and water spectacles at the port of Piraieus made the whole city "a fairylike spectacle." The American manager, Matt Halpin, on the last day of competition (May 2) led his team in "three deafening cheers in honor of the King." The King, in turn, invited 400 to a gala dinner. Young Myer Prinstein recalled that the American boys cleaned out the minister's excellent cigars, drank champagne, acted "like wild Indians," and looked forward to going to "a millionaire's villa and dance."[49] The American success in Olympic track and field athletics—the center-piece of these games—did not go unnoticed by the folks back home, but, of course, athletics could not compete with the nation's larger preoccupation with college football and professional baseball. The overarching concern of the American newspapers throughout the entire period of the Athens games was the unprecedented San Francisco earthquake disaster. Even as the sporting events in ancient Athens ended, *The Boston Globe* lamented that "Coroner Walsh of San Francisco raises the army estimate of dead...."[50]

All new or emerging nations tend to be loudly proud of their heroes, frequently being labeled nationalistic. American sport journalist's reactions to their athlete's success ranged from amusing hyperbole to sober evaluation of the nation's soaring health. One periodical concluded that "like Alexander of old, the sturdy American gladiator may soon be sighing for new worlds to conquer."[51] America's "national craving to break the record" in all things was given as another reason for her athletic domination.[52] "A nation greater than Greece has arisen," cried *The Chicago Daily Tribune* of May 4, 1906. Sullivan crowed that his boy's victories furnished "ample opportunity to allow the (American) eagle to scream."[53] The U.S.A. won eleven athletics events, he said, while Great Britain, "with all her possessions," won only four firsts.[54] A mellower approach was taken by *The Nation* editor, who perceived that for the U.S.A. to win so convincingly was "agreeable," but "to win under the shadow of the Acropolis must pass for the fine flower of athletic triumph."[55] There was much more, including unvarnished praise for James E. Sullivan as athletic genius, with "more ability ... tucked under his Derby hat than was assembled in this entire galaxy of crowned heads."[56] And from far away Paris, the Baron Pierre de Coubertin took a moment from his Olympic art and culture symposium to congratulate the American Olympians on their "brilliant success."[57]

Athletes from the leading physical culture countries—Scandinavia, Denmark, Britain, Germany, Austria, France, and Switzerland—had participated successfully in these 1906 Athenian games. In the English language press, however, the American domination in track and field athletics was perceived incorrectly as evidence of that nation's superiority in all sports. Historian Harold Underwood Faulkner noted that some took this illogic one step farther, declaring that "The astonishing success of the American athletes at the Olympics was a fresh confirmation to ardent nationalists of the superiority of the American way of life."[58] America's movement from relative barbarism in just over one hundred years had, by the early twentieth century, resulted in what many in that country saw as inexorable progress. Citizens of this new nation were, as Oscar Handlin said, "bred in the belief in their own destined mission."[59] When the White Star liner "Republic" docked at Sandy Hook, New Jersey, on May 25, 1906, Sullivan "was fairly bubbling over with enthusiasm as he read Theodore Roosevelt's telegram: "Let me heartily congratulate you and all the members of the team...."[60] The entire American contingent had vivid memories of that last prize-awarding ceremony in Athens. A journalist from the New York *Press* took record of tumultuous crowds, shimmering heat, the classic Acropolis, and the victorious Yankees receiving prizes from the King. The success of the Americans was so overwhelming that only "the special suitability of the American climate" could explain it, he concluded.[61]

As for James Edward Sullivan, the all-powerful forty-six year old New Yorker was showered with honors, including the Greek "Golden Cross," and dozens of essays as to his honesty, toughness, and athletic integrity. Sullivan testimonials spoke of his Olympic genius for organization and "a loving fealty ... not enjoyed by any other single man in sport."[62] His elevation to presidency (in January of 1907) of the A.A.U., marked the simultaneous rise of the man as omnipotent sport leader and the nearly unrivaled success of his country in future Olympic Games track and field athletics. Sullivan had consistently believed in Athens as a permanent Olympic Games site, as long as athletics remained the core of the program. The Crown Prince of Greece called on him to bring America's finest to Athens in 1910, and Sullivan in turn talked his friend, President Roosevelt, into once again serving as honorary president of the team.[63] Sullivan was an influential official at the original Athens games of 1896, played a decisive American role at the Paris games of 1900, dominated the American direction at the unofficial Olympic Games of 1906, and was in full charge at the burgeoning Olympic Games of 1908 (London) and 1912 (Stockholm). In several ideological ways, Mr. Sullivan represented the antithesis of the Coubertin preachings, and these conflicting athletic philosophies plus subtler differences in education, family background, and social standing, made these two influential Olympic leaders uneasy companions in their divergent quests to make the Olympic Games the most important sporting event in the world.

The 1906 Athenian games were completely in the hands of enthusiastic but still inexperienced Greek authorities. A great deal went wrong, organizationally, at this Athenian spring festival. But it didn't matter, for as a manifestation of Greek will and national fervor, and purely by accident, they were by comparison far better than the ill-conceived Paris and St. Louis Olympic Games of 1900 and 1904. The American contribution in Athens helped turn the Olympic Games around, giving impetus to larger numbers of participants at the 1908 London games. And the reverse was also true, for America's rise to technological and scientific success during the era 1900-1914 was aided by Sullivan's small band of athletic elitists and their noisy victories at these interesting out-of-sequence Panhellenic games of 1906. More and more, North Americans and Europeans were beginning to echo Theodore Roosevelt's theme—"Uncle Sam is all right."

NOTES

1 See Chapter 3, "Olympic Trial and Tribulation 1896-1911," in John Lucas, *The Modern Olympic Games*, (Cranbury, New Jersey: A.S. Barnes and Company, 1980) 45-63.

2 See Rufus B. Richardson, "The New Olympic Games," *Scribner's Magazine*, 20 (September, 1896) 286. A certain Eben Alexander reproduced in its entirety the 126 word American circular to the King of Greece, petitioning for permanent Athenian games. See *New York Times*, "Letters to the Editor," March 4, 1900, p. 21.

3 King George of Greece, as quoted in Timoleon J. Philemon (ed.), *Official Report—Olympic Games, 776 B.C. - 1896 A.D.*, (New York: American Olympic Committee, 1896) 69.

4 George Horton, "The Recent Olympian Games," *The Bostonian*, 4 (July, 1896) 215-216, 228.

5 Pierre de Coubertin, "The Olympic Games of 1896," *Century Magazine*, 53 (November, 1896) 53.

6 Pierre de Coubertin, *Memoires Olympiques*, (Lausanne: Bureau International de Pedagogic Sportive, 1931) 37.

7 Pierre de Coubertin, *Une Campagne de Vingt-et-un Ans (1887-1908)*, (Paris: Librairie de L'education Physique, 1908) 130.

8 See Marie-Therese Eyquern, *Pierre de Coubertin—L'Epopee Olympique,* (Paris: Caiman-Levy, 1966) 185.

9 See *Une Campagne*, 128.

10 See "The Next Olympian Games," *The Sun* (New York), November 13, 1900, p. 5.

11 Pierre de Coubertin, "Une Rectification Necessaire," *Revue Olympique* 5 July, 1902) 10-12; see Coubertin, *Memoires Olympiques*, 76, and *Une Campagne*, 170-171.

12 James B. Connolly, "The Spirit of the Olympian Games," *Outing*, 48 (April, 1906) 103.

13 "President Roosevelt Appoints J.E. Sullivan," *New York Times*, March 10, 1906, p. 8.

14 See "The Strive for Laurels," *New York Daily Tribune*, March 6, 1906, p. 5.

15 Henry Adams, *The Education of Henry Adams*, (New York: The Modern Library, Random House, 1931; original publishing date, 1918), 466-467.

16 The fifteen year animosity between the two men is recorded and analyzed by John Lucas, "Early Olympic Antagonists—Pierre de Coubertin versus James E. Sullivan," *Stadion* III (1977) 258-272.

17 Coubertin, *Memoires Olympiques*, 79.

18 See *New York Times,* March 10, 1906, p. 8, and Caspar Whitney's comments in *Outing,* 47 (September, 1905) 786.

19 Biographical sketches were included; see "America's Best Athletes to Compete in the Olympic Games at Athens," *Washington Post*, March 25, 1906, p. 2 of the "Magazine Section."

20 See "Plan Athletic Union," *New York Daily Tribune*, March 23, 1906, p. 10; also see Lucas, "Early Olympic Antagonists," 261.

21 See "Friend Writes of Voyage of American Athletes," *Chicago Sunday Tribune*, April 29, 1906, p. 35.

22 Myer Prinstein, Hotel Hermes, Athens, to his fiancée, Etta, May 4, 1906. Personal files of John Lucas.

23 For days, the major newspapers of the world were preoccupied with the disaster. See, for example, *Philadelphia Inquirer,* April 9 and 11, 1906.

24 Prinstein to Etta. British Olympic athletes also witnessed the horror at Vesuvius. "Soldiers were still taking out the mummified bodies of victims who had been caught in the last lava-flow, looking exactly like bodies we had just seen in Pompeii of the victims of 1800 years before." See Theodore Andrea Cook, *The Sunlit Hours—A Record of Sport and Life*, (New York: George H. Doran Co., n.d.) 227.

25 See "Athletes' Trip Near End," *Chicago Daily Tribune*, April 17, 1906, p. 10.

26 See *New York Herald*, April 19, 1906, p. 1.

27 Robert *Edgren*, "Athletes Reach Athens," *Boston Globe*, April 20, 1906, p. 1.

28 See *New York Herald*, April 20, 1906, 1.

29 Prinstein, letter to Etta; Johannes *Runge*, "From Athens to Berlin", *Olympic Games 1936*, No. 7, Berlin: German Organizing Committee (October, 1935) 15.

30 Pierre de Coubertin in a letter dated 10 April, 1906, as found in *Bulletin du Comite des Jeux Olympiques a Athenes*, p. 190. This 204 page manuscript is located in the library of the IOC, Lausanne, Switzerland.

31 Matt Hatpin to the *New York Evening Mail*, as quoted in Dick Schaap, *An Illustrated History of the Olympics*, (New York: Alfred A. Knopf, 1975) 96.

32 James B. Connolly, "The Capitalization of Amateur Athletics," *Metropolitan Magazine*, 32 (July, 1910) 452.

33 James E. Sullivan to Marquard Schwartz, 8 March, 1906, University of Illinois, Archives of the Alumni Association, Avery Brundage Collection, Box 103, International Olympic Committee Subject File, Pierre de Coubertin.

34 James E. Sullivan, "American Athletes in Ancient Athens," *American Monthly Review of Reviews*, 34 (July, 1906) 48.

35 See Erich Kamper, *Encyclopedia of the Olympic Games*, (New York: McGraw-Hill Book Co., 1972) 61.

36 See Harvey Lee Abrams, "The History of the United States Wrestling Team From 1896 to 1920," (M.A. thesis, Southeast Missouri State University, 1979) 21.

37 "Americans in Good Form," *Washington Post*, April 24, 1906, p. 8.

38 Sullivan, "American Athletes in Ancient Athens," p. 44.

39 Sullivan as quoted in "Athletes Reach Port," *New York Daily Tribune*, May 26, 1906, p. 10.

40 See "The American Victory at Athens," *Colliers*, 37 (June 9, 1906) 13.

41 Connolly, "The Capitalization of Amateur Athletics," 452-453.

42 See "Wants Colors of Ireland to be Seen at Greek Games," *Chicago Daily Tribune*, April 27, 1906, p. 10 and May 1, 1906, p. 10.

43 See "Sure to Win," *Boston Globe*, April 28, 1906, p. 1.

44 Edgren, "Athletes Reach Athens," p. 1.

45 Cook, *The Sunlit Hours*, 232.

46 See "Our Athens Record," *Washington Post*, April 29, 1906, p. 1, sporting section.

47 "President Congratulates Victors," *New York Daily Tribune*, May 4, 1906, p. 1.

48 See James E. Sullivan (ed.), *The Olympic Games of 1906 at Athens*, (New York: American Sports Publishing Co., 1906) 44-45.

49 Prinstein, letter to Etta.

50 *Boston Globe*, April 29, 1906, p. 1.

51 See "American Victors at Athens," *Public Opinion*, 40 (May 12, 1906) 584.

52 See "American Triumphs in the Olympic Games," *American Monthly Review of Reviews,* 33 (June, 1906) 664.

53 Sullivan, "American Athletes in Ancient Athens," 44.

54 James E. Sullivan, "American Athletes Champions of the World," *Outing,* 48 (August, 1906) 626.

55 See *Nation,* 82 (May 10, 1906) 377.

56 See "The American Victory at Athens," 13. Several more accolades may be found in *New York Times,* May 4, 1906, p. 8, and May 6, 1906, p. 4; *Literary Digest,* 32 (May 12, 1906) 712-713; *New York Herald,* May 26, 1906, p. 12; *Harper's Weekly,* 50 (June 2, 1906) 774-775.

57 See "Prizes at Olympian Games," *New York Daily Tribune,* May 27, 1906, p. 3.

58 Harold Underwood Faulkner, *The Quest For Social Justice 1898-1914.* Vol. II: *A History of American Life* by Arthur M. *Schlesinger* and Dixon Ryan *Fox* (editors), (New York: Macmillan, 1931) 293.

59 Oscar Handlin, *Truth in History,* (Cambridge, Massachusetts: Harvard University Press, 1979) 89.

60 Theodore Roosevelt, as quoted in "Olympic Champions Return from Athens," *New York Herald,* May 26, 1906, p. 12.

61 See the New York Press release as located in *The Literary Digest,* 32 (May 12, 1906) 713.

62 See "Sullivan Testimonial Enthusiastic Tribute," *New York Times,* January 10, 1907, p. 7.

63 See "President and the Games," *New York Times,* December 16, 1906, p. 11.

7.
Origins of the Academy Award Film
"Chariots of Fire"*

I talked with David Puttnam, Producer of "Chariots of Fire," and he told me that the film title was revealed to him after recalling the lines of an old school and church hymn called "Jerusalem" sung by British children. "Listen carefully to the boy's choir at the beginning of the film," he told me in a cross-country telephone conversation, "and you'll hear the line 'Bring me my chariot of fire!'"[1] The image itself may have been handed down to us from Greek mythology; the actual phrase "chariot of fire" comes from *The Holy Bible* where the great prophet Elijah beheld "a chariot of fire, and horses of fire," and parting both asunder he "went up by a whirlwind into heaven."[2] Elijah had remained steadfast in his faith and was rewarded by being "translated to heaven without dying" in a chariot and horses of fire.[3] Elijah's companion, Elisha, in answer to his master's question "Before I am taken from you, ask me what I can do for you," answered "Let me fall heir to your spirit." A difficult request answered the prophet. "If you see me taken from you," said Elijah, "may your wish be granted." Suddenly "a chariot of fire with horses of fire drove between them and Elijah went up by a whirlwind into heaven."[4] The 1701 illustrated edition of *The History of the Old and New Testament* vividly depicts the extraordinary scene in two full-page drawings titled "Elijah taken up in a fiery chariot" and "Elijah taken up into heaven."[5]

A hundred years later the mystical English poet-engraver, William Blake (1757-1827), was in the midst of his most productive anti-rational, myth-making writings. Blake, who spanned the transition to Romanticism, "lived on mystery, rejected science, doubted God, worshiped Christ, transformed the Bible, emulated the Prophets, and called for a Utopia of earthbound saints."[6] Thus Blake's mythopoeia (deliberate myth-making and return to primitive non-logical anthropomorphism) was his response to the immediately preceding era of the Enlightenment. Listen to his exquisite poetical selection from "Milton":

> And did those feet in ancient time
> Walk upon England's mountains green?
> And was the holy Lamb of God
> On England's pleasant pastures seen?
> And did the Countenance Divine
> Shine forth upon our clouded hills?
> And was Jerusalem builded here
> Among these dark Satanic Mills?
> Bring me my bow of burning gold!
> Bring me my arrows of desire!
> Bring me my spear! O clouds unfold!
> Bring me my chariot of fire!
> I will not cease from mental fight,
> Nor shall my sword sleep in my hand,
> Till we have built Jerusalem
> In England's green and pleasant land.[8]

Blake knew the Bible story well and illustrated "Elijah and Elisha" and "Elijah in the chariot of fire" in two of his extraordinary engravings.[9] The poem was never lost to the people of England and during the last decades of the nineteenth century became a clarion call for a Christian Socialist society called the Guild of St. Matthew, made up of "keen and able men ... including such young writers as Bernard Shaw."[10]

In the midst of the war, 1916, England was in a fever of patriotism and at the same time the House of Commons had the good sense to pass a Women's Suffrage law. A great service of thanksgiving was held in the Albert Hall, Lon-

John Lucas was an observer at the XIth Olympic Congress in Baden-Baden in 1981.

don. Sir Hubert Parry, composer and suffragist, took William Blake's poem "Milton," composed tune for it, renamed it "Jerusalem," and it "speedily attained the position of a new national anthem."[11] Several years later, on the centenary anniversary of Blake's death, August 12, 1927, *The Times* of London said of Blake's and Parry's "Jerusalem" that it in some ways surpassed in meaning the national anthem, that it expressed "the feelings that lie below the conscious loyalties of 'God Save the King'...." The haunting melody and message went beyond "the inadequacy of official patriotism."[12]

Rumors continue to persist that "Chariots of Fire" won the 1981 Academy Award not because it was the best film of the year but rather by default, since the judges could not settle decisively on a winner. It was simply too complicated a film to be liked by all the critics. The *New Yorker* reviewer hated the simple values displayed, was turned off by synthesized music, and considered the effort a form of "retrograde moviemaking, presented with fake bravura."[13] Robert Hatch in *The Nation* "grew weary of Abrahams' hot-eyed obsession with victory and of Liddell's smug righteousness."[14] The favorable comments far outweigh criticism of the "Chariots" film, but before looking at several of them another look at origins is in order. Producer David Puttnam already indicated the long-time popularity of the rousing British World War I hymn "Jerusalem." He and fellow Englishman, Director Hugh Hudson, were vaguely aware of the famous Blake poem "Milton" put to music by Parry, but the inspiration to tie that song to high drama at the 1924 Olympic Games and call it "Chariots of Fire" belongs to the persistent genius of the first-named David Puttnam.

David Puttnam got the idea for "Chariots" in 1977 while staying in the guesthouse of Los Angeles Athletic Club President, Charles Hathaway.[15] Puttnam was struck by the heroic stories of Eric Liddell and Harold Abrahams as described by Bill Henry and his daughter Pat Henry Yeomans in their 1976 *Approved History of the Olympic Games*.[16] Mrs. Yeomans wrote that Puttnam found the idea for the project on pages 116 and 201 of the *Approved History*. "He pursued the project," she said, "and used authentic documents from the International Olympic Committee and the 1924 Official Report."[17] Mr. Hathaway confirmed this in a letter addressed to Pat Yeomans in which he reminded her "that it was our home Puttnam rented and our library where he ran across your book, so we both can accept some responsibility and credit for the movie!"[18]

"'Chariots of Fire' appealed to me because the characters were so passionate," said Director Hudson of Colin Welland's original screenplay.[19] It was a sensation at the Spring 1981 Cannes Film Festival, a prize winner at the fall Toronto Festival, and highly acclaimed at the 19th New York City showing.[20] The accolades poured in as they always do for an Academy Award winner, but there was something different about this one—an air of incredulity. No sex, no violence; unbelievable! said some of the reviewers. Scott Ostler's *Los Angeles Times* comment was that the public was apparently "ready for a sports movie dealing with the simplistic theme of two men striving for excellence."[21] Dale Pollock called "Chariots" victory "a stunning upset ... a film without artifice ... a very uncool film. People aren't embarrassed to react to it. They cry while they're watching it."[22] Of course the film's success surprised many, and Mr. Puttnam supplied the reason. "This is an expedient world," he said. "For people to behave in an unexpedient manner is extraordinary."[23]

The modest-priced $6,000,000 film was pure romance and everyone knew it; only a few thought it would make it. Eric Liddell's exclamation in the film, "When I run I feel His pleasure," is, as *Sports Illustrated* journalist Frank Deford said, a sort of "continuum that brings with the Victorian concept of 'muscular Christianity' ... and extends to the present Fellowship of Christian Athletes."[24] Both David Puttnam and Colin Welland—producer and scriptwriter—were extremely good at their trade. But for Puttnam especially "the taste of success was never as sweet as he had imagined it would be."[25] Somehow the chemistry was right. A powerful and holy story from the *Old Testament* was given heightened mysticism and a patriotic flavor by the great William Blake, which in turn was crafted by a famous World War I musician and finally given a worldwide Olympic Games scenario by the team of Puttnam-Hudson-Welland. Joy Gould Boyum in the staid *Wall Street Journal* thought it all a "convincing evocation of the '24 Olympics," a film conveying "the extraordinary feeling of authenticity ... of overwhelming realistic texture ... of lovely cinematography, muted in tone and softly lit."[26]

There were misgivings about the film and *The Christian Science Monitor* critic, David Sterritt, called it a bracing film, "more stimulating to the eye than to the mind."[27] He was quickly criticized by *Monitor* readers as far away as Swanbourne, Australia.[28] Sterritt shot back that with all of the film's clear and buoyant air, the movie was still superficial. Cleanliness and decency, he said:

... are only the starting points for works of art, as for human relations. Here's hoping 'Chariots of Fire' is a starting point, ushering in a brand new wave of wholesomeness and cinematic skill....[29]

Howard Reich of the *Chicago Tribune* was intrigued by the film's photography and low cost;[30] John Simon in the *National Review* called "Chariots" a superficial film but one that "is genteel, well-crafted, eminently worthy...."[31] Reviewers in *Films in Review* and *Films and Filming* were taken with the rare mixture of religion, national and triumphant exhilaration shown in the film.[32] Almost every paper had something to say about the award-winning production, including the *Dallas Times Herald* and even the Boca Raton, Florida, weekly.[33] Kenneth Turan found the opening scene symbolic of the whole film—the British Olympic team running through the surf of the English Channel. They are running hard, said Turan:

... but they are supremely, almost mystically happy; they are in training but they are simultaneously very much in love with what they're doing, and it is the film's triumph to explain how they've come to feel the way they do.[34]

There's strong evidence that the actors themselves got caught up in this evangelic fervor, and George Vecsey in the *New York Times* described the involvement.[35] A careful reading of Colin

Paris 1924 : Start of the 100 m final.

Welland's exquisite script, now in a paperback book, will tell you why many of these professionals got "caught up" in the film's animated atmosphere.[36] And lastly (although there are scores of reviews unmentioned) there is the recent review in *People's Weekly,* which forgave a half score historical errors in the film, giving it an "A" for "courage, discipline and character."[37]

There's no need to make too much of "Chariots of Fire." It is a very fine film with an uplifting message, a true melodrama that runs counter to present-day individual and collective mediocrity and narcissism. William Blake, I think, would have enjoyed the film. All his life he had visions, declaring that he was daily visited by a messenger from heaven.[38] Blake's "elaborate symbolic mythology"[39] invited phrases such as "Chariot of Fire," and late in his extraordinary life he wrote an intensely personal "interpretation of the Gospel of Christ"[40] called "The Everlasting Gospel." On pages 100 and 101, lines 31-34, Blake identified God and the fiery chariot as one of the same:

Paris 1924: The two heroes of the film "Chariots of Fire," Harold Abrahams (l.) and Eric Liddell (r.).

THERE IS THE SPIRIT OF YOUTH AND ADVENTURE, IN

CHARIOTS OF FIRE

The God of this World raged in vain
He bound old Satan in his chain
And bursting forth
His furious ire
Became a Chariot of Fire.[41]

But Blake's "Milton" poem and its middle stanza will, I think, be remembered longer as identified with the 1981 Academy Award winning film:

Bring me my bow of burning gold!
Bring me my arrows of desire!
Bring me my spear! O clouds unfold!
Bring me my chariot of fire![42]
*****

1. William Blake (1757-1827): English poet, painter, engraver, and mystic. His early works, e.g. "Songs of Innocence," were predominantly lyrical, but his later works, e.g. "Milton" (1804-8) and "Jerusalem" (1804-20), were almost entirely symbolic, portraying the conflict of restrictive morality and anarchical liberty. A professional engraver all his life, he also painted in watercolors. Most of his books were self-manufactured by his original process of "illuminated printing"; text and pictures were

done in reverse on metal with acid-proof ink, then treated with acid, printed by hand, and hand-colored.

2. The reference in the second verse to "Jerusalem" being built "among these dark Satanic mills" means (I think) the establishment of Christian values and morality in place of the uncaring exploitation and materialism of the industrial age. ("Mills" means "industrial workshops" or "ateliers.") The poem continues in verses 3 and 4 with a rousing declaration of determination to fight through to victory, presumably with the Lord's help. However, the reference to a "chariot of fire" from the clouds is Biblical; the Book of Kings: "Lo there came a fiery chariot with fiery horses and he went by a whirlwind to Heaven." This refers to the prophet Elijah, and perhaps Blake regarded himself as something of a prophet!

3. The poem was set to music by Parry and has become a kind of national hymn. It is called "Jerusalem" and is sung on patriotic occasions. With a cathedral organ and a big choir and congregation, it sounds magnificent.

NOTES

1 Telephone conversation with David Puttnam on Thursday, April 29, 1982.

2 *The Holy Bible.* Authorized King James version; II Kings 2:11.

3 See "Elijah" in Henry Snyder Gehman (ed.), *The New Westminster Dictionary of the Bible* (Philadelphia: The Westminster Press, 1974), p. 261.

4 *A New Translation of the Bible* by James Moffatt (New York : Harperand Row, Pub., 1954), p. 417. See also *The New Standard English Bible* (New York : Oxford University Press, 1972), pp. 409-410.

5 *The History of the Old and New Testament* (London : R. Blome S., 1701), pp. 155, 156.

6 Will and Ariel Durant, *The Age of Napoleon*, Vol. XI of *The Story of Civilisation* (New York : Simon and Schuster, 1975), p. 413.

7 The word "Mythopoeia" is defined in *The Harper Dictionary of Modern Thought*, edited by Alan Bullock and Oliver Stallybrass (New York : Harper and Row, Pub., 1977), p. 407.

8 John Sampson (ed.), *The Poetical Works of William Blake* (London: Oxford University Press, 1961), p. 370.

9 *William Blake's Illustrations to the Bible* (London : Trianon Press, 1957), Plates 64 and 65a.

10 Percy Dearmer, *Songs of Praise* (London: Oxford University Press, 1933), p. 240.

11 Ibid.

12 "William Blake—a True Englishman," *The Times,* London, August 12, 1927, p. 11.

13 "Chariots of Fire," *New Yorker,* 57 (October 26, 1981), 178.

14 Robert Hatch, "Films," *The Nation,* 233 (October 10, 1981), 357.

15 See *Runner's World,* 17 (January, 1982), 60.

16 Bill Henry and Pat Henry Yeomans, *An Approved History of the Olympic Games* (New York : G. P. Putnam's Sons, 1976).

17 Letter from Patricia Henry Yeomans to John Lucas dated March 30, 1982.

18 Letter from Charles F. Hathaway to Patricia Henry Yeomans dated January 28, 1982.

19 Clarke Taylor, "Director Hudson Winning with 'Chariots of Fire," *Los Angeles Times,* September 30, 1981, p. 1.

20 Ibid.

21 Scott Ostler, "Is This Any Way to Make a Movie ?" Los *Angeles Times,* March 31, 1982, p. 3.

22 Dale Pollock, et al., "The 'Fire' that Lit Up Oscar's Night," *Los Angeles Times* March 30, 1982, Part II.

23 Malcolm Moran, "A Study of Ambition and Morality to Open the Film Festival," *New York Times,* September 20, 1981, p. D1.

24 Frank Deford, "Nearly Picture-Perfect," Sports *Illustrated,* 55 (September 28, 1981), 63.

25 Sally Magnusson, *The Flying Scotsman—A Biography of Eric Liddell* (New York : Quartet Books, 1981, p. 184.

26 Jay Gould Boyum, "Convincing Evocation of the '24 Olympics," *Wall Street Journal,* October 2, 1981, p. 21.

27 David Sterritt, "Short Takes," *Christian Science Monitor,* October 8, 1981, p. 18.

28 "Chariots of Fire, *"Christian Science Monitor,* December 1, 1981, p. 22.

29 David Sterritt, "... Another Look at 'Chariots of Fire'...," *Christian Science Monitor,* May 13, 1982, p. 18.

30 Howard Reich "Low Budget, Unknown Faces: 'Chariots' Races to a Winning Finish," *Chicago Tribune,* October 18, 1981, Part. 6, pp. 17, 18.

31 John Simon, "Fancy Footwork," *National Review,* 33 (November 13, 1981), 1360.

32 *Films in Review,* 33 (January, 1982), 50, and *Films and Filming,* 330 (March, 1982), 15-20.

33 *Dallas Times Herald,* February 21, 1982, pp. 1,6-7; Boca (Boca-Raton, Florida), January 28 - February 3, 1982, p. 1.

34 Kenneth Turan, "Chariots of Fire," *The Runner,* 4 (January, 1982), 76.

35 George Vecsey, "An Actor's Sprint in Two Eras," *New York Times,* February 28, 1982, p. 53.

36 W. J. Weatherby, *Chariots of Fire—A True Story* (New York: Dell Publishing Co., Enigma Productions, 1981).

37 'Britain's 1974 Olympic Champs Live Again in 'Chariots of Fire'— and Run Away with the Oscars," *People's Weekly,* 17 (May 10, 1982), 95.

38 See "William Blake (1757-1827) in Seymour Kurtz (ed.), The *Columbia Encyclopedia* (New York: Columbia University Press, 1963), p. 228.

39 Ibid.

40 This phrase comes from Sir Paul Harvey (ed.), *The Oxford Companion to English Literature* (New York : The Oxford Press, 1967), p. 94.

41 William Blake, "The Everlasting Gospel" as found in David V. Erdman (ed.), *The Poetry and Prose of William Blake* (Garden City, New York: Doubleday and Co., 1965), p. 515.

42 Ibid.

*****

"Additional Commentaries on 'Chariots',," see:

a) *The Times* of London, 1 November 1981, p. 29a.

b) Robert Barnett, "'Chariots of Fire' Won Because None of the Experts Could Decide on a 81 Winner," The *Runner,* 4 (June, 1982), 9.

c) Ben Rothenbuecher, "Chariots of Fire," *Christian Century,* 98. (December 9, 1981), 1292.

d) Colin L. Westerbeck, "Not Cricket, Que Vadis, Lads?," *Commonwealth,* 108 (December 4, 1981), 687-688.

e) Michael H. Seitz, "Thatcher in the Theater," The *Progressive,* 45 (December, 1981), 53-54.

f) "Chariots of Fire," *Senior Scholastic,* 114 (October 16, 1981), 27.

g) George F. Will, "'Chariots of Fire'—a Noble Character Steals the Show," *Detriot News,* December 11, 1981, p. 19A.

* A presentation made prior to the viewing of "Chariots of Fire" on June 23, 1982, at the United States Olympic Academy VI, Pepperdine University, Malibu, California.

8.
Theodore Roosevelt and Baron Pierre de Coubertin: Entangling Olympic Games Involvement, 1901-1918*

In a remarkably seminal manner, Theodore Roosevelt (1858-1919), during his seven and one half years (September, 1901-January, 1909) as American president, embodied many of the larger virtues and some vices of that rapidly industrializing society. He was quixotic, chauvinistic, bellicose, very physical, a real intellectual, and generally acknowledged as one of the five greatest leaders of the American republic.[1] During this same time period, the founder of the modern Olympic Games, Pierre de Coubertin (1863-1937), was extremely conscious of the emerging American giant—a capitalist entity where, as cultural historian Richard Mandell noted, "performance-oriented, disciplined, democratic, theatrically presented sport suits well [the nation's] spiritual and mythic needs...."[2] During the years 1907 through 1918, the two exchanged admiring correspondences, and, also, when, despite the usual backbreaking schedule of an American president, Theodore Roosevelt found time to intervene into the affairs of the American Olympic Committee (AOC) and Coubertin's International Olympic Committee (IOC).

Both men were precocious intellects, restless, and maintained a personal, national, and global interest in sport throughout their lives. Both were wealthy enough to always perceive sport in the idealized and narrow sense. For them, always, amateur sport was "good," and professional sport was "bad." Coubertin married

*STADION, VIII/IX (1982-83), 137-150.

Marie Rothan in 1895, and, regrettably, the two children born of that union, Jacques and Renee, were unwell all their lives.[3]

Roosevelt's first wife, Alice Lee, gave birth in 1884, to a child of the same name, but Mrs. Roosevelt died in childbirth. His second wife and life-long companion, Edith (they married in December of 1886), presented to the world Theodore (1887); Kermit (1889); Ethel (1891); Archie (1894), and Quentin (1897). The elder Roosevelt—college boxer, football player, rough-and-tumble physical culturist and superb horseman—treated his six children in the same vein. Hermann Hagedorn, in his engaging biography *The Roosevelt Family of Sagamore Hill,* recalled that "Theodore taught the children to swim by dropping them off the dock into deep water."[4]

Prior to any personal exchange of correspondences between Coubertin and Roosevelt, the two of them as young men, between the years 1883 and 1900, had already written scores of journal articles, newspaper essays, and each of them had completed several books. Coubertin's *Souvenirs d'Oxford et de Cambridge* (1887), were followed quickly by *L'Education en Anglettere* and *L'Education Anglaise en France* in 1888 and 1889. His *Universites Transatlantiques* (1890) and *Souvenirs d'Amerique et de Grece* (1897), along with the earlier works, discussed politics, education, religion, social, and cultural life in the new and old worlds. Throughout, the Baron de Coubertin spoke rhapsodically about the value of physical culture, leisure sport, and competitive athletics to individual participants, and, especially, to the nation. His unflagging efforts resulted in the revival of the Olympic Games in 1896, and Coubertin crowed, "Athens is doubly beautiful this spring, the atmosphere itself redolent with light and spirit. The Olympic Games have no enemies."[5] Coubertin's most important work, The *Evolution of France under the Third Republic* was completed (1897) when the Baron was thirty-four years of age. In the "Introduction," the distinguished American journal editor, Albert Shaw, called the young French aristocrat "a philosophical observer and a constructive reformer."[6]

Theodore Roosevelt, the well-read Harvard University graduate, rancher, cowboy, unvarnished outdoorsman-hunter, war hero, President of the New York City Police Board, Assistant Secretary of the Navy, and Governor of New York State—all by the age of forty—epitomized "the strenuous life." The ebullient Roosevelt, the moral crusader of "optimism and opportunism"[7] exemplified a philosophy that "ran with, rather than against the main current of American life."[8] Among many things, this emerging national mind-set glorified in masculine physicality and vigorous sport. Roosevelt's first book on naval warfare was written in 1882, to be followed by the 4-volume work *The Winning of the West* (1889-1896); *American Ideals* (1897); *The Rough Riders* (1899), and *The Strenuous Life* in 1900. If one believed in destiny, it would almost seem that by the first year of the new century the two men, Coubertin and Roosevelt, would be drawn to one another through their mutual attraction to love of country, to the concept of physical vigor as a contributor to national salvation, to love of scholarship, as well as personal and vicarious joy of highly competitive athletic competition.

Anarchist Leon Czolgosz killed President McKinley on September 6, 1901, at the Buffalo Pan-Exposition, and Theodore Roosevelt immediately took his place as the leader of an extraordinary, emerging, vigorous nation of nearly 80 million inhabitants. Coubertin's first autobiography noted that "le plus sportif des chefs d'Etat etait naturellement plein de sympathies a l'endroit des Jeux Olympiques."[9] Coubertin was impious enough many years later to remark about Theodore Roosevelt: "Celui-la etait un courainen, un ami et, des lors les horizons de la IIIe Olympiade [America in 1904] s'eclairement."[10] Coubertin lost little time in writing to the new American president, conferring on him the title of honorary Olympic Games president. "Your great reputation as a sportsman," said the artful IOC leader (in the French language), "will add much to our efforts in holding these games in your great nation."[11] Fearful of entangling alliances and "after consultation with the members of the Cabinet," President Roosevelt regretfully declined the honor. "Personally, my dear sir," he wrote Coubertin on December 7, 1901, "I shall most cordially aid you in any way that I properly can. I have ... the most thorough sympathy with your aims...."[12]

Of course the President sympathized with Coubertin's sporting pedagogical goals. Had not Roosevelt's Harvard University classmate, Owen Wister (1860-1938)—the brilliant portraitist of chivalric Wyoming ranchers, noble red men, and the author of *The Virginian*—called him in 1901 "a conspicuous throwback to all that was great and good and wholly virile about America"?[13] Between 1890 and 1901, had not Roosevelt written essays with such titles as "Professionalism in Sports"; "The Boone and Crocket Club"; "The Value of Athletic Training"; "The Manly Virtues and Practical Politics"; "Character and Success"; "The Strenuous Life"; "Health and Courage"; "The Essence of Heroism"; and "What Can We Expect of the American Boy"?[14] And these are only representative selections of Roosevelt's compulsion for individual morality, his impulse for combining intellectual and physical action. One sport historian's study of the turn of the century era called Theodore Roosevelt "the undisputed leader of the cult of manliness."[15] Pierre de Coubertin was never a good athlete himself, but enjoyed dabbling in fencing, swimming, riding, and rowing. More importantly, like Roosevelt, he believed in a visionary "muscular Christianity"—concentric circles of a strong body, an educated mind, and in the center bulls-eye, a person of integrity … of high character. They both put an unrealistically heavy burden on sport as contributing to all three dimensions.

No sooner had the Baron received Roosevelt's declination to serve as honorary president of the 1904 Olympic Games, than he replied with thanks for the President's promise of support for an American games. "But I am astonished," said Coubertin, "that you cannot fully support the city of Chicago as the site of the games. But I hope that it will become possible later."[16] Coubertin, who would eventually write twenty-four books (and nearly a thousand published essays), sent Roosevelt several of his books, including his recently published *Notes sur Education Publique.* Early in January of 1902, Roosevelt, pleased that his French colleague had dedicated his most recent book to him, thanked the Baron, asked if he was fond of big-game hunting, and invited him to his home on his next visit to America "in order that we might discuss the Olympic Games."[17]

The print media loved to peek in at Roosevelt's family life on Sagamore Hill, Oyster Bay, Long Island. It was such a cacophony of sounds, stress, and family energies. The *Chicago Tribune* described it this way: The president chopped wood, rode cross-country, walked briskly 20 miles, gave his children a wheelbarrow ride, rested a moment or two, "by which time he was ready for *breakfast!*"[18] Coubertin read everything on the new man in the White House and was no less amazed at Roosevelt's energy. In March of 1902, he wrote that Roosevelt's strenuous life "est une conception de l'humanite qui est a la fais simple et rude, … a kind of primitive fanfare."[19] Both Coubertin and Roosevelt—in their own special spheres—worked from compulsion more than from duty; driven men who, in the last analysis, felt that their lives were of value only in so far as they might influence for good the characters of those whom they touched.

On May 21, 1901, the IOC officially voted for the city of Chicago as host for the Olympic Games of 1904.[20] Before the year's end, Baron de Coubertin had asked, almost pleaded once again with President Roosevelt to accept the position of honorary referee of these first American Olympic Games. There were two letters—one published in the *New York Daily Tribune*[21] and the other, the already-mentioned polite refusal by Roosevelt. Coubertin was obliged to remind his new friend that King George of Greece and French President Emil Loubet "held honorary leadership at the 1896 and 1900 Olympic Games." Why was it not possible for him to do the same, implied the Frenchman?[22] Henry J. Furber, President of the Olympic Organizing Committee in Chicago, vigorously sought help from both Pierre de Coubertin and endorsement for his little understood international games from Theodore Roosevelt during the middle months of 1902.[23] It was a critical time because the well-organized Louisiana Purchase Exposition in St. Louis was getting ready for its giant world's fair, and the organizers wanted the 1904 Olympic Games in their city rather than in Chicago. However, David R. Francis of St. Louis admitted no such thing in an August 9, 1902 letter to Roosevelt:

> I understand you are taking great interest in the Olympian Games to be held in Chicago in 1904, and can see no reason why there should be any conflict between that event and our Exposition. We have no fear that the Olympian Games will detract from our Physical Culture Exhibit.[24]

Roosevelt, too busy to follow all the Olympic machinations between the two cities, was now ready to support Chicago, but he regretted that "the United States cannot officially take charge or be responsible for the games."[25] He did repeat to Coubertin that he would do "everything I can for the Olympian Games...."[26] Despite Roosevelt's endorsement, the Chicago organizers could take it no longer—informed Coubertin on November 26, 1902, that St. Louis could have the games, and on December 23, the IOC voted for the transfer.[27]

For the moment, both Coubertin and Roosevelt could exchange correspondence of a less serious nature. But first the American political leader went on a tour of college campuses, reminding Minnesota students to "study hard, play hard, keep the senses of proportion." In Kansas, he spoke of bodily and mental strength ... the "gift of the original Greeks." At Stanford University and at Berkeley, he repeated the same themes, emphasizing the gospel of work and play and the upliftment of the human soul.[28] Coubertin was not much of an athlete, but on March 8,

1903, he conducted an experiment on himself. At the French Riviera near Cannes, Coubertin engaged in a well-paced exercise regimen of six consecutive hours of lawn tennis, riding a "motor tricycle," bicycling, horseback riding, and fencing with foil, sword and sabre—all, as he wrote President Roosevelt, "to show that even an ordinary physical specimen could do it without harm."[29] Roosevelt was absolutely delighted and replied in kind:

> I never was a champion at anything. I think you preach just the right form of the gospel of physical development.... I would like you to pay me a visit here in Washington and we will take some walks and ride together ... row or chop trees or shoot at a target, as well as ride and swim.[30]

In a truly extraordinary 1400-word essay, the president of the United States "talked" with Coubertin about all his children, the "sport-for-all" pedagogy, the real dangers of excessive "athleticism," and, as he said, although not a good athlete, "I can ride 50 miles and walk 20."[31]

Roosevelt was plenty busy in his first term of office. Wrestling with the Sherman anti-trust laws, dealing with the United Mine Workers' strike, trying to speak and act rationally regarding growing unrest in Latin America and the Far East, and, necessarily, working towards his election in 1904. But he managed time for several "muscular Christian" orations as well as accepting the honorary presidency of the St. Louis 1904 Olympic Games. "I cannot be there in person," he told Olympic Commissioner James Edward Sullivan and organizing chairman David R. Francis, but promised to help in every way that he could.[32]

Coubertin wasn't exactly loafing, either. His amorphous Olympic committee was giving him fits; the Greek government was planning a tenth anniversary celebration of the first Olympic Games in 1896; and to the Baron's great consternation, they were going to call these out-of-sequence games "Olympian." He wanted no part of them, burdened as he was in trying to convince European sport societies to send their athletes on the hazardous 4,000-mile journey to a remote mid-western American city in the summer of 1904. Amidst it all, he wrote an essay titled "Roosevelt et Tolstoi," praising the creative genius of the Russian and also calling the American: "Theodore Roosevelt est un lettre; sa vie de *rough-rider* a ete aussi pleine d'efforts cerebraux que d'efforts musculaires."[33] The Baron wrote Roosevelt directly after the November elections, congratulated him on victory, presented him with his latest book *La Gymnastique Utilitaire*—a provocative text on sporting activities for the masses. Until I received a letter from you, Mr. President, noted Coubertin, "I was unsure of the direction the book should take.... The IOC awards you an 'Honorary Diploma' as the world's first sportsman."[34]

Both James E. Sullivan's official *Report of the Olympic Games of 1904* and the unofficial Charles J. P. Lucas' *Olympic Games of 1904* were dedicated to the "Honorable Theodore Roosevelt." The president wrote Coubertin on May 13, 1905, offering his undivided help in future Olympic endeavors, including contacting university and club athletes, and even sending a delegation of the U.S. Army to the games.[35] Coubertin's IOC meeting in Brussels (June 9-14, 1905) discussed the perpetually insoluble question "What is an amateur athlete?" Also, Brazilian aeronaut Santos, English diplomat W. H. Grenfell, arctic explorer Fridtjof Nansen, and Theodore Roosevelt were honored as "men of noble character, sportsmen, possessing enterprising spirit."[36] Almost in a childlike way, Roosevelt was pleased to receive the award and wrote Coubertin, inviting him and the Baroness to the White House. America has already become too materialistic, abandoning to a large degree personal health and fitness, said the American. Sport for all must become a national mandate, he told Coubertin. "Of course," he added, "sport can be grossly exaggerated, ... but this is true of almost every serious occupation also."[37]

Thanks to James Sullivan, a powerful American track and field team dominated the unofficial Olympian Games in Athens. "Uncle Sam is all right," chortled Roosevelt, in a cablegram to Sullivan. Journalists from the Athens' newspaper *Estia* were puzzled and asked "to know the identity of the mysterious person called 'Uncle Sam.'"[38] Another ebullient telegram awaited the American team as its ship, the White Star liner "Republic" docked at Sandy Hook, New Jersey on May 25, 1906.[39] Roosevelt couldn't get enough of the American victories in Athens and wrote Coubertin "for some really good accounts of the games."[40] One is reminded of the fact that Roosevelt's interests ranged over a wide spectrum, of which sport was one. It was at about this time, 1906, that his son Kermit remembered:

> I have heard him speak to the foremost Bible student in the world, a prominent ornithologist, a diplomat and a French general, all of whom agreed that Father knew more about the subjects on which they had specialized than they did.[41]

There remains significant evidence that between 1906 and the completion of the London, England, Olympic Games 1908, America's Olympic boss, James E. Sullivan, visited Roosevelt in the White House and at his home in Oyster Bay, as well as conducted two-way correspondences in the form of letters and telegrams. Sullivan took his American team to London, succeeded in transforming and escalating a healthy patriotism among his men into an anti-British sentiment. This attitude, combined with their obvious athletic superiority merged with innumerable bunglings by the British officials, and resulted in serious tensions between the two athletic nations. Repercussions reached President Roosevelt in the White House following nearly violent and repeated arguments between English officials and America's Sullivan, Gustavus Town Kirby, and Bartow Weeks. The most inflammatory event of all was the 400-meter dash final where USA's Carpenter was accused of hindering Britain's Halswelle. The American was disqualified instantaneously, without a meeting of officials, and Halswelle ran the finals all alone—the remaining Americans refusing to take part. Every major American and British newspaper carried the story on both the sport pages and, regrettably, on page one. President Roosevelt penned a detailed 2,000 word letter to his Ambassador in London—an explicit reply to George Candee Buell's comments that quite possibly the Americans were at fault, and the President might wish to think twice before offering support to his team. Roosevelt was angry and questioned the alleged evidence that Carpenter had indeed fouled the English army lieutenant. In greatest detail, the President instructed Buell on events leading up to the 400-meter race that preconditioned the British (in Roosevelt's opinion) to a psychological anticipation of American irregularities. Let me repeat, said the President:

> that if Carpenter was guilty of the offense the comments of this British paper [The Sportsman] itself deliberately inviting attention the day before to the probability of what it now says actually happened (and thereby of course giving the excuse to everybody who so desired), and who wished to make believe that it happened, to pretend that it did actually happen.[42]

The unseemly details of the marathon drama and disqualification were discussed by Roosevelt in this same letter, and he warned Buell of irresponsible gossip, suggesting that he and all Americans in London "refrain from every statement which will tend to cause international bitterness...." Roosevelt got in a last shot, upbraiding Buell and all those that consistently supported so-called British sportsmanship as compared with American aggressiveness. Was it not the English tug-of-war team, asked the President rhetorically, that wore illegal iron boots, embarrassing the U.S.A. team by easily outpulling them? Let us all give credit, he ended, to our team "for its remarkable aggregate of victories...."[43] Roosevelt was at his best and worst, athletically and politically speaking, in this remarkable outburst.

Writing to the Japanese ambassador in the summer of 1908, Roosevelt admitted that because "feeling is so intense.... I do not believe in these international matches."[44] However, none of these negative feelings prevented the essentially patriotic Roosevelt from sending Sullivan a cable on July 27 with "Heartiest congratulations to you and your team. Wish I could shake hands with each man."[45] In an extraordinary series of vituperative remarks about British athletic "stupidity, ineptness and lack of fairness," American Olympic boss Sullivan's remarks finally alarmed Theodore Roosevelt sufficiently to write his friend:

> We won a remarkable victory anyhow, and for us to make complaints of unfair treatment does us no good.... The dignified and wise thing for us to do is to make no public comment of any kind.... I look forward greatly to seeing you and the team next Monday.[46]

The president threw caution to wind, however, and supported a giant ticker-tape parade of "his" Olympic team, down New York City's Fifth Avenue, and then hosted the entire team of men and women at his home on Oyster Bay. "Everyone in America is proud of you," he ventured. "Here is the top notcher," he noted as he grasped marathon winner Johnny Hayes' hand. "You did nobly," he said to black sprinter John B. Taylor.[47] *The Theodore Roosevelt Papers* on microfilm revealed another dozen letters from the president to James Sullivan during October and November of 1908. They represented only a small fraction of Roosevelt's astounding correspondence, but it typifies his life-long interest in sport. It also reveals the classic dilemma of a person in high office sometimes unsure of exactly how unvarnished should be his feelings on a popular issue that has stirred wide controversy. The last gasp out of Roosevelt on these London Olympic Games occurred on January 6, 1909, in a long letter to Whitelaw Reid—the new American ambassador to Britain and former editor of the *New York Tribune:*

I think that the Olympic games squabble is dying a natural death, ... the thing [is] a screaming farce.... They
[Hayes, Dorando, and Longboat] are all three of the professional type pure and simple, and to have had all the
yell and trouble concerning them as amateurs at the
Olympic Games does seem a little absurd.[48]

Mr. Roosevelt announced that he would abide by George
Washington's precedent against serving more than one reelec-
tion. Restless as always, he plunged into plans for a stupendous
1909 African hunting trip—one of the most exciting and widely
publicized expeditions in American history. Scores of journal articles and several books flowed from his pen before he and son
Kermit emerged from the jungles in the spring of 1910. On April
22, he arrived in Paris, "greeted as a king," with 25,000 people
cheering him in the streets. He wanted no part of politics and
for a week "from noon until midnight, he was the guest of intellectual Paris." On that same day, Mr. Roosevelt "was the guest
at luncheon of Baron Pierre de Coubertin"—his correspondence
friend since the turn of the century.[49]

Roosevelt's stunningly successful speech at the Paris Sorbonne on April 23, titled "The Duties of a Citizen in a Republic,"
was reproduced in the press all over Europe and North America.[50] This "greatest voice of the New World" had, said one paper,
proved to all that the great American had devoted a life-time effort to practice what he preached, "a kind of sane and vigorous
life, of which he is the embodiment." Coubertin was transported,
and upon returning home wrote Roosevelt that they had spent
too little time together in Paris. "I long to see you again and not
for so short a time," wrote the Baron. He added: "I am going
to spend the winter in Switzerland because I have two books to
write and at the same time enjoy ski-touring."[51] The ex-president
promptly replied, thanked his old friend for the latest honor, the
"Diplome des Debrouillards," and noted: "I shall always remember the enjoyable time I had at your house."[52]

There's an exchange of letters between the two men in 1911,
dealing with the elevation of American Evert Jansen Wendell to
the IOC, and again in December of that year from Coubertin to
Roosevelt, wishing the family:

... on the eve of this New Year—the Fifth Olympiad—my
warmest wishes.... I'm enjoying winter sports here in
Switzerland. Hope you've received my new books. The

Stockholm Games are preparing nicely, but I have great trouble in keeping peace among my colleagues belonging to 32 different nations.[53]

Roosevelt replied right away, but rather wistfully, lamenting, "I do almost nothing [athletically] but a little wood chopping, a little riding and walk." My dear Coubertin, he ended:

I know no man who has done more than you have done for the healthy development not only of sport but also of manliness of character, which is essential if our civilized nations of today are not to grow effete.[54]

The two men had never been apart in most of the things that matter, that is to say the role of the individual unto himself (not "herself"; both men were classic Victorian chauvinists), the role of the individual in society; the 'gospel of hard work'; the essential role of recreational activities in everyone's lives, and the very special and precious role of competitive athletics in the lives of boys and with some young men. It was a marvelous example of environmental and educational compatibility—both men driven by inner visions of personal ambitions, but, far more importantly, of a national sense of power for Roosevelt, and, for Coubertin, after his early fervor for French glory had cooled, an international dream of fitness and friendship through participation in the Olympic Games.

Coubertin held a straight course in his dream to make the Olympic movement a universal "sport-for-all" phenomenon and to make his Olympic Games a high-minded, peaceful gathering of the amateur athletic youth of the world. The IOC meeting in Lausanne, Switzerland, in the spring of 1913, was convened for these exact purposes ... and Theodore Roosevelt was invited to present a paper. He could not make it, but sent a paper titled "The Vigor of Life," which was read to those assembled. The three letters exchanged between the two men in April and May of 1913, dealing with the Congress, express their mutual admiration.[55] Much of Roosevelt's paper was autobiographical—the story of a sickly boy who grew robust through boxing and riding, and, more importantly, developed a kind of "moral courage" that stayed with him all his life.[56] In Roosevelt's own autobiography, published that same year, he repeated the theme that bodily vigor counts for nothing if it is not accompanied by and subordinate to "vigor of soul."[57]

Theodore Roosevelt came back from a four-month expedition in the Brazilian jungles (October, 1913, to April, 1914) a very sick man—"pallid, hollow-cheeked, leaning on a cane and lighter in weight by 55 pounds."[58] All agree that the illness led to his death in 1919 at age 60. He did have strength enough to return to Paris and then Madrid in the spring of 1914, for his son Kermit's marriage. But Coubertin had already permanently abandoned Paris and was living in Lausanne. The two did not meet again, and there was a lull in their correspondence during the terrible war years. But on July 29 1918, Coubertin wrote his friend expressing his deepest sadness at Quentin Roosevelt's death at the battlefront. Possibly we can meet again, concluded the Baron, speaking of what for him had been a nearly endless World War I, "in Paris when the day comes of the final victory."[59] And just three weeks before the so-called "Great War" came to an end, the Roosevelt-Coubertin correspondence terminated. The former American president had but four months longer to live, while Baron de Coubertin would live out his full measure another nineteen years. "My dear Baron," wrote Roosevelt, "I thank you for your letter and I appreciate these fine photographs. I congratulate you upon the work you are doing. Faithfully yours."[60]

It was done. The president of the United States of America had for nearly two decades reached out and touched the president of the International Olympic Committee, and a number of key Olympian personalities. Almost none of the correspondence is profound or momentous. There is a homeyness about the correspondence reminiscent to what many of us write to good friends—warm and human exchanges that must, to historians, give insight into the real personalities of these men. And since the public actions of important and visible men are often reflections of their "real personalities," these present revelations might prove useful in helping to understand why they acted the way that they did and may give some explanation for what they said. Coubertin was always the unreconstructed visionary—the dreamer of universal understanding through sport, and this vision "ultimately … became his monument."[61] The Baron, remembering the days of his youth and his two favorite teachers at the Sorbonne, Leroy-Beaulieu and Albert Sorel, admitted: "I left the lecture hall with mind filled with light."[62]

Long after Roosevelt's death, Olympic track coach Mike Murphy was talking to long-time Olympic official Gustavus Town Kirby about the glorious day back in 1908, when the entire American Olympic team had been made to feel so good by President

Roosevelt at his Sagamore Hill home. Returning home that night, Murphy admitted to Kirby that for years he had perceived himself as the greatest track coach in the world. He had changed his mind after meeting the president. "Mike, that's nonsense!" exclaimed Kirby. "No," said Murphy, quietly:

> Give me sixty men, every one a champion, and let that man [Roosevelt] have sixty other men, and every one of 'em a dub, and his team would lick mine every time. You see it's this way. That man down there would tell a miler that he could reel off a mile in four minutes [an impossible task in 1908]. And not only would that man *think* he could run a milc in four minutes, but, by God, he'd go and do it.[63]

The book is not yet closed on Pierre de Coubertin. Nearly fifty years after his passing, new documents by and about the man unfold. It is the way of history. The absolute Coubertin, the perfect reincarnation of Theodore Roosevelt, and a perfect recapitulation of the times that lived in can never be. We can only agonize in the effort, and revel in possibly getting close to the mark.

NOTES

1 Only Lincoln, Washington, Franklin Roosevelt and Jefferson, in that order, rank higher than Theodore Roosevelt. See R. K. Murray and T. H. Blessing, "The Presidential Performance Study: A Progress Report," *Journal of American History,* 70 (December, 1983) 551.

2 R. D. Mandell, *Sport: A Cultural History,* New York 1984, p. 200.

3 See M.-Th. Eyquem, *Pierre de Coubertin-L'Epopee Olympique,* Paris 1966, p. 178; also J. J. Macaloon, *This Great Symbol-Pierre de Coubertin and the Origins of the Modern Olympic Games,* Chicago 1981, pp. 272-273, 333, note 47.

4 H. Hagedorn, *The Roosevelt Family of Sagamore Hill,* New York 1954 p. 33.

5 P. de Coubertin quotation translated by B. Henry, *An Approved History of the Olympia Games,* New York 1948, p. 45. Coubertin's original statement may be found in his *Souvenirs d'Amerique et de Grece,* Paris 1897, p. 139.

6 Albert Shaw as quoted in P. De Coubertin, *The Evolution of France Under the Third Republic.* Translated by I. F. Hapgood, New York 1897, p. iv.

7 R. E. Spiller, et al., *Literary History of the United States* in: *History.* 1969, p. 1110.

8 Ibid., p. 945.

9 P. de Coubertin, *Une Campagne de Vingt-et-un Ans, 1887-1908,* Paris 1908, p. 157.

10 P. de Coubertin, *Memoires Olympiques,* Lausanne 1931, p. 62.

11 Coubertin to Theodore Roosevelt, November 15, 1901, *Theodore Roosevelt Papers* (microfilm); series 1; reel 22.

12 Roosevelt to Pierre de Coubertin, December 7, 1901, *Theodore Roosevelt Papers* (microfilm); series 2; volume 32; reel 327. See also *New York Daily Tribune,* December 5, 1901, p. 5.

13 See O. Wister, "Theodore Roosevelt—The Sportsman and the Man," *Outing,* 38 (June, 1901) 243-248.

14 See *The North American Review,* 151 (August, 1890) 187-191; *Harper's Weekly,* 37 (March 18, 1893) 267; *Harper's Weekly,* 38 (December 23, 1893) 1236; *The Forum,* 17 (July, 1894) 551-557; *The Outlook,* 64 (March 31, 1900) 725-727; *The Roosevelt Book Selections,* New York 1909, pp. 21-29; *The Outlook,* 61 (February 25, 1899) 444-446; *The Youth's Companion,* 75 (April 18, 1901) 202, and St. *Nicholas,* 37 (May, 1900) 571-574.

15 G. F. Roberts, "The Strenuous Life: The Cult of Manliness in the Era of Theodore Roosevelt," Ph. D. dissertation, University of Michigan, 1970, p. 2 of abstract.

16 Coubertin to Theodore Roosevelt, December 23, 1901, *Theodore Roosevelt Papers* (microfilm); series 1; reel 23.

17 Roosevelt to Pierre de Coubertin, January 9, 1902, *Theodore Roosevelt Papers* (microfilm); series 2; volume 33; reel 328. See also *Revue Olympique,* 5 (January, 1902) 12.

18 Hagedorn, p. 172.

19 Coubertin as quoted in *Revue du Pays de Caux—Politique et Litteraire,* 1 (Mars 1902) 10-11.

20 For details see J. Lucas, "Early Olympic Antagonists—Pierre de Coubertin versus James E. Sullivan," *Stadion, III* (1977) 261-265.

21 "Asks Roosevelt to Preside," *New York Daily Tribune,* Dec. 5, 1901, p. 5.

22 Coubertin to Theodore Roosevelt, December 23, 1901, *Theodore Roosevelt Papers* (microfilm), series 1; real 23.

23 See Coubertin, *Une Campagne,* pp. 157-158; Henry J. Furber to Theodore Roosevelt, May 24, 1902; University of Chicago Library.

24 Francis to Theodore Roosevelt, August 9, 1902, *Theodore Roosevelt Papers* (microfilm); series 1; reel 28.

25 See *New York Times,* August 22, 1902, p. 9, and *New York Daily Tribune,* August 22, 1902, p. 14.

26 Roosevelt to Pierre de Coubertin, October 6, 1902, *Theodore Roosevelt Papers* (microfilm); series 2; volume 37; reel 329.

27 Furber to Pierre de Coubertin, November 26, 1902. See *Revue Olympique* (February, 1903) 5; and *Memoires Olympiques,* p. 63.

28 See Th. Roosevelt, *Presidential Addresses and State Papers,* volume 1, New York, 1904, pp. 293-294, 379, 407; *Addresses and Presi-*

dential Messages of Theodore Roosevelt 1902-1904, New York 1904, p. 183.

29 Coubertin to Theodore Roosevelt, June 2, 1903, *Theodore Roosevelt Papers* (microfilm); series 1; reel 34.

30 Roosevelt to Pierre de Coubertin, June 15; 1903, *Theodore Roosevelt Papers* (microfilm); series 2; volume 40; reel 331. The entire letter is reproduced in E. E. Morison (ed.), *The Letters of Theodore Roosevelt,* volume 3, Cambridge, Mass. 1951, pp. 489-491.

31 Ibid.

32 Roosevelt to J. E. Sullivan, March 15, 1904, *Theodore Roosevelt Papers* (microfilm); series 2; volume 46; reel 333; see also Roosevelt to Francis, April 1, 1904, series 1; reel 43 and Sullivan to Roosevelt, July 15, 1904, series 1; reel 45.

33 P. de Coubertin, "Roosevelt et Tolstoi," *Le Figaro* (September 1903) 1.

34 Coubertin to Theodore Roosevelt, November 11, 1904, *Theodore Roosevelt Papers* (microfilm); series 1; reel 50.

35 Roosevelt to Pierre de Coubertin, May 13, 1905, *Theodore Roosevelt Papers* (microfilm); series 2; volume 55; reel 337.

36 See Ch. L. Bonnameaux, "The Second International Convention of Sports and Physical Education," *American Physical Education Review,* 11 (December, 1906) 244.

37 Roosevelt to Pierre de Coubertin, July 21, 1905, *Theodore Roosevelt Papers* (microfilm); volume 56; reel 338.

38 See *New York Daily Tribune,* May 4, 1906, p. 1; also see J. E. Sullivan (ed.), *The Olympic Games of 1906 at Athens,* New York 1906, pp. 44-45.

39 Roosevelt, cablegram to James E. Sullivan, May 26, 1906; *Theodore Roosevelt Papers* (microfilm); series 2; volume 64; reel 341; also J. Lucas, "American Involvement in the Athens Olympian Games of 1906," *Stadion* VI (1980) 224—225; and *New York Herald,* May 26, 1906, p. 12.

40 Roosevelt to Pierre de Coubertin, May 31, 1906, *Theodore Roosevelt Papers* (microfilm); series 2; volume 64; reel 341.

41 Kermit Roosevelt as quoted in Hagedorn, *The Roosevelt Family,* p. 236.

42 Roosevelt to George Candee Buell, August 18, 1908, Morrison, *The Letters of Theodore Roosevelt,* volume 6, p. 1182.

43 Ibid., p. 1185.

44 Roosevelt to Baron Kogoro Takahira, undated, Morison, ibid., p. 1190.

45 Roosevelt, telegram to James Sullivan, July 27, 1908; *Theodore Roosevelt Papers* (microfilm); series 2; volume 83; reel 350.

46 Roosevelt to James Sullivan, August 24, 1908, *Theodore Roosevelt Papers* (microfilm); series 2; volume 84; reel 350.

47 Almost every single major eastern newspaper covered the Roosevelt congratulations, the parade, and the Oyster Bay reception. For example, see *Boston Globe,* September 1, 1908, p. 5; *New York Times,* Sep-

tember 1, 1908, p. 5; Roosevelt to James Sullivan, September 1, 1908, *Theodore Roosevelt Papers* (microfilm); series 2; volume 84; reel 351.

48 Morison, volume 6, pp. 1465-1466.

49 "Roosevelt Cements French Friendship," *New York Tribune,* April 23, 1910, p. 2; *Washington Post* of April 25, 1910, p. 3, reported, "Col. and Mrs. Roosevelt had luncheon with ... Coubertin." *The Times* [London], April 22, 1910, p. 7, reported "after lunching quietly with Baron Pierre de Coubertin, Mr. Roosevelt visited this afternoon, the galleries of the Louvre...."

50 *The Journal des Debates,* as quoted in *New York Times,* April 25, 1910, p. 3. See also *The Times* [London], April 25, 1910, p. 5; *The Outlook,* 94 (30 April 1910) 983-993; *L'Illustrations* [Paris], 30 April 1910, p. 409; J. L. Gardner, *Departing Glory: Theodore Roosevelt as Ex-President,* New York 1973, p. 152; *New York Times,* April 24, 1910, pp. 1, 2, 9; *New York Tribune,* April 24, 1910, pp. 1, 4, and *Scribner's Magazine* 48 (September, 1910) 370-377.

51 Coubertin to Theodore Roosevelt, November 10, 1910, *Theodore Roosevelt Papers* (microfilm); series 1; reel 94.

52 Roosevelt to Pierre de Coubertin, December 6, 1910, *Theodore Roosevelt Papers* (microfilm); series 3A; volume 5; reel 364.

53 Coubertin to Theodore Roosevelt, circa December 1912; *Theodore Roosevelt Papers* (microfilm); series 1; reel 163. (Author's note: this letter was almost certainly written in December of 1911, and not a year later which would have put it after the Olympic Games).

54 Roosevelt to Pierre de Coubertin, January 16, 1912, *Theodore Roosevelt Papers* (microfilm); series 3A; volume 40; reel 372.

55 See *Theodore Roosevelt Papers* (microfilm); series 2; volume 96; reel 356; series 1; reel 172, and series 1; reel 174.

56 Olympic historian N. Muller discussed this Roosevelt paper in his *Von Paris bis Baden-Baden. Die Olympischen Kongresse 1894-1981,* Niedernhausen 1981, pp. 68-69. See also Y. P. Boulongne, *La Vie et l'œuvre Pedagogiqtte de Pierre de Coubertin 1863-1937,* Ottawa 1975, p. 253.

57 Th. Roosevelt, *An Autobiography,* New York 1913, p. 50.

58 Hagedorn, *The Roosevelt Family,* p. 335.

59 Coubertin to Theodore Roosevelt, July 28, 1918, *Theodore Roosevelt Papers* (microfilm); series 1; reel 287.

60 Roosevelt to Pierre de Coubertin, August 26, 1918, *Theodore Roosevelt Papers* (microfilm); series 3A; volume 177; reel 407.

61 B. Dates, "The Father of the Olympics," *Los Angeles Times,* November 21, 1983, part. 3, p. 1.

62 Coubertin quoted in H. Pouret, "The Men Who Influenced Coubertin's Thought," *Proceedings 1973,* International Olympic Academy, Athens 1973, p. 85.

63 Hagedorn, *The Roosevelt Family,* p. 247.

9.
"Three Specially Selected Athletes" and a Recapitulation of the Pennsylvania Walking Purchase of 1737*

William Penn's "Holy Experiment," like all human endeavors, worked imperfectly, and yet in several significant ways surpassed the experiments of religious and political freedom in Massachusetts, Rhode Island, and Virginia. Samuel Eliot Morison called Pennsylvania "a portent of the America to be" (Morison, 1965). As could be expected, human conduct in this early colonial state at times approached the divine, and at other times encompassed every form of rascality. William Penn was a good man and left a legacy of pacific relations with the seventeenth-century Indians in the Philadelphia and eastern Commonwealth regions. His instructions to his commissioners were to "Be tender of offending the Indians ... let them know you have come to sit down lovingly among them" (Memoirs, 1826). Penn spoke the language of the local Indians "and to their great delight, participated in their athletic exercises" (Cribbs, 1919). William Penn, the visionary Quaker, successfully solved the problem of bringing settlers to the Province.

Penn's son Thomas, however, was far from a saint, and after the elder Penn's death in 1718, faced serious financial problems as well as the difficulties of restraining settlers from crowding upon land belonging to the Indians. For several years prior to Thomas Penn's residency in Philadelphia (1732-1741), it had become evident to all that the Whites were per-

*Research Quarterly for Exercise and Sport, 54, (March 1983), 41-47.

manent residents "and no amount of presents or 'pay' could blind the Delawares to the fact that, long before the Walking Purchase, they were being relentlessly pushed out of their homes" (Wallace, 1937).

Historians of colonial Pennsylvania have correctly looked upon the 1737 Walking Purchase as essentially a political event, a highly controversial confrontation between second generation Quaker colonial proprietary agents[1] and Indian leaders in the eastern part of the state, all of it with strong overtones of deceit and venality. This paper will underscore this position, the one taken by almost all historians of Pennsylvania. The importance of the Walking Purchase aftermath will also be reaffirmed, though without overstating its importance. Thirdly, the paper will emphasize the magnitude of the physical feat involved in the eighteen-hour forced run-walk marathon, and expand on the reasons why those involved were not called "athletes" at the time and could only be so labeled long after the fact.

Pennsylvania Sport During the First Half-Century

For the period of Pennsylvania history from 1686 to 1736, the moral rectitude, piety, and conservative Puritanism of William Penn discouraged play, sport, and diversions during the working week, and forbade any such goings on during the holy Sabbath day (Lucas & Smith, 1978; Jable, 1973). A series of laws passed by the Philadelphia leadership in 1695, 1700, 1705, and 1710, severely restricted conspicuous play and sporting activities. The Quaker oligarchy, inheritors of a modified Calvinist theology, inflicted on the larger population the strongest admonition against all organized sport and non-utilitarian diversions. The pure Quakerism of founder George Fox and his first disciple William Penn became diluted during the second and especially the third generations of colonists. But still, during the early 1700s, there were no individuals who on a full-time or even part-time basis wore the rubric "athlete" or "sportsman." Thus, several of the main actors in the unfolding drama of the Walking Purchase have consistently and correctly been labeled "woodsmen," "chain-haulers," "wood-cutters," or "farmers," even though the primary sources emphasize that the three participants were specially selected for their physical strength, endurance, and courage—attributes much treasured in the latter-day athletic community.

Politics in the Period 1686-1736

William Penn came into peaceable possession of Indian lands in 1686, the terms of the treaty stating that white men were to be given as much land along the western shore of the Delaware River as a man could traverse on foot in a day and a half. No physical evidence of this treaty was ever found, but it is generally agreed by Pennsylvania historians not only that there had been a treaty but that the tempo of the day and a half tramp through the heavy forest would be leisurely and in the traditional unhurried way. Penn's Deputy Governor, William Markham, and Penn himself had settled (in 1682 and 1689) what seemed an amicable distribution of land *(Pennsylvania Archives, 1).*

As the new century wore on, however, there grew a desperate need for westward expansion out of the city of Philadelphia by the new immigrants. Between 1727 and 1745, approximately 22,000 people arrived in the already overcrowded city (Adams, 1927). A series of confrontations involving physical violence left both the Indians and the new settlers unhappy. In 1732, Chief Sasoonan of the Schuylkill Indians, "for substantial reward" sold land along all tributaries of the Philadelphia River *(Pennsylvania Archives, 1, 345).* The sale did not meet the approval of the Delaware Indians in that southeast pocket of Pennsylvania, and "did much to alienate the Indians" (Early, 1905). Thomas Penn arrived in Pennsylvania in 1732, and immediately decided to deal only with the dominant Indian group—the Iroquois. Thus "these Delaware Indians had no principal role in further land sales ... " and mutual understanding between colonist and Indian grew more tenuous (Klein & Hoogenboom, 1973; Kent, 1974). Thomas Penn plunged "at once into the strange world of forest diplomacy," renegotiating for all lands on the Schuylkill River "between the Lehigh Hills and ... the Endless Mountains" (Franklin, 1938). The un-liberal Thomas Penn, unskilled and unfriendly in his dealings with the Indians, relied heavily on James Logan and interpreter Conrad Weiser. The Philadelphia meeting of August 25 to September 2, 1732, with representatives of the Six Nations, gained more land from the Indians *(Pennsylvania Colonial Records, 3).* The next year, in the month of June, Penn met with the friendly Chief Nutimus of the Munsee clan of Delawares, exchanged gifts and discussed the knotty problem of land distribution. The Indians, uneasy at the inexorable encroachments on the land by the new settlers, met with them outside of Philadelphia in October of 1734, reviewing together the original land division treaty of 1686. Another similar meeting took place on May 5, 1735, at Pennsbury, where plans for another eighteen-hour walk were probably discussed (Jacobson, 1911). Strong evidence exists that during the very time of the Pennsbury conference, Thomas Penn had completed instructions to associates for a secret walk over the exact route to be traveled in the forthcoming land-division walking tour (Fackenthal, 1932). Penn's copy of the 1686 deed (the original, it seems, having been lost) called for a tract of land along the Delaware River, the bounds of which extended from a certain point "back into the woods, as far as a man can go in a day and a half," and then a line drawn back to the river again. As Pennsylvania historian Paul Wallace (1945) said, such vague terms were common in the days of Indian occupation, and "did not encourage precise measurement."

Three persons "who can travel well" were employed by Thomas Penn to force walk for a day and a half out of the city in a northwesterly direction in order to see "how far they will reach up the country." Surveyors, horses and riders with provisions accompanied the walkers. The secret time trial was accomplished and Thomas Penn was informed that "with the use of a little plane geometry, a walk of a day and a half could be made to take in a stretch of some 150 [square] miles of the best land along the river" (Wallace, 1945). Historian Francis Jennings (1970), like Paul Wallace, confirmed the actions of "the secret walkers" by quoting from letters exchanged between Thomas Penn's men, dated April 25, April 29, May 5, and July 23, 1735, all pertaining to preparation for the "official" walk in 1737. Edward Marshall, Joseph Doane, and James Yeates, the best woodsmen in the area, literally blazed a trail through the forest regions of Bucks and Northampton County. They worked swiftly and thoroughly, anticipating the Pennsbury Council in May of that year—a meeting between the Indians and Thomas Penn to determine the nature of the land divisor agreement. James Steele, Receiver General under Thomas Penn, wrote twice in April to Timothy Smith, Sheriff of Bucks County, urging haste in completing the secret trial run, as well as all haste in relaying essential information about the walk back to the Proprietors prior to the all-important meeting with the Indians. Steele wrote, "The time is now spent that not one moment is to be lost; and as soon as they have traveled the day and a half journey, the Proprietaries [sic] desire that a messenger may be sent to give them account without delay, how far that day and a half travel will reach up country" (Fackenthal, 1932; Franklin, 1938).

Thomas Penn had cause to act hastily and, regrettably, unethically, in this time period 1735-1737. Mounting population pressures in the city of Philadelphia demanded expansion,[2] and yet the Indians refused to sell another acre of land. A Philadelphia meeting in October of 1736 between the Six Nations' chiefs and their antagonists was unfruitful, the Indians standing firm "in declaring that the Delaware nation had no lands to sell" (Sipe, 1927). All that was left for Thomas Penn was to bring to fruition the tentative agreement between himself and the Indians that a recapitulation of the ancient 1686 agreement of land division take place.

The Walking Purchase of 1737

On August 25, 1737, four Delaware Indian chiefs signed the "Walking Purchase" deed, agreeing to give to the white man all the land covered in a day and a half. The complex details of the deed were unknown to the illiterate Indians, and strong evidence exists that they expected the journey to cover "as the crow flies

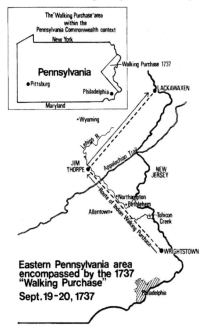

The "Walking Purchase" area within the Pennsylvania Commonwealth context

Eastern Pennsylvania area encompassed by the 1737 "Walking Purchase" Sept. 19-20, 1737

from the southern end of the Walking Purchase lands to the most northerly elbow of Tohiccon Creek" (Wallace, 1949)—about twenty miles. "The unwilling and resentful Indians," said C. A. Weslager (1972) in his *The Delaware Indians,* "aware that control of lands in the Lehigh Valley was at issue, were forced to agree that the line should be paced off as specified in the document." The famous walk was set for the morning of September 19, 1737, starting at the landmark chestnut tree near the Friends Meeting House in Wrightstown, Pennsylvania. Deputized to see that the walk was fairly conducted were Indians John Combush, Neepaheilo-mon, more commonly called Joe Tuneam (who spoke fluent English), and Tom, his brother-in-law. Standing on the line of the Durham road in the shadow of a large chestnut tree were the three principals involved, Edward Marshall, James Yeates, and Solomon Jennings (substituting for Doane, who helped blaze the undisclosed trial walk of 1735). Also present were Sheriff Timothy Smith, Benjamin Eastburn, Surveyor General, and his two deputies, Nicholas Scull and John Chapman. James Steele, Jr. was there to report back to Thomas Penn. Also present were Enoch Pearson, Edward Marshall's brother, Samuel Hughes, Joseph Knowles, and Thomas Furniss. Horses, bedding, provisions, and liquors accompanied the party (Buck, 1886).

The proprietors had engaged the services of those 1735 trail walkers who had "held out the best," and were instructed "to choose the best ground and shortest way that can be found." Trees had been felled and a path cleared (Wallace, 1945). The north and westerly direction was carefully chosen "and had been used probably for many years, as it was one of the principal thoroughfares from the Delaware River near Burlington, to the great hunting grounds at the Susquehanna, near Wyoming" (Henry, 1860).

Completely unprepared for what happened next, the Indians "were stunned to see the three selected athletes move off so briskly ... totally unaware that their route had been prearranged and a party with provisions sent ahead on horseback" (Kelley, 1980). The walkers were well suited to their activity. Edward Marshall was a noted hunter and surveyor's chain carrier. "James Yeates [was] a tall slim man of much agility and speed of foot, and Solomon Jennings a remarkable stout and strongman" (Egle, 1876). Each was promised five English pounds and 500 acres of the newly acquired land for his athletic performance—a feat made easier by woodsman Joseph Knowles who, preceding the three resolute walker-runners on horseback, carried his chain saw[3] and helped "to clear a road, as directed by my uncle, Timothy Smith" (Thomson, 1759).

Yeates led the way "with a light step," followed closely by Jennings and two of the Indians; Marshall and the third Delaware walked a controlled pace at the back. Gradually Marshall picked up his tempo, reaching Ottsville, nearly twenty miles from the starting chestnut tree, in three hours. The party took a hurried lunch in Wilson's meadow and rushed onward in the direction of the Lehigh River and what is now the city of Bethlehem. The

Indians complained bitterly at the unrelenting pace and, according to young Knowles:

> The Indians then began to look sullen and murmured that the men walked so fast, and several times that afternoon called out and said to them, you run, that's not fair, you was to walk. The men appointed to walk, paid no regard to the Indians, but was urged by Timothy Smith and the rest of the Proprietors party to proceed until the sun was down. (Thomson, 1759)

The disgusted Indians fell further behind as "Penn's Athletes," (Wildes, 1940) "fastest backwoodsmen in the Province," (Sipe, 1931) struck a relentless course toward the Lehigh River. Moving at a gait somewhere between fast walking and jogging (a hundred years later in Britain and America this sporting gait was called "go-as-you-please"), the company left behind an exhausted Solomon Jennings, who quit and left for his home several miles away. Previously slashed or marked trees provided navigation and assured uninterrupted progress. The Indians' moccasins fell apart, and they expressed dissatisfaction that the Penn party failed to replace them. "Some of the company out of compassion let them ride their horses by turns," noted William Buck (1886) in his *History of the Indian Walk*.

Thomas Furniss, one of the supply men in attendance, testified that just before sunset, two of the Indians gave up the chase, "having often called Marshall that afternoon and forbid him to run," and were deeply angered that "the walkers would pass all the good land" (Thomson, 1759). By late afternoon, Yeates, Marshall, and the lone Indian Combush, were well beyond present Bethlehem. A little after 4 p.m., Marshall slowed slightly, dropped behind Yeates, but then recovered with an acceleration that brought him even with his partner. Combush, according to William Buck, "called to him that he must walk fair." They struggled on, guided by marked trees, beyond a party of waiting Indians who expected they would stop for the day, not understanding that a "day" meant exactly twelve hours—plus fifteen minutes lost at lunch. As the first day's agony drew to a close, Timothy Smith stood atop a small incline, watch in hand, urging Marshall to keep up his pace to the summit and the 6:15 p.m. deadline. Marshall hung on till the top, then nearly collapsed from exhaustion, grasping a sapling tree with both hands to stay upright. Thomas Furniss recalled, incredulously, that Sheriff Smith asked Marshall "What was the matter?" Marshall replied he was "almost gone, and that, if he had proceeded a few poles further he must have fallen" (Thomson, 1759). Constant murmurings by the Indians about too fast walking were ignored by the hardworking Yeates and Marshall, both of whom had been continually urged onward by leader Timothy Smith and the whole Proprietary party. They had covered approximately 60 miles through heavy timber on this first day—a good day's work for these early colonial marathoners.

They camped that night a half mile from the Indian town of Nockyondocquay, enjoyed a big campfire and ample provisions— neither of which shut out angry voices from the Indians at a "cantico" or traditional chant. Dissatisfactions among the local Delaware, noted Furniss, remained "common subjects of conversation in our neighborhood for some considerable time after [the Walking Purchase] was done" (Thomson, 1759). Rainy weather and stray horses delayed departure the next morning. Local chief Lappawinzo declined to assign any of his people to accompany the white men's party, but shortly before eight o'clock Combush returned with two other Indians. These, however, after managing several miles in heavy rain, decided to "proceed no farther" (Buck, 1886). At this point the party was well beyond the Lehigh River, headed for the ridge of the Pocono Mountains (containing the present-day Appalachian Trail). Marshall and Yeates pressed on in a northwesterly direction, accompanied by the official entourage. Somewhere beyond the Lehigh River, where the hills become almost mountains, Yeates collapsed, having grown "lame and tired," as eyewitness Timothy Smith said (Buck, 1886). The irascible Marshall hung on a little longer, struggling to the north side of the mountain to present-day Jim Thorpe, Pennsylvania (formerly Mauch Chunk), and into a grove of five chestnut trees. It was 2 p.m., and he threw himself to the ground in a state of near catalepsy. Marshall had accomplished an athletic feat of considerable magnitude. As the crow flies the distance he covered is seventy-five miles. Marshall's circuitous path through heavily wooded territory, most of it rough, undulating, and continuously interspersed with hills and low mountains, must have made the total mileage nearer ninety miles. Marathon champions of the 1980s, under the best conditions and on the smoothest roads, can cover somewhat more than 100 miles in eighteen hours. And yet it is highly unlikely that a modern distance star would have an easy time duplicating exactly the feat of 1737. Modern day army rangers consider five miles per hour for long distances very acceptable, while well-conditioned all-day hikers consider a four-mile per hour average speed very challenging.[4] By any standard and in any age, Marshall's achievement was most impressive—the work of a strong-legged, strong winded outdoorsman, an athletic feat of singular proportion. Though not formally trained for his achievement in the manner of a modern athlete, Marshall lived a life of great physical robustness. As a lumberjack, big game hunter and "surveyor's chain carrier" on the frontier, he had built up his physical reserves to an unusually high degree.[5]

The Division of Land and Its Aftermath

Marshall's footrace of seventy-five miles to the foot of the Kittatinny Mountain clearly established the southern border of the new territory belonging to the Quaker government in Philadelphia. The noted historian Francis Parkman observed bitterly:

> And now it only remained to adjust the northern boundary. Instead of running the line directly to the Delaware ... the Proprietors inclined it so far to the north as to form an acute angle with the river, and enclose many hundred thousand acres of valuable land, which would otherwise have remained in the hands of the Indians (Parkman, 1895).

The surveyors immediately went to work, projecting a line not due east to the Lehigh River but northeast, at right angles to the now established southern border, to Laxawaken, Pennsylvania, and "encompassing a tract much larger than that which the Indians had initially envisioned; it comprised nearly the entire homeland of the Delawares" (Klein, 1973). The enraged Indians refused to quit this area of more than 500,000 acres, claiming "foul" for many years to come. Their first formal protest occurred in 1742 to the Quaker Assembly, resulting in a dramatic confrontation between the Delawares and the new ally of the Philadelphia Proprietors, the Iroquois chief, Canassatego. In a stinging admonition, he called the Delawares "women," and demanded their removal from the contested land *(Smith's Laws, 1700-1810)*. Parkman (1895) commented bitingly, "The unhappy Delawares dared not disobey. They left their ancient homes ... as they had been ordered." The troublemakers had been removed. The Six Nations chiefs, plied with presents worth 300 English pounds, pronounced that the white men's conduct was blameless, and that the Walking

110 / John Apostal Lucas

Purchase was legal and binding *(Pennsylvania Colonial Records,* 4).* The Delaware chief Nutimus and his people collected their families and goods, burned their cabins, and headed west, perceiving all too clearly "that the league between the whites and the Six Nations was irresistible" (Sharpless, 1900). Frequent but fruitless meetings between the Indians and the Philadelphia establishment took place in 1740, 1742, 1744, 1754, 1756, 1757, and 1758. All of them reviewed the Walking Purchase of 1737, and none of them resulted in any restitution to the American natives. At the Easton council of 1758, when the old warrior Teedyuscung was asked to state the cause of the bloody Indian attacks on the settlers, he replied "Walking Purchase" (Thayer, 1943).

The bitterness of the Indians extended to the principals themselves, especially to Edward Marshall. Following the Purchase, Marshall lived in Northampton County, Pennsylvania, where the Delaware Indians of the Munsee Clan were quite aware of his part in the questionable purchase. They are said to have killed one of his sons in 1748, severely wounded his daughter in 1757, and succeeded in murdering his wife in the same year. Some historians also believe that Marshall was never paid for his feat.

The Walking Purchase was the largest land transaction of the Penn family, and the overtones of fraud connected with the episode mark the beginnings of serious troubles between the Indians and the colonists. The native Americans turned more and more to violence, as they perceived that no land would be returned to them, land for which they said they had not been paid "and for which they had never voluntarily and honestly passed title" (Early, 1905). The Indians were not altogether blameless, as the extant Pennsylvania records clearly show, but the burden remained with Thomas Penn and his associates. There is irony in the fact that one of Pennsylvania's earliest political and social problems was solved by dubious manipulations of a member of the Penn family, in tandem with the physical prowess and athletic skill of one Edward Marshall.

Direct cause and effect are of course difficult to establish in complex historical phenomena. Julian P. Boyd in his *Indian Treaties Printed by Benjamin Franklin 1736-1762,* tended to exonerate the Proprietors, stating that "the generally accepted conclusion that the Walking Purchase had far-reaching consequences and a direct relation with the warfare of 1755-1756 is even more tenuous than the charge of fraud and deception" (Franklin, 1938). And yet *Smith's Laws of Pennsylvania, 1781-1790,* hints broadly at some kind of cause and effect:

The walkers were expert, and the Indians who could not keep up with them complained that they ran.... It is not our intention to enter further into the controversy than to exhibit the general grounds which are said to have estranged the Delawares from our interest, and drove them into that of the French ... *(Smith's Laws, 1781-1790).*

By far the majority of historians dealing with this Pennsylvania time period condemn the actions of the Philadelphia political establishment, employing terms such as "unsavory," "infamous," and "most serious offense against the Red Men." One historian concluded that the Quaker "Holy Experiment" worked for a while, but that, people being neither saints nor devils, the ideal of pacifism gradually weakened. The new proprietors regarded the sale and rental of land as more important "than a 'good neighbor' policy toward the Indians" (Davidson, 1957). For many years after the 1737 walk and controversial land sale, the Indians of what is now Bucks County voiced "great dissatisfaction" (Davis, 1876), while another local historian presented evidence that "the Walking Purchase directly and indirectly led to the gravest of consequences so far as the warlike Munsee Clan of the Delaware was concerned" (Donehee, 1926).

Throughout Western history, from the marathon feat of the Greek warrior-courier Pheidippides in 490 B.C. to Davy Crockett, the most robust of early nineteenth-century Americans, physical prowess and athletic skill have given evidence of playing an important role in the political and cultural maelstrom of nations. Alexander the Great, Spartacus, Roland, and Saladin were no less athletic than George Washington and Abraham Lincoln. Each of them possessed physical vigor and athletic ability along with more important talents. All of their skills combined to influence history. Until the most recent era of the past 150 years in America, athletic ability of itself was of little value and not commercially useful. But it had always existed. Edward Marshall was a major actor in the drama of the 1737 Pennsylvania Walking Purchase. His athletic feat of covering approximately ninety miles on foot over rugged terrain in exactly eighteen hours is without parallel in colonial history, and it was another hundred years before recognized professional athletes surpassed Marshall's record, doing so on smooth tanbark tracks, and surrounded by the adulation of the crowd (Lucas, 1968). Whatever kind of rogue or luckless woodsman Edward Marshall may have been, were he living today and chose to do so, his athletic ability could earn him

five thousand fold more than the twenty dollars he earned during
that fateful march in September of 1837.

REFERENCES

Adams, J. T. *Provincial Societies 1690-1763.* Volume 3 of *A History of American Life,* A. M. Schlesinger and D. R. Fox, (eds.) New York: MacMillan, 1927, 183.

Buck, W. *History of the Indian Walk.* Printed by author in 1886.

Cribbs, G. A. *The Frontier Policy of Pennsylvania.* Pittsburgh, 1919, 5.

Davidson, R. L. *War Comes to Quaker Pennsylvania 1682-1756.* New York: Temple University. Published by Columbia University Press, 1957, 69.

Davis, W. W. *The History of Bucks County, Pennsylvania..* Doylestown, PA: Democratic Book and Job Office, 1876, 489.

Donahee, G. P. *Pennsylvania—A History.* New York: Lewis Historical Publishing Company, 1926, vol. 3, 348.

Early, J. W. "Indian Massacres in Berks County," *Transactions of the Historical Society of Berks County,* 2 (1905-1909), 110-111.

Egle, W. H. *An Illustrated History of the Commonwealth of Pennsylvania.* Harrisburg: DeWitt C. Goodrich and Company, 1876, 442-444.

Fackenthal, B. F. "The Indian Walking Purchase." *Bucks County Historical Society,* 6 (1932), 14-15.

Franklin, B. (Comp.). *Indian Treaties Printed by Benjamin Franklin 1736-1762.* Philadelphia: The Historical Society of Pennsylvania, 1938, fn. 28.

Henry, M. S. *History of the Lehigh Valley.* Easton, PA: Bixler and Corwin, 1860, 15-16.

Jable, J. T. "The Pennsylvania Sunday Blue Laws of 1779." *Pennsylvania History, 40* (1973), 413-417.

Jacobson, M. A. "The Walking Purchase." *Moravian Historical Society Transactions* (1911), 9, 22.

Jennings, F. "The Scandalous Indian Policy of William Penn's Sons." *Pennsylvania History, 37* (1970), 31.

Kelley, J. J., Jr. *Pennsylvania—The Colonial Years 1681-1776.* Garden City, NY: Doubleday, 1980, 202.

Kent, D. H. *Historical Report on Pennsylvania's Purchase from the Indians.* New York: Garland Publishing Company, 1974, 15.

Klein, P. S. & Hoogenboom, A., *A History of Pennsylvania.* New York: McGraw-Hill, 1973, 54-55.

Lucas, J. A. "Pedestrianism and the Struggle for the Sir John Astley Belt, 1878-1879." *Research Quarterly, 39* (1968), 587-594.

Lucas, J. A. and Smith, R. A. *Saga of American Sport.* Philadelphia: Lea and Febiger, 1978, 33-35.

Memoirs of the Historical Society of Pennsylvania. Philadelphia: McCarty and Davis, 1826-1895,2, Part 1, 218. Morison, S. E. *The Oxford*

History of the American People. New York: Oxford University Press, 1965, 131. Parkman, F. *The Conspiracy of Pontiac and the Indian War after the Conquest of Canada.* Boston: Little, Brown and Company, 1895, 84, 86-87.

Pennsylvania Archives, 1, Series 1, 1664-1747, 47-48, 540-543.

Pennsylvania Colonial Records, 3, 435-452.

Pennsylvania Colonial Records, 4, 597.

Sharpless, I. *A Quaker Experiment in Government.* Philadelphia: T. S. Leach and Company, 1900, 174-175.

Sipe, C. H. *The Indian Chiefs of Pennsylvania.* Butler, PA: Ziegler Printing Company, 1927, 165.

Sipe, C. H. *The Indian Wars of Pennsylvania.* Harrisburg: Telegraph Press, 1931, 112, 790.

Smith's Laws of the Commonwealth of Pennsylvania from 1700-1810, vol. 2, 116.

Thayer, T. "The Friendly Association." *Pennsylvania Magazine of History and Biography,* 67 (1943), 365.

Thomson, C. *Enquiry into the Causes of the Alienation of the Delaware and Shawnee Indians from the British Interest.* London: 1759, 36-40.

Wallace, A. F. C. *King of the Delawares: Teedyuscung 1700-1763.* Philadelphia: University of Pennsylvania Press, 1949, 26.

Wallace, P. A. W. "Conrad Weiser and the Delawares." *Pennsylvania History, 4* (1937) 146.

Wallace, P. A. W. *Conrad Weiser 1696-1760: Friend of Colonist and Mohawk.* Philadelphia: University of Pennsylvania Press, 1945, 96-99.

Weslager, C. A. *The Delaware Indians—A History.* New Brunswick, NJ: Rutgers University Press, 1972, 189. Wildes, H. E. *The Delaware.* New York: Farrar and Rinehart, 1940, 103-104.

Williams, J. S. "An Old Burying Ground Grave of Edward Marshall." *Bucks County Historical Society,* 2 (1909). 351.

NOTES

1 Proprietary agents were employees of English business firms working in the colonies. The proprietorship succeeded the trading company as a device employed to build England's colonial empire. It was expected that every agent's decision would be in England's best interest. Thus "the proprietary Province was virtually a feudal jurisdiction in which ... the lord proprietor exercised sovereign powers." See Thomas C. Cochrane (ed.), *Concise Dictionary of American History* (New York: Charles Scribner's Sons, 1962), p. 772.

2 "In the thirty-year period from 1725 to 1755 the number of colonists nearly quadrupled from about 40,000 to 150,000. The population of the city of Philadelphia probably doubled to about 16,000 during this same span." See R. S. Howald, "The Structure of Pennsylvania Politics, 1739-1766," Ph.D. dissertation, Princeton University, 1978, p. 19.

3 The chain saw of 1737 was of course not a power implement. It consisted of a series of links, each with saw teeth on one side. At each end of the chain was a handle. In effect it was a flexible cross-cut saw, and had the additional advantage of curling neatly onto itself for storage on horseback.

4 These estimates were obtained after discussions with recreational, fitness, and ROTC specialists on the campus of The Pennsylvania State University. The author is also a long-distance runner with 35 years' experience.

5 Edward Marshall lived to the age of about seventy-nine years *(Williams, 1909).* Details of his violent life are given by Sipe (1931) and Buck (1886).

10.
American Preparations for the First Post-World War Olympic Games, 1919-1920*

No single Olympic Games in modern history got off to such modest, even tentative beginnings than did the 1920 Games of the Seventh Olympiad in Antwerp, Belgium. The so-called "Great War" had raged only twenty months before, and signatures were obtained on the Treaty of Versailles, June 28, 1919—a little more than a year before the Olympic Games. The conflict had been utterly devastating, with ten million dead, twenty million wounded, and more than $300 billion in damages.[1] And yet Baron Pierre de Coubertin, founder of the modern Olympic Games, was able to convince the most cruelly damaged nation, Belgium, to host an Olympic Games—the first in eight years. Belgium was grievously unprepared to do so, nor were any European and even North American countries ready to fully participate in this revived "festival of youth." An analysis of the American Olympic Committee's (hereafter called AOC) unvarnished support for its nation's re-entry into Olympic competition, an analysis of the United States preparations, or rather more accurately, lack of administrative preparations, that country's frequently awkward but eventually partly successful efforts to field a representative Olympic team in 1920, and certain implications regarding the importance of this uneven success on the whole American Olympic movement form the essence of this essay.

What could possibly have provoked the AOC president, Gustavus Town Kirby, in a post-Olympic Games interview, to call for

*Journal of Sport History, 10 (Summer, 1983), 30-44.

a complete committee overhaul and thus preclude in the future "any possibility of such conditions as existed ... in the preparations for the last Olympic Games"?[2] Was AOC secretary Frederick Rubien grossly overreacting when asked to comment on disharmony aboard ship as the athletes headed for the Games in Belgium and answered: "There was an element of dissatisfaction in the team which assumed the aspect of a Bolshevik outburst as we were nearing Antwerp"? Was the veteran of many Olympic Games, New York City Police Lieutenant Matt McGrath, upon returning from the 1920 Games, justified in angrily stating: "I will never enter an Olympic Games again"?[3] Was there collusion between track and field champion McGrath and American Olympic swimmers, boxers, and fencers who stated collectively that their own officials were to blame for abominable conditions aboard the transport ship *Princess Matoika*?[4] How typical was the remark made by a returning American Olympian: "It was horrible; you can't believe what we've been through"?[5] A look at the immediate past history of the AOC and the international Olympic movement is necessary in order to propose disinterested answers to these questions.

Portent of American Olympic Disharmony

Track and field athletics was the dominant sport in each of the five Olympic Games, 1896-1912. The United States was the world leader in this sport during this period and thus emerged, on the eve of World War I, as the paragon of Olympic Games participants. A great deal of credit for such success was due to the brilliant and tyrannical leadership of James Edward Sullivan.[6] Sullivan's brand of leadership—ruthless, autocratic, aristocratic, single-minded, and utterly efficient—had been very much in tune with the organizational nature of American amateur athletics in that era, 1896-1914. It was very sorely missed at his death. But Sullivan died on September 16, 1914; the Berlin Games of 1916 were cancelled; America's greatest Olympic track coach, Michael C. Murphy, died the year before Sullivan; and, American athletic hero and representative to the International Olympic Committee (IOC), Evert Jansen Wendell, died in battle at Nevilly, France, on August 25, 1917. Lastly, as if to compound American amateur athletic miseries, both Colonel Robert Thompson, esteemed longtime president of the AOC, and Judge Bartow S. Weeks (Sullivan's successor) resigned their positions in late 1919. Thompson had served well, was old, and stepped down from leadership, while Weeks had been co-opted by the IOC. It was a tenuous situation, one that led eye-witness Alexander M. Weyand to observe that the years 1913 to 1919 "had not dealt kindly" with the AOC. "It was small wonder," he said, "that the 'cream' turned slightly sour."[7]

The persistent dreamer, Pierre de Coubertin, self-exiled in Switzerland during the years 1914-1918, occupied much of his time in planning for the post-war Olympic Games. Consumed with keeping the Olympic idea alive, the Baron addressed the Greek Liberal Club of Lausanne, Switzerland, on February 24, 1918, calling for an end to the war, a universal sport-for-all mandate, and a restoration of the Olympic Games—and in that order of importance.[8] In a euphoric outburst of letter-writing following the war's end, Coubertin, in one of these homilies, called for the brotherhood of nations to emulate the new and exciting American idea of pervasive physical education and intercollegiate athletics.[9] Coubertin's blizzard of correspondence to athletic leaders around the world prepared them for the first post-war IOC meeting in Lausanne on April 28, 1919—the twenty-fifth anniversary of that body. IOC member from Belgium, Count Henri Baillet-Latour, very much wanted the 1920 Olympic Games to be held in his own country and convinced some government officials that the successful fruition of an Olympic Games in that country would be visible proof of Belgium's vigor and recovery from the carnage of war. Baillet-Latour and Coubertin were close friends and the Frenchman took little convincing to give Antwerp the nod. Rome's bid for the 1920 Olympic Games fell through; no one else wanted the Games, and Coubertin with veiled enthusiasm pronounced Antwerp, Belgium's credentials as "incomparable," and so that utterly decimated city, having requested the Games, began preparations.[10] The Baron looked heavenward and predicted a successful Olympic Games—a festival whose origins were rooted in "Anglo-Saxon sporting utilitarianism and the lofty and resounding concepts bequeathed by ancient Greece."[11]

Three-way communication between the IOC, the Belgian Olympic Organizing Committee and the AOC were non-existent between May and October of 1919. It was not until late November that the AOC announced plans to send a team to Antwerp "worthy of upholding the dignity of the nation." Kirby was chosen AOC president and made a plea for $200,000—a sum desperately needed to fund the American team. He reminded all that the most powerful athletic nations would be in Antwerp (except Germany), a "foreshadow of stiffer opposition for the American standard bearers."[12] President of the United States Woodrow Wilson was chosen honorary president of the AOC; retired Colonel Thompson and ex-president of the U.S., William Howard Taft, agreed to accept titles of honorary vice-presidents of the AOC.[13] A certain smugness at having so many high-powered government officials in their Olympic corner was lost in late December of 1919, when the Belgian Committee announced the Olympic program of events. Ice hockey and figure skating events would begin in early April while swimming and rowing finals would take place on September 30—a half-year of Olympic Games competition! "Separate and distinct expeditions" would be needed by a beleaguered AOC that had no money and no ships with which to transport their fractured teams to Europe.

Some solace was obtained in early 1920 when Secretary of War Newton Baker and Secretary of the Navy Josephus Daniels agreed to become honorary vice-presidents of the Olympic Committee. Gustavus Kirby had obtained the patronage of some of Washington, D.C.'s most important people.[14] Nevertheless, the struggle for monies and the near impossibility of obtaining transportation overseas remained unsolved in the spring of 1920—only three months before the Opening Day Ceremonies of the Olympic Games. AOC boss Kirby convened an emergency meeting on March 13, 1920; IOC member Weeks was annoyed that the American track and field Olympic trials were scheduled *after* final entries were due in Belgium. Kirby was pleased to announce the first donation, a $5,000 gift from Colonel Thompson. Any thought of easy victories in Antwerp "must be discarded," warned Kirby.[15]

The Olympic Dilemma Compounds Itself

The Olympic Committee's dilemma was of classic proportions. America's athletic youth, both in and out of the universities, both young men and young women with expanding horizons, were eager to contest for places on the Olympic team. But the AOC had no monies and no way to get the athletes to Europe. Powerful political and military leaders in Washington, D.C., had accepted honorary invitations to the Committee. The Army and the Navy were especially important to the Olympic Committee since much of the nation was still on a war-time basis and all large transport ships, commandeered by the military, were not available to civilian organizations such as the Olympic organization. The few private steamship lines were "fully booked to August 1."[16] The United States Army of Occupation on the Rhine River had its base at Antwerp and ships plied that 4,000-mile trip on a regular basis. The War Department admitted "that so far as passengers were concerned, transports were running with many staterooms and most of their troopship quarters empty."[17] It seemed to be the logistic and fiscal solution of the AOC's major headache. There was only one thing wrong, however; it was illegal for civilian athletes and officials to travel on Army and Navy ships. A painful and protracted period of Congressional hearings and testimonies by AOC president Kirby and his associates occupied all their energies between March and June of 1920. The Games of the Seventh Olympiad were "right around the corner" and the mightiest athletic nation was wholly unprepared.

Gustavus Town Kirby was a well-educated, experienced, and resolute athletic administrator, born in Philadelphia (1874) of ancestors on his mother's side who went back to John Wesley Neveling —George Washington's chaplain. Kirby's father, Thomas E., was wealthy and "perhaps the greatest art auctioneer of all times."[18] G. T. Kirby had engineering and law degrees from Columbia University, had presided over the Intercollegiate Amateur Athletic Association of America (IC4A), the AAU, and was, in the spring of 1920, an experienced AOC president who had officiated at every Olympic Games 1900 through 1912. He entered Congressional debates with coolness and an Olympian sense that his cause was just. Kirby immediately sought help from Brigadier General Hines, Chief of Transportation Services, U.S.S., Secretary Baker, the Honorable James Wadsworth of New York, Chairman of the Committee on Military Affairs of the Senate, and the Honorable Julius Kahn of California, Chairman of the Committee on Military Affairs of the House.[19] On March 20, 1920, House Joint Bill 319 was introduced by Representative Rollin B. Sanford of New York State, and thereafter, Senate Joint Resolution 179 by Senator Wadsworth, stating in part:

> That authority be, and is hereby, given to the Secretary of War, under such rules and regulations as he may prescribe, to use such army transports as may be available for the transportation of teams, individuals, and their equipment representing the United States in Olympic Games and other international competitions during the present year.[20]

Senate Joint Resolution 179 passed the Senate without difficulty[21] but the House insisted on hearings before its Committee on Military Affairs on April 7 and May 8, 1920. Appearing on behalf of the bill before chairman Julius Kahn of California and his committee were Secretary of War Newton D. Baker; Lieutenant General Robert L. Bullard, Eastern Division, U.S. Army; Commander C. B. Mayo, Chief of the Morale Division, U.S. Navy; Honorable Bartow S. Weeks, Associate Justice of the Supreme Court of New York State; General F. H. Phillips, Secretary of the National Rifle Association; and Honorable Murray Hulbert, Commissioner of Docks, New York City. Chairman Kahn opened the April meeting by making it perfectly clear that transportation on military vessels was against the law and allowing Olympic athletes passage to Europe "would be setting a dangerous precedent that would hound the members of Congress in the years to come."[22] These are the first Olympic Games in nearly a decade, pointed out Secretary Baker. Military transportation for civilian athletes is a one-time affair, a war-related emergency and ought not to be done if it would create a precedent; it is a singular event, pointed out the secretary, bringing "the athletes of all the nations together."[23] Obtuse discussions followed, touching on the Boy Scouts, the Red Cross, the International Association of Churches; finally, the meeting was adjourned without decision.

The Spiraling Bureaucratic Labyrinth

A meeting on Saturday, May 8, was arranged and President Kirby brought his most persuasive advocates to the House Military Affairs Committee. The eloquent Kirby led the parade of speakers, emphasizing the utter futility of trying to obtain civilian ships when the nation was still on a wartime footing. He underscored the "one-time" nature of this request and reminded the good gentlemen of the Committee that these Olympics athletes—young men and women "from coast to coast and from the Gulf to Canada" represented the glorious United States of America and would bring honor to the nation ... but only if they were allowed to go to Antwerp.[24] General Bullard was of the opinion that these August Olympic Games would be even more valuable than the Inter-Allied Games held in Paris the year before. Commander Mayo reminded the Committee that one-fifth of the American Olympic team would be soldiers and sailors and only good could come from their participation in the Games. Judge Weeks was a member of the prestigious IOC and spoke with the authority of that office as well as the Supreme Court of New York State. "The United States must help brave little Belgium," said the Judge, striking at the soft side of the Committee's hide. Other nations far smaller than the U.S.A. have already outspent her in Olympic preparations, he said. Our fine young men and women, he concluded in his *coup de grace,* "... are going to carry our flag to victory over there on the battle fields of peace, just as they carried our flag to victory on the battlefields of war."[25] Committee members seemed obsessed with the problem of "paternalism" if a private group of specially selected athletes were allowed free passage overseas. There is no paternalism involved, repeated Weeks and Kirby, this time with a note of peevishness in their words. Since the American Olympic team is not funded by the government, several committee members wondered how Kirby and Weeks could constantly invoke flag, country, and patriotism. Justice Weeks got in the last word and concluded his part of the testimony by repeating the triple invocation of flag, country, patriotism, *plus* "nation defense," as splendid reasons for allowing some of the country's finest youth such a rare opportunity.[26]

General Phillips informed the Committee that the Olympic rifle team was easily the best in the world and should be allowed to prove it. "The world is out of joint," said the last witness, the shrewd Commissioner of the New York City Docks, Murray Hulbert, and it is essential therefore that the government cooperate in order that the athletes "may uphold and maintain the honor and dignity of the United States ... upon the field of peaceful competition."[27] Before adjourning, a letter was read from the legendary football coach, Walter Camp, noting that no dangerous precedent would be set in helping the Olympic team get to Europe, for not only would they be the beneficiaries but our entire "industrial population" would be "stimulated."[28]

Senate Joint Resolution 179 made its tortuous way through the House of Representatives. Slight changes in wording, small additions and deletions took ten weeks of work and revision. Sharper focus on the resolution took place in April and May of 1920.[29] Several members of the House considered it unconscionable that the government would be burdened with huge costs for transporting and feeding several hundred "civilians" in a little understood venture to a European city still smoldering from the bombs of the recent war. The bill's sponsor repeated, it seemed almost interminably, that:

> These boys will come from all over the United States ...
> and the Army and the Navy are interested in the mat-
> ter on account of the athletic features involved. We want
> these boys to compete in the service in order to hold up
> the name of America in these Olympic Games this year.[30]

Will there be any "joy rides" involved, asked several lawmak-
ers? "Absolutely not" was the quick reply. Every person has been
carefully selected and will fulfill a specific vital role was the essence of lengthy debate in late May. Mr. Gallivan of Massachusetts nodded approval, pointing out to the doubting Thomases
that these athletes were "the very best" and "will not be able to go
to Antwerp unless they have a helping hand from Uncle Sam."[31]
It was easier going now, and on May 24, the Vice-President of the
United States laid before the Senate the amendment of the House
of Representatives. On June 2, 1920, Woodrow Wilson, American president, "approved and signed Joint Resolution 179."[32] For
several weeks prior to Mr. Wilson's approbation, AOC President
Kirby was sure of victory. We still need a quarter-million dollars, he said, but government support will save $80,000 and,
more importantly, "it will be a truly American invasion," the best
American team ever, and "the first time that the government has
given official recognition to the participation of American athletes
in the Olympics."[33]

An Olympian Ocean Crossing

Olympic athletes in the Armed Services had no problems and
would travel first class aboard the armored cruiser *Frederick*.[34]
The ship selected to carry the majority of team members was
the "fine and fast" *Northern Pacific*.[35] But on the eve of its July
20 departure date the ship was declared "unseaworthy" and the
254 members of the Olympic team appeared stranded. President
Kirby hadn't planned on sailing with the athletes as he was ur-
gently needed at home to support a team threatened with money
shortages and a reduction in team size.[36] Incredibly, the only
ship available to the U.S. Navy for use by the Olympic Committee
was the transport *Princess Matoika*, and she was in mid-ocean on
her way to New York City. Even the AOC, ever apologetic about
the very halting progress being made about getting the team to
Europe, called the *Matoika* a slow ship "and of ancient vintage."[37]
Many years later, passenger Daniel J. Ferris, AAU and Olympic
official, remembered the nightmare trip:

... The government gave us this great rusty old army transport, the *Princess Matoika*. Oh, it was a terrible, terrible ship. When we arrived to board, they had just taken off the bodies of 1,800 war dead from Europe. When the team filed up the gangplank, the caskets were sitting there on the docks, lines and lines of coffins. It was a shocking way to start.the athletes were quartered down in the hold. The smell of formaldehyde was dreadful. What a black hole that was for them. The athletes had to sleep in triple-decker bunks that hung on chains. The place was infested with rats. The athletes used to throw bottles at the rats. It was terrible, but we had to go this way because we had no money. No money at all.[38]

The Atlantic crossing took exactly 14 days—July 26 to August 8, 1920. The perpetual motion Kirby, before departure, raised $60,000,[39] made a quick round trip to Antwerp, inspected the *Matoika* and promised "comfortable quarters."[40] However, after the first night aboard ship, some of the athletes complained about crowded sleeping quarters below the water line. Joey Ray and Charley Paddock lodged protests with Mr. Kirby, who called their allegations exaggerated, although he admitted that the athletes "will sail under severe conditions."[41] The *Matoika's* captain took the southern course to avoid ice, but ran into heavy fog and rain. On deck, training was nearly futile; below decks the transport was dirty, infested with rats, the food was "from poor to bad," and sanitary arrangements were wholly insufficient.

But a beleaguered Olympic officer responded that the athletes were insensitive to "the many little conveniences and luxuries installed for their comfort." He further pointed out that earlier that same summer the *Princess Matoika* had transported 600 Boy Scouts to Antwerp and without a peep of complaint.[42]

But within days some of the athletes were in a mean mood—an attitude that sport journalists John Kieran and Arthur Daley called "the Mutiny of the *Matoika*." The giant New York City Policeman, Lieutenant Matthew McGarth—respected by both the athletes and Olympic officials—was frequently called up to smooth matters between management and "the self-confessed 'cream of the athletic world.'"[43] Everyday aboard ship was a crisis, and even the placid McGarth, in retrospect, said that conditions had been so bad that he would never enter an Olympic Games again. The ship's officers gave us extra food and blankets, he added. "Without the army and navy," he ended, "we would have suffered a terrible defeat."[44] American athletes, returning home early from Antwerp for failure to advance beyond the trials, returned to New York, complaining bitterly about the wretched conditions aboard the *Princess Matoika*.[45] Another athlete, requesting anonymity, called conditions aboard ship "Horrible. You can't believe what we've been through."[46] Spokesman for the AOC, Frederick Rubien, pointed out ominously that under the circumstances conditions were as good as possible, but that "There was an element of dissatisfaction in the team which assumed the aspect of a Bolshevik outburst...."[47]

American athletes aboard the *Princess* trained as best they could. Boxers and wrestlers worked on the decks. Track and field athletes ran in place and sprinted along a 70 yard cork track, while swimmers tried to stay fit in a 12 X 9 foot long canvas pool. "Everyone is perfectly satisfied; it looks like one big family," was AOC member R. S. Weaver's message to the wire services.[48] But things got ugly; injuries occurred; P. J. McDonald injured his thumb; steeplechaser Max Bohland got three stitches due to "rolling of the ship;" heavy rains forced one athlete to murmur aloud "Our quarters are absolutely unlivable."[49] Seasickness prompted several to "swear they would never part with dry land again." Paul Lowry of the *Los Angeles Times* caustically noted that the pending crisis was "not mustard gas, but the revived Olympic Games."[50] Social critic W. O. McGeehan, quoting a fictitious Olympian, wailed, "No, I ain't going over to the Olympic Games; I wouldn't travel steerich." His phantom athlete "Izzy" complained about the "stinking government ship" and how the AOC seems "never to do anything in the right way."[51]

The lid blew on August 6, the twelfth day aboard the *Matoika*. The great Olympic 800-meter champion of 1912—James E. "Ted" Meredith—was aboard as a Universal Service Staff Correspondent as well as a member of the 400-meter dash Olympic team and described the "indignation meeting" held by the athletes. They simply would not tolerate conditions in Antwerp similar to those on ship, and blamed their own officials, all of whom were aboard—for insensitivity and ineptness. "U.S. Olympic athletes threaten to go on strike," cried the sporting headline of the *New York Tribune*. Several midnight meetings were held, the whole Olympic Committee hierarchy was castigated in a frontal assault, and a formal protest to Secretary of War Baker was written. The incensed athletes chose representatives from all geographic areas of the United States to protest their recent fate aboard the

Princess and to demand first-rate accommodations at the little red schoolhouse already set aside for them in Antwerp.[52]

Brave and Ill-Prepared Antwerp Welcomes the World

Nothing in nearly a quarter-century of American involvement in the Olympic Games had reached such vitriolic levels of anger between athletes and their own officials. Inefficiency was the least of the charges brought against Justice Weeks, Mr. Kirby, AAU boss Samuel J. Dallas, Everett C. Brown, and AOC secretary Rubien. Nearly 200 athletes signed the resolution. The bottom line was, finally, that they would compete in Antwerp "no matter what" and in spite of hard bunks and decks, endless rain, poor ventilation, and "evil-smelling holds overrun by rats."[53] Upon arrival in Antwerp's harbor at 9 p.m. of August 6, the mood of the team was not enhanced when it was announced that they would have to sleep aboard ship one more night. The next morning the American young men and women found their housing at a local school and YMCA, respectively—all adequately comfortable, although the men had no privacy in the schoolroom filled with rows of cots; nor was there hot water in the showers. The female swimmers found the pool "icy cold" and therefore were probably unimpressed by Belgian onlookers who said, "They swim like men."[54] Head track coach Jack Moakley from Cornell University found the stadium's cinder track wholly unsuitable, while hammer thrower Pat Ryan went around declaring that all athletes would get "cauliflower ears" sleeping on hard bunks decorated with hay-filled pillows.[55] The emotional dam broke once again when two more incidents occurred. A letter was read from the Belgian committee to the American team urging them to refrain from boisterous conduct about the schoolhouse quarters. Far more serious was Dan Ahearn's instant dismissal from the team when he moved out of the primary school and into a local hotel. Two American boxers were also ordered home on the first available ship, having been accused of "boxing for a purse."[56]

Many of the American athletes were in no mood for such antics by their own AOC members and retaliated with an angry outburst that "left the committee stunned." Catcalls and heckling were aimed at President Kirby and Judge Weeks. Ahearn's case was especially galling to team members, but Weeks pointed out several acts of insubordination by the triple jump champion. Weeks pleaded for teamwork, discipline, and duty. "What position would you be in if the Committee refused to continue its duty?" A chorus of angry voices shouted, "Go ahead! We will get a better committee."[57] Almost immediately President Kirby and his associates changed their minds and reinstated the independent Ahearn, but only after the athlete apologized and in time for the American participation in Opening Ceremonies of these Games of the VII Olympiad.[58]

The Antwerp Games Try to Stand Tall and Straight

For the Baron, the interregnum period 1912-1920 had been a double horror. The war had been a personal and international disaster. And, of course, it marked eight long years without an Olympic celebration. The great day had arrived, a day that the 57-year-old Baron Pierre de Coubertin had, with extraordinary impatience, waited 8 years to celebrate. Some 1,800 athletes from 27 countries were greeted by King Albert and Queen Elizabeth. The Antwerp stadium seemed "pathetically tiny," but, nevertheless, Arthur S. Draper said, "It was the best League of Nations meeting since the war."[59] All the Coubertin trappings were present: royalty, parade of athletes, soaring airplanes, and a solemn ceremony at Antwerp's Cathedral where Cardinal Mercier compared the athlete's glory with a higher glory—that of "man's union to the glory of God himself."[60] Coubertin was understandably elated, exclaiming "Sport is King." Speaking to the 18th session of the IOC, Coubertin maintained that 3 elements would emerge from these Games: (1) a belief in mankind's inexorable progress, (2) a conviction that peace is attainable only through a sense of universal objectivity or disinterestedness, and (3) a long-held faith that every nation needs to embrace a sport-for-all position.[61]

Probably the American athletes, coaches, and officials were not thinking such thoughts on this Opening Day Ceremony, August 14, 1920. What did concern them was to continue their domination of the Olympic Games, especially in track and field athletics—a national surge that had brought a harvest of 38 gold, silver, and bronze medals in that one sport at the Stockholm, Sweden, Games 8 years earlier. American generosity in exporting track and field coaches to Europe during the periods 1910-1914 and 1919-1920, contributed to slightly closing the gap. Yankee athletes won 29 medals in this sport at the Antwerp Games, ahead of the awesome athletic power—little Finland. America still ruled the Olympic Games—and in more than one sport. Returning home with precious gold medals were track and field athletes Charlie Paddock, Alan Woodring, Frank Loomis, members of the 3,000-meter team race and 400-meter relay, Richard London, Frank Foss, Pat Ryan, and P. J. McDonald. In swimming, the American victors were Duke Kahanamoku, P. Kealoha, Norman Ross, the 800-meter relay team (men), L. Kuehn, Ethelda Bleibtrey, the 400-meter relay for women, and tiny 13-year-old Aeileen Riggin in fancy diving. DeGennaro, Mosberg, and Eddie Egan won boxing crowns while Ackerly won the featherweight class in catch-as-catch-can wrestling. There was but a single finals match in Rugby football and the U.S.A. overpowered France, 8-0. The United States Naval Academy 8-oared crew won a stunning, very close victory over England's Leander crew. The famous John B. Kelly won at single sculls and won again in double sculls with Paul V. Costello. American marksmen were awesome, dominating almost all rifle and pistol shooting, with Mark P. Arie, Karl T. Frederick, Carl T. Osburn, Morris Fisher, and Lawrence Nuesslein especially effective.[62]

By all systems of athletic scoring used in 1920—and there were many— the United States emerged as the dominant nation at these Olympic Games, with Finland in surprisingly close attendance. There was murmuring, however, among some AOC members and especially among journalists that the country had not done as well as the great 1912 U.S. team, and that poor management by the AAU and the AOC was the reason. Matthew P. Halpin, four-time manager of the American Olympic team, wagged his finger at complacent associates, noting that "had it not been for the tremendous loss of life in the world war, which depleted much of the athletic material of our Allies, we might not have fared so well."[63] In a moment of candor, AOC and AAU secretary Rubien admitted that the Europeans were catching up to the American athletes.[64] President Kirby himself returned home and told the press, "If I had it to do over again, I would do many things differently."[65] Limply, the official chronicler of America's activities in Antwerp said that "The difficulties and mistakes of the last Olympiad were largely due to lack of time and to early uncertainties."[66] After complementing Belgium for its bravery in hosting the Games, the same writer became more specific:

> But to ignore mistakes and shortcomings on the part of the Belgian management and of even more glaring ones on the part of international sport federations which laid down the rules and provided the officials for the contests would be mere pretense.[67]

One of the most perceptive remarks was made in the post Olympic Games AOC report which admitted that "the continuity of the AOC ... was severely strained by the Great War" and that some of the most success-oriented American sport leaders were gone by the year 1920.[68] U.S. athletes performed admirably, but unreasonably high expectations by journalists generated as much criticism as praise. Some of the former came from Roy Lewis in the January 1921 issue of *Outing* magazine. The American team was filled with complacency, he said: "sixty percent did nothing but have a joy ride and join the ranks of 'also rans.'" He quoted fellow journalist Sparrow Robertson of the *New York Herald*—that there was "too much deadwood" among the U.S. athletes. His most damaging cut was at AOC leadership. "The team seems never to have been in hand," was his conclusion.[69] Lastly, the author of the *Literary Digest* essay titled "Was the recent Olympiad a failure?" concluded that he did not find "in the seventh Olympiad a pleasant retrospect." Bad weather, injuries, a swollen team of non-scorers, a drop in medal wins compared to 1912, and even a negative comparison in male physiques compared to the Finns were all comments by John J. Hallinan in the *Boston Globe*. As far as America is concerned, he said, the Games "will go down in history as a failure." Hallinan was present at both the Stockholm and the Antwerp Games and the Belgian organizers suffered by comparison. Injuries and poor physical condition of many of our athletes were laid at the feet of the AOC. Dreadful conditions aboard a very slow tub were inexcusable, he lamented and "While the Committee, no doubt, failed in its mission, the athletes, too, were not above censure for the way they acted." Hallinan's very detailed and balanced view of conditions aboard the *Princess Matoika* tended to find the athletes not without fault, but the burden of ineptitudes lay with American Olympic officials. Hallinan's series of essays in the *Boston Globe*, August 22-28, 1920, was widely quoted in American newspapers and magazines.[70]

The Bottom Line on America's Olympic Preparations

The World War I carnage interrupted America's Olympic Games success. There was a loss of international athletic leadership among Americans after the death of James E. Sullivan in 1914. The AOC had never solicited monies from its government, and in the difficult days immediately after the war precious little cash was located in the public and private sectors. All of this was compounded by slow, painful progress by the Belgians. Coubertin was responsible for all this precipitousness. "Everything had to be created from scratch," he admitted, and was hardly comparable to the London and Stockholm Games of 1908 and 1912.[71] All countries had trouble getting to Antwerp, none more so than the British—and they had only a short trip across the lowest portion of the North Sea to the Olympic city. Latent ill will against American athletic aggressiveness and a long-standing coolness toward any sporting event without a British label resulted in almost no monies for a team to be sent to Belgium. The Reverend R. S. de Coursey Laffin and Sir Theodore A. Cook worked unceasingly to heighten national enthusiasm and raise the needed funds. They succeeded somewhat, and a small British team performed well at the Games.[72]

The bottom line regarding American difficulties in preparing for the Antwerp Olympic Games of 1920 was that, in addition to a myriad of serious handicaps for which it could not be held responsible, the American Olympic Committee was sadly lacking in vision, forcefulness, and in its capacity to raise monies. General Palmer E. Pierce, President of the National Collegiate Athletic Association (NCAA), in his 1920 annual address, blamed the AOC for a poorly managed Olympic effort.[73] The AAU was the most powerful arm of the AOC and there were those that said the root of the problem lay with them; but the AAU "disclaimed all responsibility for the alleged mismanagement" of our Olympic involvement during the difficult years 1919 and 1920.[74] The AOC was acutely aware of its own shortcomings and after a series of meetings in October, November, and December of 1920, and in 1921, a significant restructuring of the organization took place. Permanent subcommittees were formed, mandated to work year-round and every year rather than just during the Olympic Games period. Fund raising was given the highest priority, and men whose memories easily went back to America's first Olympic Games' involvement in 1896—and to each of that country's successive unrivaled Olympic success—forged ahead and changed the name of their own committee to "The American Olympic Association (AOA)." The old guard—Sloane, Armour, Mills, Weeks, Halpin, Rubien, all were there to nod approval to AOA president Kirby's remark that these changes were but precursors and "will preclude any possibility of such conditions existing as did exist in the preparations for the last Olympic Games.[75]

James Edward Sullivan had been for twenty years an extraordinarily able leader for both the AAU and the AOC. His notes were directives; he never issued suggestions but always mandates. He was honest, extremely intelligent, brutally direct, and above all, totally dedicated to keeping his country the supreme track and field power in international contests and Olympic Games. He was very successful at his work. This "aggressive American patriot" without "a shred of cosmopolitanism," as Lucas called him,[76] had no comparable successors in American amateur athletics following the First World War. Kirby and his athletic entourage were worthy men with considerable experience, but some of the steadiest men in the American Olympic movement were gone, and were missed. Besides, it was a new era—the 1920s and an age of heightened individual awareness and independence. For the first time in significant numbers, American amateur athletes were speaking their minds, refusing to "knuckle-under" to the AAU and the AOA. It was a disconcerting period for the athletic leadership.[77]

Internecine struggles all through the decade of the 1920s between the AAU, the NCAA, and the Olympic Committee were to reach unprecedented proportions. In other words, the dismal U.S. Olympics administrative problems of the period of 1919-1920 were the result of a sudden loss of leadership, the encompassing trauma of the war, a certain "touchiness" and new independence on the part of American athletes and the special frenzy of Pierre de Coubertin during these years. All of them were precursors of a nearly permanent discontinuity between the American amateur sporting bodies. And in a quite extraordinary way that goes well beyond the boundaries of this paper, the Olympic Committee of the United States was, for two more generations, caught inbetween the two most powerful of these "sporting bodies"—the NCAA and the AAU. It was no place to be. Part of the reason for such juxtaposition can be traced to the several years of indecision and lack of genuine leadership by the American Olympic Committee during those years of trial 1919 and 1920.

NOTES

1 William L. Langer, Comp. and ed. *An Encyclopedia of World History* (Boston: Houghton Mifflin Company, 1948), p. 951.

2 Gustavus T. Kirby as quoted in "Olympic Officials Plan for Future," *New York Times,* December 5, 1920, section 9, p. 2.

3 Matthew McGrath as quoted in "U.S. Athletes Return Angry at Committee," *New York Tribune,* September 12, 1920, p. 14.

4 "Several Members of Olympic Team Back from Abroad," *New York Tribune,* September 5, 1920, p. 16.

5 "Olympians Return, Condemn Officials," *New York Times,* September 12, 1920, p. 2.

6 For Sullivan's influence, see John Lucas. "Early Olympic Antagonists—Pierre de Coubertin versus James E. Sullivan," *Stadion,* III (1977), 258-272.

7 Alexander M, Weyand, *The Olympic Pageant* (New York: The Macmillan Company, 1952), p. 136.

8 Pierre de Coubertin, *Ce que nous pouvons mainlenant demander an sport* (Lausanne: Edition de l'Association des Hellenes Liberaux de Lausanne, 1918), passim.

9 Coubertin letter dated January 5, 1919, as found in *The Olympic Idea: Pierre de Coubertin Discourses and Essays* (Cologne: Carl Diem Institute, 1966), p. 59.

10 Pierre de Coubertin, *Memoires Olympiques* (Lausanne: Bureau International de Pedagogic Sportive, 1931), p. 155.

11 Coubertin, "Address ... Lausanne, April, 1919," as found in *The Olympic Idea,* p. 74.

12 "Official Decision is Made to Send an American Team to Olympic Games," *New York Times,* November 18, 1919, p. 15; "To Plan U.S. Part in Olympic Meet," *New York Times,* November 17, 1919, p. 21.

13 "Gustavus Kirby Chosen to Head Olympic Committee," *New York Herald,* November 29, 1919, p. 14.

14 *Report of the American Olympic Committee—Seventh Olympic Games—Antwerp, Belgium 1920* (New York City: AOC, 1920), p. 18, 20; also see "Government to aid Olympic officials," *New York Times,* February 13, 1920, p. 12.

15 "Take Long Strides in Olympic Plans," *New York Times,* March 14, 1920, p. 20; also Robert Korsgaard, "A History of the Amateur Athletic Union of the United States," Ed.Dissertation, Teachers College, Columbia University, 1952, pp. 194-195.

16 *Report of AOC,* p. 21.

17 Ibid.

18 Gustavus Town Kirby, *I WonderWhy?* (New York: Coward-McCann, 1954), p. 18, 111.

19 *Report of AOC,* p. 23.

20 See "Olympic Games," *Monthly Catalogue of U.S. Government Publications,* 20 (July 1919 to June 1920), p. 634, 695; *Congressio-*

nal Record, 59, part 5, 66th Congress. 2nd session, March 20, 1920, p. 4670; also March 30, 1920, p. 4993; April 3, 1920, p. 5151; April 5, 1920, p. 5224, and *Report of AOC,* p. 23.

21 *Congressional Record,* 59, part 5, 66th Congress, 2nd session, April 6, 1920, p. 5235.

22 Kahn as quoted in "Transportation of Olympic Teams," Hearing Before the Committee on Military Affairs, House of Representatives, 66th Congress, 2nd session, April 7, 1920, and May 8, 1920 (Washington, D.C.: Government Printing Office, 1921), p. 3.

23 Ibid.

24 Ibid., p. 9.

25 Ibid., p. 18.

26 Ibid., p. 26.

27 Ibid., p. 28,

28 Ibid., p. 34.

29 *Congressional Record,* 59, part 5, 66th Congress, 2nd session, p. 5307, April 7, 1920; part 7, May 12, 1920, p. 6970; May 13, p. 7028; "Use of Army Transports to Olympic Games," May 21, 1920, pp. 7456-7457; May 23, 1920, pp. 7490-7949; May 24, 1920, p. 7511; part 8, May 26, 1920, p. 7711; May 27, 1920, p. 7713.

30 Ibid., May 21, 1920, p. 7456.

31 Ibid., May 22, 1920, p. 7492.

32 Ibid., May 24, 1920, p. 7511; June 3, 1920, p. 8308.

33 Gustavus T. Kirby, "U.S. Government Supports U.S. Olympics," Walter Camp Papers, Box 50, "1908-1920," Yale University Stirling Library; *New York Times,* May 23, 1920, p. 4, sec. 8; *New York Tribune,* June 5, 1920, p. 13; *New York Times,* June 5, 1920, p. 21.

34 J. T. Boone, "Hospital Corpsmen in Olympic Games," *Hospital Corps Quarterly,* January, 1921; *New York Times,* May 21, 1920, p. 13.

35 The small 12-person ice hockey and figure skating group left America for Antwerp on April 7, 1920, aboard the liner *Finland*; the 23 rifle team left aboard the transport *Antigone* on June 21; the 8 trapshooters departed June 23 on the *Fort Victoria*; while the revolver and pistol team (16) left on July 6 on the transport *Pocahontas.* See *AOC Report,* pp. 42-43.

36 "May Have to Cut Olympic Entries," *New York Times,* July 7, 1920, p. 13; "Our 'Athletic Ambassadors' in Need of Financial Backing," *The Literary Digest,* 66 (July 24, 1920), 68-70; "American Olympic Committee Report Explains Adverse Condition," *New York Times,* November 1, 1920, p. 18.

37 *AOC Report,* p. 26.

38 Daniel J. Ferris as quoted in William O. Johnson, *All That Glitters is Not Gold. An Irreverent Look at the Olympic Games* (New York: G. P. Putnam's Sons, 1972), p. 141.

39 *New York Times,* November 1, 1920, p. 18.

40 "Kirby Back from Europe," *New York Times*, July 3, 1920, p. 11 and July 5, 1920, p. 11; "Matoika to Carry American Athletes," *New York Times*, July 10, 1920, p. 9.

41 "Olympic Athletes Sail for Antwerp," *New York Times*, July 27, 1920, p. 15.

42 *AOC Report,* p. 30.

43 Weyand, *Olympic Pageant,* p. 135. Captain Weyand was an Olympic boxer and endured the Atlantic crossing like the rest.

44 Matt McGrath as quoted in "U.S. Athletes Return Angry at Committee," *New York Tribune,* September 12, 1920, p. 14.

45 "Several Members of the Olympic Team Back from Abroad," *New York Tribune,* September 5, 1920. p. 16 and "Olympic Athletes Back; Angered at Treatment," *New York Tribune,* September 7, 1920, p. 14.

46 "Olympians Return, Condemn Officials," *New York Times*, September 12, 1920, p. 21.

47 "Rubien Defends Olympic Committee," *New York Times,* September 26, 1920, p. 21.

48 "Conditions Good on Athlete's Arc," *New York Times,* August 1, 1920, p. 19.

49 "Athletes Suffer Injuries on Ship," *Public Ledger* [Philadelphia], August 5, 1920, p. 10; "American Track Team Ruffled," *Public Ledger* [Philadelphia], August 7, 1920, p. 10.

50 Paul Lowry, "Ready for the Olympic Games," *Los Angeles Times,* August 13, 1920, part III, pp. 1, 2 and August 3, 1920, part III, p. 1.

51 W. O. McGeehan, "Izzy Quits Olympic Team," *New York Tribune,* August 1, 1920, p. 19 and McGeehan, "In all Fairness," *New York Tribune,* August 2, 1920, p. 11.

52 J. E. Meredith, "Olympians Put on Indignation Meet; May Not Compete," *Pittsburgh Post,* August 7, 1920, p. 7; "U.S. Team Stages Protests Meeting," *New York Times,* August 7, 1920, p.7; "U.S. Olympic Athletes Threaten to Go on Strike," *New York Tribune,* August 7, 1920, p. 9; "Olympic Team Protest to be Sent to Baker," *New York Tribune,* August 8, 1920, p. 20.

53 "Athletes Blame U.S. Committee for Poor Conditions," *Pittsburgh Sunday Post,* August 8, 1920, p. 3. sec. 3; "Officials Blamed by U.S. Athletes," *New York Times,* August 8, 1920, Sports sec., p. 19; "Ted" Meredith, "Olympic Athletes Place Responsibility of Poor Treatment on Officials," *Pittsburgh Post,* August 9, 1920, p. 6.

54 "U.S. Athletes in Olympic Quarters," *New York Times,* August 9, 1920, p. 11.

55 Kieran and Daley, p. 125.

56 "Olympic Stadium Ready for Opening," *Public Ledger* [Philadelphia], August 13, 1920, p. 11; Arthur S. Draper, "Three Americans are Barred from the Olympic Games," *New York Tribune,* August 14, 1920, p. 9.

57 "Committee Members Heckled by Athletes at Protest Meeting," *New York Tribune,* August 14, 1920, p. 9; *Public Ledger* [Philadelphia], August 14, 1920, p. 9; *New York Times,* August 14, 1920, p. 9.

58 James E. Meredith, "Great Olympic Stadium at Antwerp Officially Opened," *Pittsburgh Sunday Post*, August 15, 1920, Sec. 3, p. 3.

59 Arthur S. Draper, "Ahearn Reinstated by AOC," *New York Tribune*, August 15, 1920, p. 19. During the parade of nations all flags except the USA dipped: "The Americans executed 'eyes right' and did not dip their flag." *Public Ledger* [Philadelphia], August 15, 1920, p. 11.

60 As quoted in *Bulletin du Comité Internationale Olympique*, 19 (January, 1950), 24.

61 Pierre de Coubertin, "Discours Prononce a la Seance d'Ouverture de la XVIII me Session Pleniere du CIO," 17 August, 1920, p. 1, passim.

62 *Olympic Games Handbook* (New York: American Sports Publishing Company; Spalding's Athletic Library, 1921), passim.

63 Ibid., p. 9.

64 Ibid., p. 4.

65 Kirby as quoted in "Olympic Committee to Make a Report," *New York Times*, October 5, 1920, p. 9.

66 Report of AOC, p. 46.

67 Ibid., pp. 36-37.

68 "American Olympic Committee Reports," *New York Times*, November 1, 1920, p. 8.

69 Roy Lewis, "Our 'Scintillating' Stars at Antwerp," *Outing*, 11 (January, 1921), pp. 162-163.

70 As quoted in "Was the Recent Olympiad a Failure?" *The Literary Digest*, 67 (October 16, 1920), p. 70, 78. Hallinan's original articles appeared in the *Boston Globe*, August 22, 1920; p. 1, 16; August 23, 1920, p. 12; August 27, 1920, p. 7; August 28, 1920, p. 10.

71 Coubertin, *Memoires Olympiques*, p. 157.

72 Examples of British indifference to the Antwerp games may be found in *New York Tribune*, May 22, 1920, p. 15; *The Times* [London], August 14, 1920, p. 6; *The Egyptian Gazette* (Cairo), August 10, 1920, p. 5; *Public Ledger* [Philadelphia], August 16, 1920, p. 14; *The Times* [London], August 23, 1920, p. 8; *The Times* [London], August 27, 1920, p. 6.

73 Palmer E. Pierce, "President's Address," *Proceedings*, 15th NCAA, December 29, 1920, p. 56.

74 Korsgaard, "Amateur Athletic Union," p. 194.

75 Kirby as quoted in "Olympic Officials Plan for Future," *New York Times*, Decembers, 1920, Sec.IX, p. 2; "American Olympic Association Meeting," November 25, 1921 (New York Public Library under Kirby, Gustavus Town); "New Olympic Body Formed at Meeting," *New York Times*, November 26, 1921, p. 16.

76 Lucas, "Early Olympic Antagonists," p. 65.

77 A classic and representative case was that of the multiple Olympic Games champion, Charlie Paddock—an angry thorn in the side of the AAU and Olympic officials from his first competition in the Paris, France, Inter-Allied Games of 1919 to his retirement on the eve of the 1932 Olympic Games.

11.
Chasing the Chill*

Despite the Frigid Temperature, Cunningham Burned Up the Track

The veteran track coach at Dartmouth College, Harry Hillman, had a couple of things he wanted to prove when he invited the great miler Glenn Cunningham up to Dartmouth in the winter of 1938. "Our old oversized wooden track at Dartmouth College is the fastest in the world, indoors or outside," Hillman, a three-time gold-medal winner from the 1904 Olympics in St. Louis, had been saying for years. Second, the crafty coach had been watching the 28-year-old Cunningham in all eight of his indoor race victories that winter. "He's never been sharper," observed Hillman correctly. "He's a cinch to break the world's mile record on our track."

It was news for the former University of Kansas star, winner of an Olympic silver medal, to set aside his Ph.D. studies at New York University and take the train to Hanover. Big-city journalists and photographers from New York City and Boston made the trip with Cunningham. All were apprehensive. Especially Cunningham.

He arrived on the afternoon of Thursday, March 3. The race was scheduled for eight o'clock that night. All day a bitter wind howled down from the hills, and the temperature hovered around 10 below zero—unseasonably cold, even for Hanover. Cunningham knew that the ancient, barnlike fieldhouse would be bitter cold. He checked the cavernous building, noted the futility of the bubbling hot radiators, and resigned himself to running that night in 40-degree chill.

Sports Heritage, 2 (Spring, 1988), 36-37.

Glenn Cunningham (left) ran to win, not to set records. He did both.

Getting properly warm for the race would be difficult. When Cunningham was eight years old, he had tried to rescue his brother from a schoolhouse fire in Elkhart, Kansas. The fire took his brother's life, and left Cunningham with legs so severely burned that it was thought he would never walk again. Walk again— and run—he did, but his legs were horribly disfigured. Cunningham remembers, "My legs were always so painful; there was little blood circulation in them." However, he would be, as always, up to the challenge. The fastest outdoor mile time was 4:06.4 by England's Sydney Wooderson, while Cunningham's 4:08.6 was the indoor record. All those who knew about these things predicted that the perfectly fit Cunningham and the giant $6^2/_3$-laps-to-the-mile, three-foot-high banked springy wooden track would combine to shatter both marks.

Racing with the Spirit

Thirty-five hundred folks packed Alumni Fieldhouse and Webster Hall to celebrate the 42nd Dartmouth Night, the Hanover program celebrating "the Dartmouth Spirit" with singing, dancing, alumni speakers, and messages from grads from all over the world. Interrupting these international messages "proving the transcendental power of the Dartmouth Spirit," Cunningham would race six undergraduate students, all of them given generous handicaps.

Cunningham arrived at the track at 7:15 p.m. during the 45-yard high hurdles and the mile relay race. All eyes turned to the powerfully built Kansas Olympian in his two warm-up suits, trying to prepare for the feature mile. The campus paper, *The Dartmouth,* described Cunningham as "dancing up and down, shrugging his shoulders, stretching his arms and legs"—all in an effort to fight off the cold and loosen his fire-damaged legs. Finally, two miles of jogging, twice his normal preparation, satisfied him. Coach Hillman anticipated almost everything. Four official Amateur Athletic Union (AAU) timers were provided, their stopwatches carefully checked and accurately synchronized. The track was measured twice, with an inside border added to make it official. Professors L.F. Murch and Gordon S. Hull of the Dartmouth faculty and Charles A. Proctor also held watches. The whole scenario was supervised by 40-year-veteran referee Dr. John W. Bowler, while the equally famous J. Frank Facey personally handicapped the six youngsters, putting all of them far enough ahead of Cunningham to "bring out the competitive fight in the star."

Cunningham was asked to start six inches behind the starting line, just to be sure. The no-smoking rule was rigidly enforced, with one exception; Coach Hillman puffed nervously on cigarettes throughout the evening. Finally, Cunningham responded to starter Elliot Noyes's pistol.

The springy boards placed over a spongy cinder track plus the three-foot-high banked track made running an even greater joy for Cunningham. The initial quarter mile in 58.5 seconds was astonishingly easy. "Like mechanical rabbits," the Dartmouth youngsters ahead of him fell to Cunningham one by one. But he thought the time too fast, and slowed to 64 seconds for the next interval, a 2:02.5 half-mile. Running with tremendous power, even more than he himself realized that evening, Cunningham flew the next quarter mile in 61.7 (3:04.2 at three-quarters.) He was running with astonishing power, without strain, "hardly human" as one eyewitness journalist said—"an automaton geared to speed." Too bad, as Cunningham said later, that the second quarter was so slow.

The Fastest Mile

Cunningham ignored the exhausted youngsters running out of his way in lane two and unleashed his famous last-lap "kick," carrying him through the last 440 yards in a bit over one minute (60.2 seconds). Not even out of breath following a postrace jog, Cunningham grinned at the time: four minutes four and four-tenths seconds, the fastest mile ever run by anyone, anywhere. Curiously, this fastest mile yet was not considered a world's record. Since it had been run indoors, on an odd-size track, with

"rabbits," it was not eligible for world-record status. No matter—
it was still "the fastest mile run by a human being," and proved
Hillman's points. Moreover, it set up the inevitable four-minute
mile.

Accolades poured in from all over the nation and the European continent at Cunningham's New Hampshire feat. The great
analyst from the *New York Herald,* Jesse Abramson, prophetically stood firm that "Cunningham's record stamps the four-minute
mile as a possibility." Cunningham himself said, "I never set out
to break records; I always ran to win, but Mr. Hillman kept after
me all winter to come up to Hanover, and I'm glad I did."

12.
A Centennial Retrospective—
The 1889 Boston Conference
on Physical Training*

Two thousand people crowded Huntington Hall at MIT on post-Thanksgiving day Friday and filled the auditorium again on Saturday. It was the first time that the new profession of physical education received national attention.

The American Alliance for Health, Physical Education, Recreation and Dance (AAHPERD) was born in 1885 (at that time called the Association for the Advancement of Physical Education), four years before the Boston Conference in the Interest of Physical Training (Barrows, 1889). The new association was hardly noticed by the academic community, given little consideration by the educational leadership of city public schools or university scholars, and nearly ignored by newspaper and journal writers. Not so with the 1889 Boston Conference of 100 years ago, held November 29-30, 1889. A score of eastern newspapers and a dozen scientific and medical journals published accounts of the speeches delivered at the Massachusetts Institute of Technology (MIT) by 16 medical doctors; one general of the Army; one English earl; two Barons; one doctor of law; one Ph.D., and a dozen male and female gymnastic and sporting specialists. Two thousand people crowded Huntington Hall on the post-Thanksgiving Day Friday and filled the auditorium again on Saturday. It was the first time that the new profession of physical education received national attention.

*Journal of Physical Education, Recreation and Dance, 60 (November/December 1989), 30-33.

The Female Triumvirate

Three women subsidized, organized, and recorded this historic conference. Mary Porter Tileston Hemenway (1820-1894) was a public-spirited philanthropist and, as "the wealthiest woman in Boston," devoted much of her life to girls' education: the construction of the Harvard University Hemenway Gymnasium; the creation of the Boston Normal School of [Swedish] Gymnastics (BNSG) for women; the introduction of Swedish gymnastics into the Boston Public Schools; and the co-organization of the Boston Conference (Tileston, 1927; Dunton, 1894; Spears, 1971 and 1974). Her assistant, and for many years the director of the BNSG, Amy Morris Homans (1848-1933), helped significantly in the selection of speakers for the 1889 conference (Spears, 1986; Skarstrom, 1941). The third person, Isabel Chapin Barrows (1845-1913), was a well-educated liberal social worker, feminist, and reformer—the first American woman to study both undergraduate and graduate medicine in New York City, Leipzig, and Vienna ("Her Devotion to Ideals," *Outlook,* 1913). These three—Hemenway, Homans, and Barrows—occupied center stage in the conference, the first effort to clarify the various physical training and physical education ideologies in the land (Leonard & Affleck, 1947).

A Brief Look at Several "Systems"

German gymnastics were imported into Northampton, Cambridge, and Boston, Massachusetts by disciples of Friedrich Ludwig Jahn, the founder of popular and nationalistic gymnastics. Their eclectic German programs professed mind-body harmony and were recommended year-round on outdoor plazas and indoor gymnasia. Girls were encouraged to engage in appropriate games, exercise, and dance, while the boys participated in running, jumping, wrestling, crosscountry hiking, tactics, and military marching. Serious work was done on horizontal bars, wooden bucks, and horses. Ladder- and rope-climbing and standing-in-place exercise routines, with and without heavy dumbbells, also challenged students. Discussions were held to improve morals, morale, and the competitive spirit. Jokes, bantering, and storytelling were sometimes used to raise spirits and as diversions from vaulting, climbing, throwing, pulling, lifting, jumping, and running routines. Rhythmic free exercise with music was used in coeducational classes. It was vigorous hard work with effective psychological camouflage.

The legendary Per Henrik Ling, a Swede, created an exercise experience allegedly different from the emotional and experiential German method. He and his followers claimed the exercises were soothing, medically therapeutic, educational, and accessible to both sexes and all ages. Above all else, Ling's "theory ... has survived the scrutiny of scientists all over the world" (Posse, 1894, p. v). Exercises were to be pleasing and aesthetic; movements emphasized physiological soundness rather than muscularity. Simplicity, beauty, and emphasis on the psychological domain were central to the system. Freestanding rational movements dominated rather than unnatural apparatus "circus tricks." Scientific use of stall-bars, poles, vertical and inclined ropes, and vaulting boxes were encouraged. A Swedish gymnastic movement must always emphasize the integral unity and harmony of mind-body, it was said, and such movements must be "defined as to space, time, force, and purpose" (Posse, 1894, p. 36).

The verdant British Isles had for centuries spawned an incredible variety of outdoor children's games. In the English public schools of the late eighteenth century and through the next century, highly competitive athletic games for boys became a tradition and were carried to Harvard, Yale, and Princeton before and after the American Civil War. Such manifestations of British "muscular Christianity" were chauvinistic, rugged, all-male, and immensely popular in America's version of the Victorian Era. Cricket, rugby, crew, and track and field found their way into nearly every American university, but on the eve of the 1889 conference there was little room for the athletically-inclined young woman.

The cacophony of voices, domestic and European, was impressive in the penultimate decade of the nineteenth century. German and Swedish systems competed with Danish physical education and French and Slovak approaches, while England and Scotland found it awkward to reconcile traditional competitive games with new physical training imports from the continent. In the United States, pluralism reigned supreme, and Americans could pick and choose one or more hybrid "systems" offered by Catharine Beecher, Dio Lewis, the Hitchcock and Sargent efforts at scientific eclecticism, and dozens of variations offered at ethnic societies, teacher's colleges, private universities, women's "finishing" schools, academies, and teacher training institutions. Nothing stood out except, of course, the growing national preoccupation with intercollegiate spectator sports—for men. The pot was boiling and advocate voices for a single "American system" were heard. Not nearly so ambitious, the formidable team of Hemenway and Homans felt strongly that the Swedish, or Ling, system of physical culture was best for the boys and girls in the Boston Public Schools. But they were sufficiently visionary to recognize the merits of other approaches and invited an impressive number of male and female lecturers to come to Boston-Cambridge and tell their story.

Day One of the Boston Conference

November 29, 1889. University presidents Charles Eliot (Harvard), A. W. Small (Colby), Helen Shafer (Wellesley), and General Francis A. Walker (MIT), plus 2,000 delegates, listened attentively as William T. Harris, United States Commissioner of Education, opened and presided over the conference. The perceptive Isabel Barrows wrote that:

> The object of the Conference is to place before educators different systems of gymnastics and to secure discussions of the same, with a view to clearly ascertaining the needs of schools, and determining how they may best be met. (1889)

Harris opened the meeting with the comment that the platonic mind-body duality "is a myth," that the union of intelligence and physical fitness is not coincidental, and that this historic conference was convened to discuss "the new physical education" (Barrows, 1889, p. 3). The mood was set when Emil Gröner led 20 children in a German gymnastics routine. This was followed by an American version of dumbbell exercises by YMCA children led by H. L. Chadwick, who reminded the audience that they were a nation of borrowers, "including this routine."

Edward Mussey Hartwell's keynote speech was long and erudite—an extraordinary presentation which sounds well today, 100 years after delivery. Hartwell's paper supported all systems of gymnastics and all outdoor competitive athletics, provided they were based on science and morality (Barrows, 1889). Brief expositions by H. Metzner (his paper "German Gymnastics" was read by Carl Eberhard) and Dr. John P. Reynolds supported the Ling system. The famous speech by Nils Posse underscored that same theme. He praised the Ling system as faultless, based on the "laws of nature" and needing no musical accompaniment because the methodology "is rational, since it seeks a reason for everything that it uses or adopts: it makes theory and practice harmonize" (Barrows, 1889, pp. 38, 42-51).

The tempo switched with The Right Honorable Earl of Meath, who seemed less than enthusiastic in informing the audience that London schools had recently adopted the Swedish system. "We have done so," he admitted, "only because it is so economical and taxpayers are pleased with this." Medical doctors Jay W. Seaver of Yale University and William G. Anderson, then at the Brooklyn School of Physical Training, found difficulty in pushing any single system, both pointing out that Americans will play competitive games "on any available lot" and that no European system is satisfactory to Americans for "we have ideas of our own." Anderson ended with a prediction that the nation would watch Hemenway's persistent efforts to introduce the Swedish system into the Boston schools. "I cannot say just now which system is best, but when we find out, we will adopt it. Variety is essential; we borrow and modify ideas from other systems." That first day ended with Amherst College's Edward Hitchcock, who was both funny and revealing. "I do not know what to say about children, except that we have ten of them at home" (Barrows, 1889, pp. 53-56). Americans chafe at accepting systems untouched, he said, and the present domestic status of mixing competitive athletics with gymnastics "is best." His proposition that scientifically trained physical educators can be found only if they are well-paid was well-understood by the audience.

Day Two of the Boston Conference

November 30, 1889. Dudley Sargent began promptly at 10:00 a.m., and his blockbuster panegyric was mostly about himself, his Harvard University fitness program, and his "wonderful Summer School for teachers." When finally finished with this heavy advertisement, he ventured that the best of Europe's systems plus America's already strong "athletic sports" would be more than satisfactory for the nation (Barrows, 1889, pp. 62-67). Medical doctor Walter Channing followed and emphasized the individuality of every single child's physical needs. Ray Green Huling of New Bedford revived the ancient Greek equilateral concept of mind, body, and spirit and then gave way to L. V. Ingraham, who underscored that old Hellenic idea and added that "manual training" should be included in the school curriculum (Barrows, 1889, pp. 65-66).

Chairman Harris excused himself and was replaced by host president Francis Amasa Walker, one of the era's great educators (Munro, 1923). He was unable to refrain from commenting that every school in the land should have a program of "school gymnastics for our boys and girls." Historians of this 1889 convention have largely ignored the address by C. W. Emerson, president of the Monroe College of Oratory in Boston—which is unfortunate, because it was a good one. Entitled "Laws to be Followed in Teaching Physical Culture," Emerson's measured and scholarly look at the Grecian middle way urged the audience to avoid mindlessly adopting a single system. "The moment that you establish any system by law, all progress in that system stops then and there; there is no more growth—except towards China" (Barrows, 1889, p. 88).

Baron Pierre de Coubertin was in Boston during this 1889 Physical Training Congress. The future founder of the modern Olympic Games was the French government's 26-year-old education representative to the Chicago's World Fair. He accepted an invitation to speak and as an unashamed Anglophile was unequivocal in praising English "muscular Christianity" and its ubiquitous British Isles competitive athletic system for boys and men. By implication, he was critical of American ambivalence and their "battlefield of systems" (Barrows, 1889, pp. 112-115).

The afternoon and the convention rapidly closed with three mini presentations praising Mary Hemenway. S. S. Curry, Hobart Moore, and J. G. Blake praised both that "noble lady" as well as the "genius of Ling" and his system. A committee of eight men and three women was charged with the immediate task of physically educating the teachers and children of Boston. Luther Gulick, M.D. and physical director at Springfield College, stepped forward and publicly thanked Hemenway and Amy Homans adding that "the whole cause of physical education in America has received a great impetus from this meeting" (Barrows, 1889, p. 132). It was over.

Recapitulation and Personal Assessment

In a restricted reading of the Barrows Report, it is difficult to agree with Betty Spears' assertion made at the 1981 AAHPERD convention "that the conference was not planned to further the general interest in physical training, but to advance Mary Hemenway's specific interest in having Swedish gymnastics adopted by the Boston public schools (Spears, 1981). Of course, Spears may be right, for she has done extensive research on the "dynamic duo" of Hemenway and Homans. However, careful study of the 34 speakers during the two days of oratory shows no visible evidence that the two organizers had "loaded" the meeting with Ling disciples. Barrows was a professional editor and showed only disinterested skill rather than bias in her collation. In an 1890 letter written from his Boston office as editor of the *Journal of Education* and the *American Teacher*, A. E. Winship thanked Hemenway for "the work [she had] done for humanity by the generous and intelligent provision made for the physical training of manhood and womanhood tomorrow through the boys and girls of today" (Winship, 1890, p. 37). Barrows went on to edit the "First Mohonk Conference on 'The Negro Question'" and to do similar professional and humanitarian projects until her passing in 1913. Amy Morris Homans became the director of the BNSG and remained in that role until 1918. All three had been major players in the Boston conference of 1889, a gathering that resolved nothing and yet captured the attention of most major Eastern newspapers and several influential journals, raising the level of understanding among many educators and helping to launch the fledgling profession of physical education. It brought together in one place almost all the nation's leaders where the unspoken word of agreement among the major players was to disagree. No higher compliment could be directed at any national congress, then, 100 years ago, or now.

REFERENCES

Barrows, I. C., *Physical Training. A Full Rreport of the Papers and Discussions on the Conference Held in Boston in November 1889.* Boston: George H. Ellis Press, 1889.

Dunton, L. (ed.), *Memorial Services in Honor of Mrs. Mary Hemenway by the Boston Public School Teachers.* Boston: George H. Ellis Press, 1894.

"Her Devotion to Ideals and to Humanity was Evident," *The Outlook, 15 (November 8, 1913),* 513.

Leonard, F. E., & Affleck, G. B., *Guide to the History of Physical Education.* Philadelphia: Lea and Febiger, 1947.

Munro, J. P., *A Life of Francis Amasa Walker.* New York: Henry Holt and Co, 1923.

Posse, N., *The Special Kinesiology of Educational Gymnastics.* Boston: Lostrop, Lee and Shepard Co., 1894.

Skarstrom, W. (1941, October). "Life and Work of Amy Morris Homans," *Research Quarterly, 12* (October 1941, Supplement), 616-627.

Spears, B., " A Glimpse of the Life of Mary Hemenway," *Journal of Health, Physical Education & Recreation*, 42 *(March 1971)*, 93-94.

Spears, B., "The Philanthropist and the Physical Educator," *The New England Quarterly*, 47 *(December 1974)*, 594-602.

Spears, B., *"The 1889 Cconference in the Interest of Physical Training: Whose interest?"* Paper presented at the AAHPERD convention, 1981.

Spears, B., *Leading the Way. Amy Morris Homans and the Beginnings of Professional Education for Women.* New York: Greenwood Press, 1986.

Tileston, M. W., *A Memorial of the Life and Benefaction of Mary Hemenway.* Boston: printed privately, 1927.

Winship, A. E. to Mary Hemenway, October 13, 1890, *Scrapbook Boston Normal School of Gymnastics #1*, 37.

13.
Whirr, Whizz, Hum:
Mile-a-Minute Murphy Breaks the Record*

In the last year of the 19th century, when professional cycling was second only to baseball in public popularity, Charles M. Murphy's foolhardy and nearly unbelievable feat of bicycling 63 miles an hour was important enough to make page one on the full sports page spread in almost every major newspaper in America. Eyebrows were raised in London and Paris, and instantly the Brooklyn native was labeled the great "Mile-A-Minute Murphy."

For seven years it had been the dream of this professional sprint cyclist to achieve the impossible. On June 21, 1899, the 154-pound, 29-year-old member of the King's County Wheelmen was given permission to follow, very closely, a Long Island train specially equipped with a five-foot-long extension hood at the rear of the caboose. For a full two miles, expert carpenters laid down perfectly-fitting hardwood planks between the tracks. A level and lonely spot in Maywood, Long Island, some 35 miles from New York City's Times Square, was chosen for the "daredevil stunt." Samuel Booth, the company's most experienced engineer, was ordered by Railroad Special Agent Hal Fullerton to get the train's speed to just under 60 miles per hour, and Murphy's job was to stay tight within the "hooded vestibule."

Murphy was confident. Twice-a-day hard training for weeks had prepared him to pedal so fast that "the human eye was unable to follow the movement." Psychologically Murphy was ready and

* Bicycle USA, 26 (June 1990), 18-19

was heard to say, "I have not the slightest fear, and if I'm going to die today, I'm going to die."

No, Murphy didn't die, nor did he reach the cherished goal of sprint racing 60 miles an hour. Instead, the horde of expert timers caught him in exactly a click of the watch under 65 seconds for the accurately measured mile of smooth boards. It had been tough, and as he ran out of smooth boards he bellowed, "For God's sake, make the track longer or I'll be killed." They did just that and scheduled another run at the record in nine days, same time, same place. This first great effort had been a failure, but Murphy told his wife and two young children that he was

determined to ride a bike faster than anyone else had—to reach 60 miles an hour, a mile in a minute on pure muscle power and total body-mind control.

Late on the afternoon of June 30, at a flat stretch of railroad bed between Maywood and Patchogue, halfway up Long Island, Charlie Murphy warmed up for a second attempt at the ultimate sprint cycle goal. Blond and blue-eyed, rock-hard muscled from years of training, Murphy approved of the longer 2 3/8-mile special track. Five planks, each 10 inches wide and carefully planed, were laid together along the length of the course. The joiner work was perfect and fitted so neatly without tongue and groove that "a billiard table is no smoother or more mathematically level than the track over which Murphy rode." In the hands of Sam Booth old Engine Number 74 moved out, pulling one car and equipped with the ingenious hood that protected Murphy from the deadly rush of air and of course significantly reduced the air resistance.

Murphy wore blue woolen tights and a thin, light blue jersey with long sleeves. The gathering crowd saw that he was deadly serious, his eyes focused straight ahead on his awesome challenge.

Head down, completely enclosed, Murphy was intent on following orders and keeping only inches away from his face a long strip of unpainted white pine, five inches wide, attached eye level to the platform of the caboose. Under no circumstances must he fall away from that piece of pine or he might be blown away to his death like a chip in a hurricane. The train gathered speed rapidly, for there was less than 2 1/2 miles of smooth wooden track for Murphy to do his thing. Mr. James Edward Sullivan and his team of expert timers from the Amateur Athletic Union appeared anxious, even grim, at the back of the train, watches cocked for the red and green flag at the start of the mile. "Murphy was pedaling frantically but seemed to have no trouble in following the terrific pace," and they flashed by the quarter-mile black line painted on the track in 15 seconds flat.

Murphy, teeth showing, stuck within inches of the pine board, his years of disciplined training focused on his bike and the flashing pedals. All seemed chaos to those at the back of the train. A rush, a roar, and as one eyewitness journalist wrote the next day: "He rode like a demon, his legs moving like piston rods, so fast they appeared a blur, and above all, everything was whirr, whizz, and hum of rushing air." The half-mile black line flashed by in 29 2/5 seconds. Murphy appeared to be in trouble. A whirlwind of dust and grit struck his face, now drawn up in agony as his bike fell back inch-by-inch, the train gradually drawing away from him. Another two-foot loss and he would be blown to kingdom come. Horrified observers thought it was all over as the train exceeded 60 miles an hour and a grimace of effort clouded Murphy's face. He was not to be left behind, despite a front wheel that wobbled from edge to edge of the middle boards directly beneath him. His head rolled from side to side and he rode unsteadily in

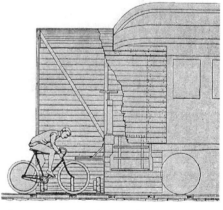

A cutaway view shows details of the windshield used during Murphy's historic ride.

his superhuman effort to regain the lost ground. His front wheel touched the rubber pad on the back of the train as the collective stop watches read 44 seconds flat for the three-quarters of a mile, the third portion done in an incredible 14 $^1/_5$ seconds.

Once again the train began to inch away from the flying Murphy, and six times he refused to let it go. "I can't see a thing," he screamed when one of the men on the rear platform leaned over and asked him how he was. His feet whirled at nearly four revolutions per second, fast enough to make up the five feet he had lost, and the bike passed over the black finish line as the train roared by the double-colored flag. Only a short stretch of wooden track remained as Murphy and his bike were violently yanked to safety inside the train by Hal Fullerton and the strong-armed railroad man J. H. Cummings, both of whom had been lying on their stomachs waiting to catch Murphy. Dazed and in shock, Murphy lay on the floor mumbling incoherently, "The wooden track came flying apart. The wooden track came up and hit me in the face." Above him, Sullivan and his timers jubilantly agreed that Murphy's mile was covered in 57 $^4/_5$ seconds, far and away a world's record. By the time the train had slowed, the new champion had recovered and was already basking in his new title, "Mile-A-Minute Murphy."

Sullivan declared, "That was the most horrible ride I've ever taken; my hair has turned gray." Murphy left the train and kissed his wife and two children. When asked if he would ever again undertake such a hazardous ride, he replied hesitantly, "It was awful, awful, awful, ... but if the money was right, I'd do it." It never was, but no matter; Charles M. Murphy had gained a measure of immortality.

14.
Professor William Milligan Sloane: Father of the United States Olympic Committee*

James Renwick Willson Sloane was pastor of a Scottish Presbyterian church in the village of Pittsburg, Ohio, and on November 12, 1850, in nearby Richmond, a son, William Milligan, came into the world. His mother was Margaret Anna Wylie and his Scottish grandfather, William Sloane, emigrated to America in 1820 where he preached to scattered congregations in Ohio and Illinois. Through his mother, William Milligan was a descendant of the distinguished literary, liberal Trumbull family of Revolutionary War era, and further back, from someone who went to America on the "Mayflower."[1]

When William was five years old, his father, who had completed tenures as president of Richmond, Ohio and Geneva, Pennsylvania colleges as well as professor of systematic theology at the Allegheny Theological Seminary, moved to New York City. The senior Sloane was a powerful educational and psychical influence, and the younger Sloane's first published work in 1888 was on *The Life and Work of James Renwick Willson Sloane*. The son was educated under his father's direction at New York City's Martha Washington Collegiate Institute, while his father, at the same time, was preaching in the city's Third Reformed Presbyterian Church. "I was a New York [City] boy," William Milligan told a San Francisco journalist in 1917.[2] The precocious youngster entered Columbia University, graduated at age eighteen with a Bachelor of Arts degree in Liberal Arts and entered the teach-

*Beckers, Edgar and Andreas Hub (eds). Umbruch und Kontinuität im Sportreflexion im Umfeld der Sportgeschichte, Festschrift für Horst Überhorst (1991), 230-242.

ing profession as instructor of Latin and Greek languages back in Pittsburgh, Ohio at the Newell Graduate Institute. After four years, in 1872, he went to Germany for graduate studies at Berlin and Leipzig universities and in 1876 received the Ph.D., his culminating dissertation in Oriental Studies titled "Arabic Poetry Before the Time of Mahomet." While in Berlin, he was for a time (1873-1875) attached to the American legation as private secretary and research assistant to George Bancroft, the American minister at Berlin and his country's most prestigious historian. During the writing of Bancroft's tenth volume of his *History of the United States,* the young Sloane was mastering the German and French languages and carefully learning the craft of historian.

In 1876, Sloane accepted a position at Princeton University, where he taught metaphysics, Latin, Hebrew, Arabic, and then in 1883, as part of the university restructuring, he accepted the chair of full professor of the philosophy of history. Dr. Sloane was tall, broad-shouldered, "the full measure of a man" and only thirty-three years of age. His scholarly career was in the ascendancy and would remain so for the next forty years.

Interestingly, up to this point there seems to be no evidence of interest in amateur and college sport, either as a spectator or participant. Sloane, the "Man with a Mission,"[3] as this researcher called him in 1977, became interested in the extraordinary growth of American intercollegiate athletics during the 1880s. He served on his university's athletic advisory committee in 1881; chaired that committee in 1884 during the struggle between the students and faculty for control of intercollegiate athletics and served an unhappy year during "the tumultuous football season of 1889."[4]

Sloane's scholar-athlete hero was his teacher, George Bancroft (1800-1891), "our most philosophic historian, a man who exercised two hours a day, rain or shine."[5] Just as the young Sloane began to achieve academic recognition (he had been since 1885, editor of the prestigious *New Princeton Review*), he received a visitor onto his campus, a twenty-six year old French aristocrat, Baron Pierre de Coubertin (1863-1937). In a whirlwind visit of twenty-five North American universities during the fall of 1889, this future *renovateur* of the modern Olympic Games found in Sloane a stimulating colleague and "undoubtedly the most important acquaintance made by Coubertin during his 1889 journey."[5] They talked politics, current events, architecture, professorial salaries, Anglo-Saxon characteristics, and the special ambiance that was Princeton. It was all so mesmerizing, the Frenchman remembered, "the buildings, the night air, the whole atmosphere."[7] Sloane's seven-year-old son interrupted an animated conversation about Plato and Alcibiades with the remark that the Yale football captain was his cousin.[8] Coubertin returned to Paris determined to increase the decibels of sporting interest in his country. He had seen so much in Britain and America! Apathy and tradition were against Coubertin, and his athletic-minded colleagues and the years 1890 and 1891 were difficult organizational years, but, in part, because of Dr. Sloane's efforts, rowing and football competitions did take place in 1892 between the French and the Americans and the English.[9] Coubertin's runaway enthusiasm resulted in a Sorbonne University meeting on November 25, 1892, to discuss athletic amateurism and the possibility of reviving the ancient Olympic Games. The meeting was a disaster and the young Baron was forced to "set his tune in a lower key," to work much harder than ever before, to write, to visit influential friends, and to plan for another Sorbonne meeting in eighteen months and for exactly the same purpose.

Coubertin needed help in his enterprise but received none from the athletic giants, the British Amateur Athletic Association (AAA) and the American Amateur Athletic Union (AAU). He returned to North America in the fall of 1893, seeking Sloane's help in arousing even a little interest in the Olympic Games idea. He took trains to Chicago, California, Texas, up to New England, and down to Princeton, New Jersey for a serious talk with W. M. Sloane, "my counsel and confidant in all this business."[10] Sloane had just published *The French War and the Revolution* and had done so with such sensitivity that historian Hippolyte Tame was of the opinion that "Sloane knows France better than any other foreigner."[11] Three weeks with Sloane and Coubertin felt strong enough to meet with several representatives of Harvard, Yale, Princeton, and Columbia universities on November 27, 1893. Nearly forty years later, Coubertin remembered the conversation "tres chaleureuse, intérêt sincère, mais arriè-repensée évidente d'un insuccès certain." The 'secret war' between the universities and the AAU, he said, made meaningful conversation about a European revival of the Olympic Games impossible among these gentlemen.[12] The amiable Sloane admitted that these "like-minded friends" from the world of American intercollegiate athletics were incapable of grasping "the conception of international sport on a broad basis."[13] One of those present was Columbia's Gustavus Towne Kirby (1874-1956) who remembered sixty years later telling Baron de Coubertin that "James Edward Sullivan is your man in the United States capable of organizing an Olympic committee."[14] For the first time Coubertin shared his hope for a second Sorbonne Congress in June of the following year, and the AAU pledged to send a delegate, not Sullivan, but the distinguished Professor of History from Princeton University, William Milligan Sloane.[15]

Every eye-witness account of the June 1894 Sorbonne Congress is clear about Sloane's imposing presence, his organizational skill, and his full and enthusiastic support of the younger Coubertin's efforts to organize an Olympic Games for the spring of 1896. "A few days after the Congress," wrote Coubertin, "Sloane, E. Callot, and myself joined Mr. Bikelas for a meeting in the small apartment he kept in the Rue de Babylone, in Paris. It was there that the edifice of the IOC was consolidated."[16] Somehow Sloane could juggle his formidable teaching and research role at the university with an abiding interest in athletics and now this new emerging entity, the Games of the First Olympiad scheduled for Easter Sunday of 1896. As a charter member of Coubertin's handpicked International Olympic Committee (IOC),[17] Sloane was expected in Athens and wished to be there, but he was unable to make the long voyage. His new four-volume work, his most important book, *Life of Napoleon Bonaparte,*[18] was nearly finished and the new Olympic Games, dear to his heart, were out of the question. Sloane was the acknowledged architect of the small American team that was so very visible at these first games and granted an interview to a *New York Times* journalist on March 21, 1896:

> These games will be small, but a good beginning. I am only interested in sports from a moral view and I am glad that there is an American team going over.[19]

The "Father of American Amateur Sport," William B. Curtis, called Sloane's unrelenting efforts on behalf of these first-time Olympic Games "heroic work."[20] Coubertin praised his "dear friend Sloane" for assisting him, and Sorbonne Congress participant M. Georges Bourdon lauded Sloane as "Coubertin's friend from the beginning."[21] Modern scholars Mandell, MacAloon, and Allison outlined the steady hand of the Princeton University historian.[22] Probably working overtime, Sloane also completed negotiations for his new position at Columbia University as Seth Low Professor of history—a part of "President Low's million dollar gift to the library."[23] Sloane wrote Coubertin that he missed Princeton but found Columbia attractive, especially the lighter teaching responsibility. He congratulated him on his new book, *L'Évolution Français Sous la Troisième République,* stating: "it has made a first rate impression and has added greatly to your reputation in this country."[24] The Baron de Coubertin returned the compliment and publically acclaimed Dr. Sloane's Napoleon biography a unique and "beautiful work."[25] Sloane closed out the century with a revealing essay titled, "How to Bring Out the Ethical Value of History," in which he stated that "ethical values" as well as mere facts must be the dual focus of historians.[26]

Sloane, along with Coubertin, had little patience with the inept Paris Olympic Organizing Committee. "I can give neither the universities nor the AAU any authentic information" about the 1900 Olympic Games, he wrote Coubertin.[27] Following these less than perfect games, Coubertin contemplated resignation as IOC president and then turning over leadership to Professor Sloane, who represented not only the IOC but the host Olympic Games nation for 1904. The Baron remembered that Sloane refused the generous offer with the comment that "Coubertin alone could lead the IOC and in so doing perpetuate the Olympic movement."[28] It was now time for Sloane to threaten resignation from the IOC if negotiations between Coubertin, the AAU, and the proposed Olympic Games site did not improve in clarity and efficiency. William Rainey Harper, President of the University of Chicago and key person in a 1904 Olympic Games in that city, refused to negotiate through Sloane and to Coubertin in Paris. "Now, either I have the place of American member or I resign," wrote Sloane to Coubertin on April 22, 1901.[29] He didn't stay angry long as he grew more involved with the American Historical Association (AHA) and in publishing major essays on the history of American politics, on the one hundredth anniversary of the Louisiana Purchase, on French politics, biographical sketches, and two major works: *The French Revolution and Religious Reform* and *The French War and the Revolution.* By 1905, the fifty-five year old Sloane was approaching the height of his academic powers[30] and, at the same time, seeing with ever-increasing clarity that the James Sullivan-dominated AAU and Coubertin's IOC were on different levels of intellect, commitment, and priority.

The mayor of New York City, George B. McClellan, a former Sloane student, called his teacher "one of the most brilliant intellects and the greatest teachers I have ever had the honor to come in contact with."[31] At the same time, during the end of the century's first decade, Sloane was hard at work trying to mend fences as a result of serious acrimony between the American AAU and the British AAA at the Shepherd's Bush Olympic Games of 1908. While admitting that James Sullivan was an extraordinary athletic administrator, Sloane was frank with his IOC president Coubertin and indirectly blamed his fellow countryman for much of the bitterness between athletes and officials at the Games of the Fourth Olympiad. Sullivan is a ghetto-poor Irish-American, wrote Sloane, and "his great faults are those of his birth and breeding, but he is unfortunately a representative man and holds the organized athletes of the clubs in the hollow of his hand."[32] Sullivan and Sloane were at vastly different levels, and the Baron seemed wedged between them but leaning toward Sloane. Only two years earlier Sullivan had written the IOC president:

> Professor Sloane is a lovely gentleman; I have met him once. He knows nothing about athletics ... I doubt if he ever attended an important athletic meeting in America. Certainly he is unknown in the athletic legislative halls of this country....[33]

Both Sloane and Sullivan had exaggerated one another's inadequacies. Coubertin and Sloane were socially, culturally, and intellectually compatible, while the ultimate athletic pragmatist, Sullivan, was much more comfortable *in* the office and occupying the referee-managerial catbird seat.

In a quite remarkable balancing act between 1910 and 1917, Sloane reached both the height of his intellectual powers and the apex of his career as the senior and most respected American member of the IOC. Sloane overcame "rumored animosity between himself and the AAU" and in late 1910 "appointed the American Olympic Committee," with F. B. Pratt, Julian W. Curtis, and Sullivan as chief officers. "Sullivan is rapidly becoming a gentleman," wrote Sloane, in a lefthanded compliment of the AAU czar.[34]

Sloane was elected president of the American Historical Association (AHA) in 1911, and until 1917, when his country went to war, he was in constant demand as an expert commentator on France, Germany, and the always volatile "Balkan Problem." His specialized European knowledge was supplemented by a frequently expressed philosophy of history, and he was uncommonly busy during these years, writing and speaking on both these subjects. In addition, Sloane was a capitalist to the core and a life-time defender of the solid power of America's Anglo-Saxon heritage. "The princes of America are her merchants," he said in a 1911 speech in Buffalo, and art, letters, science, family, church, universities, and "all that make for idealism" come from private munificence. "To be mercantile and commercial is not to be sordid," ended the acknowledged brilliant orator.[35]

On European politics he had much to say, defending alleged Turkish aggression, attacking "the growing strength of the Greek church," detailing university life in Germany, warning America against "meddling in the European war," pointing out similarities between the German and American political party systems, and voicing approval of "Wilson Neutrality."[36] The historian turned political scientist was unable to refrain from extremely well-publicized public utterances on "the end of American aristocracy"; the superiority of "efficient democracy over socialism"; on "the vital spirit of France"; a denial that he was "pro German" and on "German propaganda plots revealed."[37] Some said that Sloane's finest oral presentation was a 7000 word talk on "The Substance and Vision of History," in which he talked on the necessary art and science of historical inquiry and the public demand for "truth and the truth told entertainingly."[38]

W. M. Sloane was utterly devoted to the Coubertin ideology called "Olympism" and was captivated by the Frenchman himself. Sloane's letters are a testimony not only to the reality of athletic power politics in America and Europe but also a warm familial look at the small Coubertin circle and the intimacy of his own household. The historian in Sloane combined with the athletic idealist in an essay "The Olympic Idea" in which he described the best of sport as a "medium of international conciliation" and "a contest in magnanimity."[39] In a kind of spiritual symbiosis, Sloane's letters frequently mentioned family members, their illnesses and successes; concern for a litany of commiserations for persistent, unsettling crises in the Coubertin household. "I cannot get used to the gentle melancholy of your letters.... Count your mercies, dear boy, as [well as] your troubles," he wrote the Baron.[40] In a 1911 letter, Sloane assured Coubertin not to fear Sullivan and Kirby; "both feed from my hand." The letter ended: "We are so distressed that your dear wife is not entirely strong."[41] There is much more of this: "My dear, dear Pierre"[42] on "Renee's illness and operation;"[43] "your devoted friend, Will."[44] And a 1916 letter ended 'Tender love from both of us to Marie and Alouette and warmest regard to Mme. Rothan ... your true friend, Will."[45]

Much more business-like were Sloane's correspondences and meetings with American and European sport and Olympic leaders. Between 1900 and 1920, Sloane met with Gustavus Town Kirby, A. S. Mills, William B. Curtis, Caspar W. Whitney, Evert Jansen Wendell, Judge Bartow Weeks, Everett C. Brown, Colonel Robert Thompson, Joseph B. Maccabe, Julian C. Curtiss, Rodman Wanamaker, Allison Armour, Charles Sherrill, William May Garland, and many other Americans. The list of European sporting figures known to Sloane is even longer. His frequent European intellectual- academic trips to Europe were always enriched with Olympic contacts. In March of 1913, his long tenure over as distinguished lecturer on European history at the University of Berlin, Sloane went on to the Olympic Congress in Lausanne, with praises ringing in his ears from the German Kaiser, from his Berlin graduate students, and, always, from his friend Coubertin.[46] He returned home to the accolades of media, fellow scholars, and wrote a letter to his friend, the President of the United States, Woodrow Wilson, suggesting that Mrs. Wilson and Mrs. Sloane "take both lunch and dinner with us Wednesday and go to the play at night."[47] Dr. Sloane was, in this year 1916, a well-known respected intellectual, the spinal cord support of the American Olympic movement and a tortured isolationist who saw his nation marching inexorably into the nightmare of World War I.

By 1917, Professor Sloane had been selected a Chevalier of the Legion of Honor and had completed terms as president of the American Academy of Arts and Letters and president of the American Historical Association.[48] Two years later, as senior "Chancellor" of the Academy, Sloane spoke at the James Russell Lowell Centenary Celebration and repeated a personal theme of forty years, that the English language and Anglo-Saxon nations form the crucial backbone of Western civilization and won the recent world war. The agony of that same war spilled over into family illness in both the Coubertin and Sloane families, and letters were exchanged between the two friends during the years 1918 and 1919. 'We grieve deeply to hear of Marie's illness" and he talked of his own son Frank's "long, long nervous breakdown." Sloane went on at length about his athletic homework: letters to Judge Weeks, essays to be written alerting the world to plans for a post-war Olympic Games in 1920, and "... by the way, please do not address me as president of the American Olympic Association. Colonel Thompson is still that; I am merely senior member of the IOC."[50]

Sloane worked hard, not for a 1920 New York City Olympic Games as was proposed, but for a celebration in the unlikely and crushed Belgian city of Antwerp. Amidst these American preparations the Academy of Arts and Letters Chancellor, Dr. Sloane, met with the Board of Directors Daniel Chester French, Nicholas Murray Butler, Hamlin Garland, and Booth Tarkington.[51] Sloane's last letter to Pierre de Coubertin, dated April 16, 1924, was suggesting that at age seventy-four, with thirty years' service on the IOC, it might be time to retire. He spoke of his recent African trip and the newly published book on his findings, *Greater France in Africa*. "Take good care, Dear Pierre," he ended. "Your devoted Will."[52] The very next year, Sloane suffered a devastating stroke that rendered the once powerful physique and intellect nearly inoperable.[53] He passed away in mid-September of 1928, and when Robert Underwood Johnson, former American Ambassador to Italy heard the news, he called Sloane "a noble example of American character."[54] President of Columbia University, Nicholas Murray Butler, said of his friend: "He was a productive scholar of importance, ... a vigorous, understanding American gentleman and scholar and his life work may well serve as an example to the youth of today and tomorrow."[55]

Those who might champion James Edward Sullivan as the architect of the original United States Olympic Committee (USOC) are not without some position of historical strength. American sport management was nearly a full-time job for Sullivan during his fifteen years of power, 1899-1914. He was very much respected, very much feared in North America and at the Paris, Athens (1906), London, and Stockholm Olympic Games. But the very bellicosity in the national and international worlds of track and field as well as the Olympic Games that made him a power-house removed all serious possibilities for Sullivan to enter the inner sanctum of the International Olympic Committee. From the very beginning, Sloane was Coubertin's man, his link with America, his gossip-*confidant,* his source of comfort and wisdom, the Baron's spiritual elder brother. Absolutely none of these feelings existed between Sullivan, the "low-born" son of an Irish immigrant and the aristocratic Coubertin. Sloane and Coubertin were much alike in education and temperament and shared a common intellectual commitment to history and philosophy. During these years of Coubertinian power, the Baron very much chose to surround himself with men like himself, with people like Dr. Sloane and not with what he considered the epitome of the athletic and social "hoi polloi," Sullivan. Bricks and mortar laid atop a foundation form a house. Sullivan was the former but Sloane was the latter in this edifice, which was not to become officially operational on a day-to-day basis until 1921, the United States Olympic Committee. Sloane was the USOC's genius and genesis, while Sullivan was its indispensable secretary-general, its successful architect of the USA's Olympic Games gold-medal factory. These two men who lived so uneasily together for a quarter-century probably combined to influence the direction of the USOC more than the combined efforts of all the rest. Both Sullivan and Sloane were moral men with well-formed values by which they endeavored to live, but Sullivan was fanatically American while the patriot Sloane, too much conscious of his Anglo-Saxon breeding, was also a cosmopolitan, internationalist, intellectual, scholar, and comfortable in half a dozen languages. Sullivan spoke and wrote English tolerably well, but no more.

During these critical years of USOC creation, the years before the Great War, the United States needed athletic success at the fledgling Olympic Games in order to gain its wings. Sullivan supplied this manifestation of national power to an extraordinary degree. Equally necessary was the American Olympic Committee's need to be accepted by Baron de Coubertin and his European body of nobles and for an American Olympic leader to step forward, someone of "'substance," credibility, someone with impeccable credentials and acceptable Continental conduct. Sloane, not Sullivan, was their man, and the busy professor, living two lives in one, accepted the mantle of the IOC's man in America. It fit him extremely well. At the bottom and at the top of this American Olympic house stood the formidable team of James Edward Sullivan and William Milligan Sloane. The latter figure was senior to the former in age—and in a number of other critical ways.

William Milligan Sloane's Major Works*

1. *Life and Work of James Renwick Willson Sloane,* 1888.
2. *The French War and the Revolution,* 1893.
3. *Aristotle and the Arabs,* 1894.
4. *Life of James McCosh,* 1896.
5. *Napoleon Bonaparte, A History,* (four volumes) 1901.
6. *The French Revolution and Religious Reform,* 1901.
7. *Parteiherrschaft in Amerika,* 1913.
8. *The Balkans, a Laboratory of History,* 1914.
9. *Party Government in the United States,* 1914.
10. *The Treaty of Ghent,* 1914.
11. *The Powers and Aims of Western Democracy,* 1920.
12. *Greater France in Africa,* 1925.

*not included are several score essays and even greater numbers of published scholarly speeches

Many thanks to David Young, Professor of Classics, University of Florida for the loan of his complete set of correspondences between Sloane and Coubertin, which Dr. Young obtained from the IOC Archives.

NOTES

1 Sloane's "Napoleon," *Century Magazine,* 4 (November, 1894), 153, *The New England Historical and Genealogical Register,* 83 (1929), 345, *National Cyclopedia of American Biography,* 21 (1931), 95, and *Dictionary of American Biography,* 17 (1935), 214.

2 Sloane's comments in Edward P. O'Day, "William Milligan Sloane," *San Francisco Town Talk,* December 1, 1917. Also see the *New York Sun,* September 12, 1928, obituary column.

3 John Lucas, "Man With a Mission: William Milligan Sloane," *The Olympian,* 4 (September 1977), 15, 21.

4 See Ronald A. Smith, *Sports and Freedom. The Rise of Big-Time College Athletics.* New York 1988, 125, 138, and Smith, "The Harvard-Yale Dual League Plan of the 1890s," *New England Quarterly,* 61 (June 1988), 204.

5 William M. Sloane, "College Sport," *Harper's Weekly,* 3 (March 1890), 170 f.

6 John J. MacAloon, *This Great Symbol. Pierre de Coubertin and the Origins of the Modern Olympic Games.* Chicago 1981, 128.

7 Pierre de Coubertin, *Universités Transatlantiques.* Paris 1890, 17.

8 See Marie-Thérèse Eyquem, "Pierre de Coubertin," *L'Épopée Olympique.* Paris 1966, 83.

9 See Albert Shaw, "Baron Pierre de Coubertin," *American Review of Reviews,* 17 (April 1898), 437 f.; John Apostal Lucas, "Baron Pierre de Coubertin and the Formative Years of the Modern International Olympic Movement 1883-1896," University of Maryland, dissertation, 1962, 77 f.; Pierre de Coubertin, *Une Campagne de Vingt-et-un Ans (1887-1908).* Paris 1909, 54-81.

10 MacAloon, *This Great Symbol,* 166. For details of Coubertin's second and last American visit, see his: *Souvenirs d'Amerique et de Grece.* Paris 1897. He called Americans "strong and fearless, members of a very great nation" (p. 102). Coubertin's book was dedicated to "my friend William Milligan Sloane."

11 See Taine's quote in John Lucas, *The Modern Olympic Games.* New York 1980, 33 and *New York Times,* March 3, 1893, 19.

12 Pierre de Coubertin, *Memoires Olympigue.* Lausanne, 1931, 16 and Coubertin: *Une Campagne,* 92. Sloane wrote the AAU Board of Governors on November 18, 1893 that "you must see your way clear to sending representatives to the [Sorbonne] congress.... It is very important that America should be well represented in such a movement." No action was taken by the AAU, and Sloane was the lone American in Paris the next year. See *Spirit of the Times,* November 25, 1893, 613 f.

13 William M. Sloane, "Modern Olympic Games," *Report of the American Olympic Committee 1920.* New York 1920, 77. In the same volume (pp. 59-70) he wrote "The Greek Olympiads."

14 Personal interview with Kirby on August 20, 1951 by Robert Korsgaard; see his dissertation: "A History of the AAU of America," Columbia Teacher's College 1952, 183. Also Gustavus T. Kirby's autobiography: *I Wonder Why?* New York 1954, 30 f.

15 See "Amateur Athletic Union," *Spirit of the Times,* November 25, 1893, 613 f. Also Albert Shaw, "The Re-establishment of Olympic Games," *American Review of Reviews,* 10 (December 1894), 644. The Sloane-organized November, 1893 meeting in New York City is discussed in: *The Times* [London], June 18, 1894, 5. From 1896 to 1921, the American Olympic Committee was composed of a few wealthy Eastern gentlemen, and they only met occasionally. There was no office, no headquarters, and no formal structure. See Robert E. Lehr, "The American Olympic Committee, 1896-1940: From Chaos to Order." Ph.D dissertation, Pennsylvania State University, 1985, note number 27, p. 39.

16 Coubertin: *Memoires Olympiques,* 21. See also: Peter C. Diamond, "Baron Pierre de Coubertin and the Founding of the Modern Olympic Games 1892-1894." Senior History Thesis, Yale University 1973.

17 "Le Premier CIO: Bikelas, Coubertin, Callot, Boutowsky, Guth, Balck, Cuff, Sloane, Zubiaur, Lucchesi-Palli, Herbert, Lord Ampthill and Kemeny." *Bulletin du Comite International des Jeux Olympiques,* 1re annee, no. 1 (June 1894), 1.

18 William M. Sloane, *Life of Napoleon Bonaparte.* Four volumes. New York 1896-1897. "Congratulations on a great book," said critic John A. Kasson in *The Century Magazine,* 52 (October, 1896), 958. The late M.

Taine said of the American historian Professor Sloane that "he knew France better than any other foreigner he ever met." *The Critic*, April 20, 1895, 294.

19 Sloane in *New York Times* [NYT], March 22, 1896, 12. See also: Rebecca L. Trunzo, "American Anglo-Saxon Domination of the 1896 Olympic Games," in her M.S. thesis, Pennsylvania State University, 1988, 42 ff.

20 W. B. Curtis, "The New Olympian Games," *Outing*, 28 (May, 1896), 21.

21 Coubertin quoted in American Olympic Committee, *Official Report Olympic Games 776 B.C.-1896 A.D.* New York 1896, 57. Bourdon in "Comite Olympique Francais," *Les Jeux de la 8ᵉ Olympiade Paris 1924.* Paris 1924, 24.

22 Mandell, *The First Olympics*, 84, MacAloon, *This Great Symbol,* 201, and Gary Allison, "The First Olympics," *Los Angeles Tines,* July 23, 1984, part 8, p. 31.

23 "Columbia's New Professor, *NYT,* November 17, 1896, 9.

24 Sloane to Coubertin, December 6, 1897, Correspondence Coubertin-Sloane 1897-1924, CIO Archives, hereafter 'Archives.'

25 Pierre de Coubertin, "Modern History and Historians in France," *American Monthly Review of Reviews,* (July 1899), 44.

26 Sloane, *School Review,* 6 (1898), 725. MacAloon found a curious overlap in Sloane's philosophy of history and that of his younger colleague Coubertin. see MacAloon: *This Great Symbol ,* 128.

27 Sloane to Coubertin, February 12, 1900, 'Archives.' There is mistrust everywhere, wrote Coubertin, who added that Sloane found the Paris organizing committee "a band of incompetents." See Coubertin: *Memoires Olympiques,* 57.

28 Coubertin, *Une Campagne,* 153.

29 Sloane to Coubertin, April 22, 1901, 'Archives.' See Sloane's letters to Coubertin dated February 26, 1901 and March 31, 1901. Some of these domestic and international tensions are described in John Lucas, "Early Olympic Antagonists—Pierre de Coubertin versus James E. Sullivan," *Stadion,* 3 (1977), 258-272.

30 A small selection of Sloane essays during this period include: "The Philosophy of Trade and Commerce" *NYT,* February 12, 1905, 7; "Proportions and Values in American History," An Address Delivered Before the New York Historical Society. New York 1906, 27 pp.; and "The Changes in Europe's Map and Their Meaning," *NYT,* October 11, 1908, magazine section, 1.

31 George B. McClellan in the annual *Report of American Historical Association,* 1909, 66.

32 Sloane to Coubertin, August 16, 1908, 'Archives.' A dozen more letters from September 18, 1908 to February 15, 1912 attest to Sloane's constant communication with Coubertin about IOC affairs and America's preparation for the Stockholm games.

33 Sullivan to Coubertin, June 26, 1906 (personal file).

34 Sloane to Coubertin, December 13, 1910, 'Archives.' Also *New York Herald*, December 13, 1910, 13 and *New York Daily Tribune*, December 12, 1910, 8. For Sloane's unobtrusively effective work in organizing America's preparation for the 1912 Olympic Games, see Sloane to Coubertin, April 14, 1909; August 23, 1909; September 19, 1910; December 28, 1910, 'Archives.' and *NYT*, December 11, 1910, part IV, 6. "Sullivan lives for his work, and no other man in America devotes himself exclusively to athletic organizations," wrote Sloane to Coubertin, October 16, 1908, 'Archives.'

35 Sloane in the *Annual Report*, AHA 1911, vol. I, 38.

36 See *NYT*, October 18, 1911, 4, October 13, 1912, sec. Ill, 1, September 20, 1914, sec. IV, 1, 4, November 1, 1914, sec. VI, 473, March 2, 1915, 3, and *Annual Report*, AHA 1913, vol. I, 6.

37 See *NYT*, February 21, 1915, sec. III, 2, February 18, 1916, 6, March 11, 1917, 7, March 19, 1917, 3, and, December 7, 1918, 1.

38 Sloane in the *American Historical Review* , 17 (January 1912), 241.

39 William M. Sloane, "The Olympic Idea—Its Origin, Foundation, and Progress," *The Century Magazine,* 84 (July, 1912), 411.

40 Sloane to Coubertin, June 22, 1911, 'Archives.'

41 Ibid., January 7, 1911.

42 Ibid., November 9, 1914.

43 Ibid., 1915.

44 Ibid., November 9, 1914.

45 Ibid., March 30, 1916.

46 "Sorry Professor Sloane is Going," *NYT*, March 2, 1913, part IV, 3.

47 Sloane to Woodrow Wilson, May 22, 1916, *Woodrow Wilson Papers*, Series 2, reel 6. Sloane-Wilson correspondences date back to 1883, 1891, 1892, and a Wilson letter (April 6, 1914) to Sloane thanking his old friend for a copy of his new book, *The Balkans, A Laboratory of History.*" See *Wilson Papers.*

48 See Edward F. O'Day's essay "William Milligan Sloane," *San Francisco Town Talk*, December 1, 1917, 5 ff.

49 See Sloane's speech, *NYT*, February 9, 1919, sec. II, 1. The "rare gold of the Anglo-Saxon has won the day," he said to a receptive audience, in: *Commemoration of the Centenary of the Birth of James Russell Lowell*, New York 1919, 34.

50 Sloane to Coubertin, August 27, 1918, 'Archives.' In a November 21, 1918 letter, Sloane kept Coubertin abreast of American Olympic fund-raising; Olympic publications, and a plea for Coubertin's reaction to the latest news that "We in America are prepared to host a 1920 Olympic Games in New York City."

51 See Academy work in the *New York Tribune,* November 18, 1920, 13, *NYT*, February 23, 1923, 13, and "The American Academy of Arts and Letters," *Academy Papers*, 1925, where he spoke on "The American Academy and the English Language," 29-37, saying, in part, that eternal vigilance is necessary to preserve good English language in order that that language "exhibit the American spirit and temper in the fine arts."

52 Sloane to Coubertin, April 16, 1924, 'Archives.' Shortly after this, Sloane was interviewed and the *New York Times* wrote on July 13, 1924, sec. VIII, 7: "How to Live Long—by Those Who Know."
53 See "Prof. Sloane has 77th birthday, [1] *NYT*, November 13, 1927, 2.
54 *NYT*, September 15, 1928, 18.
55 *NYT*, September 12, 1928, 27. There are scores of Sloane biographies and obituaries. Several of them are: *The National Cyclopaedia of American Biography*, vol. 21 (1931), 94 ff; *Dictionary of American Biography*, vol. 17 (1935), 214; *The New England Historical and Genealogical Register*, 83 (1929), 345 ff; *The Times* (London), September 13, 1928, 7; *The Princeton Alumni Weekly*, November 12, 1928, 79 ff; *American Historical Review* 34 (October, 1928), 174; *NYT*, September 12, 1928,27, September 13, 1928, 26, September 14, 1928, 27, and September 16, 1928, 28; *New York Herald Tribune*, September 12, 1928, 23; *Who's Who in America*, 1927, 2722; Henry Van Dyke, *William Milligan Sloane;* and *Commemorative Tributes of the American Academy of Arts and Letters 1905-1941*. New York 1942. vol. 1, 229-232.

15.
Ernest Lee Jahncke:
The Expelling of an IOC Member*

The International Olympic Committee (IOC) on July 30, 1936, on the first day of their annual three-day conference in Berlin, Germany, "dropped Commodore Ernest Lee Jahncke, Sr., of New Orleans, Louisiana, from its membership, ostensibly for his failure to attend its meetings regarding a national political system that was in direct opposition to a set of values initiated a generation earlier by Baron de Coubertin.[1] This Olympic ideology went on about IOC members as servants of the movement for the greater good of all human kind.[2] Coubertin and his small cadre of ideologues and "hanger-ons" sincerely believed that IOC members should not take strong and public political positions on controversial international issues. "Democratic cosmopolitanism" should be the aim of the Olympic movement rather than taking acrimoneous, narrow political stands. We must shun "myopic nationalism" and "help reestablish universalism" he lectured in 1910.[3]

Commodore Jahncke was fully aware that his every utterance was unacceptable to his IOC colleagues, at least on the surface. Still, as the Olympic Winter Games of 1936 approached, Jahncke markedly increased his boycott rhetoric, creating cleavage with the Olympic ideology but staying the course of his personal philosophy. These actions cost him dearly, and this paper is an effort at analyzing this bifurcation. In addition, this article will expand on several powerful motivations that drove this man Jahncke, personal prime movers such as his deep sense of pride at being a German-American with an immediate idealized,

*STADION, XVII, 1 (1991) 53-78.

romanticized heritage. Jahncke loved New Orleans, the South, and the United States of America with a fervor beyond the ordinary. Thirdly, Rear Admiral Jahncke was passionate about his family, about the local and national Republican Party, as well as the sport of yacht racing and not necessarily in that order. Missing from all these "passions" was any great allegiance, let alone fondness, for the American Olympic Association (AOA) or the IOC. It is the contention of this researcher that the vortex of these personal traits coalesced in the mid 1930s, resulting in his emotional and adamant stand opposing his country's participation in the summer Olympic Games of 1936.

Jahncke's Early New Orleans Years

Ernest Lee Jahncke was born in New Orleans on October 13, 1877[4], and except for his eventful years in Washington, D.C. (1929-1933), lived his entire life there, and died there on November 16, 1960, his rank of Rear Admiral (Retired), United States Navy, entitling him to six Navy pallbearers and 'Taps' sounded by a Marine Corps bugler.[5] He was educated in that city (Tulane University '99), conducted his business there, married and helped raise a family there, and found time to practice yachting skills on "treacherous Lake Pontchartrain, the narrow channel of the Rigolets, and the Gulf of Mexico."[6] Jahncke, tall, handsome, wealthy, and with two engineering degrees from the best university in the city, plunged into the social, cultural, and business atmosphere of New Orleans. One biographer lists fifty-eight honorary, fraternal, and professional organizations to which Jahncke belonged—and this just in the state of Louisiana.[7]

Ernest Lee's father, Fritz Jahncke (1850-1911) was born in Hamburg, Germany, with some Danish ancestry, emigrated to New Orleans in 1869, started in the beer business, but soon "saw the possibilities latent in sand and shells, amassed a considerable fortune by trading in them," and from there emerged into big-time salvage and ship-building—the Jahncke Navigation Company.[8] He married Margaret Lee of New Orleans, and they had three sons —Paul F., Ernest Lee, and Walter Frederick; the three boys eventually becoming associated with Jahncke Services, which became the Jahncke Shipbuilding Company. For twenty years (1909-1929) Ernest Lee served as president, Paul as vice-president, and Walter as secretary-treasurer.[9]

Sportsman Jahncke Appointed to AOA and IOC

Jahncke's skill and daring as a yachtsman earned him local fame in Louisiana, and after winning several national competitions, his reputation among yachtsmen grew. His wealth combined easily with his marriage in June of 1907, to Cora Van Voorhis Stanton, granddaughter of Edwin McMasters Stanton, President Abraham Lincoln's Secretary of War.[10] While still a young man, the newly-crowned "Commodore" took over as president of his father's corporation, served as director of Canal Bank and Trust Company, joined the American Society of Engineers, the National Foreign Trade Council, the American Society of Mechanical Engineers, the Society of Naval Architects plus the prestigious India House, New York Yacht Club, North American Yacht Racing Union, and Metropolitan Club of Washington D.C. He was voted Commodore of the Southern Yacht Club of New Orleans and as "proof positive of his esteem and popularity, was chosen King of the Carnival in 1915, the crowning honor of each year's festivities in the Crescent City" of New Orleans.[11]

Jahncke's granddaughter, Lyn Jahncke Tomlinson wrote:

> the Commodore was a good all-around athlete. He played football for Tulane. He swam, rode horseback, hunted, fished and raced speedboats. His great love, however, was sailing, and sailed all his life as did his children. I suspect ... it is how he came to be on the IOC.[12]

Almost every summer Jahncke sailed the Gulf of Mexico in search of devilfish and on the third of July in 1914, 1915, and 1916, his yacht won the famed New Orleans to Pensacola sea race. Somehow he found time to serve as vice-president of Tulane University.[13] Altogether, Jahncke the man, sportsman, and acknowledged leader seemed prime material for consideration to membership on the Olympic Committee of America and for possible inclusion into the exclusive Coubertin club—the IOC. A larger-than-life oil painting of the Commodore on the Tulane University campus contains a bronze plaque reading "The man is splendidly virile, a thorough American with the force and strength of one who speaks his mind and inspires respect and confidence."[14] He had all the background, it seemed at the time, for exemplary membership in the exclusive men's clubs AOA and IOC.

On October 29, 1926, the President of the AOA, Colonel Robert Means Thompson (1849-1930), multimillionaire financier-industrialist, [15] sent a telegram to Commodore Jahncke:

> Have been asked to recommend representative for appointment to AOA by President of USA. If tendered will you accept and will it be possible to attend [AOA] meeting in Washington, D.C. Nov. 17, 1926?[16]

Jahncke, not wise in the ways of domestic amateur athletics outside the South (let alone about international sport), telegraphed back: "I need more information regarding my appointment to AOA. Your wire 29 Oct. received; will be in Philadelphia Nov. 8."[17] The dance continued, and Thompson wrote Jahncke a 450-word letter from his room at the Bellevue-Stratford Hotel in Philadelphia indicating that when Jahncke arrived at the same hotel, he [Thompson] would already be on his way to Washington, D.C. for the annual AOA meeting. Thompson expressed delight that Jahncke was interested in membership. "We want every geographic area of the country represented," wrote the Colonel, "and besides you represent the highest type American—the kind of man we want on our committee. Your duties would not be arduous or excessively time-consuming."

> I know of the good work you have been doing on the Merchant Marine Committee of the United States Chamber of Commerce and of the fine Navy Day celebration you organized in Louisiana this year. I sincerely hope you will permit me to place your name before The President [Calvin Coolidge] and that you may be able to be in Washington November 17.[18]

The two men, Thompson and Jahncke, went on to the Olympic committee meeting as president, and the younger member representing New Orleans and the "Federal Reserve Atlanta Olympic District."[19] The "star" speaker was General Charles Hitchcock Sherrill (1867-1936). Famous as a world-class sprinter at Yale, a lawyer, American ambassador, war hero, sport organizer, millionaire art connoisseur, and IOC member since 1922,[20] Sherrill gave a semi-autobiographical speech of 2500 words to this all-male audience in the nation's capital. He began by challenging any man over half-a-hundred years of age "to a 100-yard dash for the championship of the world." He went on at great length about the

marvels of the little-known IOC and then to the athletic challenges, difficulties facing the American team's efforts to win gold, silver, and bronze at the 1928 Olympic Games in Amsterdam. "The
President of the United States will meet with us at 12:30 this
afternoon in the White House," said Sherrill. "Our business," he
concluded, "is the sound mind and sound bodies of our amateur
athletic youth. ... There is not any body of men organized into one
association in the United States today that is doing so much good
for the citizenship of the United States as this group here today."
Those assembled gave Sherrill, and themselves, "great applause"
as he sat down.[21]

General Sherrill, ten years Jahncke's senior, took on the
younger man's increasing curiosity about international athletics, and the Southerner responded with a December 17, 1927
telegram "Comme vous croyez" (As you believe).[22] Sherrill immediately shot back a short, mysterious letter:

> My dear Commodore: When are you coming to New York?
> Important matter to talk to you concerning athletics,
> which I do not wish to discuss but it is of such a delicate
> nature that I hesitate to put it in a letter. Will you go
> abroad soon? Is it your custom to do so regularly?[23]

The answer to the penultimate question was "yes," maybe,
"I'm thinking about going to the Amsterdam Olympic Games in
the summer of 1928." The answer to the last question was "no."
The New Orleans homeboy, Jahncke, had worked hard since his
teen years (and played hard) but found no great calling in European excursions. Sherrill went to Europe every year to rest, to
study, and to purchase rare cathedral stained glass. On the eve
of Sherrill's departure for IOC meetings in Monte Carlo, he asked
Jahncke: "As one sportsman to another, do you speak French
reasonably well?"[24] On the opening day of the Monte Carlo IOC
session, Ernest Lee Jahncke, became the third American on the
committee, endorsed by Sherrill, recommended by President
Calvin Coolidge (patron of the American Olympic Association),
and joining William May Garland ("from the West") and Sherrill
("from the East") as the representative from "the South."[25] The
American Jahncke, never having met Baron Pierre de Coubertin,
nor his successor from Belgium, Count Baillet-Latour, nor any
of the European IOC members, was elected to that august body
on April 22, 1927. Olympic historian Karl Adolf Scherer wrote:
"Commodore Ernest Lee Jahncke, Assitant Secretary of the Navy

... was adopted by the IOC on the recommendation of Sherrill."[26] Jahncke was not in attendance at his own inauguration.

The Assistant Secretary of the Navy 1929-1933

Ernest Jahncke was forced to be away from his beloved New Orleans to live in Washington, D.C. and serve his government as the nation's Assistant Secretary of the Navy, the first time in sixteen years that a person with the name "Roosevelt" had not occupied that position. *The New York Times* devoted a thousand-word essay to Jahncke's appointment on May 23, 1929.[27] President Herbert Hoover's appointment of Southern Republican loyalists Jahncke and Patrick J. Hurley to major Navy and War Department posts made page one of many eastern newspapers.[28] Of course, Louisiana made a fuss over Jahncke's appointment— possibly the state's most visible Republican Party supporter, a highly regarded businessman, civic leader, and "savior" of the people devastated by flood waters in the lower Mississippi Delta. Commodore Jahncke, as chairman of the New Orleans Clearing House Reparations Committee, helped negotiate financial settlements for thousands of people in St. Bernard and Plaquemine Parishes whose homes had been washed away by the swollen waters. "Louisiana is honored to have one of its most distinguished native sons appointed to a cabinet appointment," wrote the *New Orleans States.* Jahncke immediately resigned as president of his shipbuilding corporation, wrote a biographer in *The Story of Louisiana*—the proper thing to do. Even the sophisticated *Washington Post* noted that Jahncke was one of the South's most distinguished and well-connected citizens and that the president had made an admirable choice.[29] President Hoover's press conference on March 12, 1929, praised Jahncke as a person of vast experience "with shipping, and is an enthusiastic sailor, and is a large and important businessman."[30]

Jahncke's activities during the Hoover administration are covered in detail by the *New Orleans States-Item,* the *Times-Pacayune* of New Orleans, and 140 items, short and long, in *The Washington Post,* the *New York Herald Tribune,* and *The New York Times.* Apparently Jahncke, his wife Cora, and their four children Adele, Cora, Ernest Lee Jr., and Frederick Stanton were big hits in Washington, D.C., and moved in the "best" social circles.[31] Almost immediately he was called "Commodore" and was described, at various times, as "handsome, tall, and fair," as "direct and honest," a "Southern gentleman, through and through."

An item on the editorial page of *The New York Times* titled "From Bluer Seas" took note that "This Southern Republican will bring to official Washington as complete a Louisiana setting as could be found."[32] Davis Lee Jahncke, Jr., grandnephew of Ernest Lee, Sr. wrote:

> Uncle Ernest was considered one of the most important figures in New Orleans—in politics, business, yachting, social—he was the youngest Rex [King of Mardi Gras] because he was such a leader here. In Washington, he was considered the epitome of the deep South Southern gentleman and was an intimate of Herbert Hoover and the Cabinet. His daughter Adele was presented to George V and Queen Mary at Buckingham Palace and was presented in New Orleans as a debutante for two years to satisfy her Carnival honors.[33]

This paper is no effort, conscious or unconscious, to write an impossibly heroic biography, but the man Jahncke was held in high esteem by many. This is reflected in the life-size painting of the Commodore hanging in Tulane University's ROTC Building.[34] Jahncke was nowhere close to being a humble "man of the people." He had, after all, worked for the national Republican Party in the 1928 elections to "deliver" to Mr. Hoover, the Louisiana sugar plantation owners, bankers, and manufacturers.[35] But the man was so sincere, pleasant, genuinely articulate and patriotic, that he almost never got a bad press back home or in Washington, D.C. "Ernest Lee Jahncke—American," wrote a feature writer on page one of the *New Orleans States* on the day Jahncke was chosen by President Hoover to join his "team" in Washington, D.C. Ahead of him, began the article, "looms four years of hard work in a cause he loves. He believes in the Navy. He fights for it; the Navy is a passion with Commodore Jahncke," wrote Meigs O. Frost.[36] On this special day, March 24, 1929, Jahncke (the first trained naval engineer appointed to the post) spoke with typical passion regarding his perception of the interdependency of a strong Navy and a strong America. The soundest guarantee of peace, he wrote, "is adequate preparation for war." Cynical politicians and money-mad louts are not the real America, he continued, ending with "Patriotism isn't singing the Star-Spangled Banner.... It's training yourself so you'll be some use to your country when your country needs you, and some use to yourself until she does."[37]

Two pages of *The New York Times* photographs depicted the Hoover cabinet—"The New Patriots of Peace Time," businessmen who, "at heavy pecuniary sacrifice, are now serving the nation in Washington." Jahncke's name and photo seemed to lead all the rest.[38] And the physically vigorous Jahncke lost no time in organizing an early morning exercise program for the President and his closest aids—a "medicine ball cabinet get-together in an secluded spot on White House grounds."[39] The important American historian-journalist, Mark Sullivan (1874-1952), author of the six volume work *Our Times: The United States, 1900-1925,* was a frequent guest at these medicine ball sunrise sessions. He thanked "the Honorable Ernest Lee Jahncke" for helping him with the writing of one volume, and even more importantly, as "a generous friend and high-spirited companion" who contributed further help "by seeing to it that the author started off the day's work in good physical condition and good spirits, with real appreciation."[40]

Of course no one in official Washington could spell the very German name "Jahncke." *The Literary Digest* called him "The handsome and cordial Assistant Secretary of the Navy" and quoted the smiling, affable Commodore as saying, tongue-in-cheek: "Just call me 'Yankee.'"[41] He was very serious about his work—the first cabinet member to fly tens of thousands of miles inspecting facilities all over the nation and Hawaii. "I'm tremendously impressed with the manifold advantages of this modern method of travel," he said in his first year of office.[42] Some tasks were mandated by Jahncke's job description, but the New Orleans patriot went beyond the call of duty and gave patriotic speeches all over the nation—more than anyone in the Washington government.[43] Secretary Jahncke placed a wreath on the grave of North Pole explorer, Rear Admiral Robert E. Peary, and those at Arlington National Cemetery heard just the right words from the 'Yankee.' Jahncke introduced Admiral Richard Evelyn Byrd, at a National Geographic Society luncheon, honoring the great man for his flight over the South Pole. The President, the Vice-President, Dr. Gilbert Grosvenor (Society President), and a huge group of dignitaries joined in laudatory celebration and the awarding of a special medal to the Winchester, Virginia-born Byrd (1888-1957).[44] There's much more on Jahncke's sojourns and recitations,[45] but an elaboration of just one may underscore the others. On January 8, 1931, the Louisiana Historical Society "and the Citizens of New Orleans" honored Ernest Lee Jahncke at a grand banquet in the Roosevelt Hotel. Admiral T.P. Magruder made appreciative remarks, as did Mayor T. Semmes Walmsley, the president of the Society, and the Honorable Huey P. Long, Governor of Louisiana.

Jahncke's speech, "The Navy at the Battle of New Orleans," (116 years earlier, 1815, on that same day, January 8), was a panegyric in praise of General Andrew Jackson and especially of his brave sailors aboard the two 15-gun sloops-of-war in the harbor and the seven gunboats on Lake Borgne. The enemy were routed on the land and the sea; the city and the new nation were saved. Jahncke may have been at his best when praising America and its bountiful gifts for all those who would give their own personal full measure of devotion and very hard work.

Jahncke's Empty Vessel as Olympic Member 1927-1933

Secretary Jahncke was unable to give much of himself to the American Olympic Association and even less to the IOC during his increasingly busy schedule as President Hoover's close aid, 1927-1934. It was not an uncommon occurrence among IOC members in that era and earlier. Baron de Coubertin himself had said that only the smallest cadre of IOC colleagues could be depended upon to devote large amounts of time and skill to the movement. Jahncke's case may have been a little different. He was fifty years of age, a very wealthy man and did not need an international membership requiring so much time away from his beloved New Orleans. He did make plans with a New York City travel agent for the "best Amsterdam hotel" and the possibility of IOC and Olympic Games enjoyment in the Summer of 1928. But it was not to be, and the agent wrote back: "Sorry that your plans to allow us to help you get to the games have been cancelled."[46] Jahncke's sponsor and colleague, General Sherrill, wrote on December 31, 1927: "Thanks for all the lovely gifts. Will you be at the IOC meeting in Amsterdam?"[47] That same day, Sherrill wrote to his IOC president (the third in line since 1894), Belgian Count Henri de Baillet-Latour (1876-1942), expressing apprehension about his colleague Jahncke's ability to make it to the July IOC meeting. Sherrill then resorted to puzzling phraseology and wrote "My dear Baillet":

> Yesterday that great insurgent body, the NCAA, voted to rejoin the American Olympic Committee, so you see that my prediction about what would happen if we elected their man Jahncke to our International Committee has come to pass.[48]

There seems a lack of evidence to link Jahncke with the NCAA. Rather, it was a combination of Colonel Thompson and Sherrill that recommended to the IOC hierarchy a vote of confidence in Jahncke's elevation. What is clear is Jahncke's dilemma. In a painful exchange of telegrams between Jahncke and General Sherrill in June of 1928, the former revealed that he had cancelled steamship reservations to the IOC and Olympic Games get-together. Unending business commitments make it impossible, wrote Jahncke; "I absolutely cannot leave New Orleans. I am bitterly disappointed." "Your absence from your first IOC meeting is tantamount to resignation from the committee," responded Sherrill, in considerable distress.

> It is impossible for you to resign now because vacancy only filled at [IOC] committee's July meeting, therefore losing the U.S. your vote at highly important decisions, as well as leaving NCAA unrepresented. Suggest that your patriotic duty is to represent your homeland at this world meeting instead of doing local flood relief work, where a substitute is available.[49]

Jahncke had not formally tended his resignation form the IOC and continued to receive invitations to post-Amsterdam meetings. IOC secretary A. Berdez wrote Jahncke urging his attendance at the Cairo and Alexandria, Egypt, Olympic gathering March 31 to April 12, 1929.[50] The Commodore did not attend, and honest man that he was, he tried to resign and wrote to Sherrill and sent a similar letter "to the IOC President and members of the IOC." The full-time personal and governmental responsibilities in both New Orleans and Washington:

> absolutely require my daily personal supervision. I cannot attend IOC meeting, and as I have not been active or able to fulfill my obligations to the IOC, in fairness to your good self and that of your confere, Colonel William Garland, I am herewith tending my resignation. And to you gentlemen on the IOC, it is with deepest regret that I tender my resignation. The privileged honor of being associated with the IOC is one that I have much appreciated.[51]

The matter was not dead; Jahncke agreed to meet with Sherrill in early March of 1929, and Sherrill replied: "Please don't make your intention to resign public. There would be a great unpleasant scramble." Sherrill continued:

> I am so sorry you feel you must resign. Please keep it confidential until I have a chance to present it to the IOC. By the way, the Egypt IOC meeting was cancelled. We next meet in Barcelona. Can you please try and attend this April 1929 IOC meeting?[52]

In that same month Baillet-Latour wrote Sherrill regarding in March 13, 1929 letter from the American. Jahncke seems intent on resigning, wrote the IOC president, but before you act too swiftly in nominating "Mr. Irwing [sic] Brokaw[53] to take the place of Commodore Jahncke," let me discuss it with the Executive Board. Remember, continued Baillet-Latour, that in 1927, when Jahncke was appointed "there was a very strong wish to appoint Roosevelt, and I expect that his name is certain to be mentioned again. He is qualified in every way. I will be in Lausanne on 5 April; you can communicate with me if you wish."[54]

And then, without elaboration, Charles Sherrill sent a telegram to the IOC on April 5, 1929, informing the President that "Jannekes [sic] resignation has been withdrawn."[55] This immediate crisis has passed, and Jahncke continued his unremitting hard work for the Navy, for the man in the White House, and for the National Republican Party. He attended no international Olympic meetings in 1930-1931, kept aloof from Olympic business, except for one amusing item in *The Washington Post* which proclaimed: "Olympic Games for Washington, D.C. urged by Secretary Jahncke." With all due respect to my Los Angeles and IOC colleague, William May Garland, wrote Jahncke, the city of Washington is infinitely more dignified, better qualified than his city for a 1932 Summer Olympic Games.[56] On January 26, 1933, Frederick W. Rubien, long-time secretary of the AOA, wrote Baillet-Latour that all three American IOC members, Sherrill, Garland, and Jahncke, had been "elevated to the AOA Executive Board."[57] Jahncke's life-time appointment to the IOC seemed reasonably assured, despite a perfunctory two-hour appearance at the pre-Olympic Games IOC meeting in Los Angeles 1932. He did, after all, share the Coliseum box seat with William May Garland (1866-1948) and Vice-President of the United States, Charles Curtis.[58]

Of course, Jahncke was swept out of office in late 1932, along with his president Herbert Hoover, and on March 17, 1933, Henry L. Roosevelt ("distant cousin of FDR") succeeded Jahncke, who remarked:

> I leave this association with a feeling of affectionate admiration.... I consider myself a very fortunate man to have found usefulness to my country.... Once in the Navy, always in the Navy.[59]

Jahncke's Abhorrence of the Third Reich 1934-1935

Ernest Lee Jahncke was a man of controlled passion. A minor scandal broke in Washington, D.C. in the fall of 1934, when ex-cabinet member Jahncke was accused by a congressman and by a special Senate investigatory committee of complicity in secret negotiations with the German "Third Reich" in obtaining for them certain submarine parts and munitions. No proof of impropriety was ever proven against Jahncke.[60] Back home in New Orleans, Jahncke plunged into new jobs and old responsibilities with the city's banks, trust companies, Board of Trade, National Foreign Trade Council, several key positions with Tulane University, his several beloved yacht clubs, as a trustee of several colleges, and "an appointment by Governor Alien in 1935 to be the first Louisiana State Commissioner of Commerce and Industry."[61] His plate was very full, too much so to attend American and International Olympic Committee meetings. He had given fair warnings to the leadership of these two organizations that his attendance would be, at best, limited. Six years earlier his efforts to resign from the IOC were subsumed by larger domestic cries that his presence added so much to both organizations. And so, while still a very visible member of the AOA and the IOC in the fall of 1935, Jahncke (recently promoted to "Rear Admiral Retired") began his attack on Adolf Hitler and the "Third Reich." Much more controversial than that (in the United States), Admiral Jahncke began public expressions of his unequivocal disapproval of America's participation in the Berlin Games of the Eleventh Olympiad. For him "the dice ist [sic] cast"—a double Olympic committee member speaking in opposition to the very Olympic ideology of universal competition and cooperation that he had pledged to uphold at his 1927 induction into the IOC.

Almost no sport history research can match, let alone exceed, the amount of published literature on the politics of the 1936 Olympic Games. In the German, French, and English languages, several hundred books and articles exist. Several of them have been helpful regarding the so-called boycott efforts of certain American intellectuals, church leaders, educators, and sporting persons to prevent the American Olympic team from Berlin participation.[62] The newspaper coverage in these same three languages about the 1934-1936 pre-Olympic Games machinations are nearly beyond the reading capability of any one person. Excoriating essays, revelations both domestic and foreign, internecine disputes within the AAU and the AOA, nearly daily Olympic bulletins out of the German Organizing Committee—all dealt with the American indecision about going to Germany. Admiral Jahncke, completing his ninth year as an IOC member, joined the furor with his public revelation on November 26, 1935, that it was both inhuman and immoral for the United States of America to participate in, as he called them, these Hitler and Nazi propaganda games.

Lord Killanin, the sixth IOC president (1972-1980), believed that Jahncke's decision to "go public" regarding his support of an Olympic Games boycott (an unprecedented act by an IOC member) was triggered by Adolf Hitler's virulent anti-Semitic "Nuremberg laws" of September 15, 1935.[63]

Vice-President of Tulane University, Jahncke made the trip up to New York City with prepared copies for the press of two letters dated November 25, 1935. One was addressed to "My dear Colleague Count Baillet-Latour" and the other: "My dear Dr. Lewald" [President of the German Olympic Committee]. Jahncke's letters were in reply to the two European's requests that the American use his prestigious office as IOC member to insure his country's participation in the next year's Olympic Summer Games. Jahncke shot back with 700- and 500-word letters, respectively, to the IOC president and Dr. Lewald. Almost every major newspaper in the United States carried lengthy items on Jahncke's clarion-call to "keep America out of the Olympics." Taking a stand directly at variance with Sherrill and Garland, as well as the entire IOC, Jahncke voiced the belief that the German hierarchy continued to violate every requirement of sport fair play and were exploiting the games solely for financial and political gain by the despicable Nazi regime. It will be a "calamity" if America competes, he wrote Lewald. The Olympian high principles can be saved only if America and the rest of the world stay away from sport in Berlin, he wrote. Germany lies about its treatment of Jewish athletes. I believe you to be an honorable man, he told Dr. Lewald, "but circumstances have rendered you powerless," continued the ruthlessly direct Jahncke. A physically attractive stadium is inadequate. The ambiance of the athletic field must be enriched with idealism, sportsmanship, and "I find these utterly lacking in the German preparations," he wrote in his penultimate paragraph. His final shot at Lewald, or rather what Lewald represented, went like this:

> As you know, I am of German descent. I love the Germany that was and which, I pray, will some day be again. It is as much because of my affection for that Germany as because of my devotion to the spirit of sport that I feel it my duty as an American citizen and one of three members of the IOC ... to stand for fundamental principle in this matter.[64]

The American Hebrew of December 6, 1935, reproduced both of Jahncke's letters and had lots more to say in a lengthy and strident essay "Jahncke Refuses to Aid Berlin Olympics."[65] To Baillet-Latour, he wrote: "I am the only one of the three American [IOC] members who is definitely of the Teutonic race," and yet, he continued, my every intellectual, cultural, and emotional sensibility make it impossible for me to support that which you wish me to support America's participation in Hitler's Olympic Games. Believe me, "dear Colleague," continued Jahncke, I understand Coubertin and his concept that without honor, beauty, and fair play, there is no sport. It is exactly here that Berlin is deficient, and therefore "I shall urge upon my countrymen that they should not participate in the games in Nazi Germany ... under the domination of the Nazi government...." All peoples and all lofty ideals would be compromised by an Olympic Games in that unfortunate land. It is not too late, "my dear Count," he wrote at the end of his letter, to transfer the games to another land and in so doing to trade "Coubertin instead of Hitler," to safeguard the Olympic Idea for posterity.[66]

They were carefully crafted letters, thoughtful and even eloquent. Jahncke knew precisely what ideological chasm he had dug and the inevitability of his actions. Jahncke's unsparing argument won few visible adherents, but Zack Farmer, managing director of the 1932 games, declared the Hitler government an absolute anathema and therefore America should not go to Berlin. Sherrill had "no comment" to make on the whole matter, while William May Garland broke a long silence and noted that his IOC colleague "never attended a meeting of the organization except for about fifteen minutes here in Los Angeles in 1932."[67]

Two days later, Garland told Paul Zimmerman of the *Los Angeles Times:* "To refuse to join with the nations which sacrificed a great deal to come to our celebration of the Games of '32 ... would reflect on no one as much as the U.S."[68] Thus fellow American IOC members Sherrill and Garland lined up squarely in opposition to their militant colleague, Jahncke.

This researcher wrote in his unpublished manuscript *A Century History of the American Amateur Athletic Union 1888-1988* that the December 1935 combined meeting of the AAU and the Olympic committee was probably the most acrimonious in the history of those two organizations. There were many "actors" lined up shouting either "boycott" or "participation," but Judge Jeremiah Titus Mahoney (1880-1970) led the bitter struggle against AOA President Avery Brundage (1887-1975).[69] The unhappy gathering finally took a vote on Sunday afternoon, December 8, 1935, and by the closest margin "rejected all attempts to keep American athletes out of the Olympic Games in Germany."[70] The hero-villain Jahncke was not there at New York City's Commodore Hotel but was undoubtedly saddened when he heard the decision. As was his way, he reacted with comments dealing with events within Germany even larger and more important than the pending Berlin sports festival. New York City's St. Nicholas Palace was filled with more than 3,500 persons who paid to hear the famous author Emil Ludwig, as well as Ernest Jahncke, and other distinguished speakers speak of the "horrors of the present German regime" and call for "a boycott of these Nazi Olympic Games." The German-American League for Culture audience listened to this December 15 lecture by Ludwig, who pronounced the leaders of the Third Reich as a group of "unsuccessful creatures, former floaters in vocations, men born with egotism, brutalized through the long war, determined rather to continue the life of adventure than to return to peaceful occupation."[71] The full text of Jahncke's 700-word speech is preserved in the Hill Memorial Library of Louisiana State University. I am of German stock, began Jahncke, "and take great pride in that fact." It is incumbent on us, he told the mass audience, that we "who have a spiritual stake in the good name of Germany" to rid that nation of the "clique of egotists" who now hold the nation in their power. We must help Germany return to the world of "the immortal Immanuel Kant." The demagogues must go, and we all can help by taking even greater pride "in the American spirit of sportsmanship.... Let us by faith and honor and charity and tolerance once more show the people of the earth that the immortal light kindled by the founders of our country still shines on American soil."[72] The year 1936 was only days away, an ominous one for the world and an almost fatal one for the 59-year-old Jahncke.

The Fateful IOC Decision: July 30, 1936

Baillet-Latour had completely lost patience with Jahncke, and wrote him on December 12, 1935, that his conduct was wholly unacceptable and that he should resign. A copy of the letter was sent to the highly esteemed AOC secretary, Frederick W. Rubien (1872-1951),[73] urging him to share the letter with the press. Rubien did not, and wrote Jahncke to that effect on January 6, 1936. Jahncke waited a full month till the eve of the Olympic Winter Games, before firing a February 7, 1936 letter to Baillet-Latour (a copy to Rubien[74]). Jahncke was never frivolous, and his 250-word letter to Baillet-Latour was another well-crafted exposition. There were no prefatory "My dear Latour" salutations. Jahncke's first sentence captured the crux of the matter. "In reply to your December 12 letter, let me say that I shall not resign from the IOC. It is I that has been true to highest Olympic ideals; you and the German authorities have abandoned these lofty Coubertinian ethics," wrote Jahncke. "The American AAU-AOA vote to go to Berlin was a farce and illegal," continued Jahncke, who had not been present at the New York meeting of a month earlier. The Olympic Games must be held in accordance "with the fundamental principles, which call for no discrimination by reason of race, religion or social status.... Great moral issues cannot be resolved by counting noses, but only by an appeal to what is right and what is wrong."[75]

General Charles Hitchcock Sherrill died suddenly in Paris on June 25, 1936. He was well-known in his own country as a famous athlete, sport organizer, important American diplomat to several key nations, an influential international lawyer, a highly-regarded art connoisseur, and since 1922 a member of the IOC. In the earlier Hitler years of rule 1933 and 1934, Sherrill was overtly cautious about the German commitment to human rights, especially the freedom of German Jews to move in the direction of possible Olympic team membership. A trip to Germany and voluminous correspondence with their Olympic organizing committee convinced him that the Germans were making sincere efforts at including the nation's best athletes, including Jews, on their Olympic team. Sherrill's naiveté or worst still, complicity with the Nazis, was seized upon by those opposed to an Olympic Games in

Germany, and the General was pounded on all sides. Excoriating criticism resulted after Sherrill warned that American Jews were making too much of this whole thing, that they were "overplaying their cards. There is a grave danger of an anti-Semitic wave in the United States due to the agitation of the Jews on behalf of their German brethren."[76] A certain Albert Allen, writing in the October 25, 1935 issue of *The American Hebrew and Jewish Tribune* wrote twenty paragraphs castigating Sherrill as a closet "anti-Semite who must be unmasked."[77]

There was more censure directed at the venerable Sherrill until the day he died some three weeks before the American Olympic team sailed from New York City to Hamburg and on to the Olympic Games in Berlin. There was now an important vacancy on the IOC and an American replacement needed to be chosen at the July meeting in the Olympic city. Sherrill's funeral in Paris' American Cathedral Church of the Holy Trinity was attended by the highest diplomatic and sporting dignitaries before his return to America on the ship *Normandie,* where at New York City's Madison Avenue Presbyterian Church, an enormous congregation heard the Rev. Dr. Henry Sloane Coffin "pronounce a eulogy of the many-sided virtues of General Sherrill and read a prayer on his behalf.[78] Waiting in the wing was the extremely vigorous 49-year-old Avery Brundage, and *The New York Times* of July 28, 1936, predicted his election. There are two places available for Americans on the IOC, continued the article, for had not Jahncke "presumably resigned"?[79]

President Baillet-Latour's first order of IOC business in late July was to propose the aged Pierre de Coubertin for the Nobel Peace Prize, "the first sportsman ever nominated." *The New York Times* containing this announcement also noted that William May Garland was the lone American at this July 29, 1936 meeting, thus compounding the error that Jahncke had voluntarily removed himself earlier that year.[80] Of course, Mr. Jahncke did not show up in Berlin, thus keeping his record of non-attendance intact; the axe fell on Jahncke the next day. Sherrill was gone but, as Duff Hart-Davis wrote, another American, Commodore Jahncke "was still uncomfortably alive and intransigent."[81]

"Do you remember the day that your father was evicted as IOC member?" I asked Jahncke's daughter. "Not very well," replied Coco Jahncke Seemann. "At that time in 1936, I was making my debut in New Orleans, so had my mind on other matters."[82] Nevertheless, a great many others *did* take notice and scores of America's most influential newspapers devoted significant column space to the event, including Miss Coco's *New Orleans States* and *The New Orleans Item,* which intoned "Ernest Lee Jahncke Ousted from Olympic Board." Both newspapers forwarded the "lack of attendance" theme, but they, like everyone else, knew that Jahncke's militant stance "against an Olympic Games in Nazi Germany" was the real reason.[83]

The dam broke. Count Baillet-Latour and most of his IOC had "had it" with the once-again absent Jahncke at this pre-Olympic Games convocation in Berlin on July 29, 1936. Almost the first order of business was Commodore Jahncke. According to Lord Killanin, Jahncke's February 7, 1936 letter to Baillet-Latour, a categorical refusal to resign, infuriated the Belgian and his hand-picked Executive Board. Mr. Jahncke's conduct they said "was betraying the IOC's interests, contravening its statutes and failing in good breeding toward his colleagues."[84] Long-time Chancellor of the IOC, Otto Mayer, in his definitive work, *A Travers les Anneaux Olympiques,* wrote that the IOC's attitude toward the rebellious (traitorous?) Jahncke was one of "profound disapprobation."[85] Jesse P. Abramson of the *New York Herald-Tribune* was at press conferences in Amsterdam and Los Angeles and his third Olympic Games in 1936. Jahncke's demise was a forgone conclusion. His name was not even in the official IOC roster published weeks before the July 30 meeting. Abramson asked Theodor Lewald if it was an error of omission. "He said, bluntly, that it was no error," wrote Abramson. "I would not include the name of a man who had so shamefully offended Germany," continued Lewald. Several months earlier Jahncke told Abramson that his unsuccessful effort to resign was, in part, to help to the IOC out of its dilemma and to avoid what happened to an earlier American IOC Member, David Kinsley, former president of the University of Illinois.[86] He had been dropped for lack of attendance. It was the ruse used by the IOC to drop Jahncke from membership. William May Garland told Abramson that he had refrained from voting.[87]

The other New York City journalist, Arthur Daley, pointed out that the IOC was perfectly within its rights in dismissing Jahncke since it had a clause in its constitution permitting such action. Daley, like every other journalist, pointed out the real reason. One veteran IOC member, stiff-lipped, told Daley that Jahncke was selected for the exclusive club because he was Herbert Hoover's buddy, and as such could guarantee the presence of the U.S. president in the honor box seat at the Los Angeles Olympic Games. "He didn't even do that," was the mournful comment of the interviewee.[88] "I wasn't at all surprised by Jahncke's

184 / John Apostal Lucas

dismissal," wrote the old world-record holder in the sprints, Arthur Duffey, of the *Boston Post*. "Heavy oratorical guns," brought down Jahncke early, wrote a *Boston Globe* sport reporter. Sport editor for the *Associated Press*, Alan Gould, wrote in the *Los Angeles Times* that Avery Brundage was immediately selected to succeed Jahncke. The *Boston Herald* and the *Chicago Daily Tribune* had it on good authority that "Brundage was suggested as Jahncke's successor by William May Garland." It was highly irregular, for Olympic protocol called for Brundage to have taken General Sherrill's month-old empty seat.[89] In Richard Lee Gibson's doctoral dissertation, he said, correctly, that Brundage should have filled the *first* vacancy to occur created by Sherrill's death. Why does the official *1936 AOC Report* show photos of Garland, Sherrill, and Brundage as Americans on the IOC? One must conclude, wrote Gibson "that Sherrill was honored for his stand while Jahncke was probably one of those traitors who was 'smoked out.'"[90]

Jahncke defended himself as best he could—back in the comfort of his New Orleans ambiance. For whatever reason, he told the press, Mr. Rubien never made public his February 7, 1936 letter of resignation, "even though the Committee made public Latour's letter ripping me up the back." There was no politics involved in my IOC selection, stated an angry Jahncke. "My appointment to the committee came before I was made Assistant Secretary of the Navy," he said.[91] Jahncke's last public gasp, at least on this repellent subject, occurred in a lengthy "Letter to the Editor" of *The New York Times* of November 11, 1936. I was expelled without a hearing from the IOC's "star chamber," and the real reason was not poor attendance, he wrote. He revealed a letter from Baillet-Latour, written after the July 1936 meeting of the IOC: "The Comite International Olympique has unanimously ordered, less one absence (W. May Garland), your removal, for the reason that by your attitude you have been a traitor to its interests."[92] "I feel, in view of these circumstances," concluded Jahncke's letter, "that the American people who are interested should have these facts, which conclude my part of the record, and which I feel have completely vindicated my stand."[93]

Finale on Jahncke

Alan Gould called "1936" the worst year in American Olympic Association and AAU history. Possibly the new AAU president, Judge Mahoney, "can bring better understanding on all sides."

One of his first acts was to include Ernest Lee Jahncke as delegate-at-large. Jahncke's ouster was an "outrage and was one because of the Commodore's anti-Nazi expressions" exploded Mahoney.[94] Gus Kirby immediately wrote Brundage about Mahoney's selection, castigating the new AAU leader:

> Now that the president has slapped the IOC in its face and kicked it in its backside by appointing as one of the AAU's delegates at large the discredited Jahncke, I am confident that you and Colonel Garland will find great difficulty in acting as liaison officers between the IOC, and the governing bodies of amateur sport in this country.[95]

The nearly endless "tattle-tale" continued, and Brundage wrote Baillet-Latour on January 22, 1937, about the appointment. "This gesture," wrote Brundage, "was for the sake of publicity since this position is an empty honor and means nothing."[96] The AAU lurched along in its well-meaning but imperfect way during the last days of the 1930s, while Olympic committees everywhere put their mission into "moth-balls" during cataclysmic World War II years 1939-1945. The durable Jahncke was chosen Executive Director of the Louisiana Department of Commerce and Industry (1940); selected a member of the Herbert Hoover Foundation Board of Trustees (1954); at age 76 years (1954) appointed vice-president of Tulane University Board of Administrators, and finally, in 1955, promoted to Rear Admiral Retired.[97] Finally, in the spring of 1957, the *Times-Picayune* reported that Admiral Jahncke was recovering from emergency appendectomy at his summer home at Pass Christian, Mississippi. He seems to be doing well, "this internationally-known yachtsman, this dynamic figure in building fleets, owning and sailing history-making crafts."[98] He wasn't that well, and that same newspaper reported the passing of Ernest Lee Jahncke on November 16, 1960, in Pass Christian at age 83.

Obituaries are lopsided biographies, but they are useful in the whole historic tapestry of a prominent individual. First, from his own people in New Orleans, an editor eulogized the Commodore as a man of the very highest principles, someone who "had a long, rich, useful life and left a mark of honor." Six Navy enlisted men came down, served as pallbearers while a Marine Corps bugler played "Taps."[99] Jahncke's grandchild told this researcher: "All of us, the large family of grandfather Jahncke, held him in the most high esteem, even reverence. He seemed a powerful, dignified figure, with a great personal history."¹⁰⁰ *The New York Times* remembered him well in a measured obituary about Herbert Hoover's close friend and a member of the President's "Medicine Ball Cabinet." The *New York Herald Tribune* devoted 600 words to the "tall, blonde and congenial sailor's man."

"The tang of the sea was in his bones almost from the time he was able to toddle around the family home in New Orleans and play with his toy boats." *The Washington Post* noted that Ernest Lee's father owned 40 sailing vessels and that the boy spent much of his time sailing the South Atlantic and Gulf Coasts. "During World War I he was in charge of the Sea Service Bureau and Navigation Schools of the Merchant Fleet, Gulf Section."¹⁰¹ All three big-city newspapers made a point of mentioning that powerful ideological reasons caused his IOC dismissal and not his record of non-attendance. Lewis L. Strauss, Admiral of the Navy and former chairman of the *Atomic Energy Commission,* said of his friend Jahncke: "He was a man of courage and dedication to American ideals ... vindicated by history ... a brave man who did not hesitate to fight in a good cause even when alone."¹⁰² And lastly, when Paul F. Jahncke, Ernest's brother, died on October 1, 1965, the local paper said that the Jahncke Family and the Jahncke tradition "has been one of the notable American stories."¹⁰³ No, that's not all: Commodore Jahncke's grand-nephew, Barton Jahncke, won an Olympic gold medal for himself and his country in Dragon Class Yachting at the 1968 Olympic Games.¹⁰⁴

Conclusions

All the evidence seems to indicate that there was about Ernest Lee Jahncke, Sr. not an ounce of guile, no innate sense of cunning or duplicity. This is not always the same as an unabashed compliment in the case of Jahncke. He was direct and honest, in his own mind and as he perceived the world. With such a person there is frequently little sympathy for someone else's diametrically opposing view. Such seemed the Commodore's mind-set on many important issues, and surely it was so regarding America's participation in the Games of the Eleventh Olympiad. He believed to his marrow that it was wrong for his country to participate in the Berlin Olympic Games amidst an atmosphere of Nazi mesmerism. Too bad he was an IOC member. How inconvenient that his IOC code preached "No involvement in politics." Jahncke is to be faulted for not resigning from the IOC in 1935, and announcing to all who would listen his heart-felt reasons for doing so.

Baillet-Latour must take heavy censure for obdurateness in demanding that every single IOC member think precisely the same
as he regarding America's participation in the games. The IOC
president wrote a six-page blistering open letter to the AAU dated
November 17, 1935, a response to Judge Mahoney's "open letter"
to Baillet-Latour, dated October 20, 1935. These "multitude of
misstatements prove that Mr. Mahoney is totally ignorant of all
Olympic questions, as ignorant as the German authorities were
at the time when they envisaged the Olympic Games as being
German Games, to be a German Committee and run according
to German rules and spirit.... The IOC above all is entirely free
from any political influence."[105]

Baillet-Latour, like his predecessor Coubertin, embraced
Olympic principles as the essence of humanitarianism, cosmopolitanism, and internationalism. Jahncke had, in his universal
humanism, a higher concept. Some serious scholars of the Olympic ideology, the Olympic Idea called "Olympism," would say that
the two men were at exactly the same lofty level, but looking in
opposite directions. Both were good persons, narrow, stubborn,
and consumed by their own correctness. Neither ever displayed
unsureness, ambivalence on major Olympic issues—a sure sign
of partial intellectual myopia. Mahoney, Brundage, Sherrill, Kirby were infected with the same illness of self-righteousness. But
significant evidence exists, in the case of Jahncke, that he was
a decent man, a charismatic, energetic athlete-businessman-
family person, who did much for his city, state, and nation. His
contribution to the world community, by any objective measure,
was small by comparison.

This researcher is unable, at this time, to fathom why Jahncke did not "follow through" with his intention to resign from
the IOC—to insist unequivocally, that his formal resignation be
accepted. Similar questions persist regarding Baillet-Latour and
why he did not follow every available avenue to seek Jahncke's
membership relinquishment long before the Olympic Games. The
IOC's thin veneer of righteousness in expelling Jahncke for lack
of attendance was criticized at the time as dishonest and continues to this day. Honesty is almost always the best policy, and
surely would have been in July of 1936. As for Jahncke, the domestic giant, he was an unusually talented person who made a
big mistake in 1927 when he accepted an invitation to serve the
IOC. Errors all around. But Jahncke did act consistently in late
1935 and through the next year. His own version of a moral categorical imperative, an unconditional command of conscience,

superseded any loyalty that he might have had about a personal pledge to eternal IOC political neutrality. Jahncke seemed untouched by the babble of conflicting opinion in America about participation or non-participation in dangerous Berlin 1936. He knew what it was that he must do, and he did it. In a perceptive recent essay on "Ethical Duties of Scientists," Theodore Friedmann, spoke of Dante Alighieri's *Divine Comedy* and the stations along the descent to the Inferno at which wrongdoers find their deserved final rest. There are levels reserved for all grades of miscreants, wrote Friedmann, levels determined by the severity of their offenses:

> I suspect but cannot prove that there are somewhat fewer scientists along this path than, for instance, politicians or leveraged-buyout bankers.[106]

My own feeling, as disinterested as it is possible for me to be, is that Ernest Jahncke, need not worry about joining the miscreants mentioned by Dante and alluded to by Friedmann, the Chair of Biomedical Ethics at the San Diego School of Medicine. Ernest Lee Jahncke, Sr. had since childhood set his life-yacht on a straight and narrow course, and if he could speak to us today would probably say that he would have it no other way.

NOTES

1 Fifty IOC members met in Berlin's Hotel Adlon, July 30, 1936, underscoring the Executive Committee's statement of February 12, 1936 that "Mr. Jahncke had seriously acted against the Statutes of IOC and been almost guilty of treason against the IOC and his colleagues when suggesting a complete boycott of the Berlin Games 1936. He would be given a chance to apologize before the Session in Berlin." In July, the full committee, noting that Mr. Jahncke had "no intention to retire ... unanimously decided to exclude him. W. M. Garland did not participate in the vote, but nevertheless expressed his profound disapproval of his colleague's attitude." See *Proces-Verbal de la. 34eme Session du Comite International Olympique, Garmisch-Partenkirchen 11 Fevrier 1936* and *Proces-Verbal de la 35eme Session du Comite International Olympique, Berlin, 30-31 Juillet au 15 Aout 1936*, IOC Archives, Lausanne, Switzerland (hereafter "IOC Archives"). See also J. Abramson, "American's Ouster Laid to His Criticism of Nazis," *New York Herald Tribune*, July 31, 1936, p. 21. Few print journalists surpassed J.P. Abramson in Olympic Games history. His by-lines from Olympic venues Amsterdam 1928 through Munich 1972, are classics.

2 Jahncke to IOC president Count Henri Baillet-Latour and German Olympic Organizing Committee Chief, Dr. Theodore Lewald, November 25, 1935; see "Jahncke Eager to Keep U.S. from Olympics," *New York Herald Tribune,* November 27, 1935, p. 11.

3 P. de Coubertin, *Noveaux Programmes d'Enseignement Secondaire,* Paris 1910, pp. 1-2.

4 See *Who's Who in America,* volume 4 (1961-1968), p. 489. Most references state 1877 as Jahncke's birth year, but several sources note 1880. For example, M.O. Frost's biographical sketch "Ernest Lee Jahncke" states that "Jahncke was born in 1880, entered Tulane University at 15 and graduated in 1899." See the *New Orleans States,* March 24, 1924, p. 1 (hereafter "Meigs O. Frost").

5 "Jahncke Paid Final Tribute," *The Times-Picayune* [New Orleans], November 18, 1960, p. 6.

6 L. Huger, "High Post in the Navy Goes to a Shipbuilder," *New York Times,* March 24, 1929; sec. 11, p. 9 (article "Huger").

7 "Ernest Lee Jahncke," *The Story of Louisiana,* vol.11, New Orleans 1960, pp. 584-585 (hereafter *The Story of Louisiana*). President Woodrow Wilson appointed Jahncke a major in the U.S. Army, and in separate government contracts (May, 1917 and March, 1919), contracted with the Jahncke Dry Dock and Ship Repair Company for a multi-million dollar job. See folder "J-JE (Biography)" in the Louisiana Collection Room of Tulane University Library, New Orleans, Louisiana.

8 See Huger essay.

9 See "A True Pioneer," *Jahncke Papers, Box 1,* The Historic New Orleans Collection, New Orleans, Louisiana (hereafter THNOC).

10 See "Commodore Ernest Lee Jahncke," *The Tulanee News Bulletin,* 9 (August 1929), pp. 119-120.

11 See Huger essay.

12 Tomlinson to Lucas, April 15, 1991.

13 See J. Espy, "Olympics for District Urged by Secretary Jahncke," *Washington Post,* May 20, 1929, p. 12 (hereafter "Espy").

14 The painting of Ernest Lee Jahncke Sr., hangs in the ROTC office of Tulane University, New Orleans, Louisiana, and was painted by Robert W. Crafton in 1930.

15 Biographical material on Thompson, AOA president 1912-1920, and 1924-1926, may be found in Volume XV of *The National Cyclopedia of American Biography,* pp. 202-203; *New York Times,* September 6, 1930, p. 15; *New York Herald Tribune, September 6, 1930, p. 15.*

16 Thompson telegram to Jahncke, October 29, 1926. See Jahncke Collection in the Hill Memorial Library, Louisiana State University, Baton Rouge, Louisiana (hereafter "Hill Memorial Library").

17 Jahncke telegram to Thompson, November 4, 1926, Hill Memorial Library.

18 Thompson to Jahncke, November 6, 1926, Hill Memorial Library.

19 *AOA and AOC Minutes 1926,* p. 15. Colonel Thompson, in fragile health, remained only briefly and went on to his summer home in Florida.

20 Sherrill was Yale University Class of 1889. The Stirling Library on campus has voluminous materials on Sherrill, including *The Sherrill Genealogy* (by Sherrill) and his autobiography *My Storybook*. Sherrill's Olympic business in the 1930s is covered by the young sport historian, Stephen R. Wenn, in his "A Tale of Two Diplomats: George S. Messersmith and Charles H. Sherrill on Proposed American Participation in the 1936 Olympics," *Journal of Sport History*, 16 (Spring, 1989), pp. 27-43.

21 AOA and AOC Minutes *1926*, pp. 3-12.

22 Jahncke telegram to Sherrill, December 17, 1926, Hill Memorial Library.

23 Ibid., Sherrill to Jahncke, December 20, 1926.

24 Ibid., Sherrill to Jahncke, February 13, 1927.

25 See "International Olympic Body Names Jahncke U.S. Member," *New York Times*, April 23, 1927, p. 11.

26 K.A. Scherer, *Der Männerorden. Die Geschichte des Internationalen Olympischen Komitees*, Frankfurt a.m. 1974, p. 133.

27 See Huger. So many Roosevelts had held the office now occupied by Jahncke that the post was termed facetiously in navy circles "the only hereditary public office in the United States Government." See "'Hereditary' Roosevelt Post in Navy Goes to Outsider," *New York Times*, March 13, 1929, pp. 1, 33.

28 See *New York Times*, March 13, 1929, p. 1.

29 See Huger essay; *The Story of Louisiana;* "Louisiana Honored," *New Orleans States,* March 12, 1929, n. p.; *Washington Post,* March 13, 1929, p. 5. This last essay listed 35 local, national, and professional organizations (engineering, political, fraternal, civic, yachting, and sporting) to which the new assistant-secretary Jahncke belonged.

30 H. Hoover, *Public Papers of the Presidents of the U.S. Herbert Hoover,* March 4 to Dec. 31, 1929, Washington, D.C. 1974, p. 23; also "Jahncke Assumes Naval Duties," *New York Times*, April 2, 1929, p. 20.

31 Cora Van Voorhies Stanton, the Commodore's wife lived longer than he and passed away March 18, 1970. Adela Townsend Jahncke married and became Mrs. Charles William Dotson. Cora married Mr. William H. Seemann. For more genealogy, see the New Orleans *Times-Picayune,* November 17, 1960, n. p.

32 *New York Times*, March 14, 1929, p. 26.

33 Davis Lee Jahncke, Jr. to John Lucas, February 4, 1991.

34 See note 14.

35 See B. C. Wingo, "The 1928 Presidential Election in Louisiana," *Louisiana History*, 18 (Fall 1977), p. 411.

36 See "Meigs O. Frost."

37 Jahncke as quoted in "Meigs O. Frost" article.

38 "Hoover Enlists New Patriots in Nation's Service," *New York Times,* June 17, 1929, pp. 1-3.

39 "Exercise with Hoover," *New York Times*, April 13, 1929, p. 18.

40 Mark Sullivan to Ernest Lee Jahncke; November 10, 1930. See

Jahncke Collection; Folder M 345; Tulane University Library Archives (TULA); (hereafter called "Tula").

41 Jahncke quote in "Nicknames in Washington," *The Literary Digest,* 104 (March 8, 1930), p. 41.

42 See *New York Times,* June 27, 1929, p. 3; August 9, 1929, p. 17; August 25, 1929, p. 19.

43 For a partial list, see "The Story of Louisiana."

44 See *Washington Post,* April 7, 1929, p. 3 [Peary], and for Admiral Byrd, *New York Times,* June 21, 1930, pp. 1, 3.

45 For a partial list of duties by the peripatetic Jahncke, see: *New York Times,* June 27, 1930, p. 6; August 9, 1930, p. 13 and p. 21; November 12, 1930, p. 48; December 10, 1930, p. 21; "President Appoints Jahncke a Trustee of the Hoover Foundation" [1931], New Orleans *States-Item,* September 9, 1955, n. p.; *New York Times,* May 12, 1931, p. 23; May 28, 1931, p. 35; June 8, 1931, p. 18; "Jahncke Appointed to Three Committees," *Public Papers of the Presidents—Herbert Hoover, January 1 to* December 31, 1931 (Washington, D.C.: *U.S. Government Printing Office),* pp. 290-291, 379, 519; *New York Times,* July 8, 1931, p. 29; August 5, 1931, p. 5; August 15, 1931, p. 29; August 18, 1931, p. 4; August 22, 1931. p. 28; November 4, 1931, p. 27; January 26, 1932, p. 2; February 13, 1932, p. 8; February 26, 1932, p. 3; February 27, 1932, pp. 2 and 16; April 13, 1932, p. 3; April 28, 1932, p. 2; July 5, 1932, p. 3; "Jahncke Hails Hoover as Nation's Savior," *Philadelphia Inquirer,* July 5, 1932, pp.1, 6; *New York Times,* July 20, 1932. p. 32; July 23, 1932, p. 6; September 4, 1932, p. 10; September 8, 1932, p. 3; September 11, 1932, p. 7; September 23, 1932, p. 12; October 15, 1932, p. 3.

46 Letters from travel agents Edgar Allen Forbes and J.B. Avegno (dated December 14, 1927; May 22 and June 26, 1928) are located in personal collection of Jahncke's granddaughter in New Orleans, Lyn Jahncke Tomlinson (hereafter "LJT").

47 Sherrill to Jahncke, December 31, 1927, LJT. The letter continued: "The entire Sherrill family is stuffed with ducks and very pleased and happy for these gifts ... and for the oranges and nuts. Looking forward to your IOC and Olympic Games attendance on July 26."

48 Sherrill to Baillet-Latour, December 31, 1927, IOC Archives, Lausanne, Switzerland (hereafter IOC Archives").

49 Some of the telegrams are Jahncke to Sherrill (June 12, 1928); Sherrill to Jahncke June 18, 1928); Jahncke to Sherrill (June22, 1928); Sherrill to Jahncke (June24, 1928), and Sherrill to Jahncke July 31, 1928), LJT.

50 A. Berdez to Jahncke, December 30, 1928, LJT.

51 Jahncke to Sherrill, February 18, 1929; Jahncke to the IOC, February 21, 1929, LJT.

52 Sherrill to Jahncke, March 29, LJT.

53 Irving Brokaw (1870-1939) was American national champion figure skater, an artist, author, socially-prominent New Yorker, and a multi-millionaire. See *New York Times,* March 20, 1939, p. 17.

54 Baillet-Latour to Sherrill, March 26, 1929, IOC Archives. This researcher has no knowledge, yet, as to which member of the Roosevelt family had sufficient confidence among some IOC members in 1927 to warrant such "a very strong wish." Franklin Delano Roosevelt (1882-1945) was assistant secretary of the Navy (1913-1920), entered private business, and into 1928 politics, won the governorship of New York—a background not altogether different from Ernest Lee Jahncke.

55 Sherrill telegram to the IOC Lausanne, April, 1929, IOC Archives.

56 See J. ESPY's column in *Washington Post,* May 20, 1929, p. 12.

57 Rubien to Baillet-Latour, January 26, 1931, IOC Archives.

58 LJT Collection. Also, President Hoover and Navy Secretary Adams sent Jahncke to the West Coast to represent the administration at the San Francisco Shrine convention and at the Los Angeles Olympic Games. See *New York Times,* July 23, 1932, p. 6.

59 *New York Times,* March 18, 1933, p. 4. Ernest Lee Jahncke, Jr., graduated from Annapolis with highest honors. His father was in the front row of guests. See *New York Times,* May 30, 1933, p. 10.

60 See "Reich Revealed Building U-Boats in Foreign Plants," *New York Times,* September 7, 1934, p. 6; also Jahncke to Connecticut Congressman John Q. Tilson, September 23, 1930; see *New York Herald Tribune,* September 7, 1934, p.4.

61 H. Deutsch, "Few Men Exceeded Stature of Jahncke," New Orleans *States-Item,* November 17, 1960, p. 24.

62 *Preserve the Olympic Ideal,* ed. by The Committee on Fair Play, New York 1935; *Fair Play for American Athletes,* ed. by *American Olympic Committee,* New York 1936; A. Albert, "A General Warns Jews to Lay Low or Else ... ," *The American Hebrew and Jewish Tribune* (October 25, 1935), pp. 383, 392; R. Mandell, *The Nazi Olympics,* New York 1971; J. Holmes, *Olympiad 1936,* New York 1971; H. Bernett, *Sportpolitik im Dritten Reich,* Stuttgart 1971; H. Bernett, "Das Bild der Olympischen Spiele von 1936," *Leibeserziehung* 8 (1972), pp. 275-278; M. Gottlieb, "The American Controversy over the Olympic Games," *American Jewish Historical Quarterly* 61 (1972), pp. 181-213; A. Kruger, *Die Olympischen Spiele 1936,* Berlin 1972; H.J. Teichler, "Berlin 1936—Ein Sieg der NS-Propaganda?" *Stadion* 2 (1976), pp. 265-306; A. Hellerstein, "The 1936 Olympics: A U.S. Boycott that Failed," *Potomic Review,* 8(1981), pp. 1-9; Brohm, *Jeux Olympiques a Berlin 1936,* Brussels 1983; S. Wenn, "The Commodore Hotel Re-visited: an Analysis of the 1935 AAU Convention," *Proceedings, 6th Canadian Symposium, History of Sport,* 1988, pp. 188-199; H.J. Teichler, "Zum Ausschluss der Deutschen Juden von den Olympischen Spielen 1936," *Stadion* 15 (1989), pp. 45-64; S. Wenn, "A Suitable Policy of Neutrality? FDR and the Question of American Participation in the 1936 Olympics," *The International Journal of the History of Sport* 8 (December, 1991), pp. 319-335.

63 Lord KIllanin and J. Rodda, *The Olympic Games. 80 Years of People, Events and Records,* New York 1976, p. 17.

64 See *New York Times,* November 27, 1935, p. 2; *New York Her-*

ald Tribune, November 27, 1935, p. 11; *Washington Post,* November 27, 1935, pp.1, 19-20; *Philadelphia Inquirer,* November 27, 1935, pp. 17, 20; *Los Angeles Times,* November 27, 1935, pp. 9, 11; *Chicago Daily Tribune,* November 27, 1935, p. 22.

65 *The American Hebrew* (December 6, 1935), pp. 124-126.

66 Ibid, p. 126.

67 See "Zack Farmer...," *New York Times,* November 28, 1935, p. 2, and Garland's comment on the same page.

68 *Los Angeles Times,* November 30, 1935, pp. 7-8.

69 A short biography of Mahoney is located in the *Amateur Athlete,* 29 (August, 1958), pp. 29-30, while the definitive biography of Brundage remains A. Guttmann, *The Games Must Go On: Avery Brundage and the Olympic Movement,* New York 1984.

70 See Minutes of the AAU 1935, pp. 210-211; *Los Angeles Times,* December 9, 1935, pp. 9, 12, and "Mahoney Forces Lose," *New York Times,* December 9, 1935, pp. 1, 17.

71 Ludwig, *New York Times,* December 16, 1935, p. 10. Emil Ludwig (1881-1948), German biographer, wrote highly esteemed books *Napoleon; Bismarck; Schliemann of Troy,* and other works.

72 Ernest Lee Jahncke, Jr. See this address in the Hill Memorial Library.

73 Rubien succeeded James Edward Sullivan in 1914, as both Olympic and AAU secretary. See *New York Times,* July 6, 1951, p. 23.

74 Rubien wrote his boss Avery Brundage, enclosing a copy of Jahncke's letter, and a note: "It took Jahncke a month to write this letter and he evidently wants the publicity during the winter [Olympic] sports." See *Avery Brundage Collection* (hereafter ABC], Reel 34, Box 34; letter dated February 13, 1936.

75 Ibid.

76 "Nazis and the Olympic Games," *The Times* [London], October 23, 1935, p. 13.

77 A. Allen, "A General Warns Jews to Lay Low or Else," *The American Hebrew and Jewish Tribune,* October 25, 1935, p. 384.

78 See *New York Times,* June 26, 1936, p. 19; June 27, 1936, p. 17; July 8, 1936, p. 19; July 12, 1936, p. 6 of part II; July 14, 1936, p. 19, and July 16, 1936, p. 18.

79 *New York Times,* July 28, 1936, p. 12. Murray Hulbert and Gustavus Town Kirby were in line for a spot on the IOC, continued the clipping, but Kirby "has been subjected to some criticism since he was drawn into the case that resulted in Mrs. Eleanor Holm Jarrett's losing her place on the team. Mr. Kirby was the 'judge' in a mock trial on board the *Manhattan* which Mrs. Jarrett described as 'shocking.'" This researcher has for a long time been convinced that the IOC forever eliminated Kirby (1874-1956) from possible elevation because of this alleged indiscretion. Since his student days at Columbia in the late nineteenth-century, Kirby had been deeply involved in Olympic work.

80 *New York Times,* July 30, 1936, p. 23.

81 D. Hart-Davis, *Hitler's Games. The 1936 Olympics,* New York 1986, p. 148.

82 Coco Jahncke Seemann to Lucas, April 17, 1991.

83 See *States,* July 30, 1936, p. 13, and *Item,* July 30, 1936, pp. 1, 4.

84 Baillet-Latour, as quoted in Killanin's *The Olympic Games,* p. 17.

85 O. Mayer, *A Travers les Anneaux Olympiques,* Geneve 1960, p. 152.

86 Kinsley's Olympic connections may be found in J. Lucas, "Americans in the IOC: 17 Have Served the Movement," *The Olympian,* 10 (February, 1984), pp. 22-26.

87 J. P. Abramson in the *New York Herald-Tribune,* July 31, 1936, p. 21.

88 *New York Times,* July 31, 1936, pp. 1, 3.

89 See *Boston Post,* July 31, 1936, p. 19; *The Boston Globe,* July 31, 1936, p. 21; *Los Angeles Times,* July 31, 1936, pp. 9-10; *The Boston Herald,* July 31, 1936, p. 23; *Chicago Daily Tribune,* July 31, 1936, p. 23.

90 R. L. Gibson, "Avery Brundage: Professional Amateur," Ph.D. dissertation, Kent State University 1976, p. 80.

91 *New York Times,* August 6, 1936, p. 24; *The Atlanta Journal,* August 6, 1936, p. 15, and "Jahncke Charges His Opposition to Berlin Cost Olympic Post," *New York Herald Tribune,* August 6, 1936, p. 3.

92 Baillet-Latour, as quoted in Jahncke's "Letter-to-the-Editor," *New York Times,* November 11, 1936, p. 34.

93 Ibid., Jahncke's letter was sent from New Orleans and dated November 7, 1936.

94 A. Gould, *The Amateur Athlete,* 8 (January, 1937), pp. 3, 15; Mahoney is quoted in *New York Times,* December 7, 1937, p. 29.

95 ABC, Reel 17, Box 30.

96 IOC Archives.

97 See *Louisiana Tourist Bulletin,* 3 (October, 1940), p. 16; TULA 1916-1964; New Orleans *States-Item,* September 9, 1955.

98 New Orleans *Times-Picayune,* May 31, 1957, n. p.

99 New Orleans *Times-Picayune,* November 17, 1960, pp. 1, 3, 18; November 18, 1960, p. 6; *New Orleans States-Item,* November 17, 1960, pp. 6, 24.

100 Lucas interview of Lyn Jahncke Tomlinson, May 14, 1991, New Orleans. She also said that "Grandfather Jahncke possessed a wonderful sense of justice and fair play." Tomlinson to Lucas; April 15, 1991.

101 *New York Times,* November 17, 1960, p. 37; *New York Herald Tribune,* November 17, 1960, p. 25; *The Washington Post,* November 17, 1960, p. B6.

102 See Strauss's "Letter to the Editor," *New York Times,* November 29, 1960, p. 36.

103 New Orleans *Times-Picayune,* October 2, 1965, p. 10.

104 See *Boston Globe,* October 22, 1968, p. 35, and in *Olympic Review,* 82-83 (September-October, 1974), p. 451.

105 Baillet-Latour's "Open Letter to the AAU" reproduced in Minutes of the AAU 1935, pp. 149-150.

106 Th. Friedmann, "Ethical Duties of Scientists, their Institutions, and the Guild of Science," *The Journal of NIH Research* 4 (February, 1992), p. 22.

16.
In the Eye of the Storm:
Paavo Nurmi and the American
Athletic Amateur-Professional Struggle
(1925 and 1929)*

In the contentious and irresolvable dispute about the merits of amateur athletics as compared to the sport-for-pay professionalized version, the decade of the 1920s was the most divisive. The American sprint champion, Charles Paddock (1900-1943), multiple world and Olympic champion, was the second most controversial figure of the 1920s heated debate about how much money could an amateur athlete accept.[1]

Ahead of "Charlie" Paddock and far ahead of all the rest in this nearly endless quarrel was the master long-distance runner from Finland, Paavo Nurmi (1897-1973). His nine gold and three silver medals in three Olympic Games are without a rival.[2] Nurmi was the Olympic champion at the Antwerp, Belgium Games of the Seventh Olympiad in 1920, he broke a dozen world records in the next few years, and in January of both 1925 and 1929, following incredible success at the Paris and Amsterdam Olympic Games (1924 and 1928), he came to America and raced a total of seventy-five times. Testimonies and anecdotal records indicate that Nurmi, the "Flying Finn," was paid money at every one of these American competitions, and that in both years he returned home a very wealthy man. No one has recorded the long-distance races run by Nurmi on the European continent between 1919 and 1934, but several hundred competitions would not be an exaggeration, and at many of them he won a great deal of money. Both his North American and European financial successes were direct rules violations of the Finnish Athletics Association (FAA), the Interna-

* STADION, XVIII, 2 (1992), 225-246.

tional Amateur Athletics Federation (IAAF), the Amateur Athletic
Union (AAU) of the United States, and the International Olympic
Committee (IOC). This paper was an effort to describe and analyze
track and field amateurism in the United States during the 1920s,
and to use the dramatic example of the alleged greatest perpetrator of amateur rules violations, Paavo Nurmi, as proof of the moral
dilemma faced by the "super-star" amateur athlete, but possibly,
more so by the "policemen" of the rules.

Amateur Athletic Rules in the United States 1920–1924

During the half-decade immediately following the First World
War, the American AAU was the largest amateur sports organization
in the world and remained so for an additional twenty years. The
National Collegiate Athletic Association (NCAA), founded in 1906,
helped several hundred American universities in their quest for elite
athletes, and in a peculiar way was both the partner and the implacable rival of the AAU.[3] The American Olympic Committee (AOC),
chartered by the IOC as the legal organization in the United States
to prepare for Olympic Games participation, underwent massive re-
habilitation in 1919 and 1920, and was renamed in 1921 as the
American Olympic Association (AOA).[4] The new AOA was no threat
to the thirty-three year old AAU, for the entire administrative hierarchy of the New York City-based Association were long-time AAU
leaders. For another full generation the AAU was significantly more
powerful than the nation's Olympic committee. Before the war, both
organizations were dominated by James Edward Sullivan (1860-
1914), who, for more than twenty years, imposed the elitist, English
definition of athletic amateurism, a concept grafted onto the first
modern Olympic Games (1896) by the French Baron Pierre de Coubertin. Sullivan stamped his will on the AAU-AOC leadership with
the 1913 admonition that the professional athlete must never be
allowed to participate in amateur and Olympic Games competitions
lest all semblance of the "morality of play" be lost.[5] Ten years later,
the IOC accepted the British definition of an amateur and, in turn,
the Americans wrote into their rule book:

> That the payment of players or athletes, either during
> the time they are preparing for the Games, or during the
> Games, for broken time, is contrary to the fundamental
> principles of amateurism in particular and of the Olym-
> pic movement in general, and cannot therefore, under
> any circumstances, be permitted.[6]

The AAU was in concert with the official American College track and field body, the Intercollegiate Association of Amateur Athletes of America (IC4A), both of them pronouncing that athletic competition must never be more than an avocation and that "receiving pay or financial benefits for sport competitions or exhibitions" is absolutely forbidden.[7]

Charlie Paddock was the most popular, the most flamboyant runner in America during the whole of 1923. He was also the richest, having collected a purse of money at scores of competitions, with bonuses paid for fifteen world records at distances 40 yards through 300 meters. It was, of course, contrary to all the rules. President of the AAU, William C. Prout, declared that Paddock had made a mockery of them all and that the young Californian would be denied permission to "barnstorm" Europe that summer. An angry Paddock called the AAU and AOC hierarchy a bunch of hypocrites. The national amateur athletic "climate" was unready for the profit-making Paddock, and yet, a year later, he was issued an American Olympic team vest and competed in the Paris Olympic Games, winning fifth place in the 100 meters and the silver medal in the 200 meter dash.[8]

In Paris, the venerable founder of the modern Olympic Games and the IOC president, Baron Pierre de Coubertin (1863-1937), was preparing his retirement speech and volunteered for all those that might be interested: "'Broken Time' must not be paid to the amateur athlete," adding that "the lust for money is threatening to rot its marrow the code of athletic amateurism." The 66-year-old Coubertin admitted "that there is a certain amount of cheating and swindling [in international amateur athletics], ... the direct outcome of the lowering of moral standards."[9]

In such an atmosphere of suspicion and sometimes even fear of the professional athlete, the young solitary Nurmi ran for hours every day through dark, cool Finnish forests, logging thousands of miles a year and setting brand new standards of harsh training. He was dreadfully poor and probably dreamed of wealth. He was probably unaware of new IOC legislation in 1923 that made it impossible for the amateur to make money as a result of winning races. The future president of the IOC, the Belgian Count Baillet-Latour, proposed legislation and helped get it passed, stating that there must never be circumstances, direct or indirect, in which an amateur athlete may profit from his physical prowess. Baron de Coubertin said little at this meeting, but wrote about it several years later. The amateur dilemma, especially the issue of "Broken Time" "became a fatal conflict between the modernist trends of progressive circles and the diehard conservatism of the old English idea of sport."[10]

Nurmi was simply the *nonpareil* of the Paris Olympic Games of 1924. Daily temperatures in excess of 100° F (the city newspapers called the weather "furnace-hot") seemed not to bother the "inhuman Finnish running machine." He won two gold medals in the 1,500- and 5,000-meter races, fifty minutes apart, and an additional two gold in the 3,000 meter team race and the 10,000-meter cross-country competition.[11] Grantland Rice was in the stands and cabled his *New York Herald* colleagues about Nurmi: "The superman has arrived at last."[12] The young Finn had, arguably, become the most famous athlete in the world, his performances "beyond human comprehension."[13]

Nurmi—Child of Finnish Poverty and Angst

For centuries the Finnish people suffered grave human rights injustices at the hands of Russia on the Eastern front and from the Swedes in the west. A third of Finland's population died of starvation in the great seventeenth-century famine. Nurmi was born of very poor parents on June 13, 1897, the eldest of five children, and began working at age 12 when his father died. "Life was very hard and I only ate green vegetables," remembered Nurmi. A friend of his wrote: "Sullenness and hardness were traits that remained with Paavo all through his life."[14]

Following the Bolshevik success in the Russian Revolution of 1917, Finland or "Suomi" gained independence and elected its first president in 1919. Few European nations emerged from such suffering and barest survival as did Finland, which retained both patriotism and national toughness at the highest level. The word for it in the peculiar Finnish language is "Sisu." K. P. Silberg, in a 1927 book called *The Athletic Finn,* wrote that "Sisu" was Finnish obstinacy, the result of endless national deprivation, resulting in individual grit—"A determined and co-extensive effort of mind and body to consummate a difficult task."[15] "Sisu" seemed to define the fatherless boy Nurmi, who very early in life became "harnessed to hard work ... and came to consider the grueling exercise of a 20-mile run as play."[16] William O. Johnson wrote: "Born on the nails of poverty, the young Nurmi, with only an elementary school education, turned to running in an attempt, as one of his friends said, 'to find real life.'"[17] It is almost impossible to comprehend his concentration, wrote Matti Hannus, in *Finnish Running Secrets.* Nurmi "left his early friends

and became a quiet, meditating adolescent," and then joined the
army as a teenager and won a race through the forest, with full
60-pound backpack by such a margin that he was accused of
taking short cuts.[18]

The time seemed right for Nurmi and his business manager,
Hugo Quist, to come to America, the richest nation in the world,
and in January of 1925, in the midst of a people caught up in a
"Golden Age of Sport." Grantland Rice, for one, relished the idea
of seeing Nurmi run again, and he wrote: "Nurmi is coming—a
blue-eyed, sandy-haired ghost blown in from the spirit world."[19]

Nurmi Races Forty-Eight Times in America in 1925

In the America of 1925, sport fans loved winners, and it mat-
tered little to them that some were amateurs or professionals or
a nether group who earned large sums of money and yet called
themselves "amateurs." The AAU hierarchy, headquartered in
New York city since 1888, felt differently toward the latter group,
and in the case of the 28-year-old super-star visitor from Finland, his every move was monitored. And yet, a Nurmi biographer,
Marti Jukola, said that the multiple Olympic champion enjoyed
the five-month tour. "His popularity was enormous, his success
one long sensation."[20] Certainly, the public found the "Phantom
Finn" an absolutely engaging figure and almost all Nurmi's races
were "sell-outs," with maximum ticket prices. Several millions
of dollars were made by sport promoters, from the Boston-New
York "corridor," through the mid-west and in California. There
is circumstantial evidence that the great Nurmi shared in these
profits, despite his personal insistence that he was always an
amateur—someone who engaged in an activity with passion and
with no other extrinsic motive.[21]

The Olympic champion and *Collier's* magazine journalist,
Charlie Paddock, called Paavo Nurmi "the strange, silent Man
of Abo," while another writer of the period called him "the silent,
invincible one who runs as if air was his road."[22] Journalistic hyperbole to be sure, and typical of sport writers in the 1920s. But
it did capture the flavor, the ether of New York City when Nurmi
and his secretary-manager, Quist, arrived in early January of
1925. The former was as laconic and honest as he could be, and
told the assembled media at his hotel: "All my time is used in
walking through the woods."[23] Nurmi began the first of his four-
dozen American races, most of them on small, narrow, wooden
tracks, in the Madison Square Garden, and promptly won and

broke the world indoor records for 1,500 meters, one mile, and 5,000 meters (3:56 1/5; 4:13 3/5, and 14:44 3/5). The date was January 6, 1925, and the standing room only crowd considered themselves fortunate, as thousands of New Yorkers standing outside the Garden were unable to buy a ticket.[24] In a quite extraordinary way, Nurmi, never far removed from Hugo Quist, raced forty-seven more times, winning all but a half-mile sprint to American champion from Penn State University, Alan Helffrich on May 26.[25] Along the way, Nurmi found himself in Chicago, Boston, Portland, Maine, Syracuse, Philadelphia, Newark, Washington, D.C., Baltimore, Ottawa, Hamilton and Toronto (Canada), Buffalo, Milwaukee, Cleveland, Pittsburgh, Detroit, Minneapolis, Los Angeles, San Francisco, Worcester and Cambridge, Massachusetts, and, finally, back to New York City, where he boarded ship and returned home to Finland. He had broken two-dozen world records (some at "odd" distances) and several "classic" performances, such as a 4:12 mile and an 8:58 1/5 two-mile. There is almost no question that this most famous amateur athlete returned to Helsinki a very wealthy man.

Nurmi ran for personal pride, some deep-seated yearning, for Finland, and, despite the lack of extant financial records, probably for a great deal of money. On consecutive evenings, in New York City, in Chicago, and back in New York (January 8, 9, 10, 1925), Nurmi broke three world records before enormous crowds, and slept no more than a few hours on the express train.

"He remained peerless throughout, his resting pulse rate a startling sub-40 beats a minute."[26] The evidence of Nurmi's abridgement of the amateur rules are many, colorful, circumstantial, anecdotal, usually second-hand, and did not satisfy AAU leaders. No matter. The point of this essay is to draw up in detail the frustrating rules of amateur athletics in America at the time, and the unnerving temptation for elite athletes to "cheat." Paavo Nurmi epitomized this dilemma like no other person of his time period.

Daniel Joseph Ferris (1889-1977), was secretary to the AAU president, James Edward Sullivan, in 1907, served as assistant secretary-treasurer 1914-1927. He was its chief administrative officer from 1927 to 1957, and continued on a part-time basis until 1962—a 55-year association with the AAU. He knew Paavo Nurmi very well during the 1925 indoor track season and remembered, many years later, that "the Finn had the lowest pulse rate and the highest asking price of any athlete I knew."[27] The highly regarded sport journalist, Jim Murray, was never a party to any of Nurmi's escapades, but Murray had old-time friends that claimed first-hand knowledge of money exchanges. Murray believed them and in 1973, the year of Nurmi's death, he wrote: "Nobody could match Nurmi at being paid off in the dark. He toured America like a cash register and broke records and banks with equal ease."[28] Dan Ferris told another story about the restless Nurmi and a brief stop over in Cleveland. "Meet promoter Joe Williams told me," remembered the AAU boss, "that in addition to expenses, he had to give Nurmi an extra $1,000. That was an awful lot of money in 1925."[29]

Rumor and innuendo followed Nurmi (and Hugo Quist) on their accelerated, peripatetic tour of the United States and several Canadian cities. Frantic sport promoters wanted the "Abo Antelope" from Finland in their arenas. It would insure record profits, and this in spite of the "swollen expense reimbursement" asked for by Nurmi-Quist team. The sport media was in full form by April of 1925, and one of their members, Braven Dyer, remembered that "whatever the admission, it's believed that Nurmi usually got the lion's share of the gate."[30] Despite a promise to run in the famous Drake Relays in Iowa, Nurmi and Quist took the train out of Chicago and headed directly for a big race in Los Angeles' Memorial Coliseum, bypassing the Relays. Chicago and New York City and Los Angeles newspapers shouted "Nurmi's amateur status questioned," and "Exorbitant sum demands keep Nurmi out of Drake Carnival." The close-mouthed Nurmi said almost nothing, and Hugo Quist was, again, completely unhelpful. But Kenneth L. "Tug" Wilson[31] was director of the "wounded" Drake Relays and told newspaper reporters that Nurmi and his Olympic champion countryman, Willi Ritola, had asked for $1,500 in appearances fees for the two, plus "full expenses for both of them and their manager, from New York City to Des Moines, Iowa, and all the way back to Finland."[32] Quist denied the whole thing and received surprising support from Fred Rubien, the secretary of the AAU, the official and only American agency monitoring all foreign amateur athletes. Rubien's long career of efficiency and honesty was convincing, and he asserted that no punitive actions would be taken, insisting that "I personally undertook the arrangements for Nurmi's participation in meets in this country. I was informed a month ago that the Finnish runners' schedule would not enable them to go to Des Moines.... I have been watching this Nurmi situation like a hawk ... and I am able to say that never have I found a cleaner or finer amateur than Nurmi. He has fulfilled the rules of the

202 / John Apostal Lucas

AAU as closely as any amateur who has ever visited America. Nurmi simply has no interest in money."[33]

This "Nurmi situation" became more convoluted as a Reuters dispatch, sent worldwide and dated May 7, 1925, stated that "Secretary of AAU Rubien has temporarily cancelled Paavo Nurmi's engagements following charges of exorbitant demands for expenses alleged to have been made by Hugo Quist."[34] Only a few days later *The Times* of London, announced that "Nurmi, Ritola, and Quist are exonerated on all counts of alleged excessive expenditures."[35] Of course, Nurmi raced inside the Los Angeles Coliseum and in Harvard Stadium—at both ends of the country, running with consummate ease, winning and setting world records before great crowds of awe-struck spectators.[36]

Nurmi left Boston for New York City and returned to Finland "for a long rest," noting that "America is best country." Rubien released several bulletins, one of them stating that "Nurmi has rejoiced in the retention of his amateur status." The other item noted that "Nurmi has refused 50,000 English pounds from a British circus promoter and a breakfast food manufacturer." Landing in Helsinki, the famous Finn may or may not have been impressed with the completed statue of a larger-man life Nurmi—the "world's greatest athlete."[37]

The Perplexing World of Amateur Athletics 1921-1925

Sport historian, Ronald A. Smith, encapsulated in a single sentence the origins of the unsettling amateur athletic "code." He wrote: "The heart of amateurism is social elitism, born in Victorian England by the upper classes to exclude those of the working class."[38] On the North American continent, in Europe, and especially in Britain, the highly successful amateur athlete who also happened to be poor very frequently accepted money for his skill, and in so doing broke the rules of the day. Following the First World War, in 1921, representatives of the IOC met with officers of several national Olympic committees (NOC's), the international sport federations (ISF's) delegates, and decided that "each federation shall write its own definition of an amateur."[39] In the United States, unlike other nations, there was no single ruling body for track and field athletics, but rather, the AAU controlled all major Olympic sports.[40] The rule was crystal clear: athletic competition was for fun and not profit. Pleasures of the mind, body, and spirit, and never cash, were to be the rewards of the amateur athlete. Sport must *never* be more than an avocation and therefore by definition receiving money, beyond very minimum expenses, was against the rules.

IOC president Coubertin and his people had agonized over whether poor amateur athletes should be compensated for loss of salary while they were away from their jobs for days and sometimes weeks at a time. "Absolutely not," decides the IOC, strongly influenced by the ultra-conservative British Olympic Association (BOA), which made it clear "that the payment of players or athletes, either during the time they are preparing for the Olympic Games, or during the Games, for 'broken time', is contrary to the fundamental principles of amateurism ... and cannot therefore, under any circumstances, be permitted."[41]

It is not possible to know if Coubertin had Paavo Nurmi in mind, when the French Baron wrote in January of 1924: "Everyone knows there are false amateurs, ... well-known sportsmen who have no objection to adding a useful windfall to their customary income."[42] At the important Prague Olympic Congress in May of 1925, Coubertin opened the meeting of delegates from the IOC-NOC-ISF's with agonizing observation and plea:

> A lot of cheating and lying goes on. The lust for money is threatening to rot sport to its marrow. We must ruthlessly disqualify the false amateurs who reap fat rewards....[43]

All in attendance knew that it was the Baron's swan song, as he added official notice of retirement after 29 years of IOC leadership. Belgian Count Henri Baillet-Latour (1876-1942) became the third IOC president, and repeated what he said nearly a year before at the 22nd IOC session, on July 8, 1924: "There must never be circumstances, direct or indirect, in which an amateur athlete may financially benefit from his athletic victories."[44] With pronouncements such as these, and they were expanded a hundred-fold by amateur sport leaders, Paavo Nurmi walked—and ran—on tremulous ground. But it was all he knew, as he began another assault on the long-distance record books and harsh preparations for the Games of the Ninth Olympiad, in Amsterdam, Holland, in the summer of 1928.

A Muted Nurmi Return to the United States in 1929

"Running is my life," said Nurmi on the eve of his 30th birthday. In July of 1926, he lowered his own 3,000-meter world record and shared with teammates a new record for the 6,000-meter relay. On September 11, in Berlin, Nurmi finished third behind Germany's Dr. Otto Peltzer and Sweden's Edwin Wide. All of them broke Nurmi's old world record for 1,500 meters. Another Nurmi record fell in 1927, this time at 2,000 meters.[45] At the Amsterdam Olympic Games, Nurmi won silver medals in the 5,000 meters, the 3,000-meter steeplechase, and a gold medal in the ten-kilometer "flat" race. Only Finish countrymen beat him in the shorter races. Track experts evaluate his October 7, 1928 exploits in Berlin, of 12 miles in a single hour, circling a cinder track, as his greatest world record. "Twelve consecutive five-minute miles; extraordinary," wrote Colonel F.A.M. Webster,[46] Americans were very kind to Nurmi back in 1925, and so he returned to New York City in January of 1929, to be met once again with both glory and accusations. He was accompanied by double Olympic bronze medallist, Edwin Wide, and both men were interviewed by *Outlook* magazine's Herbert Reed:

> Both men have been exceedingly cautions this time to avoid any appearance of barnstorming for a price, and have been guaranteed amateurs by their own countries and by the Amateur Athletic Union of this country.[47]

Nurmi raced only fifteen times in America, between January 20 and his two-mile victory on a muddy track in late April at Philadelphia's Penn Relays. His legs were constantly sore, and when he was not resting them and not racing, he was in and out of "hot water" with the AAU.[48] Nurmi, still unable to speak the English language, was accompanied by an interpreter at AAU headquarters on January 7 and 9, in both cases: (1) to prove that he was gainfully employed back in Finland; (2) that he was, in every way, an amateur athlete; and (3) incredibly, that he had no intention of becoming a professional.[49] On January 19, the great Finn broke three world records in a single race, "always carrying a watch in the palm of his right hand." The very next day, the AAU received word from Boston track meet promoters that Nurmi would race in that city but only "for big money."[50] But all seemed well and "the Finnish Marvel" went to Boston, winning with a hundred yards to spare.[51] Nurmi won in Newark on January 31 and lost a sensational mile to America's best runner, Ray Conger, in the Madison Square Garden on February 9th, while "15,000 cheered wildly."[52] The tired Nurmi avoided running against Sweden's Wide and teammate, Eino Purje, both of whom were earning a living by running on American tracks in that winter of 1929. Journalist Jesse Abramson wrote about an interview he had with AAU boss, Dan Ferris, who was angry and suspended Nurmi for not competing in the indoor national championships. "He refuses to run Wide and Purje. We have no choice but to suspend Nurmi."[53] But the "long suspension" lasted but two weeks, and a refreshed Nurmi was reinstated and won a March 9 race in New York's 7th Regiment Armory.[54] At the outdoor Penn Relays in Philadelphia, Nurmi ran a 9:17 4/5 two-mile, over a muddy track.[55] Nurmi's second America odyssey was over and he headed home to Finland, in poor health and with aching legs.

Nurmi's Glory and Agony 1930-1934

The AAU of America during the 1920s and 1930s helped make thieves and hypocrites of many of its own amateur athletic champions. And the same could be said of the flood of European sport champions coming to America for both fame and fortune. The amateur codes, as they were written by all amateur administrative bodies of this early twentieth century, were elitist, restrictive, unfair, and unrealistic. Of course, no one forced these athletes to remain amateur and resort to imaginative, even devious ways of earning a living at a part-time job, of training several thousand hours a year, of being away from work as many as fifty work days a year and receiving no "broken-time" salaries for their efforts. Paavo Nurmi was infinitely more talented than all the rest, and decided as a young man to take the practical route and ignore the letter, if not the spirit of the amateur rules.

There was absolutely nothing wrong with Nurmi's health and form in 1930 and 1931. He continued breaking world records all over the Continent, and opponents "appeared no more than a mouthful to Nurmi."[56] His real antagonists were the athletic bureaucrats who wrote the rulebooks. The Olympic Games were coming to Los Angeles in the summer of 1932, and the three-time Olympian wanted new success, to win the ultimate footrace, the 42 kilometer, 26 mile 385 yard marathon. So did his Finnish track and field federation, that country's Olympic Committee, the vast majority of enthusiasts around the world wished him success. The IOC and its loyal associates on the IAAF were more circumspect about the "living legend," Nurmi, and looked deeply into allegations of irregularities, rumors of big money exchanges, and made every effort to obtain records of cash payments. The latter was very hard to obtain. The IAAF's secret session in Berlin on

April 3, 1932, issued a bulletin declaring Nurmi disqualified "the evidence against him so strong that suspension was inevitable." President Edström refused to meet with the press, while Finnish authorities cried "foul," pointing out that allegations of big-money payments in Poland, Italy, and Germany, were rumors, without a shred of "hard" evidence. Sweden's Bo Eklund, federation secretary, demanded that Finnish authorities should also disqualify Nurmi. They did no such thing, requesting and even track and field president, Urho Kekkonen, declared all accusations "unwarranted." Kekkonen (1900-1986), who would become Finland's political president in 1956, accused the IAAF of acting on "absolutely unfounded reports, on second-hand tales." Let us see the unvarnished facts, he demanded.[57] The dance continued through April and May of 1932, interrupted only by Nurmi's very short-duration marriage.[58] The phlegmatic Nurmi, athletically ineligible, a man recently divorced, traveled to Vupuri, Finland, for a practice run at the full marathon distance, running it in an incredible 2 hours 22 minutes, more than ten minutes faster than the world record of country Hans Kolehmainen (1920). "Nurmi finished, seemingly without fatigue," wrote an observer.[59] Despite his status, the Finnish Olympic team asked Nurmi to join them on the long trip to Los Angeles, hoping that the IAAF might change its mind at its meeting on the eve of the Olympic Games.

All members of the IAAF, an independent but related body to that of the IOC, remembered Baillet-Latour's admonition that the successful athlete must always "perceive work as even more glorious than sport."[60] Hostility by the amateur athletic leadership was directed toward Nurmi and all of his kind. They had broken the rules of the day and had to be punished. The AAU rules of 1932 were perfectly clear. An athlete's amateur status is terminated immediately, wrote the *AAU Official and Track and Field Handbook,* if he "accepts a prize worth more than $35, if he allows his name to be used to advertise, and if he accepts a purse of money."[61]

Scores of essays on "Nurmi's agony" appeared in all major American newspapers as the Games of the Tenth Olympiad got underway on the second day of August, 1932. He appeared doomed, for the last IOC Congress in Berlin, May 25-30, 1930, had announced to the federations and the NOC's, that continued unalterable opposition to amateur athletes profiting in any way as a result of their skills would be swift and unalterable.[62] The media loved Nurmi and not the IAAF, whose president, millionaire manufacturer from Sweden, Sigfrid Edström (1870-1964), said:

Paavo Nurmi / 207

"Nurmi for the Olympics is no more. Is that all you gentlemen of the press think about?"[63] A member of the IAAF, Avery Brundage (1887-1975), president and future president of the AOC and IOC, respectively, told journalist Alan Gould, on July 28:

> I went into the [IAAF] meeting with an open mind, feeling that Nurmi should be given the benefit of any doubt. Fresh facts ... showed beyond doubt that Nurmi received financial profit from his exhibition races in Germany and elsewhere.[64]

Brundage had changed his mind, for only weeks earlier, he wrote Edström that a well-placed but anonymous member of the Finnish A.A.A. told him that all evidence against Nurmi was circumstantial and that "Nurmi is being convicted on judicially insufficient grounds." Brundage ended his letter: "Mr. Edström, I trust now that he [Nurmi] has been suspended, that you have sufficient, definite evidence to prove the case."[65] A *New York Times* article pointed out that the seven-man IAAF Executive Board and *not* the "full-congress" had expelled Nurmi. Brundage was on that "inner circle" board and he admitted that "Fresh facts, not hitherto in our possession" revealed that large sums of money went to Nurmi in Germany during September and October of 1931.[66] All that Board members would tell Jesse Abramson of the *New York Herald Tribune* was that Nurmi was banished on "good and sufficient grounds, and the case is closed."[67] Nurmi was finished as the games began, sitting inconsolable and silent amidst 102,000 spectators, some of whom shouted "Nurmi, Nurmi, where is Nurmi?" as the Finnish contingent circled the track during opening ceremonies. Hollywood's Douglas Fairbanks, Sr. and aviatrix Amelia Earhart came over and shook Nurmi's hand. He left the stadium by the wrong exit, suffering the last indignity, as a policeman shouted "G'wan now, out of here," took the Finn by the arm and attempted to twist him around. 'Nurmi's blue eyes blazed' as he headed for the Olympic Village."[68]

Nurmi—Not Just Another Casualty of the Amateur Rules

Paavo Nurmi was easily the most prominent amateur and Olympic athlete of the decade after the Great War. His banishment made sport headlines on all continents, especially in Europe and North America. The respected Arthur J. Daley of the *New York Times* found the "secret session of the IAAF a clever coup, ... high-handed ... and a murder of justice."[69] Westbrook Pegler of the *Chicago Daily Tribune* cornered the omnipresent Hugo Quist, and asked him: "How much money did Nurmi take?" Quist smiled and answered unhelpfully: "Less than you think."[70] Quick on the scent were professional sport managers, "A Posse of Promoters Hot on Nurmi's Trail," with offers of $200,000, which he refused.[71] Bitterness and near riots spread among the Helsinki, Finland population as the realization became clear that their beloved Nurmi was no more.[72] As the IAAF meeting ended, IOC leader Baillet-Latour convened his group in the Los Angeles City Hall Tower, pontificating but not mentioning Nurmi's name: "Those who love sport will not allow themselves to take money. Amateurism is a matter of the spirit, rather than of law."[73] The president's first sentence was fatuous, while the second was a form of wisdom. The Finnish long-distance runners missed Nurmi but won most of the Olympic Games medals, left Los Angeles for Chicago, where, as Avery Brundage remembered: "They agreed to run, but only for a share of gate receipts plus $1,000."[74] Back home in Sweden, Edström wrote Mr. Brundage: "The Finns are a hard lot. They crucified me in their press."[75] A very angry Urho Kekkonen, wrote Edström:

> We consider the IAAF's action regarding Nurmi as illegal, as it was a council decision and not that of all the membership, ... a grave error of organization.[76]

Journalist Charlie Paddock had endured similar treatment several years earlier and called Nurmi "an honest man, a very great athlete, with character."[77] The moody Nurmi became disconsolate and moaned: "If I did something wrong, why did they wait three years before taking action? Why turn on me now, when my heart bleeds to end my career by winning the marathon?"[78] Admittedly biased, Martti Jukola, Ph.D., wrote that the "IAAF Executive Board acted precipitously, exceeding its powers."[79] The irreconcilability of the amateur athletic "question," begun in England a hundred years earlier, seemed no closer to a resolution in the post Los Angeles Olympic Games years. Nurmi continued his hopeless efforts for reinstatement.[80]

The Executive Board of the IOC met in Vienna on June 5, 1933, and President Baillet-Latour, in what seemed an indirect slap at the Finnish Olympic Committee which had never wavered in its support of Nurmi, pontificated once again: "I accuse certain Olympic committees of complicity. May I remind all that amateurism is a state of mind and not a law."[81] He had, without possibly realizing it, anticipated the ultimate solution to the dilemma which occurred a half-century later when the words "amateur" and "professional" were stricken from the Olympic Charter. At the same 1933 meeting of the full IOC, Bailiet-Latour's words seemed irrelevant as even more restrictive rules were passed in order to "flush-out perpetrators." The amateur athlete must never be given cash money except for food and lodging. "All travel expenses must be handled by the federations." This same athlete, continued the new edict, must never be allowed to "make use of his sports fame for financial benefit."[82]

The rules allowed Nurmi to run only in Finland, following his banishment, but he made a small "mistake" in June of 1933, and slipped over to Estonia for a small competition. The Estonian authorities said that they were sorry for the error.[83] When the IAAF met on August 28, 1934, in Stockholm, a vote was taken to sustain Nurmi's suspension. "The vote was 12-5, with a great many refraining from voting.... A storm broke over the Congress."[84] The athletic world—administrators, fans, and media, simply would not let go of this Nurmi thing. It did finally come to some kind of uneasy resolution in 1934. Nurmi could still run fast, winning his national championships at 1,500 meters. The pride-filled Finns refused to forgive the IAAF president, Edström, and in that 1934 year he wrote his friend and colleague Brundage: "Why do they not leave me alone? The Finns continue to boycott my company in Helsinki—Asea Electric Ltd., on account of the Nurmi case, and the Finns are very sore about the whole thing. But we have to stand up for justice."[85]

Therein lies the problem. For Edström and Brundage, principle and "justice" were, in every case, defined differently from Nurmi and his kind. Urho Kekkonen had, in a limited sense, the last word in this unseemly story, one in which there would be no winners. He wrote Edström on January 1, 1934: "I should regard as an error of organization the granting of powers to the IAAF Executive Council—the power to punish athletes—that really belong to the entire membership of the IAAF."[86] The whole world of amateur athletics in the 1920s and 1930s was out of kilter. Everyone knew it, no one knew what to do, with a few exceptions. Paavo Nurmi knew what to do, what he had to do, and he succeeded better than anyone of his era. Nurmi was a fine runner well into his 40's, owned and operated a lucrative clothing store in Helsinki, fought bravely in the short, bloody war between Finland and Russia in the early 1940s, and made a dramatic, extraordinary return to the track in 1952, at the Helsinki Olympic Games. He and his lifelong hero, Hannes Kolehmainen (1912 champion) jogged into the stadium carrying the Olympic torch. The 70,000 Finns stood as one and cheered for a full quarter-hour. Nurmi died in 1973. There was a national day of mourning, while thousands wept. President of the nation, Kekkonen, delivered the eulogy. All international wire services carried the story, while major newspapers on two continents carried lengthy obituaries.[87]

Paavo Nurmi was the prototypical amateur-professional athlete of his time, on a grander scale because of his skills, his mysterious personality, and the exotic era in which he lived—the post-war 1920s. He was a model for the restless and rich non-professional super-star athletes of the 1980s and 1990s. He did break the rules, but probably exorcized any feelings of guilt because of his poverty and the uncounted hours of harsh training to gain his remarkable skill. The ten-year "Nurmi Case" was symbolic of the profound, universal malaise suffered by authorities who had not the faintest notion of what to do when the amateur star athlete accepted money, except, of course, to write more and more restrictive rules. It did not work. The "solution" to this dilemma, if one wishes to call it that, occurred in the late 1980s, when the half-hundred sport federations, the 180 national Olympic committees, and the IOC, ceased their endless preoccupations and fruitless efforts to disentangle the "amateur" from the "state-supported" sports-person, from the professional athlete. Never did the professional club and team owners, anywhere in the world, give even a moment's serious thought to this dilemma, let alone its solution. They knew their job and the hard road to fame and then fortune. Their cousins, the amateur athletes, for too long a time, floundered in a haze of conflicting emotion and moral decisions. It may, however, be premature, to pronounce the decade of the 1990s "better" than the 1920s.

NOTES

1 See Paddock's autobiography, *The Fastest Human,* New York 1932. See Chapter 12 "AAU Presents Difficulties" where he talks about "open war with the powerful AAU" (p. 159). Robert Lehr devoted an entire chapter on Paddock's 1923 troubles. See Lehr's *The American Olympic Committee, 1896 -1940: From Chaos to Order,* Ph.D. dissertation, Penn State University 1985.

2 See E. Kemper and B. Mallon, *The Golden Book of the Olympic Games,* Milan 1992, p. 56.

3 Insight into this "love-hate" relationship may be found in A. Flath, *A History of Relations Between the NCAA and the AAU, 1905 -1963,* Champaigne 1964.

4 A useful but not definitive history of the AOC-AOA transition is J. Lucas, "American Preparation for the First Post World War Olympic Games 1919 -1920," *Journal of Sport History,* 10 (1983), 30-44.

5 This researcher is convinced that Sullivan wrote the anonymous and lengthy essay "Definition of an Amateur Athlete," *New York Times,* October 26, 1913; sec. 4, p. 4.

6 See "IOC," *The Times* [London], April 23, 1923, p. 5. "Broken Time" is the concept that salaries of working athletes may be paid to them while they are engaged in national, international, and Olympic competitions to pay them, in essence, for labor they never did.

7 *Official Publication 1920 IC4A,* New York 1920, pp. 10-11.

8 See "Paddock Stirs Hornet's Nest," Flath, *NCAA and AAU,* 65-73; also chapter 5 "Charles W. Paddock: Symbol of AOC Problems," in: Lehr, *American Olympic Committee.* Prout's comments were taken from "AAU Head Opposes Sending Teams Abroad," *New York Times,* March 29, 1923, p. 15, and "Prout's Presidential Address," in: AAU Minutes, November 17-19, 1923, p. 7.

9 One of Coubertin's quotes is located in J. Lucas, *The Modern Olympic Games,* New York 1980, p. 109. Coubertin's comment on "lust for money" is located in P. de Coubertin, *The Olympic Idea. Discourses and Essays,* edited by L. Deim, Schorndorf 1966, p. 97, and Coubertin on "Amateurism," *Bulletin du Comite International Olympique* 25 (Janvier 1951), 15.

10 P. de Coubertin, *Olympic Memoires,* translated by Geoffroy de Navacelle, Lausanne 1979, p. 118. To this researcher the original French seemed more eloquent: "Le 'manque à gagner critallisait le conflit fatal entre les tendances modernistes de milieux evolués et le conservatisme intransigeant de la vielle formule sportive anglaise." *(Memoires Olympique,* Lausanne: Bureau international de Pedagogic Sportive 1931, p. 185). See also the IOC Minutes, Rome 1923, p. 21, in J. M. Leiper, *The International Olympic Committee: The Pursuit of Olympism 1894-1970,* Ph. D. dissertation, University of Alberta 1976, p. 170. Baillet-Latour's involvement is described in O. Mayer, *A Travers les Anneaux Olympiques,* Geneva 1961, pp. 107-108.

11 One secondary source is J. Lucas, *The Modern Olympic Games,* New York 1980, pp. 101-103.

12 Grantland Rice's quote in Ibid., p. 101.

13 E. Bergvall, member of Swedish delegation in Paris 1924, wrote this in: *Olympiska Spelen I Paris 1924,* Stockholm 1924, p. 169.

14 Nurmi's quote is from a Finnish magazine, *Tyolaisurheilijan Joulu,* and reprinted in *Time,* 5 (February 9, 1925), p. 30. The Kolkka comment is located in S. Kolkka and H. Nygren, *Paavo Nurmi – the Flying Finn,* translated by J. O. Virtanen, Helsinki 1974, p. 8. The full Nurmi autobiography appears in the *Literary Digest,* 84 (March 7, 1925) 76-79.

15 K. P. Silberg, *The Athletic Finn,* Hancock 1927, p. 84.

16 J. Murray, "Nurmi Dies," *Los Angeles Times,* October 4, 1973; part 3, p. 1.

17 See W. O. Johnson, *All That Glitters is Not Gold,* New York 1972, p. 142. Another writer, one who knew Nurmi personally, wrote: "Paavo concentrated so severely on his running future that it is almost impossible to comprehend. He abandoned all his early friends." See M. Hannus, "Then Came Paavo Nurmi," *Finnish Running Secrets* [no author or editor listed], Mountain View 1973, p. 11.

18 Hannus, *Finnish Running Secrets,* 11, 13. See also "The Flying Finn," in R. J. Condon, *The Fifty Finest Athletes of the Twentieth Century,* London 1990, p. 108: "He competed for the first time when he was 17 [1914], capturing the Finnish national junior cross-country championship ..." thus beginning the first and only "steady job" he ever held. As a child, wrote Nurmi, "I pushed heavy carts hundreds of times up the steep streets of my hometown, Turku." See Nurmi's autobiography *Olympiavoittaiien Testamenti (The Will of the Olympic Champion),* translated by H. Lehmusvuori, published by F. Wilt (ed.), in *How They Train. Long Distances,* Los Altos 1973, pp. 76-77.

19 G. Rice, "The Greatest Runner of Them All," *Collier's* 75, January 3, 1925, p. 19.

20 M. Jukola, *Athletics in Finland,* Porvoo 1932, p. 50.

21 Following Nurmi's banishment from the ranks of amateur athletics in the summer of 1932, Nurmi refused to "turn pro" – rejecting the "Posse of Promoters." *Los Angeles Times,* July 29, 1932, pp. 13-14; *New York Herald Tribune,* July 31, 1932, sec. 3, p. 3. Both newspapers said that "Paavo was offered $200,000," which in today's world of 1995 would be equivalent to two million dollars.

22 Paddock, "He Lives to Run," *Collier's,* 85 (May 31, 1930), 48. J.H. Finley, "Nurmi, Marvel of Fleetness and Grace," *New York Times,* February 1, 1925, sec. 4 magazine, p. 6. Finley interviewed the impassive Nurmi and wrote: "He is like the herogod in the *Kalevala* [Finnish epic poem] whom nothing or no one could overtake."

23 Nurmi quoted in Finnish newspaper *Tyolaisurheiligan Juolo,* and translated into English for *Time,* 5 (February 9, 1925), 30.

24 This researcher has studied all forty-eight Nurmi races on American soil between January and May of 1925. The newspaper "cuttings" alone fill several folders, each two inches thick.

25 Nurmi lost 1:56 4/5 to 1:57 3/5. In 1990, in his 90th year, Mr. Helffrich told this researcher: "It was a great race. I was privileged to run against Nurmi. He was the greatest runner of the 20th century." Interview, January 20, 1990.

26 F. G. Menke, *Sport Tales and Anecdotes,* New York 1953, pp. 287, 293.

27 D. Ferris, as quoted in Nurmi's obituary, *Los Angeles Times,* October 3, 1973, part.3, p. 8.

28 J. Murray, "The Clock Watcher," *Los Angeles Times,* October 4, 1973, part 3, pp. 1, 12. Murray called Nurmi the world's greatest athlete "harnessed to hard work ... with the pulse rate of a fish, the suspicious nature of a Paris cop ... as sere [dry and cold] as an icicle, as gloomy as the second act of an Ibsen play." (p. 1).

29 See Ferris, fn. # 27.

30 B. Dyer in a conversation with M. Florence. See "Paavo Nurmi: He was Finland's Contribution to Golden Age of Sport," *Los Angeles Times,* August 12, 1983, part 2, p. 1. On page 14, J. Lardner, writing in 1925, is quoted as saying: "Nurmi booked any town that had a track and a bank."

31 Wilson was to serve as President of the United States Olympic Committee from 1953 to 1965.

32 Wilson quoted in the *Los Angeles Times,* April 24, 1925, pp. 1-2.

33 Rubien's surprising defense of Nurmi appeared in the *New York Herald Tribune,* April 24, 1925, p. 19.

34 See "Nurmi's Expenses," *The Times* [London], May 8, 1925, p. 7.

35 See "Athletics," *The Times* [London], May 11, 1925, p. 5.

36 "Nurmi thrilled a crowed of 45,000," wrote Dyer. On consecutive days "he dispatched eight American Indians" with a 14:15 9/10 three-mile and then world records at 2,000 yards (5:03.6); 1 1/4 miles (5:35.0), and an impressive 6:42.5 mile-and-one half. Dyer exclaimed: "The man is certainly the perfect running machine." See *Los Angeles Times,* August 12, 1925, pp. 1, 7, and Dyer's reminiscences in the *Los Angeles Times,* August 12, 1983, part 2, p. 1. More than 40,000 people braved ice-cold rain in Cambridge, Massachusetts and Harvard Stadium, as Nurmi raced a mile in 4:15 1/5 – a stupendous run through mud. See "Properly Paced, From Behind, Paavo of Abo Might Have Broken the World's Record," *Boston Globe,* May 23, 1925, pp. 1, 8.

37 "Nurmi Goes Back for Long Rest," *New York Times,* May 29, 1925, p. 11: "Telegrams in Brief, *The Times* [London], May 29, 1925, p. 13, and "A Famous Athlete's Statue," *The Times* [London], February 4, 1925, p. 18.

38 R. A. Smith, *Sport and Freedom. The Rise of Big-Time College Athletics,* New York 1988, p. 166.

39 See E. A. Glader, *Amateurism and Athletics,* West Point 1978, p. 138. Glader used as his source: *Report of the American Olympic Committee. Seventh Olympic Games Antwerp, Belgium 1920,* New York 1921, p. 424, which says, in essence, the IOC passes on to the individual national Olympic committee and to the domestic and international sport

federations the full responsibility of determining a person's amateur status. The rule remains the same, at this writing, in 1995.

40 At the 1923 meeting of the *American Olympic Committee* a resolution was passed "which gave the AAU the privilege of certifying the athletes who would represent the U.S. in the sports of track and field, swimming, boxing, wrestling, gymnastics, and weight-lifting." This quote is from the Minutes of the AAU 1923, pp. 171-172, and reproduced in R. Korsgaard, *A History of the AAU of the USA*, Ed. D. dissertation, Teachers' College, Columbia University 1951 p. 195.

41 See "IOC," *The Times* [London], April 23, 1923, p. 5.

42 Coubertin quoted in *Bibliotheque Universelle et Revue des Geneve,* Janvier 1924, and reprinted in Coubertin, *Olympic Idea,* p. 93.

43 Coubertin on May 29, 1925. See *Olympic Idea,* p. 97. We cannot support the idea of paying athletes for not working, or "Broken Time" concluded the IOC Technical Committee. See *Official Bulletin, IOC,* 1 (January 1926), 15.

44 See Mayer, Travers, p. 108, for Latour's comment. But IOC delegates cared not to continue the discussion and postponed some of the hard issues until the Prague Olympic Congress of 1925. Absolutely nothing changed in Prague and an amateur athlete was defined as "one who devotes himself to sport for sport's sake without deriving from it, directly or indirectly, the means of existence." (Mayer, *Travers,* p. 111). See also *Les Congres Olympiques 1894-1981,* Sofia 1981, pp. 137-138.

45 See C. Nelson, *Track and Field. The Great Ones,* London 1970, pp. 20-21.

46 Webster, *Athletics of To-Day,* London 1929, p. 100.

47 See Reed's "Scandinavia's Speed Mission," Outlook, 151 (January 30, 1929), p. 185.

48 The combination of constant leg pain and "another kind of pain at AAU headquarters" hastened Nurmi's exit from America. See *Souvenir Program. Paavo Nurmi Classic Races,* Portland, Oregon, October 8, 1978.

49 See "AAU Enrolls Nurmi after he Denies He Will Turn Pro; He Passes Strict Cross-examination," *New York Times,* January 8, 1929, p. 32; "Registration of Nurmi Here is Questioned," *New York Times,* January 10, 1929, p. 33.

50 See "Nurmi Establishes 3 World Records," *New York Times,* January 20, 1929, sec. 10, pp. 1, 4; also "Bedlam Broke Loose When Records Announced," *New York Times,* January 21, 1929, p. 16, and "AAU Will Lift Charges on Nurmi Regarding Boston's Knights of Columbus Meet," *New York Times,* January 22, 1929, p. 24.

51 See *New York Times,* January 27, 1929, sec. 11, pp. 1, 6. The next day, A. J. Daley wrote "The 'Abo Antelope, the Great Uncommunicative Nurmi Not Happy with 9:12.0 two-miles time." See *New York Times,* January 28, 1929, p. 17. And on January 29, Daley wrote: "Nurmi's not quite the man he was four years ago." *New York Times,* p. 24.

52 See *New York Times,* February 1, 1929, p. 17; *New York Times,* February 10, 1929; sec. 11, pp. 1, 4.

53 See Abramson's long column "Nurmi's Failure to Run Laid to Fear of Defeat," *New York Herald Tribune*, February 25, 1929, p. 22. Also A. J. Daley, "Long Suspension Likely for Nurmi," *New York Times*, February 25, 1929, p. 20.

54 See *New York Herald Tribune*, March 10, 1929, sec. 4, p. 1; *New York Times*, March 10, 1929, sec. 12, p. 4 and, March 11, 1929, p. 20.

55 See *Washington Post*, April 27, 1929, pp. 13, 15 and *Philadelphia Inquirer*, April 28, 1929, pp. 1, 5.

56 See Jukola, *Athletics in Finland*, p. 50. Nurmi ran 20 kilometers in 64 minutes and two miles in 8:59.5, breaking new barriers in long-distance running. See also G. Rice's "Nurmi Portrait,"*Collier's* 88, September 19, 1931, p. 25.

57 See "IAAF Suspends Nurmi," *New York Times*, April 4, 1932, p. 20; *The Times* [London], April 4, 1932, p. 12; for Finnish anger, see *The New York Times*, April 5, 1932, p. 28; April 8, 1932, p. 29; April 11, 1932, p. 22, April 13, 1932, p. 11; April 20, 1932, p. 30; and April 28, 1932, p. 24.

58 See "Nurmi is Married to Miss Sylvia Laaksonen, Well-known Pretty Brunette and Popular Figure in Abo, Finland,"*New York Times*, May 19, 1932, p. 23. The following year a son was born and soon after, Sylvia and Paavo were divorced. He never remarried.

59 See *New York Times*, June 27, 1932, p. 21.

60 IOC president, Baillet-Latour. See Leiper, *International Olympic Committee*, p. 173, who quoted from IOC *Minutes*, Lausanne 1929 and reprinted in the *Official IOC Bulletin* 13 (July, 1929), p. 5.

61 AAU Official Track and Field Handbook 1932, pp. 160-161.

62 See N. Muller, *Van Paris bis Baden-Baden. Die Olympischen Kongresse 1894 -1981*, Niedernhausen 1981, p. 111.

63 Eström quoted in A. Gould (Associated Press Editor), "Finland's Attempt Before IAAF Fails," *Los Angeles Times*, July 30, 1932, pp. 9-10. The day before, Edström told the print media: "We have good and sufficient ground for disqualifying Nurmi," *New York Herald Tribune*, July 29, 1932, pp. 1, 19.

64 Brundage quoted in A. Gould, "Flying Finn Ruled Out After Spirited Protest," *Los Angeles Times*, July 29, 1932, pp. 13-14.

65 Brundage to Edström, June 6, 1932, *Avery Brundage Collection*, reel 25, box 42.

66 Brundage, in "Nurmi Not Invited to IAAF Meeting," *New York Times*, July 29, 1932, p. 19.

67 J. Abramson, "Ban on Nurmi Upheld," *New York Herald Tribune*, July 29, 1932, p. 19.

68 T. de Lapp, "Nurmi Sees Fete from Stands. Great Finn Sits Alone and is Mauled by Policeman," *Los Angeles Times*, July 31, 1932, p. 4. See also *New York Times*, July 81, 1932, part 3, p. 3.

69 A.J. Daley, "Edström Undemocratic," *New York Times*, July 30, 1932, p. 10.

70 Pegler in the *Chicago Daily Tribune*, August 6, 1932, pp. 13-14.

71 "Posse...," *Los Angeles Times*, July 29, 1932, pp. 13-14. See "Nurmi Cold to Cash," *New York Herald Tribune*, July 31, 1932, part 3, p. 3.

72 Crowds swarm through streets shouting "Long Live Nurmi." See *New York Times*, July 30, 1932, p. 10; "Finland Crowds Defiant," *Los Angeles Times*, July 30, 1932, p. 9; a Finnish editorial rang: "The decision is the worst shock Finland has ever received" *(New York Times*, July 31, 1932, part 3, p. 3). Poor Nurmi, not quite himself, said: "I will run the marathon alone through Los Angeles streets and break the record," *Philadelphia Inquirer*, July 30, 1932, p. 12. Nurmi's coach, Jaako Mikkola, called it all "a charade, a travesty" (see Avery Brundage Collection, reel 25, box 42). The entire Finnish team of athletes in Los Angeles threatened to boycott the games. They did not. See "Wrong to Finland," *Time* 20 (August 8, 1932), 26.

73 Baillet-Latour in the *Los Angeles Times*, July 29, 1932, p. 13.

74 Brundage to Edström, October 19, 1932; *Avery Brundage Collection*, reel 24, box 42.

75 Edström to Brundage, November 5, 1932; *Avery Brundage Collection*, reel 24, box 42.

76 Kekkonen to Edström, December 15, 1932 and January 1, 1934, *Avery Brundage Collection*, reel 25, box 42.

77 Paddock in the *Pasadena* [California] *Star News*, August 26 , 1932, n. p., located in *Avery Brundage Collection*, reel 25, box 42. "The 'Secret Seven' IAAF Executive Board acted without authority. Nurmi is an amateur at heart," wrote Paddock.

78 Nurmi quoted in G. Miller, "Paavo Nurmi," located in W. Grimsley (ed.), *The Sports Immortals*, Englewood Cliffs 1972, p. 27.

79 See Jukola, *Athletics in Finland*, p. 55. Another Finn, U. Toivola, wrote that Finnish men and women had overcome adversity for five centuries. "The Finnish character, therefore, is founded on granite." See his essay in the *Los Angeles Times*, August 11, 1932, part 1, p. 14.

80 "Move to Reinstate Nurmi is Started," *New York Times*, December 28, 1932. p. 21.

81 Mayer, *Travers*, p. 138.

82 See Leiper, *International Olympic Committee*, p. 192, who quoted from the *Official Bulletin* of the IOC 24 (June, 1933). p. 11. The French language explanation is eloquent and lengthy, epitomized by the sentence: "L'amateurisme est un etat d'ame et non une loi." See Mayer, *Travers*, p. 138.

83 See *Avery Brundage Collection*, reel 24, box 42, item 11.

84 "Nurmi Suspension Upheld by IAAF," *New York Times*, August 29, 1934. p. 20.

85 Edström to Brundage, April 9, 1934; *Avery Brundage Collection*, reel 25, box 42.

86 Kekkonen to Edström, January 1, 1934; *Avery Brundage Collection*, reel 25, box 42. Dr. Kekkonen became president of Finland in 1956, serving in that capacity until October of 1981 at age 81. See *Dictionary of Scandinavian Biography* (1972), pp. 226-227, and *The Europa World*

Yearbook, Vol. 1 (1992), p. 1050. For more than fifty years, Kekkonen and Nurmi were friends.

87 This researcher has approximately 100 Nurmi obituaries, in eight languages. Several useful English language newspaper items are: *New York Times,* October 3, 1973, pp. 1, 48; *Atlanta Constitution,* October 3, 1973, p. 2C; *Boston Globe,* October 3, 1973, p. 61; *Los Angeles Times,* October 3, 1973, part 3, pp. 1, 8; *The Times* [London], October 3, 1973, p. 17; *Washington Post,* October 3, 1973, p. D4; *Manchester Guardian,* October 3, 1973, p. 23. *Time* and *Newsweek* magazines covered the story. Good research libraries with titles akin to "The World's Greatest Athletes" almost always include Nurmi.

17.
The Hegemonic Rule of the American Amateur Athletic Union, 1888-1914: James Edward Sullivan as Prime Mover*

The Amateur Athletic Union (AAU) of the United States, founded in 1888, and still marginally active in 1994, is the oldest continuously amateur operating sporting organization in the world. It met a great need in the late nineteenth century for both athlete and spectator, and in the northeastern portion of the nation by the first half-decade of the new century it had no rival. Such hegemonic rule was, in part, an accident, an organization filling a void. In addition, such power and influence was the direct result of calculating men from the Boston to New York City 'Corridor'—an elite cadre of wealthy businessmen, self-imbued with an amateur ideology that approached a crusade. Prominent among this leadership, both in physical presence, in a kind of 'new wave' American patriotism, and in adherence to an alien elitist, British-based athletic amateurism, was the young Irish-American, James Edward Sullivan (1862-1914). This article attempts to trace the AAU's first quarter-century, and in so doing: "follow the union's successful usurpation of the older amateur sport organization, the National Association of Amateur Athletes of America (N4A); describe the AAU's skilful efforts at alliance with another even older group—the Intercollegiate Amateur Athletic Association of America (IC4A); and show something of the rise to power of James Edward Sullivan, who during his own lifetime was called "The Czar of American Amateur Athletics."

The AAU's Initial Search for Unchallenged Power 1888-92

*The International Journal of the History of Sport, 11 (December 1994), 355-371.

From its inception on 21 January 1888, the AAU was confrontational and intent on eliminating the slightly older, self-appointed overseer of non-university amateur athletics—the N4A, founded in 1879. The N4A professed as its objective the "protection, advancement, and improvement of its membership and that of amateur athletic sports" in the United States.² They had no such national constituency in fifteen years of existence, their influence confined to athletic clubs in the burgeoning sporting atmosphere of metropolitan New York City.³ Quickly, the feud between the N4A and the newly-formed AAU became a struggle between wealthy members of the Manhattan Athletic Club (MAC) and the richer, more powerful men from the New York Athletic Club (NYAC).⁴ The AAU was formed 'overnight' as officers of the NYAC, unhappy with what they called N4A ineptness, formed a new organization in late January of 1888. By March of that year, individual and club members of the N4A had defected to the AAU. One of the defectors was James Edward Sullivan, twenty-six years of age, a recently retired all-around athlete from the Pastime Athletic Club and the vice-president of N4A. The *Wilkes' Spirit of the Times* called such desertions "a series of funerals," and the article author, who chose to call himself "Mugwump," wrote critically of both the N4A and its sponsor, the Manhattan AC: "What we need is an organization that will stop this kind of stealing and protect smaller clubs."⁵

The war between the N4A and the AAU continued unabated through 1888, and, prophetically, young J. E. Sullivan somehow retained his affiliation with both groups and also joined the staff of the New York *Morning Journal.* His sporting comments so straddled the current controversy that the *Spirit of the Times* wrote, "Mr. J. E. Sullivan degrades modern journalism. He is a renegade Irishman, the purveyor of shameful and malicious falsehoods. In fact, during the existing athletic war each party has talked, written and printed a stupendous acreage of dreary twaddle, inane platitudes and personal abuse."⁶ And when the N4A put on its abortive December indoor track and field championships, and "reporter James E. Sullivan was forcibly ejected from the Madison Square Garden,"⁷ Sullivan had made his decision: to go with the AAU. Both would be shrouded in controversy. No other city but New York could have spawned such internecine athletic struggle. "The transformation of American athletics from its pre-modern to modern form," wrote historian Melvin L. Adelman, "was nowhere more evident than in New York City."⁸ The audacious Sullivan was in his element amidst the burgeoning growth of his city, the nation's largest, wealthiest, and most dynamic. In central Manhattan, the NYAC had already withdrawn its membership from N4A on 15 May 1886, and two years later became headquarters for the AAU Board of Directors. Other athletic clubs followed suit and, as AAU historian Korsgaard noted, "Other clubs soon followed with their resignations—a telling blow to the N4A,"[9] and the AAU continued to strengthen its base of power. A *Spirit* editorial commented: "The Union will have no periods of infancy and childhood."[10] On the other hand, the AAU hierarchy was aware that its influence was strictly local, and set its sights on the whole northeastern region and eventually the United States. Any athlete competing under N4A jurisdiction "shall be debarred," announced the Union Executive Board on 25 August 1888. One of its members, Otto Ruhl, the NYAC secretary, was clear in his intent on liquidating rivals; "No compromise is possible; we will carry the war into Africa if need be."[11]

The N4A track meet in December 1888 was a failure, while the counter-punching AAU affair on 19 January 1889, was described as "highly successful, with immense attendance, ... the greatest athletic meeting ever held in America."[12] The AAU leadership, in existence for exactly a year, was intent on expansion of geographical influence and increasing its paying, card-carrying membership. The AAU issued a "boycott ultimatum": all amateur, non-college athletes must register with the AAU and no other organization. "They shall be debarred," warned the Board of Managers of the AAU.[13] On 1 August 1889, the newly-elected AAU secretary, James Edward Sullivan, under instructions from both Union president Harry McMillan (1841-1921) and the AAU legal specialist Colonel Abraham G. Mills (1844-1929), wrote to N4A president Walton Storm that it would be wise to "disband and in so doing create an amalgamation of these two organizations."[14] We have won the day, wrote President McMillan at a 14 September 1889 meeting: "This assemblage celebrates the entombment of all by-gone animosities." Frederick William Janssen, editor of the newsletter *The Ace of Clubs,* agreed with McMillan and trumpeted "Salus Populi Suprema Lex Esto" (Let the welfare of the people be the supreme law).[15] The athletes, one editor wrote, care nothing for either an N4A or an AAU, but only which group will affect them positively. "He regards athletic sports as a trade by which he can earn prizes."[16] And the already influential AAU, with significant financial support from the wealthy NYAC, was the only direction to take for the amateur athlete—both "pedestrian" and elite.

The new decade spawned A. G. Mills' 1890 AAU "Redistricting Plan," in which the whole of athletic America would be under the control of a single body. The Union's secretary for forty years, Daniel J. Ferris (1889-1977), wrote: "We immediately ceased being an association of clubs and became a union of associations, active and allied."[17] Ferris exaggerated, but the Mills Plan did divide the nation into five sections (New England, Metropolitan New York City, Central, Atlantic, and Pacific), all with some autonomy or "Home Rule," all of them "active and allied" and, eventually, financially solvent.[18] But by March 1890, almost none of the 30,000 athletes "allied" to the AAU were paying membership dues, forcing McMillan to resign. Howard Perry of Washington, DC, took charge, with William Buckingham Curtis (1837-1900),[19] Treasurer, and Sullivan, Secretary. *The Brooklyn Daily Eagle* of 17 November 1891, reported a precarious AAU balance of $1,257.[20] In retrospect, the problem seemed obvious. The youthful AAU had spread itself too thinly through the northeast and, more importantly, its code was based on an unrealistic "pure amateur and elite English" athletic ideology, casting aside any young man refusing to adhere.

American Athletic Amateurism: Nineteenth-Century Anachronism 1892-96[21]

The late nineteenth-century American version of athletic amateurism was borrowed in its entirety from Great Britain, brought to a North America wrestling with heady concepts of egalitarianism and democracy, and for this reason, as historian Ronald Smith noted: 'Not until the nineteenth century did the upper classes of Victorian England invoke amateurism for their own purposes ... to exclude from sport those of the lower classes."[22] But these visions of athletic performance devoid of the profit motive and enveloped in singularly idealized motives of individuality and romanticism had European roots older and more complex than biased English Victorian class-consciousness. The American AAU's aggressive efforts in the 1890s to protect all of their registered membership from the "evils" of professionalism and expand the concept of athletic amateurism had intellectual origins in late eighteenth- and early nineteenth-century German, French and English absorption in the "sentiment and passion" of literary and philosophical romanticism. Pervasive and persistent scholarship during the century 1790-1890 about ancient Greek life, including their great pan-Hellenic festivals, was not always historically correct. David C. Young, in his book review of Donald G. Kyle's *Athletics in Ancient Athens,* commented that "Greek athletes prove to be much more like those of our day than of the nineteenth-century heyday of aristocratic amateurism."[23]

The power and light of European intellectuals during the Romantic Period masked the multiple motives of ancient Greek athletes who competed in sporting contests for religious ecstasy, for the glory of their city state, for personal fulfillment, and also, to win as much money as possible. These were exactly the motives of many American athletes in 1894, and in 1994. Scholars were temporarily blinded about the rationale for competitive athletics and in the nineteenth-century wrapped it all in a cloak of emotional and intellectual idealism, where neither "grossness nor sensuality" existed.[24] This European immersion in the contrived ambiance of the 1821 Greek Revolution against the Turks, the new-old return to the belief "in the natural goodness of man," admiration for the "heroic" and "the exaltation of the emotions and senses over reason and intellect"[25] received wide acceptance in Europe and North America at the end of the century. For many, this soaring attitude manifested itself in perceiving athletics-for-pay as an "evil" and pure amateur sport as "good." This amateur mind-set became the unlikely philosophical and administrative linchpin of the struggling American AAU in the period 1892-95. Preoccupied with "catching" those who were unable to adhere to this amateur athletic ideal plagued the AAU during this time period and was ever-present during the full tenure of AAU secretary-treasurer and president, Sullivan—and for longer than a half century beyond his death in 1914. Such time-consuming, expensive, and futile efforts may have been the single greatest weakness in the organization's whole history.

Young Sullivan's loyalty to the AAU knew no bounds, and in 1893 he coordinated the banishment of 300 boxers as "non-amateurs."[26] The never-ending and unsuccessful struggle was just beginning for the AAU secretary and his organization. Sullivan traveled to Chicago that same year to conduct sporting events at the World's Fair and also to try and bring order out of the amorphous Central AAU district. Sullivan returned to New York City just as a foreign visitor arrived in Chicago, the French aristocrat Baron de Coubertin (1863-1937)—his second visit to North America.[27] He finished his tour with a lengthy visit to William Milligan Sloane (1850-1928) of Princeton University, one of the nation's pre-eminent historians, an amateur sport enthusiast, and an architect of the not-yet-created America Olympic Committee.[28] Coubertin was desperate to drum up enthusiasm in North America for his elusive dream of reviving the ancient Olympic Games "in modern guise." Sloane suggested a meeting at his University Club in New York City, and he hoped that AAU officials would also attend. None came.[29] Coubertin remembered fifteen years later that America's amateur sporting officials were too preoccupied with "the secret war between the colleges and the AAU."[30] One person who did attend, representing Columbia University athletes and the IC4A, was Gustavus Town Kirby (1876-1956). He remembered telling the Baron, "You must go over to AAU headquarters and talk to Jim Sullivan."[31] The Frenchman had grandiose plans. Sullivan and his AAU associates were concerned with the last vestige opposition from the N4A and uneasy at the rapid rise and nation-wide strength of another rival—the League of American Wheelmen. Also worrisome to the AAU was the fact that its state of near bankruptcy might prevent them from serving every area of the United States and at the same time delay plans on taxing every member athlete and forcing on them a small entry fee for every contest in which they competed. These plans met with disapproval from most athletes, from some AAU administrators, from the editor and International Olympic Committee (IOC) member, Caspar Whitney (1864-1929).[32] Whitney attacked the AAU for its ineptitude in handling boxing, because its "inaction and indifference left the way clear for the vicious. The AAU is sapped of its former strength, its officials invalidated, its health broken."[33] In less than a decade of existence, the AAU had moved rapidly and in so doing created an atmosphere of both fierce loyalties[34] and persistent opposition.

Sullivan Emerges as the Dominant AAU Figure 1897-1906

Secretary Sullivan took on the additional title in 1897 of Metropolitan AAU president and immediately "caught forty athletes attempting to cheat by remaining unregistered." One of them was the world's fastest sprinter, Bernie Wefers.[35] The big AAU push to register thousands of athletes was coupled with a police mentality to "get" every violator of the amateur code. In retrospect, it seems difficult to understand why Sullivan and his people failed to see the inherent contradiction of spending so much time and effort to register thousands under the AAU rubric, and at the same time spend, perhaps, as much energy in apprehending all of the athletics "sinners." But it was the double course that the union had set, and Sullivan was its captain. The AAU records during these years are replete with "backsliders"—good athletes who accepted money for their successes, were caught and suspended by secretary Sullivan. Future Northwestern University track coach, Harry Gill, was accused in 1901 (while still an athlete) of "coaching for money." A water polo team, not registered by the AAU, was suspended in 1902. The AAU was "obdurate" in the 1903 case of track star George Foster Sanford, for having taken money to coach football. Yale University's great football coach, Walter Camp, was taken to task by his good friend Sullivan for not registering the university's basketball team. "Now you know we must have law and order," wrote Sullivan, "Your team is disqualified."[36] The *New York Times* of 20 November 1906 (page 10) reported that "Sullivan has suspended 288 athletes thus far this year." A St. Louis journalist, Charles J. P. Lucas, had all he could take of the 1906 version of the AAU "and of its creature, James E. Sullivan." Not only is the AAU in need of reformation, wrote Lucas, they must also receive "deliverance" from the business house of A. G. Spalding "which controls both Sullivan and the AAU."[37] World record holder in the 100-yard dash in 1905 (9 $3/5$ seconds), Arthur Duffey, wrote: "All of us fear the AAU more than revere it."[38]

The other side of all of this was that the energetic AAU had partially filled an enormous void in American popular culture. The small number of college athletes during the decade 1897-1906 cared only for their campus experiences, while an even smaller cadre of professional athletes amused the masses, collected pay checks, prizes, and prize monies domestically in Britain, New Zealand, and Australia. The majority of those interested in competitive sport fitted into neither world and saw in the AAU a new way of expression. And the AAU obliged. Even critic Lucas admitted "that the AAU has done large service to the cause of amateur sport."[39] The AAU served its constituency unevenly, providing carefully controlled competitions in some major metropolitan areas of the northeast. Prior to the Great War, the AAU influence was wildly uneven nation-wide, except in Chicago, Milwaukee, Los Angeles, San Francisco, Baltimore, and New Orleans.[40] It would be another generation before AAU volunteer workers could report to their administrators that amateur athletics were accommodated in other large and small cities. Right to the end of the AAU hegemony in 1978, they could not honestly say that the fifty states of the American union were well-served.

The Roots of Sullivan's Single-mindedness

On 19 November 1906, the 44-year-old Sullivan was elected president of the AAU, and promised modestly, "I will aim to build up the AAU to the limit of my ability."[41] There was plenty there: a bright, aggressive, New York City student-athlete; a vigorous physique coupled with a shrewd, unbending mind, and a complex ambition having to do with self, his AAU, his beloved New York City, and an unashamed patriotism. These characteristics were frequently interchanged in some kind of hierarchy of personal commitments.

Sullivan was born in New York City on 18 November 1862, the son of Daniel J. Sullivan (c. 1835-86) of County Kerry, Ireland, and Julia Haplin O'Sullivan (1830-84).[42] Their son's formal education ended at age sixteen after graduating from Grammar School 18, at which time he entered the publishing house of Frank Leslie in 1878. In the next four years he founded a little newspaper, the *Athletic News,* wrote for the New York City *Sporting News,* and the city's *Morning Journal,* served as athletes' president of the Pastime Athletic Club, and, ironically, was club delegate to the N4A. In 1892, at age 30, Sullivan became president of the American Sports Publishing Company, a major subsidiary of the giant sporting goods company founded by the brothers A. G. and J. Walter Spalding.[43] Sullivan's father was a foreman in the construction of the New York Central Railroad, spent his life at that work, passing on to his only son no financial inheritance. But, as Arthur J. Daley said: "James Sullivan was determined to succeed and was unwilling to drift into manual labor. Night study and voracious reading sharpened his quick mind."[44]

'Big Jim' Sullivan was 5'10" and 155 pounds "with handsome Irish configurations." For ten years he acted the "athletic rat"— participating in boxing matches, race walks from a mile to 25 miles, ran in sprint races, and finished well in one-hour endurance running competitions. He was captain of his athletics club, of its tug-of-war team, "enjoyed" the 100- and 200-yard dashes and "scored points in the '440'".[45] Sullivan married young, on 4 April 1882, to Margaret Eugenia Byrne, and their two children, Julia Ellsbee and James Stacey, were born in 1882 and 1893, respectively.[46] By the time of Sullivan's presidential election in 1906, the 44-year-old had behind him years of "hard" experiences as a competitive sportsman, athletic administrator, journalist, businessman, and international traveler (he was the American Olympic team assistant leader to Paris in 1900 and American

Chief to the interim Athens Olympic Games of 1906). By all criteria, Sullivan was ready to co-operate with and do battle with all domestic or overseas sport organizations. He did both.

The AAU and the Olympic Games 1896-1912

The American intercollegiate organization in control of track and field sports, the ICAAAA (IC4A), was founded in 1876,[47] and by definition separated itself from all non-college sport and from all other university athletic teams. However, after the creation of the AAU, all college runners, jumpers, and throwers interested in "open" competitions and championships, in international matches held in America and Europe, had to register with the AAU and were rigidly controlled by AAU administrators and the university-appointed coaches and trainers. There continued uneasy peace between the two organizations during the years discussed in the article. During the five official and one "unofficial" (1906) Olympic Games, 1896-1912, this IC4A supplied the majority of American team members, most of whom were track and field athletes. The AAU, always deferential to the IC4A, knew that the universities had the athletes, coaches, the facilities, and that they did not. AAU leadership was wholly indifferent to the Coubertin-inspired Games of the First Olympiad, and had it not been for Professor Sloane of Princeton University, possibly not a single American would have participated in the 1896 beginning. By 1898, Senator William Mason (Illinois) introduced a bill in the American Congress "to raise $25,000 to aid the AAU of the USA in a display of American sports at the Paris International Exposition of 1900."[48] The bill failed, but Colonel L. M. Hamburger, Special Commissioner of the AAU to Paris, both A. G. and A. S. Spalding, all co-coordinated by Sullivan, recruited a small band of college and club athletes and won 16 out of 21 contests at the Games of the Second Olympiad. On the eve of these Paris Olympics, the AAU leadership merely changed its name, for the moment, to the American Olympic Committee (AOC).[49] For the first two decades of the twentieth century, this AOC, made up almost entirely of AAU men, met shortly before the Olympic Games to raise money and then to select the Olympic team. It had no other function.

After the failed bill of 1898, the President of the United States, William McKinley, put his full support behind the AAU—Olympic effort and appointed A. G. Spalding as the "First American Director to the Olympic Games at Paris 1900."[50] The AAU was out of money on the eve of the games and Sullivan, now treasurer as well as secretary, raised athletes' membership fee to 50 cents but was forced to reduced it to 25 cents, amidst howls of protest.[51] No matter, the Americans won almost everything in Paris, and a triumphant Sullivan crowed: "We did more to open the eyes of our legislators to athletics than anything that has been done for several years."[52] He was correct, and for the next decade the loudest if not always the official spokesman for the American AAU-Olympic Committee was Sullivan.

In every way that is capable of definition, namely administratively, financially and in the selective use of power, the AAU, not the AOC, and certainly not the IC4A nor the newly-formed (1906) National Collegiate Athletic Association (NCAA) directed America's destiny at the Olympic Games in St. Louis (1904), the Athens Olympian Games (1906), the London Olympic Games of 1908, and the Games of the Fifth Olympiad in Stockholm, Sweden in 1912. At each of these festivals, the American administrative delegation was composed of AAU men, and Sullivan was five times American presidential appointee, the official and extemporaneous spokesman for the athletes, the embodiment of the AAU's expanding power, the flag-waving super-patriot, and the recipient of reluctant congratulations from his long-time enemy—Baron Pierre de Coubertin. America won almost everything in sight at the St. Louis festival and the IOC president wrote to Sullivan: "Warmest congratulations ... in organizing 3rd Olympiad. You will be awarded commemorative medal...."[53] The American minister to Greece, John B. Jackson, writing to Secretary of State, Elihu Root, lauded Sullivan and his AAU cohorts: 'I am proud of them and of our athletes for their success, their sportsmanlike qualities and their discipline ... in winning these Olympic Games."[54] The USA won almost everything—eleven gold medals, prompting Theodore Roosevelt to telegraph his friend, Sullivan: "Congratulations. America is all right."[55] The long-term secretary-treasurer of the AAU was elected its president on his return home in late 1906. The Olympic Committee went into its usual hibernation, allowing the AAU to prepare for the next games in London.

Roosevelt once again accepted honorary presidency of the American team, but he refused Sullivan's request of $100,000 in federal monies. "Please help us, Mr. President," wrote Sullivan, "the sinews of athletic war, of national pride rather than individual honor are at stake."[56] The AAU boss knew the next best source of funds, and he told his colleagues at the November 1907 annual meeting: 'Registration, gentlemen, is the backbone of this organization. It is centralization, it means control ... absolute control over the individual athlete who competes under our protection."[57]

The London Olympic Games of 1908 were the largest on record but were nearly wrecked by the two powerful antagonists, the United States and Great Britain, who found a score of ways to criticize one another. Sullivan, his AAU, and some American athletes, behaved vulgarly, with excessive nationalistic behaviors, and, sometimes in individual and collective superciliousness. Some British athletes and officials, uneasy, envious, and with a widespread sense of inferiority in the face of the aggressive and vocal Americans, also misbehaved.[58]

The AAU gained immeasurably from the 1908 Olympics. The union's stepchild, the AOC, had chosen the superb American team, financed them, sent officers and coaches to London and, literally, returned from British shores shrouded with the American red, white, and blue flag. Sullivan was lauded by his colleagues as well as by the majority of Yankee Olympians, and in November 1909 he gave up his AAU presidency to Everett C. Brown (1863-1937).[59] The AAU and the AOC were in a state of high readiness, anticipating the giant's share of medals at the next Olympic Games in Stockholm. Sullivan was asked to select the American team, and soon after received congratulations when President William H. Taft appointed him "American Commissioner to the 1912 Olympic Games."[60] Sullivan was in good humor and wrote to AOC President Thompson on 21 December 1911: "American presidents have appointed me Commissioner to the Olympic Games in 1900, 1906, 1908, and now 1912. Of course, I naturally feel I am the logical one."[61] Amidst all this self-elevation, Sullivan's health deteriorated, the result of a serious injury suffered in a rail accident on 13 August 1911.[62] No matter, a much-subdued Sullivan took his team to Stockholm, Sweden, and watched with satisfaction the "American athletic machine" dominate these Games of the Fifth Olympiad. "We were a team with a mission," wrote Sullivan after Stockholm. "American athletes are very special people, manifestations of this glorious nation of ours."[63]

The AAU Widens its Net—President Gustavus Town Kirby 1911-14

Sullivan was no longer physically vigorous after suffering serious internal injuries while riding a Chicago to New York City express train, which derailed in the summer of 1911. His debilitation continued until his death three years later. His friend Gustavus Town 'Gus' Kirby (1874-1956) took up some slack, and at age 37, he was young, an engineering graduate of Columbia University, a successful inventor, an art dealer (with his father, Thomas), a practicing lawyer, and he was wealthy. In 60 years of involvement in amateur athletics, he served as president of the IC4A, the AAU, the post-World War I American Olympic Association (AOA) and, for 20 years until his death, as the treasurer of the United States Olympic Committee (USOC).[64] During Kirby's two terms as AAU president, the organization penetrated virtually every populated area of the United States, and in a protracted three-month tour of every AAU district he pronounced its influence "profound and pervasive." Kirby also raised most of the money to send the Olympic team to Stockholm. And when the victorious team returned, Kirby sang: The United States is now the object lesson of the world as a country in which athletic supremacy is combined with honesty and amateurism.[65] He talked exactly like his ailing comrade, Sullivan. Not to be outdone by the younger man, 51-year-old Sullivan and Mrs. Sullivan retraced Kirby's AAU stops across the country. After five weeks on the road, Secretary-Treasurer Sullivan was confident that "America will win the Berlin, Germany Olympic Games of 1916.[66] The two men left for Berlin, to look over the Olympic site, and to participate in the creation of the world track and field organization (IAAF), the special project of Sweden's J. Sigfrid Edström (1870-1964) and Sullivan. Kirby reported to his AAU colleagues that the union and Colonel Thompson's AOC had "everything well in hand."[67] World War I shattered any such roseate conclusion, but before the conflict and before his death, the unceasing Sullivan convinced former president William H. Taft, and President Woodrow Wilson, to accept honorary co-leadership of the American team preparing for the 1916 games.[68] In his latest burst of energy, Sullivan traveled to both Lyon, France, and Paris—the IAAF meeting and the Baron de Coubertin's annual IOC gathering. Sullivan, away from home for a month, warned that England and Germany would be strong in Berlin. He felt somewhat improved in health, "'but had attended fifty dinners and brought home ten pounds additional weight."[69] Sullivan died on 16 September 1914, in his fifty-second year, and Bartow Sumter Weeks (1861-1922), Supreme Court Judge of the State of New York, AAU president and IOC member, tears streaming down his face, reminded AAU friends of Sullivan's imprint on national, international, and Olympic sport.[70]

The AAU's First Quarter-Century

Robert Korsgaard's doctoral dissertation on the history of the AAU concludes that it was always the American Olympic Committee that represented the nation at the early Olympic Games, but that in actually "almost the entire AOC members were officers of the AAU."[71] In the year Sullivan's death, the AAU's influence was nation-wide, its power and personnel percolating down to the AOC, and without a rival from the new NCAA. The AAU was stronger than Canada's AAU, more influential and more aggressive than England's Amateur Athletic Association (AAA), and more tightly organized than Coubertin's unsettled IOC. French sporting organizations were not yet extensive while the powerful gymnastic clubs in Germany and throughout Europe were carefully nationalistic, inward-looking, and suspicious of foreign and international gatherings like the Olympic Games. The AAU, imperfect as it was (and imperfect it would remain till its demise in the 1970s), in 1914 was the most powerful sport organization in the world. The New York City-based AAU had in its inner circle a pantheon of wealthy and powerful lawyers, medical doctors, educators, commerce, and business leaders. There is a remarkable two-page photograph in the *New York Herald* of 8 December 1911, the headline proclaiming "Plans for 1912 Olympiad at Colonel Thompson's Dinner." The multi-millionaire Thompson had a full reproduction of the Stockholm Olympic Stadium placed in the center of the sumptuous New York Athletic Club Dining Hall. "Every little detail was worked out ingeniously as Colonel Thompson's thirty special guests sat around the stadium."[72]

From its beginnings in 1888, the AAU, after a stuttering first decade, grew rapidly in size and influence—a household institution among America's recreational sportsmen as well as with the athletic elite. Women were not welcome until after Sullivan's death and then in larger numbers after women received the right to vote following the Great War.[73] In an era before the NCAA and Olympic committee were major American social and athletic forces, the AAU had found its way into every large American city. There was nothing comparable anywhere in the world in a nation so large as the United States. There were inherent flaws in the AAU structure, but they were not always evident in the period 1888-1914. Autocratic and arbitrary and elitist edicts, combined with a fanatical zeal for "simon-pure" athletic amateurism, plus a too-great pride in recruiting well-meaning but not always skilled volunteer workers, were not always recognized as weaknesses in

the early days. It is an unchallenged fact that the AAU filled an
enormous void and gave hundreds of thousands of young men
the opportunity to play and work at sport competitions. The AAU
was there, especially in metropolitan city arenas in the evening
hours, with exciting spectator sport. The great universities were
successful for two generations in football, rowing, and track and
field, but the AAU, looking at somewhat different and larger pop-
ulations, outstripped the IC4A, the rowing federation, the NCAA,
and even the university athletic departments.

There is ample evidence that most American international
athletic competitions, with the notable exception of Ivy League—
Oxford -Cambridge sporting intercourse, began with the AAU, its
executive board, with its nearly perpetual secretary-treasurer-
president, Sullivan. He worked these three jobs for a quarter-
century without salary, and when the AAU met at it annual meeting in November of 1914—only weeks after Sullivan's death—"no
one could be found to accept the time-consuming, non-paying
position." Finally, the very able New Yorker, Frederick W. Rubien
(1871-1951), was hired (on salary) at that same 1914 meeting.[74]
Sullivan, the AAU's most visible and effective warrior, was gone,
but he and his kind had done their work well, forging a giant,
unwieldy, unforgiving, as well as extraordinarily useful organization, one that for an additional half-century seemed possessed of
talismanic powers.[75]

NOTES

1 Charles J. P. Lucas in his "Commercializing Amateur Athletics,"
World Today, 10 (March 1906), 281, 284, was of the opinion that 'the
AAU today is in serious need of reformation and deliverance ... and this
body ... is largely under the control of Mr. James E. Sullivan." Lucas
used the word "czar" several times referring to Sullivan.

2 See N4A, *Constitution, By-Laws and Laws of Athletics* (New York:
Published by the Association, 1886), p. 5.

3 See Richard Wettan and Joe Willis, "A Preliminary Analysis of the
Effects of New York Elite Athletic Clubs on Amateur Athletic Governance
in the United States 1870-1915," *Research Quarterly,* 47 (Oct. 1976),
499-505.

4 See Frederick William Janssen (comp.), *Janssen 's American Amateur Athletic and Aquatic History 1829-1888* (New York: Charles R.
Bourne, 1888). Pages 9-11 are entitled "The National Association of
Amateur Athletics of America." When the New York Athletic Club gave
up its annual track and field championships early in 1879, a group of
prominent business men filled the void by creating the NAAAA (N4A).

232 / John Apostal Lucas

George W. Carr was elected president; O. T. Johnson, Vice-President; C. H. Truax, Secretary; and Otis G. Webb, Treasurer (p. 9).

5 "The Athletic Situation," *Wilkes' Spirit of the Times* [hereafter *Spirit*] 115 (17 March 1888), 258.

6 "Athletics," *Spirit,* 116 (10 Nov. 1888), 585.

7 See "Odds and Ends," *Spirit,* 116 (29 Dec. 1888), 838.

8 M. L. Adelman, *A Sporting Time, New York City and the Rise of Modern Athletics 1820-1870* (Urbana: University of Illinois Press, 1986), "Preface."

9 Robert Korsgaard, "A History of the American AAU," Ed.D. dissertation, Teachers College, Columbia University, 1952, p. 56.

10 *Spirit,* 115 (10 March 1888), 222.

11 See *Spirit,* 116 (1 Sept. 1888), 204, and "Editorial," (5 Sept. 1888), 288-9. Ruhls belligerency is located in "Trouble among Athletes," *New York Daily Tribune, 26 Sept.* 1888, p. 3.

12 "The Greatest Contest Ever," wrote the *Spirit* journalist in its 2 February 1889 edition. By contrast the early N4A version was described as "fraudulent affair," "a chilling atmosphere requiring heavy overcoats," and "a tiny crowd, organized by those deserving of condemnation." See *Spirit,* 116 (22 Dec. 1888), 788; *New York Herald,* 16 Dec. 1888, p. 16, and *Outing* magazine, 13 (Feb. 1889), 466.

13 "Caution to Amateur Athletes," *Spirit,* 116 (1 Sept. 1888), 204.

14 Sullivan to Storm, 1 August 1889, as located in the short-lived bimonthly newsletter edited by Frederick William Janssen, *The Ace of Clubs,* 1 (15 Aug. 1889), 3-4. Brief biographies of McMillan and A. G. Mills are located in their obituaries: "Harry McMillan Lays Down His Oars at Eighty," *Public Ledger* [Philadelphia], 1 Nov. 1921, p. 16; and "Col. A. G. Mills Dies at 85 Years." *New York Times (NYT),* 28 Aug. 1929, p. 25.

15 McMillan in *The Ace of Clubs,* 1 (15 Oct. 1889), 3. Janssen's remark is in the 1 July 1889 issue, p. 9.

16 *Spirit,* "Editorial," 116 (15 Sept. 1888), 288, 289.

17 Daniel J. Ferris, "The AAU is Formed," *The Amateur Athlete* (AA), 9 (Dec. 1938), 35.

18 See Korsgaard, pp. 109-10, and AAU historian, C. Robert Paul, "History of the AAU," *AA,* 33 (Dec. 1962), 6.

19 William B. "Father Bill" Curtis, editor of the *Spirit of the Times* in the year of his death (1900), was the greatest "all-around" athlete in America during the post-Civil War decade and twice president of the NYAC. "He froze to death atop Mount Washington in New Hampshire in a severe storm between July 1st and 3rd." See Caspar Whitney. "The Death of 'Father Bill' Curtis," *Outing,* 36 (Aug. 1900), 557. A much more recent essay is that of Richard G. Wettan and Joe D. Willis, "William Buckingham Curtis, the Founding Father of American Amateur Athletics, 1837-1900," *Quest,* 27 (Winter 1977), 28-37. Some two-dozen Curtis sketches appeared in print immediately following "Father Bill's" death.

20 *The Brooklyn Daily Eagle,* 2 Nov. 1891, p. 6, and in the same newspaper, "Annual Meeting of the Amateur Union," 17 Nov. 1891, p. 1.

See also "League of American Wheelmen vs. AAU," *The Ace of Clubs,* 1 (15 March 1890), 6.

21 Professor Ronald A. Smith of The Pennsylvania State University is convinced that "simon-pure athletic amateurism" never really caught on with America's elite athletes in the late nineteenth century. This researcher agrees. See Smith's *Sport and Freedom. The Rise of Big-Time College Athletics* (New York: Oxford University Press, 1988), pp. 44-6, 166-74.

22 Ronald A. Smith, "History of Amateurism in Men's Intercollegiate Athletics: The Continuance of a 19th Century Anachronism in America," *Quest,* 45 (Nov. 1993), 431.

23 David C. Young in *The American Historical Review,* 94 (Feb. 1989), 106-7. Among the many revisionist historians of Greek amateur athletics, Donald G. Kyle and David C. Young are especially illuminating. See Kyle's "E. Norman Gardiner: Historian of Ancient Sport," *International Journal of the History of Sport,* 8 (May, 1991), 28-55, and Young's *The Olympic Myth of Greek Amateur Athletics* (Chicago: Ares Publishers, 1984), p. 7, where, amidst significant elaboration and some exceptions, he says "Ancient amateurism is a myth."

24 The phrase is from an essay on "Walter Horatio Pater (1839-94)," *The Victorian Age-Prose, Poetry, and Drama,* edited by John Wilson Bowyer and John Lee Brooks (New York: F. S. Crofts and Co., 1938), pp. 721-2.

25 See p. 1827 in the lengthy essay on "Romanticism" in *The Columbia Encyclopaedia* (New York: Columbia University Press, 1963), edited by William Bridgewater and Seymour Kurtz. This researcher profited by also reading Will and Ariel Durant, *The Story of Civilization,* Vol. X: *Rousseau and Revolution* (New York: Charles Scribner's Sons, 1929), edited by Albert Cranberry Reed, xiii-xxv.

26 See Korsgaard, pp. 123-4. When Korsgaard conducted his doctoral research in the 1940s, the AAU records were intact and, additionally, several AAU men from the 1890s were still living and were interviewed by the Columbia University graduate student. The original AAU records burned. See "Fire Burns up Athletic Records." *NYT,* 6 July 1913; sec. 4, p. 2.

27 There is no evidence that in 1893 the two men knew one another, personally or by reputation. See John Lucas, "Coubertin One Hundred Years Ago: His Second American Visit in 1893," *Olympika: The Journal of Olympic Studies,* 2 (1993), 103-8.

28 See John Lucas, "Professor William Milligan Sloane: Father of the United States Olympic Committee," in *Sport-Reflexionen im Umfeld der Sportgeschichte, Festschrift für Horst Überhorst* (Andrea Luh-Edgar Beckers, ed.), pp. 230-42.

29 John Lucas described the meeting in his "Early Olympic Antagonists—Pierre de Coubertin Versus James E. Sullivan," *Stadion* 3, 2 (1977), 258-72. On p. 259, Lucas made two errors. Gustavus T. Kirby was at that meeting, but he was not yet the "AAU boss." A more grievous mistake was the statement: "Coubertin and Sullivan met for the first time at this November 1893 gathering." Sullivan was not present.

30 Pierre de Coubertin, *Une campagne de Vingt-et-un ans 1887-1908* (Paris: Librairie de l'education Physique, 1908), p. 92.

31 Korsgaard interviewed Kirby on 20 Aug. 1951. See the former's disertation, p. 183. Also, in Kirby's autobiography, *I Wonder Why?* (New York: Coward-McCann, 1954), pp. 30-1, the young fencer assured Coubertin that there were athletes interested in the possibility of an international Olympic festival. Kirby was remarkably involved, and in 60 years he served the IC4A, AAU, and United States Olympic Committee (USOC).

32 Whitney's biography and that of all Americans who served on the IOC may be found in John Lucas, "Americans in the IOC: 17 have served the Movement," *The Olympian*, 10 (Feb. 1984), 22-6.

33 Caspar Whitney, "Amateur Sport," *Harper's Weekly*, 40 (25 April 1896), 425-6. An ephemeral Amateur Athlete Company published *The Amateur Athlete*. In volume 1 (August 1896), 4, the editor, Harry Allan Ely, wrote, "The end is near." The AAU must go and will be replaced by "representatives of eight of the largest athletic clubs in the United States.... Some fine morning the AAU ... will awaken to find that their misruled kingdom has departed once and for all."

34 The nineteenth-century *Spirit of the Times*, managed by AAU president, W. B. Curtis, consistently supported the AAU. An editorial read, "AAU officers have been uniformly honest, capable, and industrious." See *Spirit*, 126 (6 Jan. 1894), 838.

35 See *New York Daily Tribune*, 16 July 1897 p. 3; 14 Aug. 1897, p. 3; 28 Aug. 1897, p. 3, and "AAU and Bernie Wefers," *NYT*, 16 Nov. 1897, p. 4. Back in 1893, A. G. Mills wrote a letter to Sullivan congratulating him for "disqualifying professionals from the ranks of amateur athletes." See *A. G. Mills Correspondence;* letter dated 12 Aug. 1893.

36 See *New York Tribune*, 3 Nov. 1901, p. l; 13 Dec. 1901, p. 5; 19 Feb. 1902, p. 5; and 12 Aug. 1902, p. 14. For Sullivan's confrontation with Camp, see *Camp Papers*, Reel 2; letters dated 9 June 1900; 11 Dec. 1900; 23 Dec. 1901; and 10 March 1902.

37 Charles J. P. Lucas, "Commercializing Amateur Athletics," *World Today*, 10 (March 1906), 281. Lucas was the author of the important book, *The Olympic Games 1904.*

38 Arthur Duffey, "Amateur Athletes Exposed," *Physical Culture* (Dec. 1905), 488. Duffey was in constant trouble with the AAU for making money from running and was suspended in 1904. Later, he was for 40 years a sport journalist for the *Boston Post*. In another article, Duffey exclaimed, "Secretary Sullivan can erase all the Duffey records he wants to. But the public will never forget that Duffey was one of the greatest sprinters the world has ever seen." See Duffey's "Amateur Athletics Exposed" (conf.) *Physical Culture* (Jan. 1906), 126.

39 Lucas, 281.

40 On the AAU's fiftieth birthday, its monthly magazine, *Amateur Athlete (AA)*, devoted its entire issue to "The AAU in the East, Mid-West, West Coast, and South." See *AA*, 9 (Dec. 1938).

41 "J. E. Sullivan Elected," *New York Daily Tribune*, 20 Nov. 1906, p. 10.

42 At a master AAU party at New York City's Waldorf-Astoria Hotel on 18 Nov. 1912, there were banners everywhere proclaiming "Today is the AAU's 25th birthday and our leader Sullivan's 50th birthday." See "AAU Celebrates Two Big Events," *NYT*, 19 Nov. 1912, p. 13. See also *Who's Who in America 1908-1909*, p. 1839; *Webster's American Biographies* (1974), p. 1006; *The New International Encyclopaedia*, 21 (1918), p. 651. An interview by this researcher of Sullivan's grandson, J. Stacey Sullivan, revealed that, "We were taught to revere our grandfather, but learned little of his youth ... and most of the records are gone." Interview in San Diego, California, 26 Dec. 1989.

43 See James S. Mitchell, *How To Be a Weight Thrower* (New York: American Sports Pub. Co., 1910), p. 2; Stephen Hardy on Sullivan in D. G. Kyle and G. D. Stark (eds.), *Essays on Sport History* (College Station: Texas A. and M. Press, 1990), pp. 64-9.

44 Daley, as quoted in *Dictionary of American Biography [DAB]*, 18 (1936), p. 191.

45 See *The New York Clipper*, 28 Jan. 1882, p. 737. On Thanksgiving Day 1881, Sullivan won a half-mile race in 2:08.5 "over muddy ground and a stinging rain," *NYT*, 25 Nov. 1881, p. 5. He was several times city "all-around" champion and in 1884 won second place in the Canadian half-mile championships, *New York Tribune*, 17 Sept. 1914, p. 14 in a Sullivan obituary.

46 Mrs. Sullivan passed away on 16 July 1923; Julia married and became Mrs. Joseph Abel, while James Stacey lived till 18 November 1957, leaving a wife, the former Katherine G. Farrell, and two sons, E. D. Farrell Sullivan, and J. Stacey Sullivan, Jr. (born 1926). See *NYT*, 17 July 1923, p. 19; *NYT*, 19 November 1957, p. 33, and interview with J. S. Sullivan, Jr., 26 Dec. 1989.

47 See John Lucas, "The IC4A Championships—A Hundred Year History," in *IC4A Record Book 1876-1976* (ECAC Office, 1976), pp. 7-19.

48 *New York Daily Tribune*, 7 Aug. 1898, part 2, p. 4, devoted a thousand-word essay on "Extensive Preparations for the Paris Olympic Games." Involved in the whole process were: Thomas W. Cridler, Third Assistant Secretary of State; the late Major Handy, Special United States Commissioner to the Paris Exposition; Louis M. Hamburger, Assistant Commissioner and Special Commissioner of the AAU; President Henry S. McMillan of the AAU and its secretary, J. E. Sullivan. Also "Baron Pierrre de Coubertin, a well-known literary man and the blue-blooded of royalists, but thoroughly republican at heart and American in his sympathies." See also: p. 1494, *Congressional Record—Senate—7 Feb. 1898*; Vol. 3, Part 2; 50th Congress—2nd Session—25 Jan. - 22 Feb. 1989. Also, *New York Chipper*, 46 (26 Feb. 1898), p. 862.

49 See Robert E. Lehr, "The American Olympic Committee, 1896-1940: from Chaos to Order," Ph.D. dissertation, Pennsylvania State University, 1985. See Chapter 2 for the temporary life of the AOC during its early year.

50 See *The Olympic Games Stockholm 1912*, ed. J. E. Sullivan (New York: American Sports Pub. Co., 1913), p. 10; also *Congressional Re-*

236 / John Apostal Lucas

cord—Senate 50th Congress; 2nd Session—25 Jan-22 Feb. 1899, p. 1494; *New York Clipper,* 46 (26 Feb. 1898), 862, and Lawrence Hilmond Chalip, "'The Framing of Policy: Explaining the Transformation of American Sport,'" (Ph.D. dissertation, University of Chicago, 1988). p. 28.

51 "Athletic Magnets Meet," *NYT,* 22 Nov. 1898, p. 2. Even 25 cents was too much for H. J. Brown of the National Interscholastic Association and with Gustavus Town Kirby and Charles H. Sherrill of the IC4A, who cried "tyranny." See *New York Clipper,* 46 (5 March 1898), 9.

52 "J. E. Sullivan on Paris Games," *New York Daily Tribune,* 17 Aug. 1900, p. 5.

53 Coubertin to Sullivan, 19 Oct. 1904. See J. E. Sullivan (ed.), *Spalding's Athletic Almanac for 1905* (New York: American Sports Pub. Co., 1905), p. 185.

54 John B. Jackson to Elihu Root, 4 May 1906. See 59th Congress; 2nd Session; House of Representatives Papers Relating to the *Foreign Relations* of the United States, Part I (Washington: Governing Printing, 1909), pp. 813-14. On p. 813, Elihu Root wrote to Jackson: "President Roosevelt has accepted the honorary presidency of the American Committee on the Olympic Games at Athens, from April 22 to May 2, 1906." Letter dated 21 Feb. 1906. On 9 March 1906, Sullivan lunched with the president in the White House, Roosevelt agreeing that the AAU leader should head the American Olympic delegation to Athens. See 'U.S. Representatives to Olympic Games; J. E. Sullivan Appointed', *NYT,* 10 March 1906, p. 8.

55. Roosevelt to Sullivan, telegram, 3 May 1906, and published in the *New York Daily Tribune,* 4 May 1906, p. l. The details of the AAU, its subsidiary, the AOC, and Sullivan's role are published in John Lucas, "American Involvement in the Athens Olympian Games of 1906," *Stadion,* 6 (1980), 217-28. See p. 223.

56 "Wants Congress to Aid Athletes," *NYT,* 20 Feb. 1907, p. 9.

57 Sullivan in the *1907 Minutes of the AAU Annual Meeting,* 18 Nov. 1907, p. 7.

58 The extant literature is large here, both eyewitness and secondary accounts. The English journal *Truth* fired heavy criticism at "the vulgar Mr. Sullivan as well as the indecisive British officials, especially 'The Silence of Rev. De Courcy Laffan,'"(Volume 64; 9 Dec. 1908), 1388-9. See also Theodore Cook, "A Forward as to Origins," in *The Fourth Olympiad, Being the Official Report of the Olympic Games of 1908* (London: BOA 1908). For the American view, see "The Olympic Games in London," by Mike Murphy, under section entitled "Olympic Games" in the *Walter Camp Papers,* Reel 44. Sullivan's acid quotes were reproduced across the United States. "British officials are hopelessly behind the times and therefore utterly inept," he wrote in the *New York Herald;* Special Sunday Sporting Section, 19 July 1908, p. l. One useful secondary source captured a small fraction of the controversy. See George R. Matthews, "The Controversial Olympic Games of 1908 as viewed by the *New York Times* and *The Times of London," Journal of Sport History,* 7 (Summer 1980), 40-53.

59 "AAU's New President," *NYT,* 21 Nov. 1909; part 4, p. 2. Brown's obituary, *NYT,* 12 April 1937, p. 17.

60 "Sullivan to Select Team," *NYT,* 11 Dec. 1910; part 4, p. 6; President Taft's secretary C. D. Hills to Sullivan, 9 April 1912; *William Taft Papers;* Series 6; reel 401, number 576. The Taft Papers, contain more than 100 letters addressed to Taft supporting Sullivan as "the only logical American Commissioner to the Olympic Games." Among them are letters from IOC members Caspar Whitney and AOC president Colonel Robert Thompson, withdrawing their names from consideration as Commissioner.

61 Sullivan to Thompson, 21 December 1911; William H. Taft Papers; Series 6; reel 401, number 572B.

62 "Sullivan Injured in Train Wreck," *New York Tribune,* 14 Aug. 1911, pp. 1, 4; "James Sullivan's Legs Crushed," *NYT,* 14 August 1911, pp. 1, 2; "Sullivan Confined to Home," *NYT,* 6 Sept. 1911, p. 10; "Sullivan Seriously Ill," *NYT,* 3 Jan. 1912, p. 10 and 4 Jan. 1912, p. 10.

63 See James E. Sullivan (ed.), *The Olympic Games Stockholm 1912* (New York: American Sports Pub. Co., 1912), pp. 83, 89, 101.

64 Biographical data on Kirby are located in *The National Cyclopaedia of American Biography,* 45 (1962), 20-1. Also Kirby's "AAU Reminiscences," *Amateur Athlete,* 9 (Dec. 1938), 4, 24, 39. "Mr. Kirby had witnessed all of the Olympic Games since their revival in 1896," wrote the *Amateur Athlete* editor (April 1956), 12, in a tribute entitled "Gustavus T. Kirby Dies at 82."

65 See *NYT,* 19 March 1912, p. 9; 24 March 1912; sport sec.; p. 8. Kirby's quote is located in *1912 Minutes of AAU Annual Meeting,* 18 Nov. 1912, p. 2.

66 "Jim Sullivan Back," *NYT,* 30 April 1913, p. 9.

67 See *1913 Minutes of AAU Annual Meeting,* 17 Nov 1913, pp. 2-7. AOC president Robert Means Thompson (1849-1931) was also in Berlin. It was at this 1913 meeting that Alfred J. Lill (1881-1956) was elected AAU president. His obituary is located in *NYT,* 19 March 1956, p. 31.

68 Fifty letters exist between Sullivan and President Wilson. Finally, in mid-April 1914, Wilson accepted the honorary presidency of the AOC. See Woodrow Wilson Papers, Series 2; reel 56, also Series 4, reel 242. Also, William H. Taft Papers; Series 8, reel 525, p. 52.

69 See *New York Herald,* 19 July 1914, part 4, p. 7 for this quote on his weight. See also Korsgaard, pp. 199-200; *NYT,* 21 June 1914, part 4, p. 2. In the *NYT,* 19 July 1914, part 4, p. 2, one reads: "A silver cup was given by Coubertin to Sullivan as a gift to the United States."

70 Judge Weeks' speech, one of the most passionate ever read by this researcher, is located in the *Minutes* of the Metropolitan AAU annual meeting, 21 Sept. 1914, p. 51. At least 100 newspapers in the United States, Canada, England, and France carried Sullivan's obituary. Sporting and literary journalists carried the news of his death. See "James E. Sullivan, Dean of American Athletics Dies," *American Physical Education Review,* 19 (Oct. 1914), 545-6; also "Sullivan Obituary," *American*

Review of Reviews, 50 (Oct. 1914), 418; "Mort de James E. Sullivan," *Bulletin du Comite International Olympique,* 1 (Jan. 1915), 1-2; Sullivan's influence on sport in Canada was strong. See Daniel B. Reid, "The AAU of the United States and the Canadian AAU 1897-1914," M.A. thesis, University of Western Ontario, 1990), *passim.*

71 Korsgaard, p. 192.

72 Seated around the giant papermachê stadium, with its real cinder track and "fine moss duplicating the turf of the arena," surrounding Colonel Thompson were: Sullivan, Evert Jansen Wendell, Matthew F. Halpin, 'Gus' Kirby, Jeremiah T. Mahoney, E. E. Babb, Graeme M. Hammond, M.D., Luther Halsey Gulick, Judge Weeks, Julian W. Curtiss, Allison V. Armour, J. B. Maccabe, and William Milligan Sloane.

73 See Mary H. Leigh, "The Evolution of Women's Participation in the Olympic Games, 1900-1948," Ph.D. dissertation, Ohio State University, 1974, passim.; Paula Dee Welch, "The Emergence of American Women in the Summer Olympics Games, 1900-1972," Ed.D. dissertation, University of North Carolina at Greensboro, 1975, passim.

74 See *New York Herald,* 16 Nov. 1914, p. 14. On Rubien, see *NYT,* 17 Nov. 1914, p. 11; also *Amateur Athlete,* 22 (Aug. 1951), 9.

75 Since 1930, the James Edward Sullivan Award has been given to the outstanding male or female amateur athlete in the United States. The AAU has from the beginning sponsored the event. Full records of all the winners are located at their national headquarters in Indianapolis, Indiana.

18.
Gustavus Town Kirby:
Doyen of American Amateur Athletics and his Inadmissibility into the International Olympic Committee*

Part I: "Preamble"

This essay is decidedly not a Paen to Gustavus Town Kirby, nor is it, hopefully, a mindless, one-sided (and therefore unscientific) vituperation of an American who for sixty years was a person of substance in American and international amateur athletics—a man of financial means ceaselessly immersed in law, technology, invention, the international art world, urban renewal, leisure-recreation at every level, and important civic affairs in New York City. Prodigious energy is insufficient when standing alone, but when combined with the deliberate effort to place himself in the eye of many storms, the man emerges large. Carefully orchestrated biography can tell an even larger story. French historian Jean-Michel Faure said it better in his Jean Borotra story: "Provided he avoids the temptation of being no more than an apologist, the biographer who sticks to facts can ... open ... horizons."[1] It is the contention of this researcher that, next to Avery Brundage (1887-1975), Kirby was the most important American amateur sport administrator of this century. And yet he is little known. Richard W. Leopold said the same thing about American jurist-diplomat, Elihu Root: "Time has a way of playing strange and cruel tricks on famous men, and he who looms large in the eyes of one generation may be forgotten by another."[2] Closer to the subject,

* STADION, XXI /XXII (1995/ 96), 171-192.

the young sport historian, Stephen Wenn, wrote: "Historians are left to speculate on the nature of Kirby's 'unfortunate mannerisms,'" and therefore his place in Olympic Games.[3] This research essay is an attempt to (1) discuss "Gus" Kirby's considerable accomplishments, (2) disclose several of these "unfortunate mannerisms," hitherto unpublished, (3) connect these positive-negative attributes to the lOC's decision not to co-opt Kirby into their select club, and (4) attempt an assessment of the whole person Kirby.

At this juncture, on the edge of the twenty-first century, it will be no easy task to evaluate Gustavus Town Kirby (1874-1956). Born in Philadelphia, Kirby attended public and private schools in New York City and Columbia University, which gave him an electrical engineering degree in 1895 and a law degree in 1898. He practiced law for 50 years, was auction partner with his father, Thomas E. Kirby, at the very prestigious American Art Association, and for an even longer period was ceaselessly involved in local, national, and world amateur and Olympic Games activities. The Public Schools Athletic League [PSAL] and the international recreation movement took up large portions of his time and energy. For long periods before the Second World War and after, he was the perpetually-frustrated treasurer of the USOC—seeking but never finding enough money to keep the organization solvent. *The National Cyclopaedia of American Biography* (volume XLV, 1962) devotes more than 500 words to Kirby, commenting that the young Kirby was associate counsel with Supreme Court judge, Charles Evans Hughes, in 1905, and forty years later was president of the Society of Medical Jurisprudence. In between these years, his several inventions were used worldwide, among them, in 1931, the Kirby instant photo camera, used in foot and horse races. A few of Kirby's significant awards were: knight first class of the Order of Gustavus Vasa, Sweden (1912); officer of the Order of Leopold II of Belgium (1920); officer, Legion of Honor, France (1926); Cross of Merit, first class, Germany (1936); Finland's Knight of the Order (1941); and Finland's Cross of Merit (1952). Another dozen American and international awards are listed. *The New York Times* obituary column of February 29, 1956, page 31, said of Kirby: He devoted so much time and energy to amateur sports and scores of other important enterprises, "that it often was wondered how he ever had enough hours left to become successful in his profession and in business."

Kirby was married in 1906 to Wilhelmina Stewart Clafflin, daughter of millionaire John Clafflin, "the merchant prince of

America." Kirby's ancestor, on his mother's side, was John Wesley Neveling, chaplain to George Washington, "while on father's side, the Kirby heritage came from Britain."[4] By this date, Kirby's active career as an athlete was over, having won the Columbia University Iron Man Trophy in fencing, cycling, and track and field—the Colonel Robert M. Thompson Award.[5] Five major divisions exist in this paper. They are: Part I, a "Preamble" on the possibility of balanced biography serving enlightened historiography; Part II, a recapitulation of Kirby's repeated but unsubstantiated claim that in the fall of 1893, in New York City's Columbia University Club, he had lunch and a long conversation with esteemed American historian William Milligan Sloane and with the thirty-year-old French Baron Pierre de Coubertin. Kirby was a well known scholar-athlete on campus, not yet twenty years of age; Part III, Kirby's life-long habit of making his views and those of the moral high ground all one. He seemed inexorably wedded to a mind-set that convinced him that he was always right on every issue. Kirby was decidedly not a humble man. Such attitudes made him staunch friends and implacable enemies ... simultaneously; Part IV, Kirby's "unfortunate mannerisms," many of them of indefinable sexual overtones, are discussed here; and Part V, "Epilogue."

Part II: Kirby, Sloane, and Coubertin 1893[6]

Coubertin's two important autobiographies confirm that in the fall of 1893, he had lunch with Sloane "at the university club in New York City." No other name is mentioned as present at the meeting.[7] At age eighty, Kirby penned his autobiography, remembering sixty years earlier. Coubertin, wrote Kirby, came to America to visit Sloane, "a man he had never met."[8]

> Sloane ... asked me to meet ... with De Coubertin .... We lunched together in the old building of the University Club, which was then on Madison Avenue at 28th Street.... I assured De Coubertin that there would be little or no difficulty in forming an American Olympic Committee and of America participating in the "Modern Olympic Games."[9]

Historian-educator Robert Korsgaard interviewed Kirby on August 20, 1951. They talked for half a day. Kirby told Korsgaard:

242 / John Apostal Lucas

I met Coubertin in 1895 at the University Club in New York City and told him that [James Edward] "Sullivan was the best person to organize a [USA] team to send to Athens."[10]

According to Kirby, at this 1951 interview, Dr. Sloane had asked him to be at this meeting because he [Sloane] was "a friend of the Kirby family." Kirby continued:

I then met with Sullivan and persuaded him to accept the chairmanship of a U.S. Olympic Committee. We then organized the first Olympic Committee which included Julian Curtiss, Treasurer, A.C. and Walter Spalding, Casper Whitney, ... Sullivan and me.[11]

At the 65th annual meeting of the AAU on November 28, 1953, Kirby reminded the delegates that no man was still alive who knew Baron de Coubertin in the nineteenth century-except himself. Kirby addressed this 1953 audience at the Washington, D.C., Willard Hotel, which included the new IOC president, Avery Brundage. Kirby captivated his colleagues with the oft-told story:

Sloane had a luncheon down at the old University Club. Coubertin was there, and I was invited. 'Can we get the United States to participate in a revived Olympic Games?' asked Coubertin. I'm sure we can and the next day I went down and saw Jim Sullivan. I told him the story and Jim Sullivan said, "We can do it."[12]

Back in 1947, Kirby, the president Emeritus of the United States Olympic Association, gave an important speech titled "This Broken Time Question." He got the date correct this time:

Fifty-four years ago Baron de Coubertin and Professor William Milligan Sloane asked me ... to confer with them ... relative to the possibility of forming an American Olympic Committee. We were in conference for several hours.... Out of this conference ... came the organization of the first American Olympic Committee and of it I am the only surviving member.[13]

Even earlier, in 1938, Kirby remembered his alleged meeting with Sloane and Coubertin in New York City's University Club:

Professor Sloane asked me who was the leader of amateur sport in the United States and when I said James Sullivan, it was to him that he took for advice and assistance the then unknown young Frenchman Coubertin.[14]

All the way back to 1931, Kirby spoke on "World-Wide Influence of Olympic Games," in which he remembered: "Back in 1895 [sic], I listened to Coubertin talk about his dream of an Olympic Games that could help with international friendship."[15]

The purpose of this "Part II" is to share Olympic Games origins and some little-known historical data. Another reason for

this section is to reveal Kirby as a complex professional—a *raconteur,* a high-voltage anecdotist, an egotist, and at the same time, an amateur sport administrator of great skill who made it his business to be amidst the vortex of American and international Olympic business for more than half a century. There is no corroborative evidence that the youth Kirby met with Coubertin and Sloane in November of 1893—except Kirby's repeated insistence that it happened, and therefore he—Kirby—must be acknowledged one of the senior American Olympic administrators, even before the Games of the First Olympiad took place.[16]

Part III: Kirby's Life-long Habit of Making his Views and Those of the "Moral High Ground" All One

This researcher believes himself above gossip, disdainful of innuendo, and one who consistently has retreated from groundless statements not based on fact. Every effort has been made in this "Part III" to avoid mindless tattletale and personal attack. There were real reasons why the veteran Olympic administrator and recognized expert on many dimensions Olympic Gustavus Town Kirby was shunned by the IOC as a serious candidate for cooptation into that exclusive body. Allegations, subtle hints, accusations, some possibly bizarre autobiographical anecdotes, a few sensational allegations, and persistent views about girls and women that would be unacceptable in the America of the late 1990s, are here accounted, verbatim and without editorializing. Possibly none of them, as a single event in a long and very meaningful life, amounts to much. But it is the contention of this researcher that the accumulated "weight" of all these "happenings" embarrassed three IOC presidents, rendered uncomfortable some members of the AOC and the IOC, resulting in the boycott of Kirby from (possibly) his rightful place in that international seat of power.

Kirby's Vituperate, Uncompromising Stance in London 1908

Coubertin despaired of the Games of the Fourth Olympiad in London 1908. There was so much anger, name-calling and three-way animosity between English, Irish, and American athletes and officials! The American team leaders, led by 48-year-old James Edward Sullivan and 34-year-old "Gus" Kirby, objected to the entry of Canadian great professional long-distance runner and native American, Tom Longboat. All the field event throwing and jumping areas are "primitive and dangerous" shouted Sullivan and his disciple, Kirby. The 400-meter "walk-over" was a travesty—"a display of ineptness and cowardice," they said. The heat and quarter-final distribution of athletes—all favoring the English—was manifestly amateurish, in the worst sense of that word. And the gift of a gold medal to Italy's Dorando Pietri instead of to America's Johnny Hayes (later overturned due to the shouting match between the British Jury of Appeals and Sullivan-Kirby) was "illegal and beyond the pale." Looking back thirty-one years, Kirby called British officiating "unfair, dishonest, insular, insolent, impossible."[17] Kirby never held back, rarely took a conciliatory view. "British officials made it as difficult as possible for Americans to win, or, for that matter anyone else, other than Englishmen," was a Kirby quote, reproduced in the major American newspapers.[18] "Passion" and "frenzy" were words—used by the Games' Founder to describe the conduct of the American officials.[19]

Kirby was past president of the IC4A and a permanent member of its executive board. He wrote a pamphlet, an "Official Report" to that organization—a horrendously critical six-page assessment of British officiating at the games. "They did almost nothing well nor efficiently," wrote the acid-tongue Kirby.[20] Theodore A. Cook, prominent Britisher, wrote a 59-page reply to Kirby, an angry rebuttal titled *A Reply to Certain Charges made by some American Officials.* "I trust that Mr. Kirby will share with his IC4A people, the British version of what happened in London," wrote Cook. "Such universities as Yale and Harvard ... are not likely to be taken in by Mr. Kirby."[21] New York State's Lt. Gov. Chanler, in the presence of Gus Kirby, called British conduct on the athletic field "a spindleshank monstrosity."[22]

Not all Americans supported Kirby's tirade. Boston, Massachusetts lawyer, Francis Peabody, Jr., from the city's most prominent Brahmin families, wrote, "I was in London. Kirby has told only half- truths. His endless angry complaints ... show an angry and prejudiced state of mind."[23] Kirby slashed back in a 35-page pamphlet, calling Peabody "uninformed" and then listed fifty individuals and British-American newspapers that agreed with his [Kirby's] viewpoint.[24] The young Kirby was making friends and enemies at an extraordinary rate.

It was inevitable. Kirby was considered as a possible IOC member, and then rejected ... as early as the 1908 Games aftermath. James Hazen Hyde (1876-1959)[25] had just resigned as IOC member and in late 1908, Coubertin was looking for an American replacement. Sloane wrote Coubertin on September 18, 1908, about the empty post. Sloane brought up the name "Kirby" without at the same time framing it as a ringing endorsement. "You met Kirby in London. What do you think of him as a possible IOC member?" wrote Sloane, continuing:

> He is fairly well bred, is very influential in university athletic associations and is well-connected. Personally he is not the entire thing; I shall not ask him yet.[26]

Sloane never found it possible to recommend Kirby. Honor and disappointments came to him early and often. Sloane wrote Coubertin again (October 16, 1908), proposing that any possible personal endorsement of Kirby as an IOC member would have to wait "until some of the [London] smoke has rolled away."[27] Nothing came of it. Kirby was the most publicized "bad guy" in the eyes of the 1908 Olympic officials (all of them English).[28] The Sloane-Coubertin correspondence continued into December of 1908, and they could not rid themselves of Kirby's specter. "I have seen a Sullivan to Kirby letter," wrote Sloane to his good friend, "which makes their absurd situation plain and in consequence Kirby has asked for an interview with me."[29] Kirby got in a last condemnation of English fairness. "I cannot believe that English officials, after the 400- meter race, are devoid of honesty." Furious at being called a liar, Kirby demanded that the unknown perpetrator "step forward."[30] Lastly, on this unseemly subject, the future president of the IOC Belgium's Count Henri Baillet-Latour—was in the London stadium in the summer of 1908, and he heard and saw "everything."

The Sloane-Coubertin correspondences of 1909-1910 are revealing, and some of it on the touchy subject of Gustavus Kirby. "The mud-slinging in London was a horror; I tried to stay aloof as a gentleman," wrote Sloane to Coubertin on January 26, 1909. "The Sullivan crowd have evidently determined not to approach me though they have announced Kirby as an [IOC] entry," wrote Sloane to Coubertin in April of that same year. In January of 1911, Sloane wrote the IOC president: "Please have no fear about Sullivan and Kirby: both 'feed from my hand.'" Sloane informed Coubertin on January 22, 1911: "We have Kirby in his place [as AAU president] where he can do no harm.... Everyone ... has a watchful eye on Kirby...." Sloane wrote the next day to his good friend: "Dear Pierre: Kirby's party at his home was the olive branch of magnanimity as he asked us to forget the past [London]." Kirby's dinner last month, wrote Sloane to Coubertin "was the last gasp of a trapped eel."[31]

Kirby's 1921 Insult of Coubertin Remembered a Long Time

Most people, including IOC members, have long and vivid memories. When "Gus" Kirby inadvertently insulted Baron de Coubertin at the 1921 Olympic Congress in Lausanne, both future IOC presidents Baillet-Latour and Sigfrid Edström were in the room when it happened. Kirby was at the height of power in his American amateur athletic world, having recently been elected president of his National Olympic Committee [NOC].[32] Kirby was the main architect in the complete reorganization of the American committee—a movement of significant, positive impulse in that country's Olympic history.[33]

The post-war years necessitated an emergency meeting in June of 1921 of the IOC with the NOC's of the world, as well as presidents of individual international sport federations (IP's)—a "Congress." Nothing was more important on the agenda than selection of the Summer Games city for 1924 and serious talks about the 1928 site. AOC member from Los Angeles, William May Garland (1866-1948) was in the front row of interested delegates (he was elected to the IOC in 1922). He loved his city and country, and he was also a powerful lobbyist for Southern California businessmen. But the conversations were not going his way. President Coubertin talked about many things and several European cities, but nothing of consequence about a small American city thousands of miles away. Kirby was present both as a member of the world track and field body, the IAAF, formed by Sullivan and Edström in 1913, and as newly-elected AOC president. The meeting progressed with Coubertin in charge of his fiefdom, orchestrating the meeting in his old-fashioned manner of benign singular control.[34] Garland said little; Kirby, as was his way, criticized Coubertin in writing after returning home, where he and Frederick Rubien (AOC secretary) had nothing good to say about Coubertin's cavalier and casual way of conducting an Olympic Congress meeting. The remarkable 4,500-word report is reported as a 1921 appendage to the 1920 *Report of the American Olympic Committee—Seventh Olympic Games.* Praise be to Coubertin, our IOC president, read the document. But in running a meeting there is "sometimes lacking ... business-like methods and courtesies which make for success"(p. 421). The president, "with much petulance and misunderstanding" directed a resolution to suit his own agenda (p. 422). The request of Los Angeles as a possible site for the 1924 or 1928 Games was ignored or remained unrecorded, possibly, continued the report, because the IOC "has no stenographer present at its meetings." The Kirby-Rubien essay refused to release Coubertin.

> It is generally understood that the minutes are made up by the president from his memory.... It thereby oftimes happens that the recollection or record of just what took place is vague or misleading with consequent misunderstanding and opportunity for trouble.[35]

The Baron was so angry at Kirby's report that he held a press conference. At an *Associated Press* release out of Geneva, dated January 3, 1921, Coubertin asked for an investigatory committee "to point out and rectify alleged errors and willfully misleading insinuations in the recent published report of the American Olympic Committee." Kirby reacted coolly: "The American committee has nothing to add to nor retract from the report in question."[36] He concluded with still another typical direct barb: "Members of the American delegation to the Lausanne meeting felt the offer on behalf of Los Angeles had not been treated by the International Committee and the President with respect and courtesy due such an invitation."[37]

That same day, General Palmer E. Pierce of the AOC Publication Committee wrote Kirby that his report was, regrettably, never edited before it was published in the *Official Report*. Please contact me, ended Pierce's letter.[38] Kirby felt the need to write Coubertin on February 14, 1922, assuring the IOC leader that he meant no personal insult, but was only critical of administrative inefficiency. The whole world, including myself, pays you "high tribute, ... highest esteem," ended Kirby's note.[39] But many years later, in 1931, Kirby wrote Avery Brundage: "No one disliked him [Coubertin] personally more than I; no one differed with him more frequently than I."[40] All of this righteous indignation may have cost Kirby a spot on the IOC. President Edström certainly thought so and expressed exactly that sentiment in a 1943 letter to Mr. Brundage. Kirby has been an inestimably important part of the Olympic movement "from the very beginning," wrote Edström. Kirby's a very good man, but "unfortunately he got in a scrap with de Coubertin in Lausanne in 1921 and therefore did not become a member of the IOC as had been the intention."[41] Gus Kirby stood for principle, as he understood it. There was no other way for this American martinet. In his case, such a stand raised him in the estimation of many contemporaries, and, at the same time labeled him pompous and opinionated with some of his friends and foes. It is a price paid by persons possessing strong wills and impenetrable positions. The man never stopped, and as a delegate to the all-important Olympic Congress in Prague 1925, Kirby was full of criticism for the hopelessly ineffective pedagogical program[42] and exasperation at the new IOC president, Baillet-Latour—"no more than an efficient businessman."[43] Kirby once again "hit on" Baillet-Latour as sexist. Edward S. Goldstein, in a "Henri de Baillet-Latour" essay, wrote about an IAAF meeting in 1930: "American delegate Gustavus Kirby angrily counterproposed (Baillet-Latour's proposal for minimum participation for women in the 1932 Games) that if women were banned, a consideration to eliminate men's track and field would be forthcoming."[44]

Kirby's 1933 Brave Resolution "Distanced Him" from the IOC

During 1933 and 1934, G. T. Kirby was a very big "player" among those Americans who wished their country not to participate in the Games of the XIth Olympiad in Berlin unless German Jewish athletes were given a chance to make their Olympic team. The fact that Kirby changed his mind (after Brundage's "fact-finding" trip to Germany in 1935) may have been less important in the eyes of IOC members than the initial two years in which he insisted that the Hitler government's treatment of Jews "is a violation of the Olympic code." "Without equivocation," shouted Kirby at the Pittsburgh AAU meeting on November 20, 1933, "Jewish athletes must be allowed to train, prepare for and participate in the Olympic Games of 1936."[45] Kirby was "front and center," the architect of this resolution which could jeopardize his nation's participation in the Games.

Much took place between 1933 and 1935—some negative; some illusory, and a little bit positive. On December 28, 1933, A.C. Gilbert (Olympic pole vault champion, multimillionaire toy maker and member of the AOC) wrote Kirby: You are a great man, Gus, but regarding IOC membership for you, "I regret that I am not in a position where I could do something to accomplish this end."[46] Enormous energy was expended in the United States by pro Olympic participation people and by those advocating a boycott. On March 7, 1934, Kirby gave a fiery speech in the Madison Square Garden, demanding Germany do an immediate "turn-around" and allow Jewish athletes full opportunity.[47] But when Kirby's friend, Brundage, returned from Berlin, Kirby softened his view and looked forward to the AAU and AOC meetings in late 1935. In a quite extraordinary scenario inside New York City's Commodore Hotel, delegates argued for five hours, finally voting 58 $1/4$ to 55 $3/4$ to go to Berlin. Kirby voted with the majority.[48] Kirby's "flip-flop" from 1933 to December of 1935, i.e. from opposition to support of his country's Olympic Games participation, may have been genuine belief that Germany had changed in 2 $1/2$ years. There may have been, perhaps, a "hidden agenda." After all, Kirby knew that the IOC would vote for new members on the days just before the Berlin Olympic Games would begin. We cannot know for sure.

Part IV: Persistent Rumors of "Unfortunate Mannerisms"[49] Were Damaging to Kirby

Innuendo can never be mistaken for the truth and must never be used as historical fact by social scientists. But persistent and consistent hints of lifestyle are used in courts of law. True or not, rumors can be damaging. This researcher is convinced that whispered allegations hurt Kirby in his relentless pursuit of a very much desired place on the IOC.

In most "western societies," for a great many centuries, men talked about "sex" more openly than did women. It has always been more acceptable for men than for women to talk and write in suggestive sexual manners. Gus Kirby enjoyed mild ribaldry, and frequently shared such jokes and anecdotes and his indefinable escapades with friends, and sometimes in private forums.

A 1940 Olympic committee meeting at the New York City Regis Hotel drew "big shot" men from the American and Japanese world of business and sport. Tokyo was the designated city for the Games of the XIIth Olympiad, and the host country delegates wanted a very big USA team to Japan in the summer of that year. A good time was had by all. Gus Kirby shared one of his many anecdotes about the "old days"—one of them about his 1902 visit to Japan: I played a gambling game of "strip"[50] with a "beautiful Japanese girl by the name of Okomo San. I lost so much clothing that after the game I was taken back to the Grand Hotel at Yokohama ... wrapped in a bath towel." This 1940 audience apparently enjoyed Kirby's recollection of 1902. The next speaker, AAU and Olympic Committee secretary, Daniel J. Ferris, commented (after he stopped laughing) and with phony Japanese accent:

Mr. Kirby played game with beautiful Japanese girl.... Mr. Kirby lost much. Mr. Kirby eager come to Japan to meet Okomo San and say "how do you do" to all his children.

Of course everyone roared.[51] At the 1930 Olympic Congress in Berlin, Kirby and delegates enjoyed a demonstration by young German female gymnasts. "I was personally not offended by their near nudity," he wrote a friend that same year.[52] There is no immorality in the intermingling of the sexes "in a nude condition" commented the liberated Kirby.[53] In a 1932 letter to his good friend, John Terrance "Terry" McGovern, Kirby shared with him a day in church, starring at "a very pretty blond who had wandered over from Greenwich Village, her legs crossed, showing a good six inches of bare skin between her rolled stockings and her panties—if she had any." "I was reminded," Kirby continued, "of long ago days, wandering around the world, days I have dubbed 'WWW'—World Wandering amongst the whores."[54] It was a private letter to a friend. No one will ever know if McGovern, the lawyer for the AOC, ever shared it with anyone. A few months earlier, Kirby shared stories with the men of the AAU at their annual convention. Brundage and I enjoyed the 1930 Congress in Berlin, said Kirby. We were:

surrounded by the most beautiful women and girls ... and I know a good-looking woman when I see one [laughter].... I am not telling you stories that you can't tell your wives....[55]

I have many friends on the IOC "and possibly one enemy, ... [Sweden's] Count von Rosen," wrote Kirby in a June 26, 1936 letter.[56] A year later, American IOC member William May Garland, received a letter from Brundage: "I'm torn regarding giving Kirby the bad news that he was not considered for IOC membership [at the recent IOC meeting] ... because of unfriendliness or prejudice of some years, he [Kirby] cannot be elected.... He knows that Count Clarence von Rosen is bitterly opposed to him...."[57]

Rosen, Swedish aristocrat, served an incredible 48 years on the IOC[58] and was an internationally prominent horseman. Born in 1867 of an American mother, he became equerry (in charge of the king's horses) to H. M. King Gustav. He and his daughter, Countess Maud von Rosen, visited the United States several times, for the two Olympic Games in 1932.[59] Maud was European equestrian champion. Kirby's daughter, Wilhelmine, was a recognized rider during the 1930s. Something occurred between von Rosen and Kirby that resulted in the Swede's intense dislike for Kirby. This researcher has not found the reason.

The giant controversy surrounding the dismissal of American double Olympic swim champion, Eleanor Holm, from the 1936 team, is very well documented. It was American Olympic Committee president, Brundage i.e. "Bad Guy Brundage" who found Miss Holm's conduct "reprehensible" and disallowed her from competing in her third games.[60] A careful look at the literature reveals that Miss Holm vented her anger at Mr. Brundage and, simultaneously, for Kirby and his ship-board conduct that was "lewd" and far more serious than "my little bit of champagne and caviar" in the small hours of the morning. From seaport Hamburg, Gus Kirby was burning angry. The AOC treasurer told a *New York Times* reporter: "All I have to say is that only an evil mind could see anything improper in the performance."[61] The shrillness continued for a week, till the athletic games began. Women listen and gossip; men listen and gossip. IOC members, all men, listened carefully and probably with some discomfort, especially at the name "Kirby."[62] The highly-respected Jesse Abramson of the *New York Herald Tribune* wrote an essay as late as August 2, 1936, titled "Gustavus Town Kirby's international cocktail party...." He revealed new details, not at all complementary to Kirby.[63] Few, if any, American or European Olympic officials, could ignore these sensational anti-Kirby allegations.

Several additional vignettes from a few years earlier seem to underscore Kirby's "zest for fun." It was probably silly "chit-chat" on Kirby's part when he wrote Brundage (1933) about "The woman who swallows her nose"; "my charming and pretty young lady," to a student studying in Germany (1933); to Brundage, he wrote (1934): "If our wives only have their husbands in their lives, life would be indeed, to them at least, dull and drab." Kirby wrote Brundage about Mrs. Brundage (1934) "her beautiful, lovely self."[64]

Judge Jeremiah T. Mahoney, former president of the AAU, had no affection for Kirby, and in a January 4, 1940 letter, he scolded Kirby for demeaning the image of the AAU. It was regrettable that a man of his background and excellent education

> should so frequently demean himself by the risqué remarks ... that you have made at gatherings ... attended by sport leaders.... Such conduct on your part is not in

keeping with the ideals and principles of the AAU.... I
had hoped for a long time that you would stop the practice for which you have been so often criticized.[65]

The unrepentant Kirby immediately answered Judge Mahoney: "I thought my stories were good ones; they were generally
laughed at...."[66] During the Second World War, the 70-year-old
Kirby was voted president of the Society of Medical Jurisprudence. The full text of his speech is preserved: "I Wonder Why?—
The Mysteries of Science." He concluded: "I love three things:
beautiful women, good rum, and a raging sea."[67] Kirby's Olympic
committee colleagues generally knew Kirby's considerable talents, his very great contributions over half a century, as well
as some of his personal habits. Owen Van Camp succeeded Kirby as Olympic committee treasurer, and at their December 10,
1945 meeting, President Brundage remarked: "We hope, Mr. Van
Carnp, that neither by inclination nor osmosis you adopt any
of Gus Kirby's bad habits" [laughter].[68] After the war Brundage
wrote Kirby about the daughter of IOC president Edström:

My astonishment at learning that you not know who
Laaere is (I always thought that you kept track of all
beautiful girls) was balanced by my pleasure to know
that you are still interested in the subject.[69]

And lastly, on this wearisome but relevant subject of "sex,"
Kirby's personal scrapbook notes on his trip to the Buenos Aires
Pan-American Games, the 77-year-old Kirby, wrote: "I saw one of
the prettiest girls you ever want to see. 'You have a beautiful face
and a beautiful figure' I said—she 'purred' like a kitten."[70]

Part V: "Epilogue"

All extant materials gathered by this researcher indicate that by
1937, Kirby was in a trough of despair and gave up all hope of joining his colleagues as a member of the IOC. In a miserable February
3, 1937 letter to Brundage, Kirby moans that Sloane's retirement
from the IOC should have meant my election, ... but it didn't happen. Back in 1921, I apparently insulted Coubertin and "he got up
and stamped out of the room," recalled Kirby, and "By reason of
this incident, Coubertin told Sloane that he would prevent my election [to] the IOC." He continued: "My only other serious enemy was
Count von Rosen. He hated me, but the fault was all his."

> When his daughter came to Lake Placid [in 1932], we took her in.... It is not for me to say here what Clarence did.... It is not a pleasant story. His associates on the IOC recognize the situation.... Clarence has unusual ability ... and apparently unlimited vindictiveness.[71]

There was one open spot on the IOC, and in this February 3rd appeal, he asked for Brundage's support. No such luck. Frederic R. Coudert (1871–1955), wealthy American lawyer, was chosen instead of Kirby. That same month, IOC member Garland wrote IOC member Brundage:

> Personally, I am a friend of Gus, but I could name a dozen of our colleagues who dislike him and particularly his personality. None are more emphatic in this respect than Baillet-Latour.[72]

Garland's memory went back to 1922, and he remembered serious opposition to Kirby's ambition to be on the IOC:

> Professor Sloane beseeched me ... to present the name of General Charles H. Sherrill to take Judge Week's place on the IOC.... Kirby is not wanted by many of my colleagues or myself.[73]

Brundage replied to Garland that several IOC members, all the way back to Coubertin in 1921, did not care for Kirby. "Although I have reservations about Coudert as a new IOC member," wrote Brundage, "I shall nominate Coudert over Kirby."[74] Kirby was finished; his friend of twenty years—Brundage—was unable to support his IOC candidature. Brundage received a "confidential" note from Garland on March 12, 1937, upset at Kirby's obsession: "The office should seek the man.... Mr. Kirby's name has been discussed and opposed.... Sir Noel Curtis Bennett of the British Committee, is strongly opposed to Mr. Kirby."[75]

Upon returning home from an IOC meeting, Garland wrote President Baillet-Latour that his choice for new IOC member was Henry Breckinridge, but that he declined and recommended Frederic Rene Coudert. Kirby's name is nowhere mentioned.[76] The IOC president wrote Brundage a week later: "Garland warns me that Kirby seems to be very anxious to have the [IOC] place filled by himself. He does not favor this candidate, more than yourself.... Advise me to present Mr. Coudert."[77] "I feel sorry in a way for Kirby, but confidentially Baillet-Latour said positively he did not want him," wrote Garland to Brundage.[78] The end of Kirby's long, personal "Holy Grail" was over, and he knew it. He admitted as much to Brundage. "I probably will never quite recover from the IOC incident."[79] In a wonderfully revealing letter from A.C. Gilbert to Kirby, he praises Kirby to the sky, telling the truth about the very great contributions that he has made decade after decade. "But you make mistakes," he told his friend. "I know of your great disappointment.... I was in a position once in Berlin to hear much of this story, and why you never would be a member of the IOC."[80] Kirby responded to this sensitive letter from a good friend:

> I preferred going down fighting than to be softly eased out of the picture ... The reasons were altogether of my own making; when I differed with others, I said so.[81]

It was an unusual form of magnanimity by the usual pride-filled Kirby. He served the USOC for another fifteen years. He continued active and valuable work in New York City planning. The legal, medical, and recreational community benefited from his life-long experience. Kirby, in old age, helped the USOC with its perpetual financial crises, and he helped his loyal, long-time buddy, Brundage, organize the 1951 Pan-American Games. Kirby lived "two lives in one," and next to the mighty Brundage was the most productive American amateur sport leader in the United States during the first half of the twentieth century; and, after careful consideration, I might include the second fifty years of the 1900's as well. In a 1933 article titled "The George Wood Wingate Memorial Foundation," the editor of the journal, E. Dana Caulkins, said of Kirby: "Kirby is perhaps the only man in the country who is close to all the groups that make up American amateur sport."[82] It was a fitting tribute and accurate. Kirby's best friend was "Terry" McGovern, author and member of the AOC. It may be unscientific to end this essay on Kirby's "inadmissibility" into the IOC by several long quotes from his friend, but this researcher found the view a balanced one. Gus Kirby, wrote McGovern, can be damaged in every conceivable way, "but he cannot be killed. If he were a toy in a window, he would be labeled 'guaranteed indestructible.'" No matter how much Kirby irritated, offended, "or repelled his audience by his manner," in the end he was never malicious nor uncivil. McGovern concluded:

There probably has never lived a man with such a propensity and power to offend, insult and irritate for the sole purpose and with the inevitable result of obtaining clean, meritorious, loftily, inspired, and humane results.[83]

It seems to me that Kirby was master of many crafts—some which gained him a lofty place in American amateur athletes and several habits, which denied him the inestimably challenging opportunity to serve on the International Olympic Committee.

NOTES

1 M.H. Roukhadze, as quoted in J.M. Faure, "National Identity and the Sporting Champion, Jean Borotra and French History," *The International Journal of the History of Sport,* 13 (1996), p. 98.

2 R.W. Leopold, *Elihu Root and the Conservative Tradition,* Boston 1954, p. 194.

3 St. R. Wenn, "A House Divided: The U.S. Amateur Sport Establishment and the Issue of Participation in the 1936 Berlin Olympics," *Research Quarterly for Exercise and Sport* [RQES] 67(June 1996), endnote 102, p. 171.

4 See Kirby's autobiography, *I Wonder Why?,* New York 1954, pp. 10-11, 94. A daughter, Wilhelmina, "a brilliant horsewoman," was born in 1914. This researcher interviewed her in 1996, and was allowed to read the Kirby scrapbooks. Additionally, see marriage news in the *New York Herald [Herald],* June 22, 1906, p. 12; *New York Tribune [Tribune],* June 22, 1906, p. 6, and *New York Times [NYT],* June 22, 1906, p. 7. Kirby obituary notices are located in *Amateur Athlete [AA],* 27 (April, 1956), 12; *NYT,* February 29, 1956, p. 31; *NYT,* March 2, 1956, p. 23; *Tribune,* February 29, 1956, p. 12; *Herald,* February 29, 1956, p. 12; *Obituaries On File,* I (A-R), 1979. Meyer Berger wrote that the "tall, blue-eyed 80 year old Kirby, on his mother's side, traced his ancestry back to Betsy Ross." (See *NYT* 1954; Kirby's scrapbook does not contain specific date and page).

5 See *The National Cyclopaedia* (1962), p.20. Col. Thompson served as president of the AOC before World War I and again after the war.

6 Late in his life, "when everyone else is gone," Kirby loved to tell the story of his meeting with Coubertin and Sloane. In almost every case, he either forgot to mention the year or remembered it as "1895" All Olympic historians agree that Coubertin visited America twice—in 1889 and in 1893. Coubertin was not in New York City in 1895, and never visited North America thereafter.

7 See *Une Campagne de Vingt-et-un ans 1887-1908,* Paris 1909, pp. 92-93. Also *Memoires Olympiques,* Lausanne 1931, p. 16.

8 Coubertin spent several weeks of conversation with Sloane in 1889.

9 Kirby, *I Wonder Why?*, pp. 30-31.

10 R. Korsgaard, "A History of the Amateur Athletic Union of the United States," Ed. D. dissertation, Teacher's College, Columbia University, 1952, p. 183.

11 Ibid.

12 Kirby's original speech located in the Kirby Files, located in the USOC Training Center, Colorado Springs, Colorado, in eleven boxes, uncatalogued. Hereafter "Kirby Files." This same speech is located in the "Kirby Scrapbook," loaned to the researcher by Kirby's daughter, Wilhelmine Steward Kirby (born January 19, 1914). This same lady, Mrs. Thomas Mercer Waller of Bedford Hills, New York, allowed me to study the personal Kirby memorabilia in the summer of 1996.

13 Kirby, "This Broken Time Question," *The Amateur Athlete [AA]*. 18 (September, 1947), p. 8.

14 Kirby, "Reminiscences," *AA*, 9 (December, 1938), p. 24.

15 See Kirby's speech in E. Dana Calkins (ed.), *Aims and Methods in School Athletics. Wingate Memorial Lectures 1931-32*, New York 1932, p. 67. When Kirby was inducted into the Helms Hall of Fame, he talked about his meeting with the great duo of Sloane and Coubertin. See *AA*, 25 (January, 1954), pp. 10, 22.

16 Immediately following the Sloane-Coubertin meeting in November of 1893, at which Kirby insisted he was present, Sloane wrote a letter dated November 18, 1893, and addressed "To the President of the AAU of the United States." AAU secretary Sullivan read the letter to the delegates and the full contents are reproduced in the *Spirit of the Times* (November 25, 1893), pp. 613-614. I enclose Coubertin's "circular," he wrote "in the hope that you may see your way clear to sending representatives to the [Sorbonne] Congress ... at Paris, France, in June, 1894...." If Kirby was correct and he was, at age 19 $^1/_2$ years, present with Coubertin and Sloane in New York City, then it is manifestly clear that he, Kirby, was present at the very beginnings of modern Olympic history. Kirby never stopped reminiscences about 1893, especially to his ancient comrade, Avery Brundage, the IOC president (who was only six years old in 1893): "Dear Avery: I shall never forget 1895 [sic], when Baron de Coubertin came to this country.... I shall never forget it.... His main quest was to have organized an American Olympic Committee. This was accomplished on my calling upon James E. Sullivan, and convincing him that it would be a great thing for sport and ... for America" (See Avery Brundage Collection [ABC]; letter dated November 26, 1952; ABC, reel 18; box 31. Kirby said the same thing to Brundage several years earlier; "We [Kirby, Coubertin and Sloane] discussed the difficulties of maintaining amateur status ... and the Ten Commandments. The year was 1894 or 1895." See Kirby to Brundage; letter dated June 4, 1947; ABC, reel 18; box 30.

17 Kirby to William J. Bingham of Harvard University, February 1, 1929 ABC; reel 17; box 30.

18 See half-page articles in the *NYT.* September 12, 1908, p. 8; *Tribune,* September 12, 1908, p. 8; and *Boston Globe,* September 12, 1908, p. 4; "All blame and censure ... fall at the feet of British officials," wrote Kirby in the *Tribune.* He always had a way with words.

19 Coubertin, *Olympic Memoires,* Transl. by G. de Navacelle (1979), of Coubertin's 1931 autobiography.

20 Kirby, *To the Intercollegiate Association of Amateur Athletes of America.* Six pages. See New York Public Library MVF p.v.3.

21 Cook's ʀᴇply, p. 30, is located in the IOC Library.

22 See Chanler's fuller comments in *NYT,* September 22, 1908, p. 9.

23 See *Boston Globe,* September 24, 1908, p. 7. "Bad losers are to be found even out of England," was Peabody's last word on the subject.

24 Kirby, *An Answer to Mr. Francis Peabody. Jr.* (1908). Pamphlet located in IOC Library.

25 Hyde was not a sportsman, but he was living in Paris and a friend of Coubertin in that city's high society. Hyde had a "checkered past" i.e. frequently called "scandalous" by the press. See *NYT,* November 14, 1913, p. 4; *Philadelphia Inquirer,* July 27, 1959, p. 8; *NYT,* March 24, 1961, p. 26; *Tribune,* July 27, 1959, p. 10; *NYT,* July 27, 1959, p. 25; *Who's Who,* 31(1960-1961), p. 1439.

26 Sloane to Coubertin, September 18, 1908. Researcher John Lucas has this letter, as does David Young of the University of Florida.

27 Sullivan holds American athletes "in the hollow of his hand," and Kirby is right there at his side, wrote Sloane. See letter to Coubertin, dated October 16, 1908 (Lucas—Young Collections).

28 See C. Whitney on the English anger, *Outing,* 53 (November, 1908), pp. 244-249); also *The Times* of London, November 17, 1908, p. 14. Mr. Kirby was confused or either told outright lies, was the essence of the very long essay.

29 Sloane to Coubertin, December 11, 1908. See Lucas' collection of Sloane-Coubertin and Coubertin-Sloane correspondences.

30 See *NYT,* February 12, 1909, sport sec., p. 3; *NYT,* February 21, 1909, sport sec., p. 3; *Tribune,* February 21, 1909, sport sec., pp. 3, 11.

31 See Sloane to Coubertin, January 26, 1909; Sloane to Coubertin, April 14, 1909; Sloane to Coubertin, January 11, 1911; Sloane to Coubertin, January 22, 23, and 24, 1911; also Sloane to Coubertin, February 11, 1911. All of these letters and more are located in IOC Archives and in the personal files of John Lucas and David Young. Many years later, Kirby unburdened himself to Brundage: "I believe that Professor Sloane was correct in his statement that I was well qualified to succeed him as a member of the IOC ... and it was [his] intention to present my name at the same time that he presented his resignation." See Kirby to Brundage; letter dated February 3, 1937, ABC, reel 17, box 29. See "Columbia at the Olympic Games," *Columbia Alumni News* (November 15, 1912), pp. 147-149.

32 See R.E. Lehr, "The American Olympic Committee; 1896-1940: From Chaos to Order," Ph. D. dissertation, Penn State University, 1985,

pp. 55-56; also *Tribune,* November 29, 1919, p. 14; *NYT,* November 29, 1919, p. 12; *Report of the AOC -Seventh Olympic Games, Antwerp, Belgium 1920,* New York 1920, p. 7.

33 So wrote Lehr, p. 89.

34 Coubertin had preordained that Paris and Amsterdam would win the 1924 and 1928 summer Olympic Games. All other city suggestions would fall on deaf ears. Mine was "a masterly coup d'etat," he wrote in his *Olympic Memoires:* "Nobody had expected such a radical and sudden presidential intervention. It was morally impossible to refuse what I was asking." See p. 106 in the Navacelle translation.

35 *Report AOC 1920,* p. 422.

36 See *NYT,* January 4, 1922, p. 14; *Tribune,* January 4, 1922, p. 12.

37 *NYT,* ibid. (last sentence).

38 Pierce to Kirby; letter dated January 4, 1922. Kirby did reply immediately. The Kirby-Rubien report is without error, wrote Kirby. See Kirby to Pierce, January 4, 1922. Both documents are in the IOC Archives.

39 Kirby to Coubertin, February 14, 1922, IOC Files.

40 Kirby to Brundage, February 13, 1931; ABC, reel 17; box 29. Several years later, Kirby almost wept: "As you know, Avery, it was planned years ago that I should succeed Professor ... Sloane ... on the IOC. That I did not was due to the fact that I was not willing either to give way to or stand the abuse of the then peppery chairman, Baron Pierre de Coubertin." See Kirby to Brundage, June 26, 1936; ABC, reel 17; box 29.

41 Edström to Brundage, July 8, 1943; ABC, reel 24; box 42.

42 Olympic historian Norbert Müller wrote that Kirby was angry at discussions that allegedly "lacked factual knowledge," and that Kirby agreed with an English delegate who said most resolutions were merely "vague generalities and pious aspirations." See Müller, One *Hundred Years of Olympic Congresses,* Lausanne 1994, p. 121.

43 G.T. Kirby, "Some Remarks Upon The Olympic and Pedagogic Congresses," Prague, Czechoslovakia, 1925. A ten-page pamphlet located in the New York Public Library, 2-MV p.v. 72, number 8.

44 See Goldstein's essay in J. E. Findling and K.D. Pelle (eds.), *Historical Dictionary of the Modern Olympic Movement,* Westport Conn. 1996, p. 359. A. Guttmann agrees. See his *The Olympics. A History of the Modern Games,* Urbana 1992, p. 50..

45 It has been said that more literature has been published on the 1936 Olympic Games than that of all previous games combined. This researcher has nearly a hundred primary and secondary references just on Kirby's famous "boycotts resolution" of 1933. Several important ones are: *Pittsburgh Post-Gazette,* November 21, 1933, pp. 17, 18; *NYT,* November, 21, 1933, pp. 1, 6, 25; AAU *Minutes,* November 20-22, 1933, pp. 70-71, and M. Gottlieb, "American Controversy over the Olympic Games," *American Jewish Historical Quarterly* (1972), pp. 181-213. On p. 185, Kirby is quoted as saying that "Garland, Brundage, Sherrill, and I feel the same way. The Olympic Games will not continue to Berlin un-

less and until there is a change in the German attitude towards Jews." Kirby wrote a remarkable letter to Brundage. We cannot go to Berlin unless fairness to Jewish athletes is a reality. See ABC, reel 17; box 30, dated November 2, 1933.

46 Gilbert to Kirby, December 28, 1933, Kirby Collection, Colorado Springs Olympic Training Center.

47 "Kirby Warns Reich on Olympic Games," *NYT*, March 8, 1934, p. 16.

48 Several valuable sources are: Guttmann, pp. 60-63; St. R. Wenn, "The Commodore Hotel Re-Visited: An Analysis of the 1935 AAU Convention," *Proceedings, 6th Canadian Symposium on the History of Sport*, pp. 188-201; *NYT*, December 9, 1935, pp. 1, 17; *Minutes* of AAU 1935, pp. 141-142; the names of each delegate and how they voted can be found in "Kirby Files 1935" located in Colorado Springs.

49 Historian Wenn was puzzled by Kirby's alleged "indiscretions." See endnote number 3 in Wenn's paper "The Commodore Hotel Re-Visited."

50 *The Random House Dictionary of the English Language* (1966), p. 1408 defines "strip[1]" in a great many ways, one of them: to remove one's clothes.

51 Kirby's quote and Dan Ferris' alleged comments are located in the Kirby autobiography, pp. 146-147.

52 See Kirby to Howard S. Braucher, June 9, 1930, ABC, box 75. A. Guttmann read the same letter. See his *The Games Must Go On: Avery Brundage and the Olympic Movement*, New York 1984, p. 59.

53 Kirby is quoted in Guttmann's *The Games Must Go On*, p. 59.

54 Kirby to J. T. McGovern, November 3, 1932, and located in "G.T. Kirby Scrapbook" stored in his daughter's suburban New York City home and read by this researcher.

55 Kirby's speech at the *Minutes* of 1931 AAU, November 15-17, 1931, in Kansas City, p. 298.

56 Kirby to Brundage, June 26, 1936, ABC, reel 17, box 29.

57 Brundage to Garland, March 9, 1937, ABC, reel 33, box 56.

58 See K.A. Scherer, *Der Männerorden. Die Geschichte des Internationalen Olympischen Komitees*, Frankfurt a.m. 1974, p. 231.

59 See "Distinguished House Guests" [Count von Rosen and his daughter, Maude]. A lengthy biography is located in ABC, reel 21, box 35. Brundage wrote Kirby: "Count von Rosen traveled the U.S. and met people interested in equestrian sports," August 16, 1937, ABC, reel 17, box 29.

60 Every serious Olympic Games history, in the French, German, and English languages, deals with the Eleanor Holm "Scandal." Front page and sport page headlines in American newspapers shouted the news. *Associated Press* (AP) releases July 19 through July 29, 1936 dealt with the beautiful Eleanor Holm (Jarrett) and her "exploits" aboard the U.S. ship *Manhattan* on its journey across the Atlantic. She drank alcohol and stayed up all night—contrary to the Brundage rules of Olympic conduct. She was dismissed; she cried uncontrollably; she begged for-

giveness; it never came, and she then accused Mr. Gustavus Town Kirby of horrible conduct aboard ship. Mr. Kirby's "mock marriage ceremony" was "so shocking that many athletes walked out of the social hall," said Mrs. Jarrett. "His [Kirby's] whole late-night affair was altogether unsuitable, for youthful ears," she revealed to eager-to-listen newspaper men. "Kirby's dialogue ... was such that it was the talk of the boat for days afterwards," revealed the distraught Holm-Jarrett. The all-night party was "offensive," and Mr. Kirby was the pretend-minister at the "mock marriage," she stated. The "AOC officials, led by Kirby, disgraced themselves," she told the ever-growing number of journalists. Kirby responded with anger, indignation, and total rejection of all accusations. Olympic track coach, Dean Cromwell, said: "It's her own fault." See same article *Los Angeles Times,* July 25, 1936; Part I, p. 13, 15. "Kirby has a chance for IOC membership. He's right here in Berlin," said Brundage. "But the Eleanor Holm case has subjected him to criticism" See *Herald Tribune,* July 28, 1936, p. 21. Kirby wrote remarkable letters. He told Brundage: "An innocent little girl, a high diver from Los Angeles, and her mother were at the 'mock marriage' .. and didn't see anything offensive about it." "That Holmes girl must be a hussey," was the alleged comment by the mother. See Kirby to Brundage, October 13, 1936; ABC, reel 17, box 29.

61 See *NYT,* July 26, 1936, sport section, p. 2. The "performance" said Kirby, in this "... was nothing to offend anybody. I acted the part of the judge and prosecuting attorney: the bride carried a bouquet of vegetables. We were all merry and the whole thing was done in the spirit of fun.... The dialogue had to do with marital situations [and] was open to questionable interpretations," responded Mrs. Jarrett (see p. 1 in this article).

62 Kirby's name was everywhere. See *Boston Evening Globe,* July 24, 1936, pages 1, 2; *Los Angeles Times,* July 24, 1936, part 1, p. 1; *Boston Evening Globe,* July 25, 1936, pp. 1, 2; *Boston Sunday Globe,* July 26, 1936, pp. 1, 31; *Boston Sunday Post,* July 26, 1936, sport sec., pages 15, 21; *The Philadelphia Inquirer,* July 26, 1936, p. 9; *Los Angeles Times,* July 26, 1936, Part I, p. 1 and Part II, p. 9; *Herald Tribune,* July 26, 1936; sec. 3; p. 1; *NYT.* July 26, 1936, p. 1; *Boston Post.* July 27, 1936, p. 16; *NYT,* July 27, 1936, part I, p. 1; *NYT,* July 28, 1936, p. 12; *Herald Tribune,* July 28, 1936, p. 21; *Time,* 28 (August 3, 1936), 21. There are many more similar "revelations" in this researcher's files. In the overall Kirby primary and secondary documents, this researcher possesses an additional half hundred correspondences, articles, and commentaries.

63 Abramson wrote, section III, p. 3: "The mock marriage of swimmer Katherine Rawls (5 feet), and basketballer Frank Lubin (6 feet 3 inches), with shotputter Jack Torrence (300 pounds) as ringmaster and Gustavus T. Kirby as minister...."

64 See ABC, reel 17, box 29, July 19, 1933; letter to Mildred McGee, December 19, 1933, Kirby Files, Colorado Springs, as is the August 7, 1934 letter; also ABC, reel 17, box 29, October 26, 1934. Kirby wrote

Brundage a silly letter in 1947: "Whilst in Chicago, in addition to looking upon your manly figure ... I trust also be permitted to look upon your lovely wife." See ABC, October 30, 1947, reel 18, box 30.

65 See this 800 word letter, January 4, 1940, ABC, reel 18, box 30.

66 Kirby to Mahoney, January 9, 1940; ABC, reel 18; box 30.

67 See this letter in "Kirby Scrapbook." In a telephone conversation with Kirby's 82-year-old daughter, Wilhemine, November 7, 1996, she said: "Dad liked attractive women, but he was 'All bark and no bite!'"

68 See Kirby Files at the USOC Training Center in Colorado Springs, Colorado.

69 Brundage to Kirby, October 24, 1946, ABC, reel 18; box 30.

70 Kirby scrapbook in Bedford Hills, New York, under *The Village*, March 28, 1951.

71 Kirby to Brundage, February 3, 1937, ABC, reel 17; box 30.

72 Garland to Brundage, February 24, 1937; ABC, reel 33, box 56.

73 See endnote 72.

74 Brundage to Garland, March 9, 1937, ABC, reel 33, box 56.

75 Garland to Brundage, March 12, 1937, ABC, reel 33, box 56.

76 Garland to Baillet-Latour, March 24, 1937, ABC, reel 33, box 56.

77 Baillet-Latour to Brundage, April 6, 1937, ABC, reel 24, box 42.

78 Garland to Brundage, August 4, 1937, ABC, reel 33, box 56.

79 Kirby to Brundage, December 14, 1937, ABC, reel 17, box 30. Kirby's disappointment was profound. He opened his heart to Brundage: I can only bear this greatest burden "without quitting or grousing." See Kirby to Brundage, October 26, 1936, ABC, reel 17, box 29.

80 Gilbert to Kirby; December 22, 1937, ABC, reel 15, box 26. Gilbert was displeased with a recent note from Kirby in which Kirby said: "I am naturally of a personal equation which makes it difficult to accept direction." See this same December 22 letter for this quote.

81 Kirby to Gilbert, December 27, 1937. See Kirby Files at Colorado Springs and Xeroxed by this researcher.

82 See *Scholastic Coach* (January, 1933), p. 3.

83 J.T. McGovern, *Diogenes Discovers Us*, New York 1933, Chapter 14 "Gustavus Town Kirby" occupies pages 275-291, and the quotes used in this essay are from pages 276-277, 289-290. McGovern was athlete, lawyer, judge, coauthor of the famous 1929 *Carnegie Report*, and a member of the AOC. See his obituary, *NYT*, May 27, 1960, 31. Judge McGovern was born in 1876. Marvelously laudatory comments are found in the 16-page pamphlet titled "Kirby Plaza Dedication Ceremony—June 15, 1958"; Mount Kisco, New York. Kirby was called a very great American and the elder statesman of American amateur athletics. Researcher Lucas has this document in his possession.

19.
Editorial: From "A" through "Z": from Albania through Zaire*

The Olympic Games and the Olympic Movement are the only two human institutions that embrace every single nation on earth. They encompass Albania and Zaire ... and all countries [in between], a total of 197—from "A" through "Z."

What a joy to see Albania back in the Games and the movement that is striving towards athletic excellence for a few elite Albanian young men and women and, at the same time, working towards sport, physical culture and leisure—recreational acivities for every single child in the land.

The National Olympic Committee of Albania understands the need for training champion male and female athletes—the direct results of tens of thousands of young people participating in "sport for all." Such activities are not a luxury for the poor but for all the Albanian people. The human spirit needs constant uplifting. Money helps, but beautiful and healthy and happy boys and girls, all engaged in wholesome, vigorous, challenging, and healthy fun sport is even more important than material possessions. The Olympic Movement in Albania can become the perfect blending of human idealism and collective pragmatism.

The mother and father of 71-year-old Lucas were born in Permet, a town in southern Albania, in 1899 and 1889 (respectively).

*ZËRI OLIMPIK, Official Newsletter of NOC of Albania, No. 1, (January-March 1998), p.1.

20.
The Death and Burial of Coubertin:
A Retrospective*

In the same year of his death, 1937, the Modern Olympic Games' founder, Baron Pierre de Coubertin (born 1863), wrote:

> I have not been able to carry out to the end what I wanted to perfect. I believe that a Centre of Olympic Studies would aid the preservation and progress of my work more than anything else, and would keep it from the fake paths which I fear.[1]

The destitute Coubertin was living alone in a small apartment in Geneva, rather than at his home and museum, *"Mon Repos,"* in the center of Lausanne, Switzerland.[2] Coubertin specialists agree that the Baron was ill in body, and also in a kind of spiritual melancholy in the months following the Berlin Olympic Games of 1936. French historian Louis Callebat hints that these so-called "Nazi-Olympics" were confusing to Coubertin, who refused an invitation to attend.

Callebat wrote that these games may have engendered within Coubertin a bewildering mix "of seduction and perversion mingling with beauty and grandeur."[3] The American "tough guy," Avery Brundage, both president of the American Olympic Committee [AOC] and a member of the International Olympic Committee [IOC], wrote his colleague Gustavus Town Kirby about Coubertin's multiple crises. "Why don't we set up a fund for him?" he wrote.[4] Olympic historian Yves-Pierre Boulongne has in his possession a Coubertin letter written on August 5, 1937, to his best friend Dr. Francis Messerli:

Journal of Olympic History, 9 (September 2001), 7-12.

These adverse circumstances have created an agonizing situation. The loss of my personal fortune threatens my life-long effort at enlightening pedagogical progress. [5]

But it was too late. The Baron died on September 2, 1937, and most major newspapers, worldwide, took notice.[6] So did Coubertin's own *Bulletin du CIO*, which pronounced, correctly, that "the memory of Coubertin will be long lasting and practical."[7] The *Times* of London wrote that "Baron Pierre de Coubertin ... died suddenly yesterday afternoon from apoplexy while walking in the park at La Grange in Geneva."[8]

Pierre Lorme's lengthy Coubertin obituary in the *Paris Illustration* of September 11, 1937, failed to mention the Olympic Games, but called Coubertin "a profoundly humanistic creator of an educational philosophy called 'Olympism.'"[9] Professor Lennartz, from the Carl Diem Institute in Cologne, Germany, wrote that "The mortal remains of the man [Coubertin] were buried in Lausanne. His heart, however, in accordance with his will, found its last resting place in Olympia."[10]

But nearly seven months passed before the heart of Coubertin was transported to the ancient ruins in the Greek Peloponnesus. It was late March of 1938 and the whole of the European continent was on the edge of the greatest of catastrophes—World War II.

IOC President, Henri de Baillet-Latour, found time to praise his friend Coubertin. "The world has lost a genius," he said.[11] Three Coubertin memorial ceremonies took place, and in order of magnitude they are: Lausanne March 26, 1938:

Coubertin's funeral took place at the Church of Notre Dame du Valentin and then his burial in the City of Lausanne Bois-de-Vaux Cemetery.[12]

A second and larger ceremony took place that same day in Paris, the birthplace of Coubertin [1863] and his residence until 1915. At 10:30 a.m., a ceremony took place in the Roman Catholic Church of the Trinity, with French Olympic Committee members, representatives of sporting groups and numerous personalities in attendance. An hour later in the Porte de Saint-Cloud Municipal Stadium and in the presence of M. Faillot (president, Municipal Council); Armand Massard (IOC member, 1946-1970); Misters Bucaille, G. Prade, J. de Castelaine, and Leo Lagrange (under-secretary of state for physical education), a solemn ceremony took place:

> Before an easel portrait of Pierre de Coubertin, draped in crepe and the national colours, a wreath of greenery and flowers was laid by a member of the French Olympic Committee [COF]. Three speeches by Faillot, Massard and Lagrange praised Coubertin whose entire life was dedicated to the Olympic Games rebirth and to the physical and intellectual development of youth everywhere. Physical education students from Joinville School and from the École Normale formed an honorary line, all accompanied by police department musicians.[13]

An imposing ceremony took place at Olympia on Saturday, March 26, 1938. Several hundred people moved around the "sacred soil," some of them prominent in the worlds of theology, politics, and the Olympic movement.[14] All honor to the Greeks on their anniversary of national independence and all glory to the memory of the late Baron de Coubertin. A journalist writing in the Paris *L'Auto* wrote of the appropriateness and importance of this gathering at Olympia:

> What a simple and yet grand ceremony took place at Olympia. The Greek Prince Royal placed the urn containing the heart of Coubeitin inside the commemorative monument. At the same time a similar religious ceremony took place in Paris, honoring this man who dedicated his life to the greater perception of the noble, idealized human, capable of attainment by all of us.[15]

Of course, the many Athens newspapers covered in detail the unique ceremony at Olympia. It was a modest but sacred ritual wrote one. A dignified ceremony for the Baron, elevating humanity through his philosophy of "Olympism," wrote another eye-witness journalist. This great heart of the Baron de Coubertin has returned to Greece, was another note from a newspaper writer that made the trip from Athens.[16]

With no disrespect for the memory of the late Olympic Games' founder, the Greek people, especially their government representatives, were also celebrating their independence day.[17]

It seemed appropriate for several foreign diplomats to make the arduous trip to Olympia from Athens. One of them was Lincoln MacVeagh of the United States Legation. He wrote a detailed report of all that he saw and heard to his Secretary of State. "The morning was one of the most beautiful imaginable," he wrote, "with Greek peasants gathered on the outskirts." He spoke of the ceremony itself, the Grand Marshall, the Crown Prince, the Minister Governor of Athens, the Ministers of both France and the USA. The remainder of MacVeagh's report is "all politics":

> The German Third Reich had taken over sacred Olympia for further exploration, but no German official was at the burial ceremony when the Crown Prince of Greece planted a Frenchman's heart squarely at the entrance of the German excavation. This burial was France's answer to the German claim at Olympia. The Olympic Committee doubtless thought that all they had done was to lay the heart of their old chief to rest near the sacred spot he loved, but those whose business keeps them aware of conflicting interests in this little corner of the world knew that what we had witnessed was also the placing of the seal of France on the German claim ... as neat a little piece of the expropriation of kudos as one could wish to see.[18]

A careful description of the 1938 "Ceremonie d'Olympie" appeared in that year's *Revue Olympique* and then an abridged version appeared in the *Olympic Review* of 1987, in recognition of the 50th year since the death of Coubertin.[19] The most careful description of this unique 1938 ceremony is contained on pages one to three of the French language, Athens-based newspaper *Le Messager d'Athenes* for March 22, 1938. Probably nothing of importance escaped the writer in this vivid 1700-word narrative, accompanied by three photographs. This researcher found no overt or veiled strident political views in this *Messager* account, unusual in a 1938 Europe, overwhelmed with the trumpets of war.[20] The lengthy ceremony is more clearly summarized in the 1938 *Revue Olympique* mentioned above.

Slowly approaching the marble upright stele and representing the Family Coubertin were Count Albert Bertier de Sauvigny of France [IOC 1904-1920] and another ancient one," Count Alexandre Mercati [Greek IOC member 1897-1925]; the young Greek Crown Prince Paul; Count Henri de Baillet-Latour, all followed by churchmen, Hellenic and IOC members, as well as the necessary diplomats from many nations. Grand Marshall Mercati was first to speak, and called Coubertin "a great Philhellene, a noble man who returned the Olympic Games to Greece during that nation's very difficult days."[21] Sauvigny was next, his whole few moments taken in reading a letter from the widow Coubertin, Madame Marie Roman [1860-1964], still living in Lausanne's "Mon Repos." I cannot be with you, but thank you to all who revere the name of Pierre de Coubertin, she wrote, and special thanks to the Royal Prince Constantine who, in 1896, allowed the first games to take place. And let us not forget:

> Those like-minded men on the first 1894 IOC: Bikelas; Balk; Sloane; Gebhardt; Boutowsky; Kemeny, and especially Mr. Firi-Guth-Jarkovsky, who survives to this day. The torch has passed from Coubertin to those who will hold it high and pass it on to others.... His flame will never be extinguished.[22]

Thus spoke with eloquence the 78-year-old Madame Coubertin, a powerful, little understood force in the life of her late husband. The Greek Minister of Culture, C. Georgacopoulos, was the next speaker and the essence of his 400-word oration was sincere as well as good history. Coubertin was the enlightened creator of the Modern Olympic Games and "Greece enthusiastically accepted [his] decision." He continued his praise of Coubertin, that man of noble soul:

> Your heart is at this moment deposited on the sacred soil of Olympia.... A block of white Hellenic marble ... will for ever mark your illuminated passage in this world and will consecrate the memory of your struggles for the Olympic Games. [23]

Just moments before Georgacopoulos spoke, the Crown Prince Paul placed the green urn containing Coubertin's heart into a resting place inside the stele, to be followed by a brief prayer by a Greek Orthodox priest acknowledging the eternal state of blessedness of Coubertin's soul. De Baillet-Latour spoke last. "Farewell Pierre de Coubertin. May thy soul rest in peace," said the IOC President and friend of the Founder for more than thirty-five years.[24]

Following this ceremony a luncheon took place at the Hotel S.P.A.P. in Olympia, hosted by the Hellenic Olympic Commit-

tee. Prince Paul recognized two Olympic athletes, "Mrs. Alin Ma-
tousevska and Mr. Peter Lann from England with olive branches.
At 2:15 p.m. the Prince and guests returned to Athens."[25]
    While at the S.P.A.P., De Baillet-Latour sent off a short hand-
written note to far away Madame Coubertin, offering condolences
and noting that her husband's friends had completed proper recognition. She immediately replied.[26]
    John J. MacAloon's research on this 1938 scenario is valu-
able. He combined sober factual data with his unique psycho-
historical, almost eurythmic interpretation:

> ... something rather more and rather different was
> achieved in these strangely appropriate last rites.   In
> them, race, moment, and milieu—the grand trinity of
> Hippolyte Taine, who had helped start Coubertin on his
> journey half a century before—were confounded one last
> time.[27]

Conclusions

    MacAloon goes on at some length, looking into the mind of
Baron de Coubertin and why he insisted on his own double funeral ceremonies—one in Switzerland, one in Greece—but none
in France.
    There is merit in reading this kind of thoughtful interpretative
history. Historical recapitulation is not a strict science and prov-
en fact must frequently blend with intuitive thinking to arrive at
something close to exactly what happened—and why.
    The International Olympic Committee and its vast network of al-
liances likes to call itself a peace movement. All well and good. So do
many other organizations call themselves world pacificatory agents.
    "One World" utterances come regularly from the European
Union [EU], from UNESCO, the UN, NATO, international courts
of arbitration, the International Red Cross and Red Crescent,
and many others. They all want peace, equality, and economic
stability for the whole human race. So does the IOC. Not one of
them has succeeded in halting a world war, holy wars, mini re-
gional conflicts. Very few call for the abolishment of these agen-
cies because of their frustrating record of failures.
    The IOC can never bring peace on earth, and the twenty books
written by Pierre de Coubertin, many dealing with the pacific
concept of Olympism, cannot ensure fairness and a world elevation of its standard of living.

The voices heard at the Coubertin funeral ceremonies [1937 and 1938] in Lausanne, Paris, and at Olympia, Greece, all spoke of Coubertin's life dream of peace on earth through sport, a special kind of Olympian sport. The armada of cynics around the world usually prefer to be called "scientific realists" and they make short shrift of some organizations mentioned above, including the Olympic Movement, for their excessive lofty aims, and, as a result, their endless failures. Coubertin was an unbridled optimist regarding his fellow creature and therefore doomed to failure. His creation cannot do all that it claims. None of this is reason enough for the dissolution of a single one of these imperfectly created unions, committees, partnerships. The world cannot exist without both idealists and pragmatists. Without expertise in philosophy or ideologies, this researcher-historian urges that what is needed in the world and in the Olympic world is what Pierre de Coubertin was, not a hyphenated leader with a strongly idealistic-realistic bent.

The Coubertin burial ceremonies brought together a segment of societies to honor an imperfect man who sought impossible perfection in himself, in his Olympic world, and in the larger social segment.

It may be that the voice of existential castle builders must not be quieted.[28]

NOTES:

1 "Letter to German Government," March 16, 1937. See: *Revue Olympique*, #1 (1938), p. 3.

2 Karl Lennartz, "The Presidency of Henri de Baillet-Latour (1925-1942)," located in volume 1 of three volumes: *The International Olympic Committee—One Hundred Years, 1894-1994* (Lausanne: CIO 1994), p. 212 (hereafter IOC 1894-1994).

3 Louis Callebat, *Pierre de Coubertin* (Paris: Librairie Artheme Fayard, 1988), p. 214.

4 See Brundage to Kirby; January 4, 1937, in the Avery Brundage Collection (hereafter ABC), reel 17, box 30. Brundage learned the bad news from a letter sent to him by Frederick W. Rubien, the Secretary of the American Olympic Committee. This December 22, 1936 letter, ABC, ibid., recommended that $100.00 "be appropriated" to be added to the fund already established by the IOC and announced "in the last issue of their *Bulletin.*"

5 See Boulongne, *La Vie et l'oeuvre Pedagogique de Pierre Coubertin 1863-1937* (Ottawa: Editions Lemeac, 1975), p. 69.

6 See *The Times* [London], September 3, 1937, p. 14, and a biography in that same newspaper, September 7, 1937. "Coubertin Dies" was the

headline in *New York Times* (hereafter NYT), September 3, 1937, p. 17. Also, see *New York Herald Tribune*, September 3, 1937, p. 14. *Le Figaro* [Paris], 3 September 1937, p. 3, had an insightful obituary of Coubertin, the modern man who emphasized the ancient Hellenic cry to health and sanity for "body, mind and spirit" (Maurice Capella, author). Another Coubertin friend wrote: "A grand and noble figure has left us, one whose contributions to Olympism and to humanity are beyond measure." See Fr. M. Messerli: *Histoire des Sports et de l'Olympisme* (Lausanne, 1950), p. 22. This researcher has read scores of Coubertin obituaries from newspapers on three continents. A newspaper journalist in Alexandria, Egypt, wrote of the late Coubertin: "He was a philosopher who lived for athletics and the Olympic spirit." See *The Egyptian Gazelle*, September 4, 1937, p. 7.

7 CJO *Bulletin* October 1937, number 35, pp. 2-3. For even greater insight, see Otto Mayer: A *Travers les Anneaux Olympiques* (Geneve, Caillier, 1960), pp. 166-167.

8 See endnote 6.

9 See Lorme in Volume *198,* p. 31.

10 See Lennartz, IOC 1894-1994, p. 213.

11 See *The Japan Magazine,* "Olympic Number 1"; vol. 28 (1938), p. 19, for De Baillet-Latour's remarks. Additional eulogies of the late Coubertin are included here: James C. Merrick, IOC member from Canada (pp. 17-18); William May Garland, IOC member from USA (pp. 19-20), and Lord Aberdare, IOC member from Great Britain (p. 20). Also included here is what was called "Coubertin's last message to IOC Technical advisor, Werner Klingeberg", Geneva, July 29, 1937. Coubertin, never a great prognosticator, looked forward to the 1940 Olympic Games, "where Hellenism might combine with the refined culture and art of Asia. R is a most enjoyable thought to me." See p. 17 of this *Japan Magazine* located in the New York Public Library "Oriental Division."

12 Christian Gillieron read the official city of Lausanne *Proces-verbaux de la Municipality. See Gillieron's Les Relations de Lausanne et du Mouvement Olympique a l'Epoque de Pierre de Coubertin 1894-1937* (Lausanne: CIO, 1993), p. 161.

13 See lengthy description titled: "Le Coeur de Pierre de Coubertin a etc Depose Hier a Olympic," *Le Figaro* [Paris], 27 March 1938, p. 3.

14 Several persons or groups not mentioned in this less than perfect list were present at Olympia on March 26, 1938:

a. Boy Scouts and Girl Scouts
b. M. Rediadis, sous-secretarie d'Etat
c. Due de Mecklenbourg [IOC]
d. M. Ritter von Halt [IOC]
e. Marquis de Polignac [IOCJ
f. Angelo C. Bolanaki [IOC]
g. "Delegates" from Poland, Norway, Sweden, USA, Hungary, Bulgaria, Japan, and Canada
h. "Members of the Hellenic Olympic Committee"

i. M. Ketseas
j. M. Rinoploulos
k. M. Gastritis
1. M. Nicolaidis
m. M. Fteris
n. M. Baltazzis
o. M. Athanassiadis
p. M. Demangel [Paris]
q. M. Klinkenberg [Berlin]
r. M. Kuntz
s. M. Apostolidis
t. M. Papavassiliou.

15 See *L'Auto* [Paris], 27 march 1938. page number unreadable
16 See *Kathimgrini* [Athens], March 27, 1938, pp. 1, 4; *Ethnos* [Athens], March 26, 1938, p. 6; *Elgfthgron Vima* [Athens], March 27, 1938, p. 3; *Praia* [Athens], March 27, 1938, p. 6.
17 The Greeks asserted themselves and won their independence from Turkish rule in early 1828. See Edwin Emerson, Jr., A *History of the Nineteenth Century By Year,* vol. 2 of three vols. [New York: P.P. Collier and Sons, 1902], p. 758.
18 MacVeagh's letter is dated April 29, 1938, and is located in the United States National Archives in Washington, D.C. See Microfilm Mil 79, reel 7.
19 *Revue Olympique 3* [1938], pp. 41-43; *Olympic Review* 239 [September 1987], pp. 448-450.
20 *Le Messager d'Athenes,* [Dimanche], 27 March 1938, pp. 1-3, is testimony to the newspaper editors of the dual importance of Coubertin's entombment and the vital significance of the nation's independence day celebrations.
21 *Ibid.,* p. 41.
22 *Ibid.,* pp. 42-43.
23 *Olympic Review* 239 [September 1987], p. 450.
24 *Ibid.* This ceremony seemed important enough to be included in the NYT, March 27, 1938, p. 29; *New York Herald Tribune,* March 27, 1938, p. 26; *The Times* [London], March 29, 1938, p. 15. The mystical writer, Marie-Therese Eyquem, spoke of this 1938 burial "amidst this sacred place of both battle and eurythmie." See Eyquem's *L'Epopee Olympique* [Paris: Calmann-Levy, 1966], p. 289. Longtime IOC member from Greece, Nikos Filaretos, was almost old enough to have been present there in 1938. See his comment in *The Centennial Presidents* [Lausanne: CIO, 1997], pp. 44-49. Coubertin's grand-nephew, Geoffroy de Navacelle, quoted the exact inscription carved on the stele: *Remise du coeur de Coubertin, par le prince-heritier Paul de Grece, dans la stele edifiee a Olympic selon son desir. Cette stele a ete transferee a l'entree de l'Academie Internationale Olympique non loin du Stade.* See *Pierre de Coubertin—Sa Vie par l'Image* [Zurich: Weidmann 1991], p. 89.

25 See endnote 16. This researcher sought the services of a Greek translator, and this quote is either from *Kathimgrini or Elgfthgron Vima.*

26 This researcher has copies of these letters, but had the greatest difficulty in reading the "hurry-up" script in the French language. See Madame Coubertin to Baillet-Latour, March 25, 1938, and Baillet-Latour to Madame Coubertin, March 26, 1938, in the IOC archives.

27 John I. MacAloon, *This Great Symbol—Pierre de Coubertin and the Origins of the Modern Olympic Games* [Chicago: University of Chicago Press, 1981], p. 7.

28 As is always true, the merits and deficiencies of this manuscript are entirely those of the researcher. But many generous colleagues supplied me with extant primary documents. Some of these individuals are: Dave Kelly, The Library of Congress; Nikos Filaretos and Dr. "Kostas" Georgiadis from the Hellenic Olympic Committee; Margo Stavros, State College, Pennsylvania; Jean-Francois Pahud, Barbara Schenkel from the IOC's archives depository, as well as the small army of scholars known to me by their books and manuscripts.

21.
Bud Greenspan:
Olympic Games Filmmaker and his Search for Athletic Excellence and Personal Nobility*

Introduction

Bud Greenspan is an immensely famous cinematographer of the Olympic Games. Raymond T. Grant, Director of Arts and Culture at the 2002 Olympic Winter Games, called Greenspan an international "icon" who understands the role the arts and culture play in these festivals and the ideology that embraces them. This brief biography was not intended as a panegyrical look at the 75-year-old Greenspan, but rather, a careful look at a gifted and driven artist, writer, producer, filmmaker and, in the special area of Olympic Games cinematography, possibly the best in the last half century.

This paper is divided into four parts, all of them efforts at historical re-creation: firstly, Greenspan's major works in films, essays and books; secondly, Greenspan biography; thirdly, a dispassionate look at Greenspan's personality and life-work "calling" in order to clarify why the man's "ever-uplifting" approach in all his efforts has been successful for more than fifty years and finally, a bibliographical essay of this researcher's sources is included to explain special direction taken, and may be useful to future sport historians. An expanded and specific list of references may be obtained from the author.

*"The Legacy of the Olympic Games, 1984-2000," International Symposium, Lausanne, 2002 (C.I.O. Publications, 2003), 331-335.

Greenspan's Major Works in Films, Essays, and Books

Films:
1952 "The Strongest Man in the World" (15 minutes)
1968 "Jesse Owens Returns to Berlin" (1 hour)
1970 "A Couple of Days in the Life of Charlie Boswell" (½ hour)
1971 "The Glory of the Time" (1 hour)
1976 "The Olympiad" (22 hours)
1977 "Wilma" (2 hours)
1979 "Numero Uno" (7 hours)
1979 "This Day in Sports" (3 hours)
1979 "Sports in America" (3 hours)
1980 "Olympic Moments—Vignettes—Events" (6 hours)
1982 "Time Capsule: The 1932 Los Angeles Olympics" (2 hours)
1984 "America at the Olympics" (2 hours)
1984 "16 Days of Glory: Los Angeles" (5 hours)
1985 "The Heisman Trophy Award" (1 hour)
1986 "Time Capsule: The 1936 Berlin Olympics" (2 hours)
1987 "For the Honor of Our Country" (6 hours)
1988 "The Golden Age of Sport" (1 hour)
1988 "16 Days of Glory—Calgary" (3½ hours)
1988 "16 Days of Glory—Seoul" (2¼ hours)
1988 "An Olympic Dream" (1 hour)
1992 "The Measure of Greatness" (25 minutes)
1992 "Mark Spitz Returns to Munich" (1 hour)
1992 "16 Days of Glory—Barcelona" (2¼ hours)
1993 "The Spirit of the Olympics"
1994 "16 Days of Glory—Lillehammer" (3½ hours)
1996 "African-Americans at the Olympics" (¾ hour)
1996 "America's Greatest Olympians" (2 hours)
1996 "Atlanta's Olympic Glory" (3½ hours)
1998 "Ageless Heroes" (1 hour)
1998 "Nagano'98" (2 hours)
2000 "Four Legends of Heavyweight Boxing" (2 hours)
2000 "Favorite Stories of Olympic Glory" (1½ hours)
2001 "Sydney 2000: Golf From Down Under" (1½ hours)
2001 "Discover Utah!" (½ hour)
2002 "Bud Greenspan's Stories of Winter Olympic Glory" (1½ hours)
2002 "Bud Greenspan Presents Michelle Kwan" (1 hour)

Essays and Books by Greenspan:
1983 "The Long Last Night ... for Benny Leonard," *New York Times*, April 10, section 5.

1991-2000 Twenty essays in "Advertising Section" of *Sports Illustrated* and *Parade Magazine.*
1994 "Sport and the Mass Media," Centennial Olympic Congress *Proceedings.*
1996 "Good News Doesn't Sell," *Olympic Message* (January-March).
1997 "How I Filmed 1896 Athens Olympics," *Journal of Olympic History* (Summer).
1973 [book] *Play it Again, Bud!*
1976 (book] *We Wuz Robbed!*
1995 [book] *100 Greatest Moments in Olympic History.*
1997 [book] *Frozen in Time; The Greatest Moments at the Winter Olympics.*
1997 *The Olympians' Guide to Winning the Game of Life.*

A Greenspan Biography

In every Bud Greenspan visual and written work, he is inspired by high human drama. "I am drawn to the inspirational, especially at the Olympic winter and summer games," he once said. He was quoted in a book review of his 1977 *We Wuz Robbed!*: "The structure of sport is based on the premise that all one can ask of an athlete is that he or she be dedicated, prepared, talented and courageous." (*New York Times*, February 20, 1977, sec. 5, p. 21.)

His first professional work was at the Games of the XIV Olympiad in London 1948, as a radio sports announcer for WHN, New York City. Several years later (1951), while serving as a spearcarrier in the chorus of "Aida" at the New York City Opera, he met African-American John Davis, the 1948 Olympian champion weight lifter. Davis won another gold medal in Helsinki, Finland (1952), prompting Greenspan to produce a short film: "The Strongest Man in the World." It was an artistic success rather than a "money-maker," but the native New Yorker knew what he had to do with the rest of his life. The United States government paid Bud $35,000 for the film "to counteract Soviet charges that blacks had no opportunities in the United States" (see *Olympic Message*, June 1996). His 1960 and 1964 "Voices of the 20th Century" and "A History of World War II," both disc sound recordings, were artistic-historical successes and featured Greenspan's brother, David Perry, as the voice beautiful low-key narrator. And then, in 1968, Greenspan escorted the very great Olympic champion, Jesse Owens, to Berlin, the scene of his 1936 triumphs.

The 51-year-old Owens was featured in an hour-long "Jesse Owens Returns to Berlin" and it won writer-producer-director Greenspan three television "Emmy" nominations.

The ascending career of Greenspan continued in the early 1970's, reaching one of several plateaus of excellence, with the release of his world-famous 22-hour "The Olympiad." This researcher read scores of film reviews in North American-European print media and found only superlatives about the film. A quarter-century "apprenticeship" and his cinematographic excellence were assured. Greenspan won Emmy awards from his peers and the International Olympic Committee's highest award, the Olympic Order (1985). His wife and co-filmmaker Cappy Petrash passed away in 1983, but the corporation Cappy Productions carried on the work and the commitment to entertain, educate, and to do injury to no person. He had a small, able staff of professionals, especially his closest collaborator, Nancy Beffa.

For some, Bud's approach to filmmaking is the ultimate naiveté: "I'm not comfortable doing scandal." This unlikely formula won him eight Emmy Awards; the 1995 lifetime Achievement Award by Directors' Guild of America and, in 1999, the George Foster Peabody Award, television's most prestigious honor.

He was born in New York City (18 September 1926), son of Benjamin E. (a judge) and Rachel P. (a lawyer), and he was a graduate of Long Island University (1947) after performing military service in World War II. He married Constance "Cappy" Petrash in 1965, collaborating on many films together until her death in 1983. His brother, David Perry, was for many years the exquisite narrator in many Greenspan's films, until David's passing in 1992 at age 68. Both believed that human drama, well told and filmed speak for themselves. Too much talk detracts, they said. Bud wrote in Olympic Update (1993-1994): "The mistake so often made by the television networks ... is to comment on absolutely everything."

Greenspan's Personality and Life-Work Calling

Good historians attempt to study specific past events and recapture a mass of nearly irrefutable factual evidence regarding that topic, to write with lucidity and with an absolute minimum of personal bias. Deeply held values are impossible to purge, but the good historian must subsume them in the search for truth. Bud Greenspan knows all this. He is not a professional historian, he has said many times, but rather a filmmaker, writer, editor, producer, who makes conscious decisions about how to deal with the individual thread of life. He prefers the uplifting, courageous, and noble rather than their opposite.

Visual images are more important than clever or even "profound" dialogue and they mark Greenspan's films. His 1976 "Olympic Symphony" was a "wordless celebration, ... a meld of Beethoven and Borzov" (the 1972 sprint champion). When done right, Greenspan said, sport has the capacity to touch "very deep human values ... provided competition is always kept in perspective." Aesthetic beauty, history and tradition, story-telling, and "unhindered drama" are infused into all of Greenspan's works. Gary Deeb *(Chicago Tribune,* June 22, 1979) wrote that Bud is a true artist, unlike some television salesmen "who will telecast donkey races if they think they'll attract good audience ratings."

Greenspan, "one of the very greatest storytellers," is only interested in sporting competitions that display athletes with skill, unbounded heroic histories who are measured, he said, "by their qualities of heart." Freed from the rules of the scientist, Greenspan seeks out the humanity, the drama, and the romanticism of sport, especially at the Olympic Games. "We always took the position," he said, "we would rather spend time on the 90 percent that is good and uplifting and happy about the Olympics, rather than the 10 percent that is not so good" (see Barry Wilner's column in the *Olympian Magazine* of February 1993).

Meters and millimeters, hours, seconds and milliseconds interest Greenspan and his people little. High human drama, "putting a face" on competition is always their goal. Overcoming personal, individual challenges are more important and therefore more interesting than running 1,500 meters in a little bit more than 200 seconds. Richard Sadomke knows Greenspan well and in a *New York Times* column, August 4, 1996, he wrote that all of Greenspan's work "are told straight forwardly, but emotionally, with a tersely written, stentorian narration." The description of his films is the essence of the man. Lawrence Van Gelder wrote in *The New York Times* of 11 November 1988: "A guy in Washington wrote 'Isn't it nice that Bud Greenspan still sees sports through the eyes of a young boy?'" Greenspan responded, "When I stop doing that, it'll be over."

"I'm not comfortable doing scandal," Greenspan told Karen Rosen of the *Atlanta Journal.* Drama, rather than exploitative stories, is his forte (see February 19, 1994). In that same year, Greenspan spoke at International Olympic Committee's Centennial Congress:

The visual development in coverage of the [Olympic] Games was forever changed by Leni Riefenstahl's five-hour film of the Berlin Games entitled "Olympia." For the first time the talent, dedication, beauty, and classicism of world-class athletes was seen in action, not heard or read.

The Greenspan mantra, so dear to him for his entire life, as he said in the *Olympic Review* of August 1990, is that "You can win by losing, because you make the effort." Bud made famous the 1968 Olympic Games marathoner from Tanzania, John Stephen Akhwari. He finished in last place, limping very badly into a stadium empty of spectators—with all camera crews gone, except Bud Greenspan. "Why do you continue running, more than an hour after the winner? Why did you not quit the race?" He seemed confused by the question from Greenspan, but answered "My country did not have to send me to Mexico City to start the race. They sent me to finish." Here we have, by coincidence, two men from different continents, with precisely the same mind-set.

The Olympic Games are the most important sporting event in the world. As an American and an internationalist, Greenspan's poignant films are pure universal. "Eye-glasses atop his shaved head, ... Bud has become the official keeper of the Olympic Flame," wrote Richard Sandomir, in the *New York Times* (August 4, 1996). This consummately good storyteller has brought us a humanistic vision of the Olympic athletes and possibly a larger human segment. Lastly, when asked, "Why were the '68 Mexico City Olympics your favorite?" Greenspan spoke of this first poor nation to host an Olympic Games and the ceremony of 80,000 joy-filled Mexicans inside the stadium, and of 1,000 "mariachis" singing "La Golondrina." It was a story of a caged swallow, singing its head off. But the family released the bird to give joy to the world. Bud took note of the crying Mexicans in the stands: "And they wouldn't let the mariachis leave. The crowd kept singing for an hour. As soon as they'd finish the last stanza ... the 80,000 people would sing it again. It was probably the most spontaneous surge of emotion I've ever felt. Nobody wanted to let the swallow go home." Bud Greenspan in Lawrence Linderman's interview in *Modern Maturity* (July-August 1996).

A Bibliographical Essay of Sources

This researcher first met Bud Greenspan in 1973, thirty years ago. An exchange of letters and "fax" correspondences now number forty-one and were useful in this biography. For much more than this period of time, newspaper and journal film critic reviews of Greenspan's works have been collected, read, and studied. Just from Canada and the USA, the number exceeds 175 analyses and essays, and many are from the most widely read and often scholarly sources. An extremely popular, syndicated Sunday newspaper, *Parade Magazine*, featured Greenspan's favorite heroes and heroines—Olympian figures of skill, courage and largess. All of them were read by the author. The United States Olympic Committee's (USOC) *Olympian* magazine and the *Olympic Review, Olympic Magazine* and *Olympic Message*, office organs of the International Olympic Committee featured a score of essays on the always-busy Greenspan. After he reached the senior citizen age category, the magazine *Modem Maturity* (July-August 1996) wrote a surprising insightful essay. Three decades of reviews in the *New York Times* (1973-2002), by expert observers, provided valuable insights. *Sports Illustrated* writers provided useful comments on the special Greenspan approach. Other North American sources came from the *Washington Post*; *Newsweek*; the *Atlanta Journal*; *Toronto Globe and Mail*; the *Boston Globe*; the *Desert News* of Salt Lake City; the *Los Angeles Times,* and a great many more. Insufficient research on non-American popular sources resulted in far fewer sources; The *London Free Press; The Times* of London; Sydney, Australia's the *Daily Telegraph* and the *Sun-Herald* of Sydney. Another useful look at Greenspan was located in a long essay in the "Early June 1992" Land's End Direct Merchants catalogue.

Still more of Greenspan's artistry is located in national and international essays by film reviewers, critics, and advertising specialists. The number of these commentaries, while not infinite, are impressive. He stayed away from Hollywood, treasured his home and business in Brooklyn and Manhattan, traveled the entire world, and called most of humanity brother and sister. A certain Anthony P. Montesano wrote in the American Film of September 1998: "Greenspan realizes the dramatic content of the individual's story and does not feel the need, like some to add to what already is the most dramatic story of all, the will of the human spirit to compete."

Lastly, Bud Greenspan visited this researcher's university campus in 1976 and 1992, the first time with his wife and his co-producer "Cappy" and the second time with the brilliant film editor and life companion, Nancy Beffa. The essence of who I am, he told this researcher, is in my film, "to be used for good by this generation, future generations ... and therefore a kind of immortality." More on Greenspan can be found in Les Brown's *Encyclopedia of Television* (1992), and detailed materials are also available in *Contemporary Authors*: Vol. 103 (1982).

22.
Olympic Idea, Questions of Ethics*

Even more important than winning the precious Olympic gold, silver, or bronze medals is to embrace, for all of one's sporting and personal life, the concepts of fair play, sportsmanship, and respect for all those that sincerely try to live by this universally-accepted code of honor. Far more Olympic athletes never cheat than those who ignore the rules, thus dishonoring themselves and the good nation whose uniform they wear.

There is in most languages a homely phrase: "The squeaky wheel gets the grease." Those who disobey the civil law and those who find the moral law irrelevant constantly are in the print media headlines and are everlastingly making television appearances. And so it is at the Olympic Winter and Summer Games: a few "rule breakers" will always be there, and so it will be always. All of us must work toward the gradual reduction of the number of those athletes with "easy morals" regarding the rules of athletic competition. Such a goal must be admirable although difficult to achieve. But then, was there ever anything of real value that was easy to capture? Olympic athletes do not lead an easy life. They do not work, play, and train a thousand hours a year in an idyllic, Pollyanna, "pie-in-the-sky" world. But this is never enough to break the moral law and the rules of sport. No matter who they are: male and female Olympic athletes from two hundred and two nations must abide by the international and Olympic code of honor to never cheat, no matter how difficult and challenging the circumstances. For the sake of self, nation, the Olympic Games, and humanity, one must never disobey the rules, the moral and

*What an Olympian Should Know, Compiled by Pal Schmidt, International Olympic Committee, (2003), 47-54.

ethical code. An American writer said it well. Eric Nager, in his essay "U.S. College Football—With a Difference," wrote:

> Sports are a way to express such qualities as joy, vitality, fair play, and order, which trace back to their inexhaustible spiritual source.

How very fashionable (and important) it was during the 1950's and 1960's—my own era of long-distance running competition—to read dozens of pamphlets, brochures, and articles dealing with fair play and sportsmanship. I read them all, listened to my comrades, and watched their conduct. Almost all of us decided to follow the rules. As I remember, even when the "going was tough," most decided not to cheat. And so it must be today, without equivocation. Despite what some may say, the elite athletic world of today is no different from fifty years ago. What is right is right, then and now.

One of the greatest modern sport philosophers is Dr. Hans Lenk of Germany. He was an Olympic gold medal rower on Lake Albano in 1960, continued his life as brilliant mathematician and philosopher. "The two disciplines have the same origin," he said. "The Olympic philosophy of ever-lasting fair play and honesty is under attack, as it always has been. All Olympic athletes who prepare well, compete fiercely and with uncompromising honesty, are "Olympic champions." It is certainly inappropriate, he wrote:

> to overcharge the Olympic Idea with a direct world peace mission and with immediate political functions.... The Olympic movement is too important a humanistic idea to get sacrificed or to fall victim in the jungle of commercialism ... and nationalism.

Fair play is never old-fashioned, nor is it dead, said the author of the 1960 document, *Fair Play,* a thoughtful, important statement of the French Committee for Fair Play. Ignore rule breakers, and those with easy moral standards in life and the world of sport, and "begin with the strict observance of the written rule." Examples of fair play abound in this 16-page pamphlet. It should be published again, distributed to every single one of the two hundred and two National Olympic Committees. Listen to the story of the immortal Italian Olympian, Eugenia Monti, at the 1964 Innsbruck Olympic Games. In the two-man bobsled trials,

Monti had just made his final run at a remarkable speed. Only the English team with Tony Nash and Robin Dixon could still beat his time. But it was then learnt that Nash and Dixon could not take off because a part of their sled was broken. Monti then detached the part in question from his own sled and sent it up to Nash and Dixon, who made his repair, finished in record time and won the gold medal. The International Pierre de Coubertin Fair Play Trophies Committee made its first award to Monti. We need more of his kind today, in this first decade of the 21ˢᵗ century. And they are "out there" from every land. The world and the IOC must find them, recognize them, call out their names, men and women, to the whole of the Olympic world.

Treat your strongest athletic competitor as you would wish him or her to treat you. Make no mistake, this is an achievable Olympian "Golden Rule." Without near universal compliance, the Olympic Movement around the world and its quadrennial winter and summer Games are doomed. Hans Lenk knew this instinctively, intellectually, and from the bottom of his heart. Forty-four years have passed since gold medals were awarded to that German crew. Nothing has changed since then, with the possible sense of even greater urgency. Fair play is the essence of all sport, Olympian or otherwise. Possibly it is not hyperbole that the "ancient" French Fair Play brochure concludes with a statement from the founder of this movement, the brilliant Jean Borotra and his committee:

> A task of cardinal importance lies before us all: to preserve for the modern world this great asset affair play and, through it, sport in general. And, through sport, to help man, not only to secure his physical and moral advancement, but perhaps also to save his soul.

Journalists of the world, please look around you with equal intensity for acts of nobility as well as sub-human conduct. Tough but fair-minded sports writer of *The Times* of London, Simon Barnes, wrote in a June 5, 1993 column that sportsmanship and human sensitivity are still alive and well. "Quixotic deeds still lift the heart," he wrote. At an international competition, a Swiss gymnast was badly injured, and could take no further part in the competition, apparently handing the victory to the British team. But no, British coach, Eddie Van Hoof, noticed that the Swiss number one gymnast, Daniel Giubellini, was on the floor, but out of the competition. Van Hoof suggested that he should join the team competition. The Swiss won a narrow victory and the coach won the Pierre de Coubertin Fair Play award as hero of the year.

We need to look to the distant past for similar examples. Genuine "fair play" are acts of high civility on the competitive athletic field and always when the issue of winning or not winning is still in doubt. This kind of conduct is significantly beyond the important hand shaking before and following the struggle. Read the no-nonsense *Wall Street Journal* of June 2, 1992, pages 1, A9, for a 1700-word essay on the nobility of "Fair Play and Sportsmanship." The founder of modern Olympic Games, the aristocrat and nobleman, Pierre de Coubertin (1863-1937), said a thousand times, "Above all, honor, is infinitely more important than a gold medal." The complex humanist, Fekrou Kidane, coordinator of the IOC's International Sport, the Olympic Ideal, and the Olympic Truce, once quoted, in 1994, Boutros-Ghali, Secretary General of the United Nations:

> The Olympic ideal is a hymn to tolerance and understanding between people and culture. In its way, Olympism is a school of democracy ... a natural link between the ethics of the Olympic Games and ... the United Nations.

Coubertin called his philosophy-ideology of instinctive and unfailing fair play, in life as in sport, "Olympism." In his nineteenth-century French language (translated), he said, "Olympism is a great silent machine, whose movement never stops." Dr. Deanna Binder, from the University of Alberta, has devoted twenty-five years to the study of global education through sport. Her essay is in the journal, *Quest* (vol. 53, 2001). Children of the planet must be exposed to high-minded sport conduct, and, wherever possible, taught "Olympic education" in their schools. This fair play imperative, is absolutely essential in a twenty-first century world where a billion children play games, and is carefully discussed in a 1999 book, *Sports Ethics: Applications For Fair Play,* authors Angela Lumpkin, Sharon Stull, and Jennifer M. Better.

Seventy years after his best days as an international and Olympic tennis competitor, the great Jean Borotra awarded Fair Play trophies to Frenchman, Jean-Pierre Labro, whose rugby team played an entire season without a rule violation. In a match against the Toulouse team, he and his team "accepted on principle, a refereeing decision which was nevertheless wrong."

Future Olympic Games are scheduled for Turin, Italy, 2006, Beijing, China, 2008, Vancouver, British Columbia, Canada in 2010, and candidates for the Olympic Summer Games of 2012 include New York City, Moscow, London, Paris, Rio de Janeiro, Madrid, Havana, Leipzig, and Istanbul. The IOC will select only one of them on July 6, 2005. No matter what happens and which city will host these Games of the future, and regardless of how efficiently they function, or how much money is generated, any one of them can become a failure if poor conduct by athletes, judges, and spectators are common place. They will no longer be "good" Olympic Games if individual and team conduct are vulgar, harsh, impolite, gross, mechanistic, and without sporting merit. High-level skill and world records are important and exciting. But they take, in every case, a secondary role in comparison with high moral conduct and unswerving allegiance to fair play amidst the "heat of competition." The Olympic Games badly needs such conduct, as does the much larger humanity. My hope is that it will come to pass in this way, and that the Olympic Games of the immediate future will be soaring in all dimensions, physical and metaphysical, and thus be better than any Games organized before.

23.
A Recapitulation of the United States Olympic Committee's Very Earliest Years, 1906-1922*

The National Olympic Committee (NOC) of the United States of America, the USOC, is one hundred years old. During much of that time, its headquarters was in the heart of the nation's amateur sports—New York City. Mike Moran, the USOC's media director for a quarter-century, wrote:

> ... until 1978 [the USOC] conducted modest business and organizational functions at 57 Park Avenue in New York City, operating as a small travel agency at times and often struggling in the winds of change and politics.[1]

Historian George M. Constable wrote that the USOC moved into new offices at 57 Park Avenue in I960.[2] Prior to this date and for decades, the early USOC called itself the American Olympic Committee (AOC) and met in the city's best hotels, such as the Waldorf, the Astor, or at the sumptuous and exclusive New York Athletic Club (NYAC). On January 10, 1906, wrote Fred G. Jarvis, the future United States Olympic Committee (USOC) met, calling themselves at that early date "The American Committee of the Olympic Games," with Caspar Whitney presiding.[3] The *New York Tribune [Tribune]* of March 6, 1906, wrote that Mr. Whitney's "American Committee has selected fames Edward Sullivan to lead the American team to Athens."[4] James Edward Sullivan (1862-1914), the powerful secretary and then president of

*Journal of Olympic History, 15 (March 2007), 22-26.

the nineteenth-century (1888) American Amateur Athletic Union (AAU), was in charge of the American team "and his decision shall be final."[5] In Robert Korsgaard's doctoral dissertation, he noted that "Caspar Whitney and Sullivan were appointed as Chairman and Secretary [respectively] for the United States team to Athens in 1906."[6] The busy Whitney served on the International Olympic Committee (IOC) from 1900-1904, without enthusiasm and therefore without distinction. He then took leadership of this new "American Committee of the Olympic Games," from 1906 through 1910, when Frederick Bayley Pratt (1865-1945), wealthy industrialist from Brooklyn, New York, became President of the recently re-configured American Olympic Committee (AOC). The date was December 10, 1910, and Mr. Pratt asked Mr. Whitney to accept a position on the Executive Board ... a pantheon of twenty-five of New York City's richest, most influential men, all lovers of amateur sport and advocates for America's success in the upcoming Games of the Fifth Olympiad in Stockholm, Sweden 1912.[7] Pratt served but one year, 1911, and was succeeded by a "giant" in the American Olympic business—Colonel Robert Means Thompson (1849-1930). This very wealthy businessman was already sixty-two years of age when he accepted the AOC leadership. He made few enemies, while many admired him, and an even greater number gave time and money for the "national cause" (with no governmental contribution whatsoever). Colonel Thompson served till 1919, and then, remarkably, again from 1922 until 1926, several years before his death in 1930, at age eighty-one.[8]

The new AOC tried hard to work closely with the AAU in the years before the First World War (which began in 1914). Even though many members of the older AAU also served on the AOC, and vice versa, at the highest level, tension existed regarding which of the two committees would select the best men for the Olympic Games team. For exactly a dozen years in the nineteenth century, the AAU did creditable work for those boys and girls, men and women not in high school or college, all over the country.

It was all less-than-perfect, but there was nothing else. The AOC was committed to the singular task of selecting an Olympic team, financing that team, and escorting them to the Olympic Games city, domestic and in Europe. There was an uneasy sharing of this responsibility between these two American amateur sporting organizations.

Neither the AAU nor the AOC had ownership of outdoor or indoor sporting facilities, nor did they have under their immediate direction, coaches, trainers, and certainly not a medical staff. Most importantly, they had no athletes on a day-to-day basis to coach, teach, guide, and direct. All of these enterprises took place in the country's small and large colleges and universities, and in the powerful network of athletic clubs located in every geographic area of the contiguous United States. The Olympic world in Europe would soon become aware of this wellspring of athletic talent. The AAU and AOC liked it this way, and it continued far beyond the parameters of this research paper. Their leadership continued their civilized meetings in the city's best hotels and clubs.[9]

The new AOC (1910), a recent emanation of the 1906 "American Committee of the Olympic Games," had no money in its New York City office, except for regular donations from wealthy local sportsmen. The AAU had an equally small office, but managed to sell membership cards to several thousand young men. In James Edward Sullivan's second term as president, he announced "We have $8,509.39 in the treasury, ... the most ever, largely due to [AAU] volunteers."[10] Unlike other nations at this time, the American AAU and the AOC had a Niagara of talented male athletes at its direct disposal. In this age of powerful individual, collective, and especially, governmental patriotism, the Army, the Navy and United States Marines "loaned" to the Olympic Committee their very best athletes for possible selection (by the AAU-AOC combined) as members of the United States Olympic Team. They were few in number, but significant in Olympic Games success. An avalanche of skillful male athletes emerged from the country's several hundred universities, and the AOC needed only to invite the very best of them and accompany them to Paris (1900); St. Louis (1904); to Athens for an out-of-sequence 1906 Games; London (1908), and Stockholm in 1912. There was nothing like it anywhere else in the world. Thanks to Bill Mallon, Ian Buchanan, with help from Jeffrey Tishman, in their *Quest for Gold* text, one becomes aware of the gold medals won by American athletic club members. They came from the NYAC and the Olympic Club of San Francisco, and in the Mid-West: Chicago's Cherry Circle Club, the Chicago A.C., the Chicago A.A., as well as that city's Central YMCA. Productive athletic clubs in Newark, Milwaukee, St. Louis, Portland, Oregon, Philadelphia and from the Independent Rowing Club of New Orleans trained young men and proudly sent them on to their Olympic Committee in New York City, and shepherded them to the Olympic Games venues.[11]

The elderly Colonel Thompson served as AOC president from 1911 through 1919, and again, following the so-called "Great War," from 1922-1926, this time as both AOC president and president of the new, expanded, full-time American Olympic Association (AOA). The main architect of this AOA was Gustavus Town Kirby (1874-1956). Most of Europe and North America were in a war-devastated, traumatic state when Kirby became AOC president on November 28, 1919.[12] The committee's treasury was empty and its officers utterly unprepared for an Olympic Games scheduled a half-year later in Antwerp, Belgium. The AOC's "dilemma was of classic proportions," wrote John Lucas in his essay "American Preparations for the First Post-World War Olympic Games, 1919-1920."[13] Ellen Phillips said the same thing:

> Kirby and his AOC were well aware that their own house was in chaos. The AOC had never had a constitution or by-laws or even a real existence.... The new American Olympic Association was a permanent body ... composed of AAU and NCAA representatives as well as people from a range of interested sports federations.[14]

This new reconfigured AOA may have saved the National Olympic Committee of the United States from obscurity, or worse. Hopes were high, but the 1920 games were "around the corner" and the joint AOC-AOA descended into bankruptcy, bitter internecine struggle among committee members, and, much worse, between some very angry American Olympic athletes traveling to the ruined city of Antwerp and their own officials. Alice Lord Landon, looking back fifty years to her diving competition and life in Antwerp, told journalist William O. Johnson, Jr.:

> Poor Antwerp wasn't really ready for something like the Olympics. We had cornhusk mattresses ... in a YWCA hostess house, the boys were in a horrible school barracks.... The swimming and diving competition was held in the old moat that used to surround the city in ancient times. It was the clammiest, darkest place, and the water was frigid.[15]

Johnson also interviewed the AAU secretary in 1920, Daniel Ferris, and he vividly recalled the dreadful Atlantic Ocean crossing on the "death ship," *Princess Matoika,* "that had just taken off the bodies of 1800 war dead from Europe.... The smell of formaldehyde was dreadful."[16] Certainly the fault was not that of the courageous Belgian Olympic Committee, their government, and their royal family. Olympic historian from Belgium, Roland Renson, devotes but a paragraph to America's terrible ocean voyage, and says nothing of the AOC disfunction.[17]

Back home in New York City, there was no roaring ticker-tape parade down Fifth Avenue for the returning American male and female Olympians—and this in spite of Bill Mallon's careful analysis of all competitors at these Games of the Seventh Olympiad. The USA won more medals than anyone else.[18] AOC leader Kirby called a meeting at the NYAC on December 4, 1920, and asked for a sophisticated, full-time committee—an American Olympic Association, "which will prevent snafus such as occurred at the last Olympic Games preparations."[19] Penn State University scholar, Robert E. Lehr, wrote: "Kirby was the person most singularly responsible for the eventual realignment of the AOC."[20] The AOC did most of its work during the year of the Olympic Games. Kirby found this unacceptable, and in his not always pleasant, but abrupt manner, he told his colleagues at a sumptuous dinner in his suburban rural New York City thirty-room mansion:

> We must have a permanent body to carry on, in the interim between the Olympic Games, the work of American preparation for the international classic....[21]

Kirby's Reorganization Committee of five colleagues had to wait for the full AOC meeting on November 25, 1921, where the optimistic Kirby trumpeted:

> The American Olympic Committee is at an end. The American Olympic Association is about to be born. May it be a potent force in ushering in a new era at peace and goodwill toward men.[22]

Mr. Kirby finished his brief and event-filled AOC presidency and returned the AOA leadership back to seventy-three year old Colonel R. M. Thompson.[23] Always the gentleman, his immediate task was to bring a semblance of shared control of the nation's Olympic teams. But the advantage lay with the AAU, not the AOA. The former was a generation older and richer, with athletes and Union representatives in all geographic regions of the United States. Sullivan, the brilliant autocrat, had, in two decades, placed before hundreds of thousands of

men and women, boys and girls, those inclined towards competitive sport (and not attending a university-college)—the opportunity to become involved in eight sports. From 1890 until
his death in 1914, Sullivan's AAU dominated domestic, non-
school sport, and, beginning in 1900, filled the void and took
charge of the nation's Olympic Games team. The AOC and
then AOA came later, their only mission (reluctantly shared
with the AAU) was to select the best Olympic team and take
them to the games. Thompson's first task was to share less
power with the AAU, and he said so in his acceptance speech
on October 22, 1922.[24] But the AAU's Secretary-Treasurer,
Fred Rubien disagreed:

> The Amateur-Athletic Union is the accepted Olympic au-
> thority in this country because the organization enjoys
> membership in all the international federations identi-
> fied with the Olympic Games.[25]

The AAU, in spite of its power, or possibly, because it was
so omnipotent in the United States, was not without enemies.
Journalist Newton Fuessle, in a vituperative essay in *The Outlook* magazine for April 1922, called the AAU inefficient, excessively authoritarian. "A curious war is raging.... It is a fight to a
finish for the reform of amateur athletics," he wrote, and added
that the AAU was the main but not the only culprit in this story
of "usurped authority" and that amateur athletes were in "the
control of an autocratic hierarchy." Fuessle may have weakened
his case by finding little use for the brand new, untested AOA
as a mere "subsidiary" of the AAU (see pages 642 and 644, volume 130). These were discordant times for the nation, and for
its amateur sporting organizations, in the wake of the hideous
war and the unhappy experiences of some American Olympians at the Antwerp Olympic Games. President of National Collegiate Athletic Association (NCAA), Brigadier-General Palmer
E. Pierce, wrote his friend at the University of Pennsylvania,
the influential medical doctor, Robert Tait McKenzie, about a
new organization, not yet "born" that might act as an arbitra-
tor for the angry AOC-AOA and AAU to make more possible an
even stronger USA Olympic team for the 1924 Olympic Games
in Paris.[26] Pierce wrote again to McKenzie on May 2, 1922. "I
am pleased," he wrote, "that you spoke with Kirby and Colonel
Thompson regarding the new formation of a National Amateur
Athletic Federation (NAAF)":

The conference in Washington next week promises to be
of great importance ... Thompson ... has been interviewing Amateur Athletic Union men in an endeavor to se-
cure an amicable adjustment of all athletic matters.[27]

One thing stands out, possibly above all others. The AAU "pro-
duced" not a single Olympic athlete, let alone supported them in
their long years of daily physical fitness preparations and in ac-
quiring very special Olympic skills. The same is true of the AOC-
AOA. Exactly like the AAU, they selected from a very great "harvest" of thousands upon thousands of athletic club members, and
from a forest of American universities, an equal number of young
men, ready to represent themselves (firstly), their school, club,
and country in the Olympic summer games. They won scores
of gold, silver, and bronze medals. The rest of the world stood
agape, but retained sufficient composure to eventually emulate
the "Yankee winners," but, with their own systems in Europe,
Asia, South America, and in Oceania's Australia—New Zealand,
and much later, from the great African continent. Make no mistake, the precursor was the United States of America. It is still
very much too early to state with certainty whether this Olympic
medal factory, the USA, turned out a great gift, or a small curse
to humankind, or, possibly, some kind of exotic meld.

Although beyond the scope of this paper, the "misunderstand-
ings" between the tripartite amateur sport organizations, AAU,
NCAA, and the NOC of the United States (AOC-AOA) continued
for another half-century. The NAAF "dematerialized" without
fulfilling its alleged function of acting as a "balm" between and
among the above-mentioned groups.[28] The United States government two generations later, was forced to interfere in the country's governance of amateur athletics. One of the three (AAU,
USOC, NCAA) was deemed superfluous, and the *Final Report of
the Presidents on Olympic Sport* was published in 1977.[29]

In summation, the men who chose to affiliate themselves with
the AOC-AOA in these early years (1906-1922) held the same
"ideology" as did members of the AAU, that is to say, "their" athletes must not deviate from a theoretical concept of never profiting from their athletic skills. It was a difficult but attainable
"mind-set" for most American Olympic champions in this long-
ago time. But not all, and, unfortunately, the AAU and the nation's Olympic committee "minutes" are filled-to-suffocation with
the discussions, far into the night, of the specter of sporting professionalism. It was a great inhibiting factor in the halting prog-

ress of the AAU, and in the uneven wisdom of the Olympic committee. But to their credit, these men, and a few women, were, in the main, intelligent and good people, who did believe in the innate high-mindedness of most athletes. These same AAU and Olympic bureaucrats did find personal joy and national pride in the Olympian performances of their young men and women.

Everything evolves. This writer finds no fault that, at the time, the USOC had no "home" to call their own, then rented a building, and remained beholden to schools and clubs for their Olympic teams. All has changed in this first decade of the Twenty-First Century. The very first beginnings, I believe, took place when "Gus" Kirby had a vision of a bold and permanent and fully-funded AOA. I believe, because the evidence seems to sustain it, that Kirby, the shrewd art dealer-inventor millionaire, saw clearly the unproductiveness, but great manly comradeships of bimonthly meetings of the AOA at the NYAC that included leisurely nine-course dinners, wine, the finest cigars, civilized conversations, and, then, late at night, a business meeting. Kirby apparently enjoyed these affairs, but knew them to be not the way of a "new age" Olympic committee should function.

NOTES

1 See his *USOC Fact Book 2001-2002*, p. 2 (USOC in Colorado Springs, Colorado).

2 George M. Constable, *The XXI Olympiad Montreal 1976 and Lake Placid* (1980); volume 19 of 24 volumes of *The Olympic Century*, Los Angeles 1998, p. 100. A revealing telephone call from this writer to Mr. C. Robert Paul took place on February 9, 2006. His essential role as AAU Director of Development in the 1950's, and then Director of Media Relations for the USOC from 1961-1996, allowed him insight into amateur athletic activities before these years. He told me: "Tlie Olympic Committee never really had a home until 1960. For years they rented a room in the Biltmore Hotel, with a couple of part-time workers. The AAU wasn't much better in their little place over at 233 Broadway. When I moved into 57 Park Avenue—the national Olympic headquarters—I was full-time, with a couple of ladies helping me. The four story building belonged to billionaire banker J.P. Morgan, a gift to his girlfriend. Arthur Lentz, our Executive Director, bought the lovely building in 1960 for $100,000. The USOC sold it for a million dollars just before abandoning New York in the mid-1970's, and moving to Colorado Springs."

3 Fred G. Jarvis, *From Vision to Victory. America's Role in Establishing the Modern Olympic Games 1894-1912*, New York City 1996, p. 53. This first meeting in early 1906 "sought $25,000 to send a team to Ath-

ens." See New York *Daily Tribune* [hereafter *Tribune*], (January 11, 1906),
p. 11. *The New York Times* [hereafter (NYT)] on that same date, p. 10,
wrote that the "American Committee to send a team to Athens." Even
earlier, Caspar Whitney wrote in his influential magazine *Outlook* 47
(September 1905), p. 788., that "The American Committee of the Olympic Games has decided that $25,000 is the amount necessary to take
the team to Athens."

4 See the *Tribune* (March 6, 1906), p. 5. More on Sullivan might
be gleaned from John A. Lucas, "Early Olympic Antagonists—Pierre de
Coubertin versus James E. Sullivan," *Stadion. International Journal for
the History of Sport* 3 (1977), pp. 258-272. For a substantive look at
Whitney and his times, see John A. Lucas, "Caspar Whitney -The Imperial Advocate of Athletic Amateurism and His Involvement with the IOC
and the American Olympic Committee 1899-1912," *Journal of Olympic
History,* 8 (2000), pp. 30-38.

5 *Tribune,* (March 6, 1906), 5.

6 See Robert Korsgaard, *A History of the Amateur Athletic Union of the
United States,* Ph.D. dissertation, Teachers College, Columbia University
1952, p. 188. There is a brief history of the American AAU in the *Official
Athletic Rules of the AAU, 1939,* New York City, pp. 12-16. John A. Lucas
was commissioned by the AAU and did complete a limited edition, titled
Centennial History of the American AAU 1889-1989, 101 pp.

7 See "American Olympic Committee Named," NYT (December 11,
1910), part 4, p. 6; see "Olympic Games Committee Prepares for Stockholm," *New York Herald* [hereafter *Herald*] (December 13, 1910), p. 13.
F.B. Pratt was important enough to find a place in *Who Was Who in
America,* Vol. 2 (1943-1950), p. 430; *Current Biography, 1945,* p. 480,
and *Facts On File, 1945,* p. 146.

8 See John A. Lucas, "Setting the Foundation and Governance of
the American Olympic Association: The Efforts of Robert Means Thompson, 1911-1919 and 1922-1926," *Journal of Sport History,* 29 (2002),
pp. 457-468.

9 The *Tribune, NYT,* the *Herald,* and the widely-read *Brooklyn Eagle*
contain numerous essays of AAU and AOC meetings, followed by glorious social affairs, and they wrote about them in the morning papers, all
at great length and detail. This researcher is old enough to remember, on
occasion, in the late 1940s and 1950's, invitations to the NYAC's three
large dinning rooms, not to eat but for a few moments with members of
the AAU-AOC "family," members, ephemeral meetings as an athlete and
researcher seeking historical information.

10 See *Minutes of the Annual Meeting of the AAU of the U.S., 1907,*
p. 8. We need more money, he announced "in order that we maintain
absolute control over the individual athlete who competes under our
protection."

11 *Quest For Gold. The Encyclopedia of American Olympians,* New
York 1984. Mallon and his colleagues identify Olympic champions that
represented the National Guard; the Miami-Biltmore Aquatic Club; the

Illinois A.C.; the Missouri A.C.; Boston's Posse Gymnasium; the Outrigger Canal Club in Hawaii, and many more in the greater New York City area, like the Manhattan A.C.; the Atlanta Boat Club, and the Seawankaka Boat Club. The Boston Athletic Association (BAA) was "there" (at the Athens 1896 Victory Podium) and at subsequent games in these tenuous early Olympic Games.

12 See *NYT* (November 29, 1919), p. 12, and *Tribune* (November 29, 1919), p. 14.

13 See *Journal of Sport History*, 10 (1983), p. 33. For biographical data on Kirby, see John A. Lucas, "Architects of the Modernized American Olympic Committee 1921-1928: Gustavus Town Kirby, Robert Means Thompson, and General Douglas MacArthur," *Journal of Sport History*, 22 (1995), pp. 38-45.

14 See *The. VII Olympiad Antwerp 1920 and Chamomx 1924;* vol. 1 of 25 vols. *The Olympic Century*, Los Angeles 1998, pp. 110-111.

15. See Johnson's *All That Glitters is Not Gold: An Irreverent Look at the Olympic Games*, New York 1972, pp. 139-140.

16 Ibid., p. 141.

17 *La VIIieme Olympiade Anvers 1920. Les Jeux Ressuscites*, Comite Olympique et Interfederal Beige 1995, pp. 31-32. He does show a photo of the rotting hulk, *Princess Matoika*, on p. 31. An unacceptably muted view of American athlete's extreme discomfort is located in the 451-page *Report of the American Olympic Committee—Seventh Olympic Games—Antwerp, Belgium 1920*, New York City 1920, pp. 205-210.

18 As is his way, medical doctor Bill Mallon's 281-page factual treasure *The Games of the VIIth Olympiad 1920* reveals that despite primitive conditions, the Olympic Games and the Olympic Movement somehow survived the ultimate carnage of the World War. His book was published in 1992 by Most Publications in Durham, North Carolina.

19 "Olympic Officials Plan for Future," *NYT* (December 5, 1920), section 10, p. 2.

20 Robert E. Lehr, "The American Olympic Committee, 1896-1940: From Chaos to Order, Ph.D. dissertation, Pennsylvania State University Department of Kinesiology, 1985, p. 89.

21 "Permanent Olympic Body to be Formed," *NYT* (February 6, 1921), p. 20.

22 *AOA Minutes* (25 November 1921), p. 14. The reporter present at the NYAC wrote: "After a stormy session ... the AOA was created." See *NYT* (November 26, 1921), p. 16. The always verbose Kirby and now victorious Kirby wrote, in overheated language: "The work going on in Washington of destroying mastodon war is as splendid as it is epoch-making, but the work which is primarily ours [the spread of amateur sport] – of conducting a better humanity – is certainly ... vital and important. [In the New York Public Library, see "Kirby" and his "USOA Organizing Meeting, November 25, 1921."] Earlier that month, on November 9, Secretary of War, John W. Weeks, wrote Kirby a letter supporting his bold AOA concept. However, he added, "I must instruct my representatives [on the Army and Navy] to only join an organization whose scope

is not wider than the one outlined in your constitution." See *Tribune* (November 11, 1921), p. 13, and the *NYT* (November 10, 1921), p. 24. The Secretary knew that members of the Army and Navy, experts in pistol and rifle shooting, had contributed to the USA's success in previous Olympic Games. Mere gold medals are not all that our Army-Navy boys seek, he said, but more importantly, "We are desirous of uplifting American manhood." *NYT* (November 10, 1921), p. 24.

23 "Col. R. M. Thomnson re-elected President," *NYT* (October 23, 1922), p. 13.

24 See "American Olympic Association advocates reduction in voting strength of AAU," *NYT* (October 23, 1922), p. 13. Robert E. Lehr's dissertation deals with AAU-Olympic committee tension in the early 1920s (endnote 20). Also illuminating this topic is Ying Wushanley, *Playing Nice and Losing. The Struggle for Control of Women's Intercollegiate Athletics, 1960-2000*, Syracuse, NY, 2004, pp. 20-23.

25 All these federations do recognize the AOA, he added, somewhat deferentially. See "Rubien Defends the AAU," NYT (April 18, 1922), p. 6. For forty-eight years, Mr. Rubien worked full-time for New York City's Department of Taxes and Assessments. He also rarely missed a day working at the AAU office, part-time. His obituary is located in *NYT* (July 6, 1951), p. 23, and the *New York Herald Tribune* (July 6, *1951*), p. 10.

26 An April 27, 1922 letter. See the Robert Kozar Collection of McKenzie correspondences in the University of Tennessee Archives. On that same day, R.M. Thompson issued for release to the press a letter stating that the NAAF had only the noblest of intentions. "It is the hope of the Federation," he said: "to take care of these [amateur] sports [and] not to supplant the Amateur Athletic Union ... [and] to join the Olympic Association, thus assuring a hearty co-operation among all the governing bodies interested in athletics." See Kozar at University of Tennessee Archives.

27 Pierce to McKenzie, May 2, 1922, University of Tennessee Archives.

28 This statement is not good history. In a confusing story involving the U.S. Secretary of War, the Secretary of the Navy, the United States Army, the YMCA, and, of course, the AAU and the AOA, the NAAF ceased to exist in 1927, according to Arnold Flath, "A History of Relations Between the NCAA and the AAU 1905-1963," Ph.D. dissertation, University of Illinois, 1964, pp. 105, 108, 110, 112, 117-121.

29 See the *United States Olympic Crisis—The Problem that Won't Go Away;* 31 pp., published by the NCAA on November 24, 1972. Also, *President's Commission on Olympic Sports—First Report to the President,* 123 pp. and dated February 9, 1975 (U.S. Government Printing Office); *The Final Report of the President's Commission on Olympic Sports 1975-1977,* vol. 1 (1977), 140 pp. (U. S. Government Printing Office), and vol. 2 (473 pp.) titled *Findings of Fact and Supporting Material.* This researcher has these books in his collection. The AAU was told to remain active in national children's sport competitions. And they have done so in the ensuing decades, to its credit.

Books, Monographs, and Privately-Published Works by John A. Lucas

1978   *Saga of American Sport* (Philadelphia: Lea and Febiger, 1978),439 pp, co-author Ronald A. Smith.

1979   *Thirty and More Jogging Trails in State College* (University Park, PA: Penn State University Press, 1979), 50 pp.

1980   *The Modern Olympic Games* (New York: A. S. Barnes, 1980), 242 pp.

1988   *Every Woman's Club House: The Original Penn State University Mary Beaver White Recreational Hall 1938-1968.* (University Park, PA: Published privately), 95 pp.

1988   *A Hundred Year History of the Amateur Athletic Union of the United States 1888-1988* (University Park, PA: Published privately), 190 pp.

1992   *Future of the Olympic Games* (Champaign, IL: Human Kinetics, 1992), 231 pp.

1995   *A History of the Department of Kinesiology, Pennsylvania State University 1930-1995* (University Park, PA: Privately printed) 61pp.

1996   "The IC4A Indoor Track and Field Championships 75th Celebration History 1922-1996" (an insert in the 1996 *Program* at Harvard University, March 2-3, 1996.

Published Articles by John A. Lucas

1. 1955, "Nicholas Costes—Marathon Champion," *Amateur Athlete* 26 (August 1955), 22.

2. 1957   "Interval Training for the High School Half-mile," *Athletic Journal* 37 (April 1957), 30.

3. 1957 "John Kelley—Marathon Champion," *Amateur Athlete* 28 (November 1957), 30-33.

4. 1958 "Progressive Work-Outs for Cross-country," *Scholastic Coach* 28 (September 1958), 24.

5. 1959 "555 Seconds of Running," *Athletic Journal*, 39 (April 1959), 42.

6. 1959 "Special Foods," *Athletic Journal*, 40 (November 1959), 62.

7. 1960 "Motor Fitness Program at the University of Maryland," *Maryland Physical Education Newsletter* (February 1960).

8. 1962 "The Challenge of the Intercollegiate Three-mile," *Athletic Journal*, 41 (March 1962).

9. 1962 "Maximum Leg Power in the Shot, Discus, Javelin, and Hammer," *Scholastic Coach* (March 1962).

10. 1962 "Running Records and Human Performance," *Amateur Athlete* (April 1962), 16.

11. 1963 "The All-Around," *Amateur Athlete* (August 1963).

12. 1963 "Power Thrust in Track and Field Athletics," *Modern Athletics* [British] (November 1963).

13. 1964 "Coubertin's Philosophy of Pedagogical Sport," *Journal of Health and Physical Education*, 35 (September 1964), 26-27, 56.

14. 1965 "Historical Research and the Formative Years of the Modern Olympic Movement," *Proceedings*, National College Physical Education Association for Men, January 1965, pp. 50-51.

15. 1966 "Telescoping—the Acid Test of Middle Distance Training," *Track Techniques*, 26 (September 1966).

16. 1967 "Summary of Altitude Research," *Quarterly Review* of the U.S. Track Coaches (March 1967), 57.

17. 1967 "Le Baron de Coubertin et Thomas Arnold," *Bulletin du Comité International Olympique*, 98-99 (August 18, 1967), 58-60.

18. 1968 "Pedestrianism and the Struggle for the Sir John Astley Belt 1878-1879," *Research Quarterly*, 39 (October 1968), 587-594.

19. 1968 "The Professional Marathon Craze in America 1908-1909," *Quarterly Review* of the U.S. Track Coaches (December 1968), 31-36.

20. 1968 "A Prelude to the Rise of Sport: Antebellum America 1850-1860," *Quest*, 11 (Winter 1968), 50-57.

21. 1969 "The Mile of the Century—1939 Princeton Invitation Games," *Quarterly Review* of the U.S. Track Coaches (June 1969), 11-16.

22. 1969 "The Most Amazing Feat of Human Endurance," *By-Line Track and Field.* Track and Field News Publications, 1969, pp. 58-62.

23. 1969 "Historical Survey of Middle and Long-Distance Running," *Quarterly Review* of U.S. Track Coaches (December 1969), 31-37.

24. 1970 "Le Baron Pierre de Coubertin et sa Philosophie de la Pedagogie Sportive," *Revue Olympique,* 331 (March-April, 1970), 193-202.

25. 1970 "Some Athletic Superlatives," *Quarterly Review* of U.S. Track Coaches (November 1970), 20-23.

26. 1971 "The Unholy Experiment—Professional Baseball's Struggle Against Pennsylvania's Sunday Blue Law 1926-1934," *Pennsylvania History,* 38 (April 1971), 163-175.

27. 1971 Book review of *The Nazi Olympics* by Richard Mandell in *Canadian Journal of Sport History,* 2 (May 1971), 82-85.

28. 1971 "Action through Conviction: A Fun and Fitness Program," *Pennsylvania Journal of Physical Education,* 41 (June 1971), 14-15.

29. 1971 Book review of Ellen Gerber's *Innovations and Institutions in Physical Education,* in *Pennsylvania Journal of Physical Education,* 41 (June 1971), 25.

30. 1971 Book review of Gerald Redmond's *The Caladonian Games in Nineteenth Century America,* in *Canadian Journal of Sport History,* 2 (December 1971), 84-88.

31. 1971 "The Princeton Invitation Meet—Aristocrat of international Track and Field Meets, 1934-1940," *Proceedings,* National College Physical Education for Men (1971), 197-202.

32. 1972 "Olympism and the Genesis of Modern International Olympic Games Philosophy," *Proceedings,* National College Physical Education Association for Men (1972), 26-30.

33. 1972 "The First Great International Track Meet," *Sports Illustrated,* 37 (October 23, 1972, mid-west edition), M6-M8.

34. 1972 "Olympics on a Crash Course," *The Penn Stater Magazine,* 59 (November 1972), 24-25.

35. 1972 "An Open Letter; Change for the Future Olympics," *Pennsylvania Journal of Health, Physical Education, Recreation,* 42 (December, 1972), 5-6.

36. 1973 "Open Letter to Lord Killanin," *Journal of Health, Physical Education, Recreation,* 44 (February 1973), 8-10.

37. 1973 "Los Angeles 1932—the Games are On," *Olympic Review*, 66-67 (May-June 1973), 184-186.

38. 1973 "The Modern Olympic Games: Fanfare and Philosophy," *The Maryland Historian*, 4 (Fall 1973), 70-87. Also published in *Quest*, 22 (Spring 1974), 6-18.

39. 1973 "Genesis of the Olympics"; Chapter 28 in *A History of Sport and Physical Education to 1900* (Champaign, Illinois: Stipes Pub. Co., 1973), 331-340.

40. 1974 "Olympic Genesis: The Sorbonne Conferences of 1892 and 1894," *Olympic Review*, 85-86 (November-December 1974), 607-610; also in the *Proceedings*, Third Canadian Symposium on Sport History, no p. nos.

41. 1974 Book review of *Joe Louis* by A. O. Edmonds, in the *Journal of Sport History*, 1 (Fall 1974), 168-170.

42. 1974 "History of Cross-Country," in *The Official Associated Press Sports Almanac 1974*, pp. 241-244.

43. 1974 "A String of Pearls: Avery Brundage Discources 1929-1972," *Proceedings*, North American Society of Sport History (1974), 4-5. Published in full, *The History, Evolution and Diffusion of Sports and Games in Different Cultures*, Brussels, HISPA World Sport History Conference 1976, pp. 289-299.

44. 1975 "Victorian 'Muscular Christianity"—Prologue to the Olympic Games Philosophy," *Olympic Review*, 97-98, Part 1 (Nov.-Dec., 1975), 456-460; Part 2 in volumes 99-100 (Jan.-Feb., 1976), 49-52. Also published in *Proceedings*, International Congress for Health, Physical Education, Recreation, 18 (1975), 214-224; also in *Proceedings 1975* of the International Olympic Academy, pp. 66-77.

45. 1975 "Reaction to Peter Wagner's 'Puritan Attitudes Toward Physical Recreation in 17th Century New England,'" *Proceedings 1975*, North American Society of Sport History, pp. 12-13.

46. 1975 "Sport and Politics: The Infamous Pennsylvania 'Walking Purchase' of 1737," *Proceedings 1975*, North American Society of Sport History, p. 16.

47. 1975 "The NCAA Cross-Country Championships 1938-1975," *Quarterly Review* of the U. S. Track Coaches Association, 75 (Winter 1975), 46-48.

48. 1976 "Seminar on the modern Olympic Games," *Journal of Physical Education and Recreation*, 47 (March 1976), 22-24.

49. 1976 "The IC4A Championships—A Hundred Year History 1876-1976," *IC4A Centennial Track Meet Official Program* (May 21-22, 1976), pp. 7-9, 46-49; also published in *IC4A Record Book 1876-1976* (Centerville, Massachusetts: ECAC Headquarters 1976) 7-19.

50. 1976 "A History of the Marathon Race—490 B.C. to 1975," *Journal of Sport History*, 3 (Summer 1976), 120-138; also in American Medical Association Joggers *Newsletter,* Part 1 (Summer 1976); Part 2 (Fall 1976).

51. 1976 "The Modern Olympic Games—An Experiment in International Living," *The Olympian*, 3 (July-August 1976), 14-16.

52. 1976 "American Academy Presidents: Physical Education Futurists, 1926-1976," *The Academy Papers 1976*, pp. 17-26.

53. 1976 "Antecedents of the Modern Olympic Amateur Concept," *Olympic Review*, 105-106 (July-August 1976), 365-367.

54. 1976 "The Influence of Anglo-American Sport on Pierre de Coubertin, the Modern Olympic Games Founder"; Chapter 2 in *The Modern Olympics* (Cornwall, N.Y.: Leisure Press, 1976), 17-26.

55. 1976 Book review of *La vie et l'oeuvre Pedagogique de Pierre de Coubertin 1863- 1937* by Yves-Pierre Boulongne, in *Stadion*, 2 (Winter 1976), 314-317.

56. 1977 "1932—Highpoint of Olympism," *The Olympian*, 4 (April 1977), 22-23.

57. 1977 "Man with a Mission—William Milligans Sloane," *The Olympian*, 4 (September 1977), 15, 21.

58. 1977 "Olympic Games Crisis—Reform and Reaffirmation," *Journal of Physical Education and Recreation*, 48 (October 1977), 6-9.

59. 1977 Book review of *Track and Field Omnibook* by J. Kenneth Doherty, in *Journal of Physical Education and Recreation*, 48 (October 1977), 76.

60. 1977 "Charlie Paddock—The First 'World's Fastest Human,'" *The Olympian*, 4 (November 1977), 10-11.

61. 1977 "Anomalies of Human Pysical Achievement," *Canadian Journal of History of Sport and Physical Education*, 8 (December 1977), 1-9.

62. 1977 "The Final Report of the President's Commission on Olympic Sports 1977, *Proceedings 1977*, International Association for the History of Physical Education and Sport (Supplement), pp. 52-65.

63. 1977 "Early Olympic Antagonists—Pierre de Coubertin versus James E. Sullivan," *Stadion*, 3 (1977), 258-272.

64. 1977 "The Dilemma of the Revised Olympic Rule 26," *Proceedings*, United States Olympic Academy (1977), 91-101.

65. 1978 Book review of *Memories of a Bloomer Girl 1894-1924* by Mabel Lee, in *Canadian Journal of History of Sport and Physical Education*, 9 (May 1978), 93-94.

66. 1978 "Eastern District of AAHPER: 1919-1924, A History," *Journal of Physical Education and Recreation*, 49 (June 1978), 63-65.

67. 1978 "An Interlude of Olympic Philosophy," United States Olympic Committee Education Council *Newsletter* (Spring 1978), 7-11.

68. 1978 "Marathon Man—A Look at What Made Johnny Hayes Run," *The Olympian*, 4 (April 1978), 14-15.

69. 1978 "To Save the Olympics," *Track and Field News*, 31 (June 1978), 62.

70. 1978 "Pierre de Coubertin and the Modern Olympic Games," *The Olympian*, 5 (October 1978), 22-23; also in *Proceedings,* United States Olympic Academy, pp. 34-38.

71. 1978 "Olympic Reform—Implementation of Change During the 1980s," *Proceedings 1978*, International Council for Health, Physical Education, Recreation, 2 (1978), 803-807.

72. 1978 "The French Baron Pierre de Coubertin," *Proceedings 1978*, International Olympic Academy, pp. 89-95.

73. 1979 "History of Track and Field," in Norman Lewis Smith's *Almanac 1979 —Sports and Games* (New York: Facts on File, 1979), 403-415.

74. 1979 "The Eastern District Society Finds its Strength: 1925-1929," *Journal of Physical Education and Recreation*, 50 (September 1979), 58-60.

75. 1979 "A Walk around the Clock—Biography of Captain Barclay," *The Runner*, 2 (October 1979), 74-75.

76. 1979 "Sport: Mirror and Molder of American Society," in William J. Morgan, (ed.) *Sports and Humanities: A Collection of Original Essays* (Knoxville: University of Tennessee, 1979), 67-71.

77. 1979 "Sport History Through Biography," *Quest*, 31 (1979), 216-221.

78. 1979 "The Olympics in the Year 2000," *Strength and Health*, 47 (July 1979), 16-17.

79. 1979 "The First Modern Olympic Games Champion," *The Olympian*, 6 (August 1979), 16-17.

80. 1979 "The Agony and the Ecstasy of the Olympic Games," *Proceedings 1979*, United States Olympic Academy, pp. 21-25.

81. 1980 "Mabel Lee and Elmer Mitchell Reach Out and Touch One Another," *Update AAHPERD* (July-August 1980), 5.

82. 1980 "A History of World Track and Field," in Richard Lipsky (ed.), *1980 Sportguide* (New York: Sportguide Inc.), 234-237.

83. 1980 "Troubled Times for the Eastern District Society 1930-1933," *Journal of Physical Education and Recreation*, 51 (November-December 1980), 234-251.

84. 1980 "Penn State at the Olympic Games," *Town and Gown* [State College, Pa. magazine] (February 1980), 50-60.

85. 1980 "The Olympic Games Philosophy: Cooperative Competition," *Journal of Physical Education and Recreation*, 51 (April 1980), 19-20, 69.

86. 1980 "The Durable Strength of the Olympic Games Idea," *Olympic Review*, 157 (November 1980), 632-637.

87. 1980 "Future Directions of Athletic Amateurism and the Olympic Movement," *The Academy Papers 1980*, pp. 15-19. The American Academy of Physical Education.

88. 1980 "History of the Olympic Ideal," *Proceedings 1980*, United States Olympic Academy; volume 1 of 2 volumes, pp. 47-59.

89. 1980 "John Lucas, Penn State University Historian—an interview," *Proceedings 1980*, United States Olympic Academy; volume 2 of 2 volumes, pp. 738-746.

90. 1980 "American Involvement in the Athens Olympian Games of 1906—Bridge Between Failure and Success," *Stadion*, 6 (1980), 217-228.

91. 1981 Book review of Peter Arnold, *Meaning in Movement. Sport and Physical Education* in *Journal of Physical Education and Recreation*, 52 (February 1981), 68.

92. 1981 "The Eastern District: 1934-1939—Humanity as an Integrating Totality," *Journal of Physical Education, Recreation, Dance*, 51 (September 1981), 58-62.

93. 1981 Book review of Robert L. Laeffelbein, *Knight Life: Jousting in the United States* (1977), as found in *Journal of Sport History*, 8 (Summer 1981), 102-104.

94. 1981 "The Genesis of the Modern Olympic Games"; Chapter 2 in *Olympism*, Segrave and Chu (eds.) (1981), 22-32.

95. 1981 "A Decalogue of Olympic Games Reform"; Chapter 12 in *Olympism*, Segrave and Chu (eds.) (1981), 148-153.

96. 1981 "The Significance of the Eleventh World Olympic Congress in Baden-Baden," *Proceedings 1981*, North American Society for Sport History, p. 41.

97. 1981 "Symbolism at the Ancient Olympic Games," *Proceedings 1981*, United States Olympic Academy, pp. 6-10.

98. 1981 "Five Possible Olympic Games Scenarios by the Year 1992," *Proceedings 1981*, United States Olympic Academy, pp. 221-222.

99. 1982 "2001: A Running Odyssey," *Runner's World*, 17 (March 1982), 73.

100. 1982 "600 Miles in Six Days—The Ultimate Marathon Race," *Track and Field Quarterly* of the U. S. Track Coaches, 82 (Fall 1982), 55-58.

101. 1982 "Women's Sport: A Trial of Equality," in Reet Howell (ed.), *Her Story in Sport: An Historical Anthology of Women in Sport* (1982), 239-265.

102. 1982 "Baron Pierre de Coubertin: North American Bibliography," *Newsletter*, International Pierre de Coubertin Committee (1982).

103. 1982 "The Greatest Gathering of Olympians," *The Olympian*, 9 (July-August 1982), 6-8.

104. 1982 "The Way of the Modern Olympic Games," *Journal of the New York State Association for Physical Education*, 33 (Fall 1982), 15-16.

105. 1982 "Origins of the Academy Award Film 'Chariots of Fire'," *Olympic Message*, 3 (December 1982), 51-58; also published in *Proceedings 1982*, United States Olympic Academy, pp. 35-42.

106. 1982 "The Impact of the 1981 Olympic Congress in Baden-Baden," *Proceedings 1982*, United States Olympic Academy, pp. 103-109.

107. 1982 "Prelude to the Games of the Tenth Olympiad in Los Angeles," *Southern California Quarterly*, 64 (Winter 1982), 313-318.

108. 1983 "'Three Specially Selected Athletes' and a Recapitulation of the Pennsylvania 'Walking Purchase of 1737'," *Research Quarterly for Exercise and Sport*, 54 (March 1983), 41-47.

109. 1983 "Deerfoot in Britain: An Amazing Long-Distance Runner," *Journal of American Culture*, 6 (Fall 1983), 13-18.

110. 1983 "A Critique of a Recent Doctoral Dissertation—Possible Watershed in Physical Education Research," *The Physical Educator*, 40 (December 1983), 171-173.

111. 1983 "Samaranch—A Close-Up Look at the IOC President," *The Olympian*, 9 (February 1983), 16-17.

112. 1983 "American Preparation for the First Post World War Olympic Games 1919-1920," *Journal of Sport History*, 10 (Summer 1983), 30-44.

113. 1983 "The Dream Persists: The Olympic Games Comes Back to Los Angeles," *Olympic Review*, 194 (December 1983), 833-836.

114. 1984 "The Survival of the Olympic Idea," *Journal of Physical Education, Recreation, Dance*, 55 (January 1984), 29, 32.

115. 1984 "No More Amateurs—Only Professional Athletes at the Olympic Games," *Journal of Physical Education, Recreation*, 55 (February 1984), 22-23.

116. 1984 Book review of Allen Guttmann, *The Games Must Go On—Avery Brundage and the Olympic Movement*, in *Canadian Journal of Sport History* 15 (December 1984), 70-72.

117. 1984 "The Future of the International Olympic Movement," 1984 Olympic Scientific Congress *Abstracts*, pp. 19-20.

118. 1984 "Americans in the IOC: 17 Have Served the Movement," *The Olympian*, 10 (February 1984), 22-26.

119. 1984 Book review of Vsevolod Foorman, *Olympic Stamps*, in the *Journal of Physical Education, Recreation, Dance*, 55 (May-June 1984), 90, 93.

120. 1984 "The Perpetuation of the Olympic Idea by Pierre de Coubertin during the Crisis Years 1913-1919," *Proceedings 1984*, International Congress of Sport History, pp. 115-125.

121. 1984 "Some Thoughts On International Politics, the Olympic Games and the Olympic Movement," *Proceedings 1984*, International Congress for Health, Physical Education, Recreation, pp. 21-26.

122. 1985 "Tradition and Modernism—The American Academy of Physical Education Prepares for the Future," *Journal of Physical Education, Recreation, Dance*, 56 (April 1985), 80-81.

123. 1985 "War and Physical Preparedness: EDA History 1940-1949," *Journal of Physical Education, Recreation, Dance*, 56 (September 1985), 72-76.

124. 1985 "Sport for All," in W. L. Umphlett, ed., *American Sport Culture. The Humanistic Dimensions* (1985), p. 305.

125. 1985 Book review of John J. MacAloon, *This Great Symbol. Pierre de Coubertin and the Origins of the Modern Olympic Games* (1981), in the *Canadian Journal of Sport History*, 16 (May 1985), 94-95.

126. 1985 "The Future of the International Olympic Movement," *Official Report—Sports History*, edited by Norbert Müller and Joachim K. Ruhl, pp. 296-306.

127. 1985 "Theodore Roosevelt and Baron Pierre de Coubertin: Entangling Olympic Games Involvement 1901-1918," *Stadion*, 8-9 (1982-1983), but not published until 1985. See pp. 137-150; also published in *Proceedings*, International Sport History Association (1985), pp. 308-310.

128. 1986 "The Certainty of Change in American Physical Education," *The American Academy of Physical Education News*, 6 (Winter 1986), 8-9.

129. 1986 Book review of *The Anthropology of Sport* by Kendall Blanchard and Alyce Cheska, in *Journal of Physical Education, Recreation, Dance*, 57 (May-June 1986), 90-91.

130. 1986 "The Los Angeles Olympic Games: Synchronism of Success and Failure," *Proceedings 1985*, United States Olympic Academy, pp. 188-194.

131. 1986 "Coubertin's Over-arching View of Ten Olympic Games 1896-1936," *Olympic Message*, 15 (September 1986), 61-68.

132. 1987 "Albertville and Barcelona Win Center Stage for the Olympic Games of 1992," *Pennsylvania Journal of Physical Education, Recreation, Dance*, 57 (Winter 1987), 16-17.

133. 1987 "American Men at the Winter-Summer Olympic Games 1896-1984," *Proceedings* United States Olympic Academy 1986, pp. 52-57.

134. 1987 "How to Infuse Background on the Olympic 'Boycotts' of 1976, 1980, and 1984," *Proceedings 1986*, United States Olympic Academy, pp. 98-100.

135. 1987 "The Purity of Winter Sports,"—a speech by Pierre de Coubertin," translation from the French language, in *Olympic Review*, 233 (March 1987), 122-123.

136. 1987 Book review of *An Approved History of the Olympic Games* by Bill Henry and Patricia Henry Yeomans, in *The International Journal of Sport History*, 4 (May 1987), 125-126.

137. 1987 "Admirers of Pierre de Coubertin and Avery Brundage Mark the Year," *Olympic Review*, 239 (September 1987), 451-452.

138. 1987 Book review of *Making It Happen: Peter Ueberroth and the 1984 Olympics* by Kenneth Reich, in *Journal of Sport History*, 14 (Winter 1987), 342-344.

139. 1987 "Contrasting Faces of the Olympic Ideal, Past and Present: a Plea for Balance," *Proceedings 1987*, United States Olympic Academy, pp. 161-171.

140. 1988 "The AAU's 100th Anniversary: Saluting a Century of Progress," *Info AAU*, 59 (six-part series, January through December 1988).

141. 1988 "XVth Olympic Winter Games—Calgary, February 1988," *Journal of Physical Education, Recreation, Dance*, 51 (January 1988), 74-75.

142. 1988 "Chasing the Chill—The Glenn Cunningham Story," *Sport Heritage*, 2 (Spring 1988), 36-37.

143. 1988 "The First Winter Olympic Games," *The Olympian*, 14 (February 1988), 54-55.

144. 1988 "France versus USA in the 1924 Olympic Games: Efforts to Assuage Transnational Tension," *Canadian Journal of Sport History*, 19 (May 1988), 15-27.

145. 1988 "Ueberroth" in *Encyclopedia of World Biography*, 15 (1988), 463-464.

146. 1988 "Can the Games Continue?", *Apprise* 8 (South Central Pennsylvania magazine), September 1988, pp. 52-56.

147. 1988 "Pierre de Coubertin: Nineteenth Century Man With Twenty-First Century Ideas," *Proceedings 1988 Olympic Scientific Congress*; Volume 2 of five volumes, pp. 49-50.

148. 1988 Book review of *Tales of Gold. An Oral History of the Summer Olympic Games* by Lewis Carlson and John Fogarty, in *Journal of Sport History*, 15 (Summer 1988), 184-186.

149. 1988 Book review of *The Olympic Games in Transition*, edited by Jeffrey O. Segrave and Donald Chu, in the *Canadian Journal of Sport History*, 19 (December 1988), 104-106.

150. 1988 Book review of *Aussie Gold: The Story of Australia at the Olympics*, by Reet and Max Howell, in *Journal of Sport History*, 15 (Winter 1988), 377-380.

151. 1988 "1988 Seoul," in *Official Report* of the Evaluation Committee for the Seoul Olympic Organizing Committee 1988, pp. 115-138.

152. 1988 "From Coubertin to Samaranch: the Unsettling Transformation of the Olympic Ideology of Athletic Amateurism," *Stadion*, 14 (1988), 65-84.

153. 1989 "The 1889 Boston Conference on Physical Training—A Reappraisal," *Proceedings 1989*, North American Society for Sport History, p. 41.

154. 1989 "A Centennial Retrospective—the 1889 Boston Conference on Physical Training," *Journal of Physical Education, Recreation, Dance*, 60 (November-December, 1989), 30-33.

155. 1989 "Future Physical Education and Sport Activities Will Occur After School," *Journal of Physical Education, Recreation, Dance*, 60 (September 1989), 45.

156. 1989 "The Historical Development of the Modern Olympic Movement 1980-1988," in volume 6 of *Geschichte der Leibesubungen*, Horst Überhorst (ed.), 1989, pp. 1135-1146.

157. 1989 "Thorpe's Record Assult," *Sport History*, 2 (March 1989), 19-25.

158. 1989 Book review of *Sport and Politics: The Olympics and the Los Angeles Games* by B. Shaikin, *Journal of Sport History*, 16 (Spring 1989), 99-101.

159. 1989 "The Demystification of Politics and the Olympic Games During the Administration of H. E. Juan Antonio Samaranch," *Proceedings 1989*, United States Olympic Academy, pp. 195-199.

160. 1990 "Whirr, Whizz, Hum: Mile-a-Minute Murphy Breaks the Record," *Bicycle USA*, 26 (June 1990), 181-189.

161. 1990 Book review of *American Sport—A Documentary IHstory* by Peter Levine, compiler, in *Journal of Comparative Physical Education and Sport*, 12, no. 1 (1990), 34-36.

162. 1990 "Female Competitors in the Early Years of the Olympic Games, and a Modern-Day 52 Percent Solution," *Proceedings 1990*, International Olympic Academy, pp. 94-101.

163. 1991 "Professor William Milligan Sloane: Father of the United States Olympic Committee," in *Reflexionen in Umfelt der Sportgeschichte, Festschrift für Horst Überhorst* (Andreas Luh: Edgar Beckers, eds., 1991), 230-242.

164. 1991 "Contrasting Giants of the Olympic Movement: Pierre de Coubertin and Juan Antonio Samaranch," in Fernand Landry et al, eds., *Sport...the Third Millenium. International Symposium 1991* (Quebec City: Les Press de l'Universite/ Laval, 1991), 721-727.

165. 1991 "Ernest Lee Jahncke: The Expelling of an IOC Member," *Stadion*, 17 (1991), 53-78.

166. 1991 "The 'Perfect' Physical Educator: The Blend of the Old and the New," *Journal of Physical Education, Recreation, Dance*, 62 (February 1991), 7.

167. 1991 "A Romantic Moment in Cycling History," *The Bicyclist's Sourcebook* (1991), 326-327.

168. 1992 "Taikwondo, Pelote Basque Jai-Alai, and Roller Hockey—Three Unusual Olympic Demonstration Sports," *Journal of Physical Education, Recreation, Dance*, 63 (April 1992), 80-82.

169. 1992 "The Consummate Olympian—Philip Noel-Baker," *International Journal of Physical Education*, 29 (1992), 33-38.

170. 1992 "In the Eye of the Storm: Paavo Nurmi and the American Athletic Amateur-Professional Struggle," *Stadion*, 18 (1992), 225-246.

171. 1992 "Baron Pierre de Coubertin," in *The Spirit of Olympia*, Terry Wood, compiler (Milwaukee: Narada Productions Pub., 1992), 14-17.

172. 1992 Book review of Richard Mandell, *A Munich Diary: The Olympics of 1972*. *Olympika. International Journal of Olympic Studies*, 1 (1992), 168-170.

173. 1993 Book review of *The Lords of the Rings* by Vyr Simson and Andrew Jennings, published in *The International Society of Olympic Historians' Journal*, 1 (Spring 1993), 18-19.

174. 1993 Book review of *The Complete Book of the Olympics (1992)* by David Wallechinsky, published in *The International Society of Olympic Historians' Journal*, 1 (Spring 1993), 19-20.

175. 1993 Book review of David Miller, *Olympic Revolution: The Olympic Biography of Juan Antonio Samaranch* (London: Pavillion Books, 1992); review also in *Citius, Altius, Fortius. The International Society of Olympic Historians' Journal*, 1 (Autumn 1993), 29-30.

176. 1993 "Coubertin One Hundred Years Ago: His Second American Visit in 1893," in *Olympika: The International Journal of Olympic Studies*, 2 (1993), 103-108.

177. 1994 Book review of *The Golden Book of the Olympic Games* by Erich Kamper and Bill Mallon, 672 pp., located in *Citius, Altius, Fortius. The International Society of Olympic Historians' Journal*, 2 (May 1994), 42-44.

178. 1994 "Commentary on Ture Widlund's research essay "Ethelbert Talbot —His Life and Place in Olympic History." Review located in *Citius, Altius, Fortius. The International Society of Olympic Historians' Journal*, 2 (May 1994), 7-14.

179. 1994 "Olympism in the United States of America," *Olympic Message*, 39 (1994), 59-63.

180. 1994 "USOC President Douglas MacArthur and His Olympic Moment 1927-1928," 1994 *Proceedings, Second International Symposium For Olympic Research* (October 1994), 67-69. Also located in *Olympika,* 3 (1994), 111-115.

181. 1994 "A Reflection: Madame Berlioux Revisited," *Olympika. The International Journal of Olympic Studies*, (1994), 153-155.

182. 1994 "The Hegemonic Rule of the American Amateur Athletic Union 1888-1914: James Edward Sullivan as Prime Mover," *International Journal of the History of Sport*, 11 (December 1994), 355-371.

183. 1994 "The Impact of International Politics on the Olympic Movement (1952-1972). The Concepts of Avery Brundage on Olympism," *Proceedings 1994* of the International Olympic Academy [Greek Language edition], pp. 171-176.

184. 1995 "Architects of the Modernized American Olympic Committee, 1921-1928: Gustavus Town Kirby, Robert Means Thompson and General Douglas MacArthur," *Journal of Sport History*, 22 (Spring 1995), 38-45.

185. 1995 [Co-author Ian Jobling], "Troubled Waters: Fanny Durack's 1919 Swimming Tour of America amidst Transnational Amateur Athletic Prudery and Bureacracy," *Olympika*, 4 (1995), 93-112.

186. 1996 "Faithfully Pursuing an Olympic Ideal," *The Christian Science Monitor* (newspaper), July 10, 1996, p. 16.

187. 1996 Contributing editor, *Olympism—A Basic Guide to History, Ideals and Sports of the Olympic Movement.* An Official USOC Sport Series (Glendale, Calif.: Griffin Pub., 1996), 150 pp.

188. 1996 "Coubertin and the Double Dream," *The Active Voice.* Newsletter of the American Association for Active Lifestyles and Fitness, 2 (Winter 1996), 5, 12.

189. 1996 "If Coubertin Were in America," *Olympic Review*, 25 (June-July 1996), 34-35.

190. 1996 "Gustavus Town Kirby: Doyen of American Amateur Athletics and his Inadmissability into the International Olympic Committee," *Stadion* 21-22 (1995-1996), 171-192.

191. 1996 Book review of *Historical Dictionary of the Modern Olympic Games* (1996), by John E. Findling and Kimberly D. Pelle; review in *International Journal of the History of Sport*, 13 December 1996), 472-474.

192. 1997 "Pat 'Babe' McDonald: Olympic Champion and Paragon of the Irish-American Whales," *Journal of Olympic History*, 5 (Fall 1997), 8-9.

193. 1998 "From 'A' through 'Z': from Albania Through Zaire," *Zeri Olympik* [Tirana, Albania N.O.C.], January-March 1998, pp. 1-2.

194. 1998 "Making a Statement: Annette Kellerman Advances the Worlds of Swimming, Diving and Entertainment," *Sporting Traditions: Journal of the Australian Society for Sport History*, 14 (May 1998), 25-35.

195. 1998 "Penn State's Olympic Family," *Town and Gown* [State College, Pennsylvania], (February 1998), 30-38.

196. 1998 "Penn State University's Olympic Medal Winners and Its Olympic 'Family,'" *Pennsylvania History*, 65 (Spring 1998), 223-235.

197. 1999 "More than Three-Quarters of a Century Ago," *Official Penn Relays Program 1999*, p. R24.

198. 1999 "The Ascendancy of the Amateur Athletic Concept ... and the Role of its Premier Standard Bearer, Caspar W. Whitney," *Proceedings 1999*, North American Society for Sport History, p. 5 (abstract).

199. 1999 "Twenty-nine Years of Teaching Olympic Games History at the Pennsylvania State University, 1970-1999," *Report* of the International Olympic Academy Special Sessions and Seminars 1999, pp. 582-590.

200. 1999 "The Tremulous Evolution of the United States Olympic Committee 1896-1926," Olympic Conference, Sydney, Australia 1999 (abstract).

201. 1999 "The Greatest Gathering of Track and Field Olympians: The British Empire versus the U.S.A., 1920, 1924 and 1928," *Journal of Olympic History*, 7 (September 1999), 41-43.

202. 1999 Sixteen Essays published in the *American National Biography*, 24 vols., 1999: Eddie Eagan; John J. Flanagan; Archie Hahn; "Slats" Hardin; Willie Hoppe; William DeHart Hubbard; "Babe" McDonald; Glenn Morris; Lon Myers; Harold Osborne; James Pilkington; Ralph Rose; Jackson Scholz; Mel Sheppard; "Bernie" Wefers; Benjamin Franklin White.

203. 1999 "Ten Considerations for a Reconfiguration of the IOC by the Year 2005," *The Hong Kong Journal of Sports Medicine*, 9 (November 1999), 58-59.

204. 2000 "Charlie Paddock Brings down the Wall at the Penn Relays: A Recognition of his 100th birthday," *Journal of Olympic History*, 8 (January 2000), 34-35.

205. 2000 "Caspar Whitney—The Imperial Advocate of Athletic Amateurism and his Involvement with the IOC and the American Olympic Committee 1899-1912," *Journal of Olympic History*, 8 (May 2000), 30-38.

206. 2000 "A.C. Gilbert—1908 Co-Olympic Pole Vault Champion ... and a Lot More," *Journal of Olympic History*, 8 (September 2000), 12-14.

207. 2000 "Four 'Mysterious' Citizens of the United States Who Served on the International Olympic Committee During the Period 1900-1917: Theodore Stanton; James Hazen Hyde; Allison Vincent Armour and Evert Jansen Wendell," in *Proceedings* Fifth International Symposium for Olympic Research (September 2000), 195-206.

208. 2000 "George Washington Orton—Director of the Penn Relays 1919-1925, and Much More," *Journal of Olympic History*, 8 (September 2000), 24-25.

209. 2001 Three essays in the *Official Report* of the XXVII Olympiad—Sydney 2000 Olympic Games. Volume 2 of 3 volumes. Senior Editor, Kristine Toohey. "Athletics," co-authored with John Daley; "Badminton"; and "Volleyball."

210. 2001 "Reconfiguration or Demise? The IOC's Millennial Modernization," *Journal of the International Council of Physical Education*, H./Rec./ Sport/Dance, 37 (July 2001, 13-14.

211. 2001 "The Death and Burial of Coubertin: A Retrospective," *Journal of Olympic History*, 9 (September 2001), 7-12.

212. 2001 "About Avery Brundage," *Olympic Review*, (December 2000-January 2001), 25-26.

213. 2002 "Setting the Foundation and Governance of the American Olympic Association: The Efforts of Robert Means Thompson 1911-1919 and 1922-1926," *Journal of Sport History*, 29 (Fall 2002), 457-468.

214. 2002 "An Analysis of an 'Over-Crowded Worried Life': General Charles Hitchcock Sherrill's Tenure on the International Olympic Committee 1922-1936," *Olympika*, 11 (2002), 143-168.

215. 2003 "Bud Greenspan: Olympic Games Filmmaker and his Search for Athletic Excellence and Personal Nobility," *The Legacy of the Olympic Games 1984-2000* (Lausanne: IOC Symposium 2002), 335-335. Also published in *Olympisch Bewegt, Festschrift zum 60. Geburtstag von Prof. Dr. Manfred Lammer* [509 pp.]. Cologne: Carl und Liselott Diem Archiv., 2003, pp. 345-351.

216. 2003 "Eighty Years Ago Penn State Runners Blew Past Oxford to Set a World-Record Time," *Town and Gown* [State College, Pa., Monthly], June 2003, pp. 28, 30.

217. 2003 "The 2004 Athens Olympic Games: Boom or Bust?" (abstract), *Proceedings 2003*, North American Society for Sport History, p. 82.

218. 2003 "Olympic Idea, Questions of Ethics," a chapter in *What an Olympian Should Know*; edited by Dr. Pat Schmitt, pp. 47-54.

219. 2004 "The Great Gathering of Sport Scientists: the 1904 St. Louis Olympic Games Exposition Fair—Physical Education Lectures," *Journal of Olympic History*, 12 (January 2004), 6-12. 220. 2004 "Super Star Class Inducted. 2004 United States Olympic Committee Hall of Fame," *The Olympian* (Summer 2004), 16.

220. 2005 "There's a Great Deal More to Elizabeth Robinson's Gold Medal Sprint Victory at the 1928 Olympic Games," *Journal of Olympic History*, 13 (January 2005), 16-20.

221. 2005 "Marvin Howard Eyler: a Consummate Educator," *Journal of Sport History*, 32 (Spring 2005), 67-70.

222. 2006 "The Formative Years of the American Academy of Kinesiology and Physical Education, 1930-1938," *Quest*, 58 (February 2006), 2-5.

223. 2006 "'Almost the Last American Disciple of Pure Olympic Games—Amateurism'—John J. Garland's Tenure on the International Olympic Committee 1948-1968," in *Proceedings*, International Symposium for Olympic Research, London, Ontario, Canada (2006), pp. 244-253. This Garland essay reproduced in *Olympika* 15 (2006), 113-125.

224. 2006 "Antecedents to the Decision to Host the 2012 Olympic Games," *Journal of Contemporary Athletics*, 2 (2006), 1-9.

225. 2007 "A Recapitulation of the United States Olympic Committee's Very Earliest Years 1906-1922," *Journal of Olympic History*, 15 (March 2007), 22-26.

226. 2008 "'Pierre de Coubertin's Overarching Views of Ten Olympic Games, 1896-1936," in Manfred Messing and Norbert Müller (eds.), *Olympismus—Erbe und Verantwortung; Olympism—Heritage and Responsibility* (Frankfurt: Germany: Agon Sportverlag GMBH), 103-8.

227. 2008 "Avery Brundage and His Vision of the Olympic Games During the 'Unsettling' Years, 1938-1952," *Journal of Olympic History*, 16 (July 2008), 23-32.

Printed in the United States
214504BV00003B/2/P

9 780979 551819